ANNUAL EDITIONS

Educating Exceptional Children

Eleventh Edition

99/00

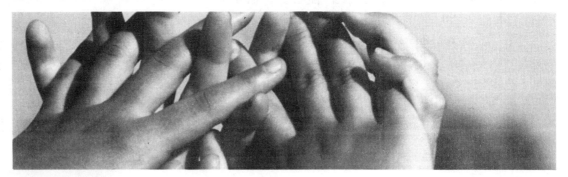

Karen L. Freiberg
University of Maryland, Baltimore County

Dr. Karen Freiberg has an interdisciplinary educational and employment background in nursing, education, and developmental psychology. She received her B.S. from the State University of New York at Plattsburgh, her M.S. from Cornell University, and her Ph.D. from Syracuse University. She has worked as a school nurse, a pediatric nurse, a public health nurse for the Navajo Indians, an associate project director for a child development clinic, a researcher in several areas of child development, and a university professor. Dr. Freiberg is the author of an award-winning textbook, *Human Development: A Life-Span Approach,* which is now in its fourth edition. She is currently on the faculty at the University of Maryland, Baltimore County.

Dushkin/McGraw-Hill
Sluice Dock, Guilford, Connecticut 06437

Visit us on the Internet
http://www.dushkin.com/annualeditions/

Credits

1. Inclusive Education
Facing overview—© 1998 by PhotoDisc, Inc.
2. Early Childhood
Facing overview—© 1998 by Cleo Photography.
3. Learning Disabilities
Facing overview—United Nations photo by O. Monsen.
4. Speech and Language Impairments
Facing overview—United Nations photo by L. Solmssen.
5. Mental Retardation, Autism, and Traumatic Brain Injuries
Facing overview—United Nations photo by S. DiMartini.
6. Emotional and Behavioral Disturbances
Facing overview—© 1998 by Cleo Photography.
7. Vision and Hearing Impairments
Facing overview—United Nations photo by S. DiMartini.
8. Multiple Disabilities
Facing overview—United Nations photo by L. Solmssen.
9. Orthopedic and Health Impairments
Facing overview—United Nations photo by J. Isaac.
10. Giftedness
Facing overview—Dushkin/McGraw-Hill photo by Pam Carley.
11. Transition
Facing overview—United Nations photo by S. DiMartini.

Copyright

Cataloging in Publication Data
Main entry under title: Annual Editions: Educating exceptional children. 1999/2000.
     1. Exceptional children—Education—United States—Periodicals. 2. Educational innovations—United States—Periodicals. I. Freiberg, Karen, *comp.* II. Title: Educating exceptional children.
ISBN 0-07-041389-4   371.9'05   76-644171   ISSN 0198-7518

Eleventh Edition

Cover image © 1999 PhotoDisc, Inc.

Printed in the United States of America   1234567890BAHBAH54321098   Printed on Recycled Paper

Members of the Advisory Board are instrumental in the final selection of articles for each edition of ANNUAL EDITIONS. Their review of articles for content, level, currentness, and appropriateness provides critical direction to the editor and staff. We think that you will find their careful consideration well reflected in this volume.

Editors/Advisory Board

Staff

iii

To the Reader

The Individuals with Disabilities Education Act (IDEA) was reauthorized in the United States in 1997. It included strong financial prods to move toward integration of most children with disabilities into regular education classes in neighborhood public schools. In the United States, about 10 percent of the childhood population in public schools is receiving some form of special educational services. About 30 billion dollars are spent each year for extra educational aides and assistances.

Is the education of exceptional children best carried out in regular education classes? Proponents of inclusion cite benefits such as socialization of both the special needs children and their nondisabled peers. Tolerance and acceptance begin with exposure and are taught by egalitarian teachers who focus on positive interaction and differential abilities. Opponents of inclusive education cite lack of preparation of regular education teachers, crowded and ill-equipped classrooms, and the negative effects of competition. They fear that children with disabilities will be ridiculed and marginalized in integrated classes.

IDEA has radically altered the ways in which children with disabilities are perceived and educated in contemporary society. First enacted into law in 1975 as the Education for All Handicapped Children Act, IDEA has been amended several times. It now guarantees that infants born at risk of developing disabilities be assessed early and frequently. An individualized family service plan (IFSP) is mandated in early childhood. The plan describes how the young child and his or her family will be followed from assessment until entrance into public school. IFSPs outline the many forms of early childhood interventions that will be provided.

IDEA guarantees that every child with a disability who is enrolled in public school will be assessed and provided with an individualized education plan (IEP). This program, to be updated every year, outlines all the interventions to be pro-vided. Every child is guaranteed a free and appropriate education in the least restrictive environment possible. Most special education schools and many full-day special education classes have been discontinued in compliance with IDEA's call for the "least restrictive environment" (LRE). The 1997 reauthorization of IDEA threatened the U.S. federal education funding to states who do not encourage LRE (inclusive classes).

IDEA guarantees the provision of transitional services to all children with disabilities through age 21. An individualized transition plan (ITP) must be written to describe all of the interventions that will be provided to help the student move into higher education, the community, or the workforce.

Annual Editions: Educating Exceptional Children 99/00, includes articles explaining how the IDEA provisions are being implemented in all areas of special education. Selections have been made with an eye to conveying information, some personal experiences, and many practical suggestions for implementation.

To improve future editions of this anthology, please complete and return the postage-paid article rating form on the last page. Your suggestions are valued and appreciated.

Good luck in using this anthology to make your own and others' lives easier and more rewarding.

Karen Freiberg

Karen Freiberg
Editor

Contents

UNIT 1

Inclusive Education

Four articles present strategies
for establishing positive
interactions between students
with and without special needs.

The concepts in bold italics are developed in the article. For further expansion please refer to the Topic Guide and the Index.

Early Childhood

Four unit articles discuss the implementation of special services to preschoolers with disabilities.

Learning Disabilities

The assessment and special needs of students with learning disabilities are addressed in this unit's three selections.

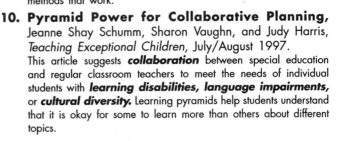

The concepts in bold italics are developed in the article. For further expansion please refer to the Topic Guide and the Index.

UNIT 4

Speech and Language Impairments

In this unit, two selections examine communication disorders and suggest ways in which students can develop their speech and language.

UNIT 5

Mental Retardation, Autism, and Traumatic Brain Injuries

Four articles in this section discuss concerns and strategies for providing optimal educational programs for students with mental retardation, autism, and traumatic brain injuries.

UNIT 6

Emotional and Behavioral Disturbances

Ways to teach emotionally and behaviorally disordered students are discussed in the unit's three articles.

The concepts in bold italics are developed in the article. For further expansion please refer to the Topic Guide and the Index.

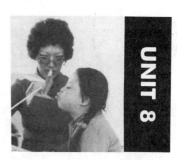

The concepts in bold italics are developed in the article. For further expansion please refer to the Topic Guide and the Index.

UNIT 9

Orthopedic and Health Impairments

In this unit, three articles discuss how health problems and mobility impairments have an impact on a child's education.

UNIT 10

Giftedness

Three articles examine the need for special services for gifted and talented students, assessment of giftedness, and ways to teach these students.

The concepts in bold italics are developed in the article. For further expansion please refer to the Topic Guide and the Index.

UNIT 11

Transition

The three articles in this section
examine the problems and issues
regarding transitions within
school or from school to the
community and workforce.

This topic guide suggests how the selections and World Wide Web sites found in the next section of this book relate to topics of traditional concern to students and professionals involved with educatibg exceptional children. It is useful for locating interrelated articles and Web sites for reading and research. The guide is arranged alphabetically according to topic.

The relevant Web sites, which are numbered and annotated on pages 4 and 5, are easily identified by the Web icon (☺) under the topic articles. By linking the articles and the Web sites by topic, this ANNUAL EDITIONS reader becomes a powerful learning and research tool.

TOPIC AREA	KNOWLEDGE	ATTITUDES	TEACHING
	(These articles provide information about a handicap or a special education concept.)	(These articles contain personal experiences of exceptional persons or discussions about changing children's attitudes toward a handicap.)	(These articles contain pratical suggestions about how to apply special education principles to teaching of exceptional children.)
Assessment ☺ **(1, 2, 5, 7, 8, 12, 14, 18)**	9. Learning Disabilities 11. Mega-Analysis of Meta-Analyses 12. Distinguishing Language Differences 14. AAMR Definition and Preschool Children 20. How to Defuse	19. How to Prevent Aggressive Behavior 25. Unexpected Benefits of High School Peer Tutoring	2. What Are Special Education Teachers Made Of?
Collaboration ☺ **(7, 8, 14, 17, 18, 20)**	5. From Philosophy to Practice 15. Collaborative Planning 26. Perspectives on Technology	3. What Do I Do Now? 4. Four Inclusion Models 8. Dyads and Data in Peer Coaching 10. Pyramid Power for Collaborative Planning 22. Child with Severe Hearing Loss	2. What Are Special Education Teachers Made Of? 24. Creating Inclusionary Opportunities 33. Making Comprehensive Inclusion of Special Needs Students Work
Computers and Technology ☺ **(5, 6, 22, 23, 24)**	11. Mega-Analysis of Meta-Analyses 26. Perspectives on Technology 29. Accessible Web Site Design	3. What Do I Do Now? 22. Child with Severe Hearing Loss	2. What Are Special Education Teachers Made Of? 23. Multimedia Stories for Deaf Children 27. "Can I Play Too?"
Cultural Diversity ☺ **(4, 7, 8, 9, 11, 15)**	12. Distinguishing Language Differences	10. Pyramid Power for Collaborative Planning 28. Listening to Parents of Children with Disabilities	2. What Are Special Education Teachers Made Of? 23. Multimedia Stories for Deaf Children
Early Childhood ☺ **(3, 4, 9, 10, 11, 12)**	5. From Philosophy to Practice 6. Together Is Better 11. Mega-Analysis of Meta-Analyses 30. Meeting the Needs of Gifted and Talented	8. Dyads and Data in Peer Coaching 16. Facilitating the Socialization of Children 28. Listening to Parents of Children with Disabilities	2. What Are Special Education Teachers Made Of? 7. "Buddy Skills" for Preschoolers 13. Language Interaction Techniques 21. Preschool Orientation
Emotional and Behavioral Disorders ☺ **(21, 25, 26)**	20. How to Defuse	8. Dyads and Data in Peer Coaching 19. How to Prevent Aggressive Behavior	17. Getting the Student with Head Injuries Back 18. Group Development for Students
Family Involvement ☺ **(10, 12, 17, 20, 22, 29)**	5. From Philosophy to Practice 15. Collaborative Planning	22. Child with Severe Hearing Loss 28. Listening to Parents of Children with Disabilities 31. Gifted Students Suggest Reforms	2. What Are Special Education Teachers Made Of?
Gifted and Talented ☺ **(29)**	32. Cluster Grouping of Gifted Students	31. Gifted Students Suggest Reforms	30. Meeting the Needs of Gifted and Talented
Hearing Impairments ☺ **(22, 25, 26)**	6. Together Is Better	22. Child with Severe Hearing Loss 29. Accessible Web Site Design	23. Multimedia Stories for Deaf Children 24. Creating Inclusionary Opportunities

TOPIC AREA	KNOWLEDGE	ATTITUDES	TEACHING
Inclusive Education ◎ *(7, 8, 9, 11, 12, 17, 18, 20, 22, 23, 24, 27, 28)*	1. Inclusion of Children with Disabilities 5. From Philosophy to Practice 6. Together Is Better 15. Collaborative Planning 20. How to Defuse Threats, Challenges, Confrontations . . . 32. Cluster Grouping of Gifted Students	3. What Do I Do Now? 16. Facilitating the Socialization of Children 22. Child with Severe Hearing Loss 25. Unexpected Benefits of High School Peer Tutoring	2. What Are Special Education Teachers Made Of? 4. Four Inclusion Models 24. Creating Inclusionary Opportunities 27. "Can I Play Too?" 33. Making Comprehensive Inclusion of Special Needs Students Work
Individualized Educational Programs ◎ *(10, 12, 13, 16, 17, 20, 21, 25, 26)*	14. AAMR Definition and Preschool Children 15. Collaborative Planning 34. Transition from High School to Work or College	3. What Do I Do Now? 28. Listening to Parents of Children with Disabilities 35. School-to-Work	2. What Are Special Education Teachers Made Of? 17. Getting the Student with Head Injuries Back
Learning Disabilities ◎ *(13, 14, 15)*	6. Together Is Better 9. Learning Disabilities	10. Pyramid Power for Collaborative Planning 29. Accessible Web Site Design	11. Mega-Analysis of Meta-Analyses
Legal Processes ◎ *(2, 4, 6, 7, 8)*	9. Learning Disabilities 14. AAMR Definition and Preschool Children	1. Inclusion of Children with Disabilities	2. What Are Special Education Teachers Made Of? 21. Preschool Orientation
Mental Retardation, Autism and Traumatic Brain Injuries ◎ *(17, 18, 19, 25, 26)*	14. AAMR Definition and Preschool Children 15. Collaborative Planning	16. Facilitating the Socialization of Children 29. Accessible Web Site Design	17. Getting the Student with Head Injuries Back
Multiple Disabilities ◎ *(25, 26)*	26. Perspectives on Technology	25. Unexpected Benefits of High School Peer Tutoring	24. Creating Inclusionary Opportunities
Orthopedic and Health Impairments ◎ *(27, 28)*	6. Together Is Better	28. Listening to Parents 29. Accessible Web Site Design	17. Getting the Student with Head Injuries Back 24. Creating Inclusionary Opportunities 27. "Can I Play Too?"
Peer Tutoring ◎ *(12, 29)*	7. "Buddy Skills" for Preschoolers 15. Collaborative Planning	3. What Do I Do Now? 25. Unexpected Benefits of High School Peer Tutoring	11. Mega-Analysis of Meta-Analyses 18. Group Development for Students 33. Making Comprehensive Inclusion of Special Needs Students Work
Speech and Language Impairments ◎ *(16)*	6. Together Is Better 12. Distinguishing Language Differences 15. Collaborative Planning	10. Pyramid Power for Collaborative Planning 16. Facilitating the Socialization of Children 22. Child with Severe Hearing Loss	13. Language Interaction Techniques 23. Multimedia Stories for Deaf Childen
Transition ◎ *(30)*	5. From Philosophy to Practice 15. Collaborative Planning 34. Transition from High School to Work or College	25. Unexpected Benefits of High School Peer Tutoring 35. School-to-Work	17. Getting the Student with Head Injuries Back 33. Making Comprehensive Inclusion of Special Needs Students Work
Visual Impairments ◎ *(23, 24)*	6. Together Is Better	29. Accessible Web Site Design	21. Preschool Orientation 24. Creating Inclusionary Opportunities

● AE: Educating Exceptional Children

The following World Wide Web sites have been carefully researched and selected to support the articles found in this reader. If you are interested in learning more about specific topics found in this book, these Web sites are a good place to start. The sites are cross-referenced by number and appear in the topic guide on the previous two pages. Also, you can link to these Web sites through our DUSHKIN ONLINE support site at *http://www.dushkin.com/online/*.

The following sites were available at the time of publication. Visit our Web site—we update DUSHKIN ONLINE regularly to reflect any changes.

General Sources

1. The Big Pages of Special Education Links
http://www.mts.net/~jgreenco/special.html
This site leads to links of all sorts that deal with disabilities related to special education.

2. Council for Exceptional Children
http://www.cec.sped.org
This is the home page for the Council for Exceptional Children, a large professional organization that is dedicated to improving education for children with exceptionalities, students with disabilities, and/or the gifted child. It leads to the ERIC Clearinghouse on disabilities and gifted education and the National Clearinghouse for Professions in Special Education.

3. National Association for the Education of Young Children (NAEYC)
http://www.naeyc.org/default.htm
The National Association for the Education of Young Children (NAEYC) is the nation's largest organization of early childhood professionals devoted to improving the quality of early childhood education programs for children from birth through age eight.

4. National Information Center for Children and Youth with Disabilities (NICHCY)
http://www.nichcy.org/index.html
NICHCY provides information and makes referrals in areas related to specific disabilities, early intervention, special education and related services, individualized education programs, and much more. The site also connects to a listing of Parent's Guides to resources for children and youth with disabilities, which is equally useful for those who work with and/or teach this population.

5. National Rehabilitation Information Center
http://www.cais.com/naric/
A series of databases that can be keyword-searched on subjects that include physical, mental, and psychiatric disabilities, vocational rehabilitation, special education, assistive technology, and more can be found on this site.

6. Other Disability-Related Sites
http://www.ici.coled.umn.edu/ici/othersites.html
A wide-ranging list of disability-related Internet sites is available here.

Inclusive Education

7. Inclusive Education: Cooperative Teaching
http://www.uni.edu/coe/inclusion/cooperative.html
This article discusses how regular education and special education teachers can work together to promote and implement inclusive education.

8. One Size Doesn't Fit All: Full Inclusion Inhibits Academic Progress of Special Education Students
http://141.218.70.183/SPED603/paperHewitt.html
Michele Hewitt, in this article, discusses the decline of academic progress of special education students in an inclusive classroom.

Early Childhood

9. Early Childhood Care and Development
http://www.ecdgroup.com
Dedicated to the improvement of conditions of young children at risk, the Consultative Group provides an International Resources site on Early Childhood Care and Development. Child development theory, programming data, parenting data, research, and other related areas that support young children (ages 0–8) and their families can be found on this site.

10. I Am Your Child
http://www.iamyourchild.org
Information regarding early childhood development is provided on this site. Resources for parents and caregivers are provided.

11. Institute on Community Integration Projects
http://www.ici.coled.umn.edu/ici/overview/projects.html#1
Research projects related to Early Childhood and early intervention services for special education are described here.

12. SERI: Special Education Resources on the Internet
http://www.hood.edu/seri/serihome.htm
This excellent resource offers helpful sites in all phases of special education in early childhood, including disabilities, mental retardation, behavior disorders, autism, gifted and talented, and other problem areas. It includes legal, inclusion, parent, educator, and transition resources.

Learning Disabilities

13. Learning Disabilities and Disorders
http://fly.hiwaay.net/~garson/learnd.htm
This is a good source for information about all kinds of learning disabilities with links to other related material.

14. Learning Disabilities Association of America
http://www.ldanatl.org
The purpose of the LDA is to advance the education and general welfare of children of normal and potentially normal intelligence who show handicaps of a perceptual, conceptual, or coordinative nature. Its home page contains What's New, Fact Sheets, Resources, Publications, and more.

15. The Instant Access Treasure Chest
http://www.fln.vcu.edu/ld/ld.html
Billed as the Foreign Language Teacher's Guide to Learning Disabilities, this site contains a very thorough list of resources for anyone interested in LD education issues.

Speech and Language Impairments

16. Speech and Language Impairment
http://www.socialnet.lu/handitel/wwwlinks/dumb.html
A thorough collection of Web sites, plus an article on the relationship between form and function in the speech of specifically language-impaired children, may be accessed here.

Mental Retardation, Autism, and Traumatic Brain Injuries

17. Autism Society Early Interventions Package
http://www.autism-society.org/packages/early_intervention.html
Answers to FAQs about early intervention in cases of autism as well as online help with obtaining early intervention services, reading lists, and organizations to contact for further information are located on this Web site.

18. Autism Society Educating Children Information Package
http://www.autism-society.org/packages/educating_children.html
This site contains a resource list, articles, a list of useful audio cassettes for parents and educators, a bibliography of useful books, a list of available instructional and educational materials, and much more.

19. Disability-Related Sources on the Web
http://www.arcofarizona.org/dislnkin.html
An excellent resource whose many links include grant resources, federally funded projects and federal agencies, assistive technology, national and international organizations, and educational resources and directories.

20. Gentle Teaching
http://utopia.knoware.nl/users/gentle/
Maintained by the foundation for Gentle Teaching in the Netherlands, this page explains a nonviolent approach for helping children and adults with special needs.

Emotional and Behavioral Disturbances

21. Resources in Emotional or Behavioral Disorders (EBD)
http://www.gwu.edu/~ebdweb/index.html
At this page, link to a collection of Web resources for teachers of students with serious emotional disturbances.

Vision and Hearing Impairments

22. British Columbia Education, Skills, and Training: Special Education Branch
http://www.bced.gov.bc.ca/specialed/hearimpair/toc.htm
At this site, a complete resource guide to support classroom teachers of hard of hearing and deaf students is available. Additional Web resources are also to be found here.

23. The New York Institute for Special Education
http://www.nyise.org/blind.htm
This school is an educational facility that serves children who are blind or visually impaired. The site includes program descriptions and resources for the blind.

24. Visual Impairment Information
http://www.mts.net/~jgreenco/special.html#Visual
There is a list of education links for visual impairment information at this site.

Multiple Disabilities

25. ADE: Exceptional Student Services
http://internet.ade.state.az.us/programs/assistance/ess/pinspals/multiple.html
This Arizona Department of Education site defines multiple disabilities, explains the effect that multiple disabilities have on a child, and offers references, resources, and lists.

26. Related Serious Research Project: Abstract
http://www.uvm.edu/~mgiangre/RSRPab1.html
This is an abstract from "Severe and Multiple Disabilities," by Michael F. Giangreco of the University of Vermont, which describes the problems that students with multiple disabilities have and offers actions that can be taken.

Orthopedic and Health Impairments

27. Association to Benefit Children (ABC)
http://www.a-b-c.org
ABC presents a network of programs that includes child advocacy, education for disabled children, care for HIV-positive children, employment, housing, foster care, and day care.

28. Resources for VE Teachers
http://cpt.fsu.edu/TREE/VE/TOFC.HTML
Effective practices for teachers of varying exceptionalities (VE) classes of physically and health-impaired students are listed here.

Giftedness

29. Kenny Anthony's Gifted and Talented and General Educational Resources
http://www2.tsixroads.com/~kva/
In addition to definitions and characteristics of giftedness and needs of the gifted, an excellent list of education resources for the gifted can be found at this site.

Transition

30. National Transition Alliance (NTA) Home Page
http://www.dssc.org/nta/index.html
This newly done site of the NTA provides state transition resources, searchable databases for keyword searching on transition, school to work, model programs in interactive format, links to other online databases, and includes a database of model transition programs.

We highly recommend that you review our Web site for expanded information and our other product lines. We are continually updating and adding links to our Web site in order to offer you the most usable and useful information that will support and expand the value of your Annual Editions. You can reach us at: *http://www.dushkin.com/annualeditions/.*

www.dushkin.com/online/

Unit Selections

1. **Inclusion of Children with Disabilities: Seeking the Appropriate Balance,** Martha M. McCarthy
2. **What Are Special Education Teachers Made Of?** Sharon Gonder
3. **What Do I Do Now? A Teacher's Guide to Including Students with Disabilities,** Michael F. Giangreco
4. **Four Inclusion Models That Work,** Dori Elliott and Merry McKenney

Key Points to Consider

❖ What does the 1997 reauthorization of IDEA require of states who fail to include children with disabilities in regular education classes?

❖ What motivates special education teachers to conquer challenges deemed impossible?

❖ What 10 recommendations can improve a regular education teacher's abilities to work with special needs children in an inclusive classroom?

❖ How do children learn best? Does specialized instruction really help? What are the three biggest challenges facing inclusive education?

 **Links** www.dushkin.com/online/

7. **Inclusive Education: Cooperative Teaching**
   http://www.uni.edu/coe/inclusion/cooperative.html
8. **One Size Doesn't Fit All: Full Inclusion Inhibits Academic Progress of Special Education Students**
   http://141.218.70.183/SPED603/paperHewitt.html

These sites are annotated on pages 4 and 5.

Public schools have an obligation to provide free educational services in the least restrictive environment possible to all children with diagnosed conditions of exceptionality. Although laws in Canada and the United States differ slightly, and laws in each state of the United States recognize different diagnostic criteria, public schools have an obligation to serve children with exceptional conditions in as normal an educational environment as possible. Inclusive education is difficult. It works very well for some students with exceptionalities in some situations, and, to the contrary, it works marginally or not at all for other students with exceptionalities in other situations.

For inclusion to succeed within a school, everyone must be committed to be part of the solution: superintendent, principal, teachers, coaches, aides, ancillary staff, students, and parents and families. High-quality education for students, regardless of abilities, requires good communication and collaboration. It is complicated to achieve. One or two persons who oppose it strongly and vocally can dramatically alter its implementation. Everyone must be educated about its philosophical antecedents and goals. Likewise, open ledgers, financial accountability, and projections of future benefits should be set out. Inclusion requires sufficient monetary support as well as extraordinary human effort. As laws and mandates call for more diagnoses to be made and more special needs to be met, the number of children who qualify for special educational services is expected to rise.

The term "least restrictive environment" is often mistakenly understood as the need for all children to be educated in a regular education classroom. Terms such as *normalization* and *inclusion* are used to describe the education of children with exceptional conditions in the regular education classroom. If students can learn and achieve better in inclusive programs, then the programs are well worth the effort. If students can succeed only marginally in inclusive education classrooms, some alternate solutions are necessary. Current laws do not require that every child be placed in a regular education classroom, but rather that every child be educated in the least restrictive environment possible. A continuum of placement options exists to maximize the goal of educating every child. For some children, a separate class, or even a separate school, is still optimal.

Special education and regular education teachers are becoming more and more intertwined. Collaboration between teachers is increasing as separate special education classes are serving fewer students. Every child with an exceptional condition is different from every other child: in symptoms, needs, and teachability. Each child is, therefore, provided with an individualized education program (IEP). This plan consists of both long- and short-term goals for education, specially designed instructional procedures with related services, and methods to evaluate the child's progress. The IEP is updated and revised annually. Special education teachers make recommendations for goals and teaching strategies on IEPs even if they are not the child's primary teacher.

The first article in this unit is a legal update written by Dr. Martha McCarthy for all persons involved in the care and/or education of children with disabilities. It discusses the impact that the 1997 reauthorization of the Individuals with Disabilities Education Act (IDEA) is having and will continue to have on our students, their teachers, and our society. Courts of law must consider the social as well as the educational benefits of including children with disabilities in the least restrictive environment possible, and the relative costs of regular classes versus special classes when adjudicating any educational placement dispute. Several 1990s cases that were resolved in favor of regular education placement are contrasted with some court decisions that were rendered in favor of more segregated placements. Dr. McCarthy summarizes her presentation with a discussion of the controversial "sticky wickets" of education which remain unresolved.

The second article gives an up-to-date view of the changed functions of special education teachers. Author Sharon Gonder provides glimpses into the lives of several special education teachers and into the lives of real students whom they have helped, and by whom, in turn, they have been helped. The vignettes are both instructive and heartwarming. They deal with important issues, such as building programs from scratch, involving parents and the community, collaboration, technology, creating individualized family service plans (IFSPs), individualized education plans (IEPs), and individualized transition plans (ITPs), and promoting a full continuum of services for students who need more than a regular classroom. They prove that students can go far beyond others' expectations for them.

The third essay addresses how to make inclusion work. Drawing on two recent books on inclusion (*Inclusion: A Guide for Educators* [1996] by W. Stainback and S. Stainback, and *Creativity and Collaborative Learning: A Practical Guide to Empowering Students and Teachers* [1994] by J. Thousand, R. Villa, and A. Nevin), Michael Giangreco presents 10 practical recommendations for teachers. All educators who find themselves faced with the task of making their classroom a good learning environment for included children with varying abilities will benefit from these 10 suggestions. The article will also initiate discussions of a hypothetical nature, such as "If I have this student, then . . . " Such exercises can generate more creative solutions to the questions about how to include unique students with very individualized abilities in regular education classrooms.

The last selection in this section on inclusive education is a discussion of the implementation of four different types of inclusion: consultation, team teaching, aide services, and limited pullout services. Dori Elliott, a regular education teacher, and Merry McKenney, a special education teacher, give many realistic and practical suggestions for success with each of these models. They expect positive outcomes and help the reader understand how they can be achieved.

Inclusive Education

Inclusion of Children with Disabilities:
Seeking the Appropriate Balance

by Martha M. McCarthy

In the 1990s courts have interpreted the Individuals with Disabilities Education Act (IDEA) as entailing a strong preference for inclusion.

The fastest-growing area of school law pertains to special education services and the rights of children with disabilities. Most of the controversies involve interpretations of the Individuals with Disabilities Education Act (IDEA), a federal funding law that guarantees all children with disabilities a free appropriate education at public expense.[1] A volatile topic is the IDEA requirement that children with disabilities must be placed in the "least restrictive environment" (LRE).

This LRE mandate means that each state education agency must ensure that "to the maximum extent appropriate, children with disabilities, including children in public or private institutions or other care facilities, are educated with children

MARTHA M. MCCARTHY is a chancellor professor at Indiana University in Bloomington, Indiana.

who are not disabled."[2] Under IDEA regulations, children may be placed in special classes or separate facilities "only when the nature or severity of the disability is such that education in regular classes with the use of supplementary aids and services cannot be achieved satisfactorily."[3] In addition, the 1997 reauthorization of the IDEA requires states to revise their special-education funding formulas if they discourage placing children with disabilities in the regular education environment.[4]

The term "inclusion" is not mentioned in the federal law. It is a popular term that refers to placing students with disabilities in the regular classrooms of their home schools *with their age and grade peers* to the maximum extent possible. In short, inclusion means bringing support services to the child rather than moving the child to a segregated setting to receive special services.[5] This concept has been extremely controversial, es-

pecially in connection with children who have *severe* mental, emotional, or physical disabilities.

IDEA's Preference for Inclusion

In the 1990s courts have interpreted the IDEA as entailing a strong preference for inclusion. Accordingly, they have placed the burden on school authorities to establish that a regular education placement is not appropriate for a given child with disabilities. Although various criteria have been proposed for making this determination, in general courts consider at least the following: the educational benefits of the inclusive versus segregated settings; the noneducational (e.g., social) benefits of both placements; the impact of the inclusive placement on other children in the class; and the costs of the respective placements.[6]

The Eleventh Circuit Court of Appeals in 1991 held that a school district had not given adequate consideration to educating a child with Down syndrome in the regular class with supplementary aids and services.[7] The court recognized that academic benefits are not the only advantages of a regular education placement; there are social, language, and role-modeling benefits as well. Assessing inclusive versus segregated placements in terms of educational and noneducational effects on the child, costs, and impact on other students, the court required placement of the child in a general education program at her neighborhood school rather than in a separate special education class.

In a significant 1993 decision, *Oberti v. Board of Education of the Borough of Clementon School District*, the Third Circuit Court of Appeals ruled that school districts have an affirmative obligation to consider placing students with disabilities in general education and supplementary aids and services before they explore other alternatives.[8] The court stated that the law's strong presumption that children should be educated in the regular classroom may be rebutted only with evidence that (a) the student's disabilities are so severe he or she will receive little or no benefit from inclusion; (b) the child is so disruptive that others' education is impaired; or (c) costs are so significant that they will have a negative effect on other students. The court declared that inclusion is a right, not a privilege for a select few.

In a subsequent California case, the Ninth Circuit Court of Appeals assessed the educational and noneducational benefits, costs, and impact on other children of an inclusive placement for a moderately mentally handicapped child.[9] The court concluded that the IDEA favors inclusion if the child can receive a satisfactory education, even if it is not the best setting for the student.[10] Because the school district had proposed a segregated placement for the child, her parents enrolled her in a private school, where she attended kindergarten through second grade in regular classes with support services. Relying on testimony of her teachers and parents, the court found that the child had made substantial progress in regular education and that there had been no detrimental effect on the regular education program. Thus, the court ordered the child placed in an inclusive environment in the public school.

It should not be assumed that school authorities generally support the more restrictive environment. In several cases parents have contested the school district's proposed inclusive placement, requesting instead residential or other segregated settings for their children. In 1996, the Seventh Circuit Court of Appeals affirmed a federal district court's conclusion that a private school for disabled students was not the LRE for a student with attention deficit hyperactivity disorder (ADHD). The court agreed with school authorities that the student could receive an appropriate education at the public high school.[11] Also, the Fifth Circuit Court of Appeals found that a school district's proposed inclusive placement for a child with learning and emotional difficulties that entailed some individualized instruction and counseling as well as some regular classes was the LRE, notwithstanding parents' request for a residential placement.[12]

The same court in 1997 affirmed a federal district court's decision that reversed a hearing officer's award of reimbursement to parents for costs of a residential placement for their child with ADHD and Tourette's syndrome.[13] The school district had attempted various placements for the child, who was quite disruptive and abusive toward other students. Noting that the individually designed education program need not be the best possible program,[14] the court found that placing the child in adaptive-behavior classes for part of the day and in the regular education program for the remainder of the day was appropriate. Thus, the parents were not entitled to reimbursement for the more restrictive residential placement.

Appropriate Noninclusive Placements

Although courts are interpreting the IDEA as entailing a presumption that children with disabilities should be placed in regular education, they are not requiring inclusive placements under all circumstances. Courts will review the specific circumstances of each case, and it is not impossible for school authorities to substantiate that the welfare of the child or classmates would be jeopardized in the regular classroom. To illustrate, the Eighth Circuit Court of Appeals upheld a centralized program for a wheelchair-bound student with spina bifida.[15] The court reasoned that school authorities satisfied the IDEA by making an appropriate program available for the student even though it was not at his home school.

In several cases dealing with hearing-impaired students, courts have upheld centralized programs, some in segregated settings, because the language needs of these children would be served more appropriately.[16] Other courts also have ruled that when more restrictive placements are superior and comparable services cannot feasibly be provided in the regular classroom, placements in segregated settings—including those away from students' home schools—are appropriate for specific children.[17]

For example, the Ninth Circuit Court of Appeals ruled that a child with Tourette's syndrome and ADHD should be placed in a special school for learning-disabled children rather than in the regular classroom.[18] The court reasoned that this child's disruptive classroom behavior, including sexual harassment of female students, prevented him from learning in the regular classroom and posed a threat to others.

Thus, placement in the special school proposed by school authorities was appropriate for this child.

In a subsequent case, the same court held that inclusion was not appropriate for a high school student who suffered from attention deficit disorder. The court noted that prior attempts to educate the child in the regular classroom had resulted in total failure, while instruction in a segregated setting produced superior results.[19]

The Third Circuit Court of Appeals held that a full-time residential facility was the least-restrictive educationally appropriate setting for a severely mentally retarded student; such a residential program was necessary for the student to make meaningful educational progress.[20] Earlier, the Seventh Circuit Court of Appeals had held that a segregated placement was appropriate for a child who was not benefiting from interaction with nonhandicapped students and who needed a more structured program with additional support services. Although the parents wanted the child placed in an integrated setting, the court noted that prior efforts at mainstreaming had proven unsuccessful: the student's behavior had regressed and he had substantially disrupted classmates.[21] In most cases upholding more restrictive placements, efforts had been made to educate the children in the regular classroom, and these efforts had not been successful.

The Continuing Controversy

Judging from the litigation to date, it appears that courts will place the burden on the party seeking a more restrictive placement. That party will have to establish that the regular education classroom with support services is not an appropriate environment for a specific child. The merits and mechanics of inclusion are likely to remain controversial among special and regular educators, school leaders, and parent advocacy groups. Teachers unions, which are skeptical at best

about full inclusion, contend that students with disabilities should not be placed in regular education unless class size is reduced and all teachers receive appropriate preparation in dealing with such children.[22] There are also fiscal concerns that inclusion might result in a reduction in funds targeted for children with disabilities. Such children, it is feared, will be placed in regular education *without* appropriate support services.

Several other issues remain unresolved. For example, how superior

The merits and mechanics of inclusion are likely to remain controversial among special and regular educators, school leaders, and parent advocacy groups.

must a segregated program be to justify placing a child there instead of in the regular classroom? Unless an inclusive placement has been tried and its impact assessed, will school authorities or parents ever be able to argue that inclusion is not appropriate for a given child? How should students with severe cognitive disabilities be integrated into the regular classroom at the high school level, where students often are tracked by ability in academic classes? If the curriculum for such children is modified beyond recognition, is this still inclusion? These and related issues seem destined to generate a steady stream of litigation

and perhaps ultimately a Supreme Court ruling to clarify the parameters of the LRE mandate.

1. 20 U.S.C. § 1401 (1997).
2. 20 U.S.C. 1412(5)(B) (1997); 34 CFR 300.550 (1997).
3. 34 CFR 300.550 (1997).
4. 20 U.S.C.A. § 1413 (1997).
5. See National Association of State Boards of Education, *Winners All: A Call For Inclusive Schools* (Alexandria, Va.: 1992); Joy Rogers, "The Inclusion Revolution," *Research Bulletin* No. 11, Phi Delta Kappa Center for Evaluation, Development and Research, May 1993; "Inclusion: What Does It Mean?" *SEAS Cable*, vol. 14, no. 7, July 1993, 1–3.
6. For a discussion of these criteria, see *Sacramento City Unified Sch. Dist. Bd. of Educ. v. Rachel H. ex rel. Holland*, 14 F.3d 1398 (9th Cir. 1994), cert. denied, 512 U.S. 1207 (1994). In earlier cases, two federal appeals courts articulated slightly different standards, but both entailed some consideration of these criteria. The Fifth Circuit Court of Appeals suggested that courts must first determine whether the child can be educated in the general classroom satisfactorily with supplementary aids and services. If not, special education must be provided and the school district must mainstream the student to the maximum extent appropriate. *Daniel R.R. v. State Bd. of Educ.*, 874 F.2d 1036, 1048 (5th Cir. 1989). The Sixth Circuit Court of Appeals noted that "where the segregated facility is considered superior, the court should determine whether the services which make that placement superior could be feasibly provided in a non-segregated setting." If so, the segregated placement would not be appropriate under the IDEA. *Roncker v. Walter*, 700 F.2d 1058, 1063 (6th Cir. 1983), cert. denied, 464 U.S. 864 (1983).
7. *Greer v. Rome City Sch. Dist.*, 950 F.2d 688 (11th Cir. 1991), opinion withdrawn, 956 F.2d 1025 (11th Cir. 1992), opinion reinstated in part, 967 F.2d 470 (11th Cir. 1992).
8. 995 F.2d 1204 (3d Cir. 1993). See also *Mavis v. Sobol*, 839 F.Supp. 968 (N.D.N.Y. 1994) (holding that school districts have the burden of proving that the LRE requirement is satisfied.)
9. *Sacramento City Unified Sch. Dist. Bd. of Educ. v. Rachel H. ex rel. Holland*, 14 F.3d 1398 (9th Cir. 1994), cert. denied, 114 S.Ct. 2679 (1994).
10. See also *Kerkam v. Superintendent, D.C. Pub. Schs.*, 931 F.2d 84 (D.C. Cir. 1991) (holding that local extended-day program conferred education benefit on severely retarded student in the LRE and thus satisfied the IDEA even if student could have made more progress in a residential placement); *Schreiber v. Ridgewood Bd. of Educ.*, 952 F.Supp. 205 (D.N.J. 1997) (holding that day program in alternative middle school that provided educational benefit to neurologically impaired student, even though residential program might be more intense); *P. J. v.*

Connecticut Bd. of Educ., 788 F.Supp. 673 (D.C. Conn. 1992) (ruling that a Down syndrome child with mild to moderate mental impairment was entitled to a fully integrated setting with appropriate special education services or the individualized program must detail a strong justification for any segregation).

11. *Monticello Sch. Dist. No. 125 v. Illinois State Bd. of Educ.,* 910 F.Supp. 446 (C.D. Ill. 1995), aff'd, 102 F.3d 895 (7th Cir. 1996). See also *School Dist. of Kettle Moraine v. Grover,* 755 F.Supp. 243 (E.D. Wis. 1990) (holding that despite parents' desire to have student placed in segregated program, student's educational and socialization needs would be met in an integrated program at the neighborhood high school).

12. *Salley v. St. Tammany Parish Sch. Bd.,* 57 F.3d 458 (5th Cir. 1995). See also *Doe v. Board of Educ. of Tullahoma City Schs.,* 9 F.3d 455 (6th Cir. 1993), cert. denied, 511 U.S. 1108 (1994) (denying parents reimbursement for the private placement of a child with learning disabilities; the proposed public regular education program with support services was appropriate); *Jonathan G. v. Lower Merion Sch. Dist.,* 955 F.Supp. 413 (E.D. Pa. 1997) (upholding inclusive placement for a child with learning disabilities despite parental objections); *Mather v. Hartford Sch. Dist.,* 928 F.Supp. 437 (D. Vt. 1996) (rejecting reimbursement to parents for private education of a learning disabled child; placement in regular education with intensive instruction in a resource room was appropriate, even though the private program might be better).

13. *Cypress-Fairbanks Indep. Sch. Dist. v. Michael F.,* 118 F.3d 245 (5th Cir. 1997) (also assessing the school district's costs incurred in the litigation against the par-

ents). The Supreme Court has ruled that parents who unilaterally enroll their children with disabilities in private programs may be entitled to reimbursement if the proposed public school placements are challenged through proper procedures and found to be inappropriate. See *Florence County Sch. Dist. v. Carter,* 510 U.S. 7 (1993); *Burlington Sch. Committee v. Department of Educ.,* 471 U.S. 359 (1985).

14. See *Board of Educ. of the Hendrick Hudson Cent. Sch. Dist. v. Rowley,* 458 U.S. 176 (1982).

15. *Schuldt v. Mankato Indep. Sch. Dist.,* 937 F.2d 1357 (8th Cir. 1991), cert. denied, 502 U.S. 1059 (1992).

16. Upholding placements of hearing-impaired students in centralized programs rather than in schools closer to the students' homes, see, e.g., *Flour Bluff Indep. Sch. Dist. v. Katherine M.,* 91 F.3d 689 (5th Cir. 1996), cert. denied, 117 S.Ct. 948 (1997); *Poolaw v. Bishop,* 67 F.3d 830 (9th Cir. 1995); *Barnett v. Fairfax County Sch. Bd.,* 927 F.2d 146 (4th Cir. 1991), cert. denied, 502 U.S. 859 (1991); *Briggs v. Board of Educ. of Conn.,* 882 F.2d 688 (2d Cir. 1989); *Lachman v. Illinois State Bd. of Educ.,* 852 F.2d 290 (7th Cir. 1988), cert. denied, 488 U.S. 925 (1988).

17. See, e.g., *Murray v. Montrose County Sch. Dist. RE-1J,* 51 F.3d 921 (10th Cir. 1995) (upholding removal of child from neighborhood school and placement in school with program for children with severe disabilities); *Devries v. Fairfax County School Bd.,* 882 F.2d 876 (4th Cir. 1989) (holding that county vocational center thirteen miles away was the appropriate LRE for a severely autistic child); *A.W. v. Northwest R-1 Sch. Dist.,* 813 F.2d 158 (8th Cir. 1987), cert. denied, 484 U.S. 847

(1987) (upholding segregated school for a severely mentally retarded child); *Wilson v. Marana Unified School Dist. No. 6 of Pima County,* 735 F.2d 1178 (9th Cir. 1984) (upholding placement of a severely physically disabled child thirty minutes away where instruction by a teacher specially certified to address physical disabilities was available); *Thornock by Baugh v. Boise Indep. Sch. Dist. No. 1,* 767 P.2d 1241 (Idaho 1988), cert. denied, 490 U.S. 1068 (1989) (holding that inclusion may be inappropriate where educational experience would not or could not be productive or enriching to the student or where it would disrupt the classroom).

18. *Clyde K. and Sheila K. v. Puyallup School Dist.,* 35 F.3d 1396 (9th Cir. 1994).

19. *Capistrano Unified Sch. Dist. v. Wartenberg,* 59 F.3d 884 (9th Cir. 1995).

20. *M. C. v. Central Regional Sch. Dist.,* 81 F.3d 389 (3rd Cir. 1996), cert. denied, 117 S.Ct. 176 (1996).

21. *Rheinstrom v. Lincolnwood Bd. of Educ., Dist. 74,* 56 F.3d 67 (7th Cir. 1995). See also *D.F., M.F. and D.J.F. v. Western Sch. Corp. and Kokomo Area Special Educ. Coop.,* 921 F.Supp. 559 (S.D. Ind. 1996) (holding that a child with severe mental disabilities could not meet his individualized education program goals in the general education classroom and did not model or imitate other students so as to attain nonacademic benefits from inclusion).

22. See David Hoff, "NEA Policy Sets Parameters for Special Ed Inclusion," *Education Daily,* 7 July 1994, 1–2; Joanna Richardson, "A.F.T. Says Poll Shows Many Oppose 'Inclusion,'" *Education Week,* 3 August 1994, 14.

WHAT ARE SPECIAL EDUCATION TEACHERS MADE OF?

Sharon Gonder

Even before "special" laws were written, special education staffs yearly made improvements in the existing programs, but change was slow and grossly inadequate. In 1975, P.L. 94-142 was passed, with the key words "free appropriate public education" and the funds to back up this philosophy. Change was rapid; and research, teacher training, materials, and programs began to respect both the students' and the teachers' abilities to learn and to teach. With the improvement in assessment techniques, total programs could be designed to meet an individual's needs.

The examples in this article provide a glimpse into the lives of pioneers in special education—both teachers and students—and show common threads of motivation and direction. These people recognized a need, whether perceived or from personal experience, and set out to provide the research, methods, and materials necessary to improve the quality of life for people with disabilities.

These pioneers also believe that participation in professional organizations is one of the best ways to promote research, provide inservice instruction, establish and monitor professional standards, and influence legislation.

Special education teachers have accepted the challenges presented to them concerning children with special needs. These teachers have been the impetus of the movement toward mainstreaming and inclusion, which has enabled many exceptional students to receive their education in a more normal setting than in the past. Through inservice, collaborative teaching, and modeling techniques, general education teachers, on the whole, are more willing to accept students who present educational challenges; and more students in general education have learned to accept children with disabilities and are willing to give them a helping hand when needed. Students with disabilities have better opportunities to engage in normal social interactions. Many parents are comforted that their children with disabilities are able to associate with their classmates without disabilities. Students with disabilities generally spend less time each day being transported to special programs outside their general attendance areas; and more teaching aides are available to provide individualized help to those students.

"It's okay, Mrs. G. We need you."

Special education teachers have always had to be adaptable, and not easily thrown into a state of shock. Take, for example, the first day of school for one brand new teacher.

The bell is about to ring, but Mrs. G. is ready. She has carefully read the folders of her six students. There are many exceptionalities and all ages, but she feels that she already knows them. This is a new classroom—and there are no materials or books; but she has made some of her own activities and games, obtained some art materials from the art teacher, and borrowed some books from the librarian. Filled with as much anticipation as kids are on their first day, she goes out to meet the bus and escort her children to their new room. But wait, something is wrong—21 children got off the bus, yes—21! This resourceful teacher simply says: "Well, we'll all just have to sit on the floor and pretend we are on an Indian reservation and see how much we can learn about our language."

Does the year get any better? Her students range in age from 5 to 14; IQs range from 52 to 112; and disabilities range from "trainable" to culturally disadvantaged to neurologically impaired to severely emotionally disturbed. It is 2 days before the room is equipped with desks and chairs and 3 weeks before meager supplies arrive. Does she quit, saying this can't be done? No, these kids must have an education, and no one else seems to care.

The following year, a similar scenario occurs when, 1 week before school opens, she is asked to pilot a new program called "Learning Disabilities." This is in the late 1960s before the federal government has even arrived at a definition for this disability. She accepts the challenge even though those students who were placed into the program had not been diagnosed as having learning disabilities. They just didn't fit any other place. As all special education teachers learn, the job doesn't stop at the classroom door. As the year progresses, she begins to give inservice presentations to help the school staffs understand these disabilities. Gradually, she finds herself giving presentations to civic and other community groups. Finally, parents cry out for help, so she establishes a parent support group with the backing of one of the local hospitals. As the community begins to understand these children and their disabilities, support comes in the form of materials and equipment, volunteer help, park board assistance with participation in sports activities, and in school-to-work transition programs.

She had become the strongest advocate special education had seen in that town, and services began to improve. This community of 35,000 became sensitive to the needs of people with disabilities because a new teacher didn't realize that it couldn't be done.

Collaboration and technology begin to really make a difference in the mid-1970s.

"Hey, I can talk!"

Jennifer's story shows the creativeness and collaboration of many teachers in making communication and learning possible for a student and how technological advances improved her quality of life. This story also is indicative of how teachers often go the extra mile outside the classroom to make sure the student's adjustment to the adult world is made effectively. Jennifer's equipment also illustrates the progress of technology.

Jennifer had cerebral palsy and went to Goshorn Learning Center during her preschool years. This facility offered physical therapy and speech therapy but nothing in the area of academics. In the mid-'70s, she came to public school kindergarten in her wheelchair. Her classroom had easy access from the outside and from the playground. There was a restroom in the classroom, but she was not physically able to use it. She had a sweet smile and disposition but was unable to engage in verbal communication. The learning disabilities teacher and the speech/language therapist made a language board so she could point to the pictures of various nouns and verbs important to her communication. As she began to learn letters, numbers, and words, the language board was expanded to keep up with her increased skills. Her parents practiced with her at home and offered suggestions toward improving the board. The next year, Jennifer's mother's health rapidly deteriorated due to multiple sclerosis. Jennifer's father lovingly cared for both his wife and child.

During first grade, Jennifer was placed into the classroom for children with orthopedic disabilities in another building, which was accessible to wheelchairs. In this particular elementary school, children with physical disabilities were included in all school activities, including the playground where the other children of the school fought over who was going to get to play with various children with disabilities. Jennifer's self-concept remained positive, with the orthopedic disabilities, language, and learning disabilities teachers constantly upgrading her language board for better communication and modifying techniques for teaching reading and math.

When Jennifer moved to the high school, technology progressed to the point that Jennifer had a motorized wheelchair, even though only parts of the building were accessible until an elevator was finally installed. She was equipped with a machine on which she could type in responses, and it would produce the approximate sounds. She named it "Ben." Although Ben provided some liberation and flexibility in communication, it was extremely slow and spoke in a mechanical monotone so was unsuitable for classroom use.

Following Jennifer's graduation from high school, her speech/language teacher made arrangements for Jennifer to work as a volunteer at a local hospital. Her teacher rode with her on the bus and went with her to the hospital to help her learn how to sort and deliver the mail to the patients. She does this so well and enjoys it so much that it is a job she continues to do to this day. In this way she is giving a little back to the community.

Technological advancements have enabled Jennifer to communicate more effectively with society. Her current machine, the Liberator, is considerably faster than Ben. She types in chunks or morphographic units, as opposed to individual letters, and then the machine prints out the communication. This machine also has enabled her to construct sentences complete with articles and conjunctions, which makes for more socially appropriate connected speech. It also has a speaking component for short responses or questions.

Figure 1 shows a letter Jennifer recently sent to her elementary school principal following his stay in the hospital.

Classroom teachers, special education teachers, parents, community services such as the city transit handicapped-accessible bus, and civic groups all assisted with the acquisition of needed equipment for both Jennifer and her mother. This equipment has enabled Jennifer to go to work, run errands (doctor, groceries, etc.), go to the laundromat, and enjoy many of the activities people without physical disabilities enjoy. The community worked together before technology offered much assistance, and it continues to collaborate on services.

Before IEPs and self-determination, achieving full potential was hard to maintain.

"Look, Mom, no wheelchair!"

Special education teachers have long understood that the three Rs are not the only aspects of a child's young life that need attention if he or she is to have opportunities to become a self-confident and independent citizen. Betty's story shows how a teacher went beyond her own training and expectations.

Betty came to public school in third grade in a wheelchair, having had no consistent therapy or educational services. Her arms were strong, and she was a friendly child; but she couldn't stand, nor could she read or write. Betty's mother had been told that her daughter would never be able to walk or read, so she just let her scoot around the floor at home and watch TV. Betty was placed in the self-contained classroom for children with learning disabilities. No physical therapy services were available through the district (obviously, this occurred before Public Law 94-142). Because of the many children with severe physical disabilities in this classroom, an aide was hired. The aide happened to be a grandmother, whom the children loved. Betty quickly learned the alphabet and began reading, using the linguistic approach. By the end of the year, her reading skills were at the end of the second-grade level. Her teacher was not convinced that Betty could not walk so she began to do strengthening and flexibility exercises. By November, her teacher secured a walker through Shriners' Hospital in St. Louis. By Christmas, Betty could take messages from her classroom to the office using the walker unassisted. In February, her teacher had Betty fitted with forearm crutches; and by the end of April, Betty was walking to the office using crutches, unassisted.

Meanwhile, Betty continued to just scoot on the floor and watch TV at home. This behavior continued during the summer, and in September Betty was back in her wheelchair again. Her teacher began all over with the exercises, all the time stressing to Betty that it was up to her to continue her exercises and to get back into her crutches. She was in her crutches again by Christmas. But Betty, her mother, and two brothers moved over Christmas break to another town in another state. It's too bad that this was before the days of the individualized education program (IEP) so that Betty's program could have followed her. (Today Betty is 35, in a wheelchair, living in a group home, and working in a sheltered workshop.)

Before interagency collaboration was the norm, caring individuals were leading the way.

"Just look at me now!"

How many times have teachers looked at the total child and not just academic needs?

This concept has been an integral part of special education programs for many years and has been much slower to be integrated into general education programs. In most cases, outside help had to be sought; and this was never easy. John Kidd, a retired school administrator from Missouri, remembers one young girl: It was in an "EMR" class [class for students with mild mental retardation] in the St. Louis County Special School District where I, as an administrator, visited and saw grossly deformed dentition pictures. The teacher knew of no effort to treat the condition. I asked one of the Special School district nurses to take a look and see if something could be done for this girl. She reported a few days later that the student was willing to have some dental work done and that, in seeking to obtain parental approval, she found the mother to have the same deformed dentition but was willing for her daughter to have corrective surgery.

Sometime later, the nurse told me that she had found a few dollars and a benevolent dentist and that treatment was sched-

uled. Within a year the condition was corrected, and within 2 years this young lady had found employment with the assistance of a Special School District Job Placement Consultant, had received her diploma, and was engaged to be married. I subsequently lost track of her but have used the experience and the photos to remind educators that they should be alert to and report to responsible parties, including parents, any negative physical factor that might be correctable and contribute to a student's well-being.

The needs of twice-exceptional children—gifted and learning disabled—often go unrecognized.

"Listen to me read. Now it's fun."

A student is usually not placed into a special education classroom until all else has failed. A special education teacher is one who is able to look beyond the tried and true and create other methods for teaching these children. Kelly's story shows how a teacher did not give up on a child who could not learn to read and was overweight, belligerent, antagonistic, and unpleasant to be around.

Kelly came to the learning disabilities program as a third grader. She could not write her name, could read no words, and was belligerent and aggressive. Testing indicated that her ability level was above average. Many approaches were tried with Kelly, but none were successful. Finally, her teacher used a *rebus* approach—using pictures to represent words. Even though the teacher felt that this method might be demeaning, Kelly's success with it finally allowed her to break down some of her defenses and be more cooperative. By the end of third grade, Kelly was reading at a mid-second-grade level. She began to smile, and her teachers were no longer talking about transferring her into a behavioral disordered program at a nearby residential center in a town 30 miles away.

During the summer, her parents continued reading the books her special education teacher had obtained for her to maintain and strengthen her skills. During her fourth-grade year, Kelly began to participate in classroom activities without feeling embarrassed and began learning cooperative and collaborative skills. In the fifth grade, she no longer needed supportive services.

Three years ago, Kelly graduated from college magna cum laude, with a special invitation to her learning disabilities teacher. (She also won two beauty contests, which helped with her college expenses.)

Parental involvement and technology combine to provide the "extra" that led to this student's success. Recognition of the importance of these elements ensured their inclusion in law.

"Thanks for letting me use the tape recorder."

Special education teachers understand the concept of "least restrictive environment" (LRE) and know how to help parents make use of and move along a full continuum of services. This task has been made easier since the passage of Public Law 94-142 and the Individuals with Disabilities Education Act (IDEA) because now there are more steps along the continuum from residential to fully inclusive programs.

The stories of Rick and Bobby show services for the hearing impaired that teachers and parents had available to them before and after P.L. 94-142.

Sara's story shows what can happen when a continuum of services is available to a child, even though the continuum may not be in sequential steps.

Forty years go, there were no laws to guarantee a free and appropriate public education for children with disabilities. Bernice Decker, a middle school teacher, tells the story of Rick, a deaf child of hearing parents. Rick's disability was not recognized until he had surpassed the time of language acquisition and still did not talk. His doctors encouraged his parents to wait, thinking that he would "grow out of it." Finally, when speech still did not develop by age 3, Rick's hearing was tested; and he was found to have a profound binaural sensorineural hearing loss. Rick's parents were told not to allow him to use sign or gestures because he would use these signs instead of speech. After extended speech therapy with an oral focus, Rick still did not have the language base or the speech/reading skills to succeed in a public school.

Rick was sent to a residential school for the deaf, where he learned manual communication. Later, Rick's parents moved to a larger city where more services were available. At the eighth grade, Rick transferred to a public school, where the special education staff arranged for him to tape record all his classes. His parents and the special education teacher could sign or type out all instructions and all new material not included in the text. He graduated from high school. Today, Rick is married and is employed successfully at a school for the deaf.

"I understand what you're teaching."

Bernice Decker remembers Bobby, who was also deaf from birth. His hearing loss was discovered at about the time of language acquisition. Bobby was enrolled in the Special Learning Center where his teachers and speech therapist signed to him, using the Signed Exact English (SEE) system of communication. He also received daily speech therapy to improve his oral skills. With an English background presented in a way he could understand, Bobby had a language base that enabled recognition of words. At age 4, he was placed in the hearing-impaired program at a public school, where he continued to gain a language base and improve his oral communication skills. At age 7, he received a cochlear implant, which significantly improved his hearing—and learning.

Bobby currently attends school in a general educational program with the aid of a SEE II transliterater. His reading and language skills are at grade level. With the strong support of his parents, teachers, and the public school system, Bobby has a bright future.

"Finally, I'm not afraid."

Sara came to school in first grade with significant visual impairments. The teacher for the visually impaired was in the building only 1 hour a week, so the learning disabilities teacher was made the implementer of the program. Sara's behavior was difficult—she wanted her way at all times in the classroom and ignored tasks that required effort. During the second quarter, she had a grand mal seizure, and the next couple of months

Although the goal today is full inclusion for students with disabilities, the wisdom built into the law allows for a continuum of services for students who need other options.

were spent regulating medication. The school staff also felt that Sara had some visual motor impairment resembling cerebral palsy, especially on the left side. The family finally took Sara to be evaluated at a well-known university hospital, and the school's observations were confirmed.

Sara did not like the hallways at class time, would hide when the class was in the gym, and did not like to eat in front of other people because they made fun of her eating habits. Classwork, although modified, was frustrating for her; to cope, she threw temper tantrums. Sara's mother really didn't, or couldn't, understand the scope of Sara's disabilities and in her impulsive/compulsive manner made matters worse. Finally, the learning disabilities teacher appealed to Advocacy, who encouraged the family to send Sara to the residential school for the visually impaired.

While at the residential school, Sara learned independence and mobility skills, and her teachers made further academic adaptations for her. Two years later, when she returned to the public schools, she was calm and controlled and could handle herself in the school setting. Academically, she continued to be frustrated; but instead of giving up, she would ask for help and actually try again. She is now using recorded books for her content-area texts, which have been obtained from the Library for the Blind. She is in the eighth grade; and by the time she is in high school, Vocational Rehabilitation staff members hope to locate a computer that will type as she dictates. At the high school, she will also be provided with an aide who will not only help her from class to class but also make sure she has a copy that she can read of all the material illustrated on the board and overhead projector and that needed lectures are taped for later review. Now, instead of threatened lawsuits, it's hugs for the learning disabilities teacher from both Mom and Sara, who are glad that this teacher insisted they make use of the full continuum of services.

With standards affecting every area of the curriculum, the requirement that all students be given the "opportunity to learn" must not be forgotten.

"I can do it."

Much of a special education teacher's early training and knowledge was learned from the students. William Littlejohn, a professor at Indiana State University, learned a lesson from Louis that is evident in all his work since that time.

As a special education teacher at a junior high school from the mid- to late 1960s, I was responsible for initiating a special education class for educable mentally retarded students. One of my students, Louis, was a 13-year-old boy classified as educable mentally retarded. One of the classes I taught was shop. I had taught the students how to use various tools and to build simple projects and had come to a point where I wished to allow them to build a project of their choice. Students had been instructed that they had to plan the project, perhaps bring pictures or write a description of their plan, and submit it to me for my approval. Louis told me that he wanted to build a rocker, a child's rocker. My first reaction on hearing this was that I couldn't build a rocker!

How could Louis build such a piece of furniture? But rather than saying "No" to Louis I told him to either draw or find a picture of the rocker, think of what he would need, and what color he would paint it. While telling this to Louis, I was wondering how I could learn enough to help him with the project. I also asked Louis why he wanted to build a child's rocker. Louis's mother had remarried, and a new baby had been born. Louis wanted the rocker for his new half-sister.

The next time we had our shop class, Louis brought in a picture of a red rocker that he wanted to build. In the meantime, I had talked to the general education shop teacher and found that we had the forms to bend the rockers, and I was able to let Louis build the rocker. I will never forget the smile on Louis's face when he completed the project and I complimented him on the beautiful red child's rocker. It truly was a piece of furniture that he, or anyone, could be proud to have built. The pride showed in Louis's face—and it burned into my memory.

One concern in working with people with disabilities is that we might preclude some accomplishment by "drawing a line" to say that those below this line could not accomplish a particular task or learn a particular skill. I learned a life lesson from Louis: *We must be extremely careful in our tendency to jump to conclusions that someone cannot do something because of his or her disability.*

"Mom, you not only opened my doors, but the doors for many others, too."

What motivates special education teachers? Many of them see a need that's not being met—then out of either anger or despair, they set out to find the best methods for remediating or treating the disability. After a daughter was born to Natalie Carter Barraga and she realized there were no services or programs for the visually impaired, she launched an effort that has allowed the blind and partially sighted to work up to their potential.

Barraga, a professor at the University of Texas at Austin, gave birth to a premature daughter in 1944 and discovered unusual visual responses when the baby was 3 months old. Doctors said that her daughter was blind, but Mom argued that she was following light but not looking at faces (of course, the doctor meant "legally blind"). Mom kept encouraging her to look at each thing given to her to play with, but the baby brought everything close to her left eye. She reached out at

From the parents of an exceptional child, to advocates, to professionals—a common path exists for special educators and others in related services.

the usual age but, at 4 months, the baby did not draw up her knees as other babies did. The doctor said she was a little spastic and gave Mom exercises to do with her daughter's legs.

What did Mom do? She began reading everything she could find about visual impairment and about spasticity. Her daughter pulled up and tried to walk at about 9–10 months, but her heels were off the floor and her knees almost crossed. When the orthopedist was questioned, he said she wasn't walking because she couldn't see (he had never heard of cerebral palsy). Then he said, "Why don't you put this child in an institution and forget you ever had her?"—this when she was already talking, knew her colors and was sorting large play letters! That was the last visit to him.

Barraga said, "I could recall many more disappointing and insulting encounters with the medical profession. I decided then that I was my child's only hope. I had a degree in Child Development, and I would learn all I could and start to eradicate some of the ignorance of the medical, psychological, and other so-called professionals."

The challenge was on for Barraga. She moved several times—to find the needed services. While in New York, she took some courses offered through Hunter College and at that time confirmed her presumption that children who have visual impairments and motor impairments are more *like* other young children than they are different from them.

She then moved to Austin, Texas, so her daughter could attend the Texas School for the Blind as a day student. Since that time, her search for better methods and programming for the blind and partially sighted led to her doctoral dissertation, which was the first piece of research to document the fact that children with impaired vision, formerly thought to be "blind," could learn to use their vision more efficiently through an organized program of sequential learning experiences designed specifically for that purpose and through the use of selected handmade and commercial materials. Her work has continued and includes the guidelines used internationally for diagnostic assessment and instruction.

Barraga reflects on her own life lessons:

Had I not had the need to learn how to be a good mother to a gifted child with multiple physical needs, I would never have been challenged to have a very rewarding and fruitful professional life. It is nice to know that I may have made a difference in the lives of many low-vision children, and I credit my daughter as the primary stimulator and motivator in my life. Before she was 3 or 4 years of age, she was asking me questions that I had to research to find the answers. That became so fascinating that research and writing and teaching became a life, not just a job.

"Thanks for being caring and conscientious."

Perhaps some of the greatest insights are gained when we ourselves have disabilities. Kenneth Wyatt, a retired special education professor, experienced early attempts at inclusion, homebound teaching, and in-hospital schooling, which have made him sensitive to the real needs of people with physical disabilities.

Wyatt recalls his experiences with special education:

My earliest experience with special education was in 1935 as a polio victim while in the second grade in a small-town elementary school in southern Oregon. There were, of course, no educational facilities for children with physical disabilities in any of the public schools in the area. The school district had no home teacher, but my teacher would occasionally send assignments home in a vain attempt to keep me current with the class. Perhaps the greatest assistance I received was from the town librarian, who saw to it that I got the first opportunity to read new magazines and books that she thought were appropriate for my achievement level.

When I was well enough to return to school, although I was in a wheelchair and the school was in no way accessible, I was allowed to attend; and two of the largest eighth-grade boys carried me up a long flight of stairs to my classroom. As a general rule, special education students with severe and moderate disabilities as we now know them did not attend the public schools. I can recall only two students that I later recognized having mild mental retardation or learning disabilities who attended my elementary school, and they disappeared by the time we entered high school. Some might think that my attendance at school represented an early example of inclusion; however, it was probably more a function of the fact that the school superintendent was a personal friend of the family.

During the next few years, I spent the equivalent of 3 years in the Shriners' Hospital in Portland where I was provided with corrective orthopedic surgery and physical therapy. "Education" was delivered sporadically by an elderly woman with no training in special education, and likely in general education, as well. Her ineptitude as a teacher was exceeded only by her ability to alienate the nurses and other hospital staff. By 1941, a qualified teacher was provided to the hospital by the Portland Public School District. While she had no special training, she was a caring, conscientious, professional who established educational objectives for each child, and expected the patient/students to meet those objectives. I credit her with my ability to enter high school with my general classmates and graduate with them on schedule.

Then in 1946, with the assistance from Vocational Rehabilitation, I enrolled at Oregon State University and spent a year in Electrical Engineering before discovering that I was more interested in people than in things. As a result, I transferred into education and psychology programs. Eventually in 1949, I enrolled in the University of Oregon so that I could major in education. After signing up for a "snap" course entitled Diagnostic and Remedial Techniques taught by Pat Killgallon, a protege of Emmett Butts from Temple University, I was hooked and began concentrating on courses that would prepare me to work with exceptional children.

Since that time, Wyatt has worked in many areas as a teacher, administrator, and consultant, always emphasizing appropriate programming, facilities, transportation, and other important issues in special education.

And the teachers say: "We came, we saw, and we conquered much."

Sharon Gonder (*CEC Chapter #404), Resource Learning Disabilities Teacher, Jefferson City Public Schools, and Adjunct Professor, Special Education Department, Lincoln University, Jefferson City, Missouri.*

Address correspondence to the author at 213 Belair Drive, Jefferson City, 65109. (e-mail: OBPC-Gonder@juno.com).

The following contributors graciously shared a bit of their lives and their students' lives: Natalie Carter Barraga, the University of Texas at Austin; Bernice Decker, Lewis and Clark Middle School, Jefferson City, Missouri; John W. Kidd, retired, Springfield, Missouri; William Littlejohn, Indiana State University; Kenneth E. Wyatt, retired, Sidney, British Columbia, Canada.

What Do I Do Now?
A Teacher's Guide to Including Students with Disabilities

Michael F. Giangreco

Michael F. Giangreco is Research Assistant Professor, The University of Vermont, College of Education and Social Services, 499C Waterman Building, Burlington, VT 05405-0160.

Teachers who successfully teach students without disabilities have the skills to successfully teach students with disabilities. Here are 10 recommendations to guide you.

As students with disabilities are increasingly being placed in general education classrooms, teachers are asking many legitimate questions about what to do about their instruction and how to do it. For the past seven years, I've consulted with teachers, administrators, support personnel, and families who are grappling with these concerns. I've also joined with colleagues in conducting 12 research studies at some of these schools. The following suggestions are concrete actions to consider as you pursue success for both students with disabilities and their classmates.

1. Get a Little Help from Your Friends

No one expects teachers to know all the specialized information about every disability, or to do everything that may be necessary for a student with disabilities.

Thus, in schools where students with disabilities are successful in general education classes, teams usually collaborate on individualized educational programs. Team members often include the student and his or her parents, general educators, special educators, para-educators, and support staff, such as speech and language pathologists, and physical therapists. And don't forget: each classroom includes some 20–30 students who are creative and energetic sources of ideas, inspiration, and assistance.

Although teamwork is crucial, look out for some common problems. When groups become unnecessarily large and schedule too many meetings without clear purposes or outcomes, communication and decision making get complicated and may overwhelm families. Further, a group is not necessarily a team, particularly if each specialist has his or her own goals. The real team shares a single set of goals that team members pursue in a coordinated way.

2. Welcome the Student in Your Classroom

Welcoming the student with disabilities may seem like a simple thing to do, and it is. But you'd be surprised how often it doesn't happen. It can be devastating for such a student (or any student) to feel as if he or she must earn the right to belong by meeting an arbitrary standard that invariably differs from school to school.

Remember, too, that your students look to you as their primary adult model during the school day. What do you want to model for them about similarities and differences, change, diversity, individuality, and caring?

So when children with disabilities come to your classroom, talk with them, walk with them, encourage them, joke with them, and teach them. By your actions, show all your students that the child with disabilities is an important member of your class and, by extension, of society.

3. Be the Teacher of All the Students

When a student with disabilities is placed in a general education class, a common practice is for the teacher to function primarily as a host rather than a teacher. Many busy teachers actually embrace this notion because it means someone else is responsible for that student. Many teachers, in fact, think of these students as the responsibility of the special education teacher or para-educator.

Merely hosting a student with disabilities, however, doesn't work very well (Giangreco et al. 1992). Inevitably, these other professionals will work with the student, and the "host" will end up knowing very little about the student's educational program or progress. This perpetuates a lack of responsibility for the student's education and often places important curricular and instructional decisions in the hands of hardworking, but possibly underqualified, paraprofessionals.

Be flexible, but don't allow yourself to be relegated to the role of an outsider in your own classroom. Remember that teachers who successfully teach students without disabilities have the skills to successfully teach students with disabilities (Giangreco et al. 1995).

4. Make Sure Everyone Belongs to the Classroom Community

How, where, when, and with whom students spend their time is a major determinant of their affiliations and status in the classroom (Stainback and Stainback 1996). Too often, students with disabilities are placed with mainstream students, but take part in different activities and have different schedules from their peers. These practices inhibit learning with and from classmates, and may contribute to social isolation.

To ensure that students with disabilities are part of what's happening in class, seat them with their classmates, and at the same kind of desk, not on the fringe of the class.

Make sure, too, that the student participates in the same activities as the rest of the class, even though his or her goals may be different. If the class is writing a journal, the student with a disability should be creating a journal, even if it's in a nonwritten form. If you assign students homework, assign it to this student at an appropriate level. In like manner, if the class does a science experiment, so should this student. Although individualization and supports may be necessary, the student's daily schedule should allow ample opportunities to learn, socialize, and work with classmates.

THE PRESENCE OF A student with disabilities may simply highlight the need to use more active and participatory approaches.

5. Clarify Shared Expectations with Team Members

One of the most common sources of anxiety for classroom teachers is not understanding what other team members expect them to teach. "Do I teach this student most of or all of what I'm teaching the other students?" Sometimes the answer will be yes, sometimes no. In either case, team members must agree on what the student should learn and who will teach it.

To do this, the team should identify a few of the student's learning priorities, as well as a larger set of learning outcomes as part of a broad educational program. Doing so will clarify which parts of the general curriculum the student will be expected to pursue and may include learning outcomes that are not typically part of the general program.

Many students with disabilities also need supports to participate in class. These supports should be distinguished from learning outcomes. If the supports are inadvertently identified as learning outcomes, the educa-

tional program may be unnecessarily passive.

Finally, on a one- or two-page program-at-a-glance, summarize the educational program, including, for example, priority learning outcomes, additional learning outcomes, and necessary supports (Giangreco et al. 1993). This concise list will help the team plan and schedule, serve as a reminder of the student's individual needs, and help you communicate those needs to teachers in special areas, such as art, music, and physical education. By clarifying what the team expects the student to learn, you set the stage for a productive school year.

6. Adapt Activities to the Student's Needs

When the educational needs of a student with disabilities differ from those of the majority of the class, teachers often question the appropriateness of the placement. It's fair to ask, for example, why an 11-year-old functioning at a 2nd grade level is placed in a 6th grade class.

The answer is that such a student can still have a successful educational experience. In fact, many schools are purposely developing multigrade classrooms, where teachers accommodate students with a wide range of abilities.

When a student's needs differ from other members of the class, it is important to have options for including that student in activities with classmates. In some cases, the student requires instructional accommodations to achieve learning outcomes within the same curriculum area as his or her classmates, but at a different level.

The student might need to learn, for example, different vocabulary words, math problems, or science concepts. Or the student may be pursuing learning outcomes from different curriculum areas. For example, during a science activity, the student could be learning communication, literacy, or socialization skills, while the rest of the class focuses on science.

7. Provide Active and Participatory Learning Experiences

TEACHERS CAN BECOME BETTER ADVOCATES
for their students and themselves by becoming informed consumers of support services.

I've heard teachers of students with disabilities say, "He wouldn't get much out of being in that class because the teacher does a lot of lecturing, and uses worksheets and paper-and-pencil tests." My first reaction is, "You're right, that situation doesn't seem to match the student's needs." But then I wonder, Is this educational approach also a mismatch for students without disability labels?

Considering the diversity of learning styles, educators are increasingly questioning whether passive, didactic approaches meet their students' needs. Activity-based learning, on the other hand, is well suited to a wide range of students. The presence of a student with disabilities may simply highlight the need to use more active and participatory approaches, such as individual or cooperative projects and use of art media, drama, experiments, field study, computers, research, educational games, multimedia projects, or choral responding (Thousand et al. 1994). Interesting, motivating activities carry an added bonus—they encourage positive social behaviors, and can diminish behavior problems.

8. Adapt Classroom Arrangements, Materials, and Strategies
Alternate teaching methods or other adaptations may be necessary. For example, if a group lecture isn't working, try cooperative groups, computer-assisted instruction, or peer tutoring. Or make your instruction more precise and deliberate.

Adaptations may be as basic as considering a different way for a student to respond if he or she has difficulty speaking or writing, or rearranging the chairs for more proximity to peers or access to competent modeling.

You may also have to adapt materials. A student with visual impairments may need tactile or auditory cues. A student with physical disabilities may require materials that are larger or easier to manipulate. And a student who is easily bored or distracted may do better with materials that are in line with his or her interests.

Rely on the whole team and the class to assist with adaptation ideas.

9. Make Sure Support Services Help
Having many support service personnel involved with students can be a help or a hindrance. Ideally, the support staff will be competent and collaborative, making sure that what they do prevents disruptions and negative effects on students' social relationships and educational programs. They will get to know the students and classroom routines, and also understand the teacher's ideas and concerns.

Teachers can become better advocates for their students and themselves by becoming informed consumers of support services. Learn to ask good questions. Be assertive if you are being asked to do something that doesn't make sense to you. Be as explicit as you can be about what type of support you need. Sometimes you may need particular information, materials, or someone to demonstrate a technique. Other times, you may need someone with whom to exchange ideas or just validate that you are headed in the right direction.

10. Evaluate Your Teaching
We commonly judge our teaching by our students' achievements. Although you may evaluate students with disabilities in some of the same ways as you do other students (for example, through written tests, reports, or projects), some students will need alternative assessment, such as portfolios adapted to their needs.

Often it is erroneously assumed that if students get good grades, that will translate into future educational, professional, and personal success. This is a dangerous assumption for any student, but particularly for those with disabilities. Although traditional tests and evaluations may provide certain types of information, they won't predict the impact of your teaching on the student's post-school life. Unfortunately, far too many graduates with disabilities are plagued by unemployment, health problems, loneliness, or isolation—despite their glowing school progress reports.

We need to continually evaluate whether students are applying their achievements to real life, by looking at the effects on their physical and emotional health, personal growth, and positive social relationships; and at their ability to communicate, advocate for themselves, make informed choices, contribute to the community, and increasingly access places and activities that are personally meaningful.

UNFORTUNATELY, FAR TOO MANY GRADUATES
with disabilities are plagued by unemployment, despite their glowing school progress reports.

The aim is to ensure that our teaching will make a real difference in our students' lives.

References

Giangreco, M., D. Baumgart, and M. B. Doyle. (1995). "How Inclusion Can Facilitate Teaching and Learning." *Intervention in School and Clinic* 30, 5: 273–278.

Giangreco, M., C. J. Cloninger, and V. Iverson. (1993). *Choosing Options and Accommodations for Children: A Guide to Planning Inclusive Education.* Baltimore: Brookes.

Giangreco, M., R. Dennis, C. Cloninger, S. Edelman, and R. Schattman. (1992). "'I've Counted Jon': Transformational Experiences of Teachers Educating Students with Disabilities." *Exceptional Children* 59: 359–372.

Stainback, W., and S. Stainback. (1996). *Inclusion: A Guide for Educators.* Baltimore: Brookes.

Thousand, J., R. Villa, and A. Nevin. (1994). *Creativity and Collaborative Learning: A Practical Guide to Empowering Students and Teachers.* Baltimore: Brookes.

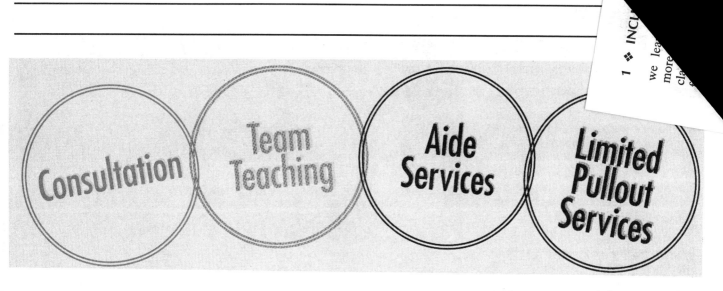

Four Inclusion Models That Work

Dori Elliott ●●●● Merry McKenney

Being a special education teacher and a general education teacher who believe in inclusion doesn't always make us the most popular teachers on staff. After 4 years of implementing inclusion in our school, we still face complaints and opposition from our colleagues. Many teachers are concerned with teacher workload and who has the most course preparations. Some colleagues believe that if students with special needs are included with the general class, then the special education teacher has nothing to do but read the newspaper or visit in the teachers' lounge. If the success of inclusion were dependent on positive feedback from teachers, whether that be in planning meetings or in casual conversation among staff, the program would not survive. On the other hand, complaints from parents and students have been almost nonexistent.

Our philosophy of education is what drives our belief in inclusion. We believe that all students learn better within a single-system approach, instead of separation of general and special education services (Stainback & Stainback, 1989). All students have the right to an education in the least restrictive environment possible (P.L. 94–142). Interactions with students, parents, and teachers have led us to believe that inclusion is more successful than a dual system. We believe that for students to be included, they must be a regular part of the classroom routine, feel a sense of belonging within that group, and have the opportunity to be a contributing member. In our district, we are working toward a single educational system that serves all children, with special and general education sharing resources rather than co-existing side by side. (Stainback & Stainback, 1989).

Special Education Law and Outcomes

Looking back on history, we've basically come around in a full circle, at least concerning students with learning disabilities. Before legislation in 1975, students were always integrated within the general classroom, unless their disabilities were so severe that they were institutionalized. In fact, it wasn't until P.L. 94–142 came along that we started changing education for students with disabilities. Students with disabilities were to be assessed and labeled with a disability so that their individual needs could be addressed. In theory all students were to be given equal educational opportunities.

Added to this law was the concept of least restrictive environment (LRE), which gave students with disabilities a chance to be with their peers as much as possible. LRE favored integration, but allowed for segregation. A free, public education is not available in different degrees. LRE, however, depends on the degree of disability, the degree of services available, and therefore a subjective decision for the child study team to make at the individualized education program (IEP) meeting. Regarding LRE, it is difficult to distinguish the difference between students' *rights* versus students' *needs*. Thus, people often debate the theory and practice of least restrictive environment, which may result in due process.

After P.L. 94–142, educators designed new assessments, teaching strategies, and materials to better the education for students with learning disabilities. Special education teachers were supposed to possess specialized skills that would benefit these children. They learned *direct instruction* through task analysis and reduction. Through all these painstaking methods, what have

We believe that all students learn better within a single-system approach, instead of separation of general and special education services.

...ned? Do these students learn ... quickly than if they were in the ...ssroom, retain greater amounts of in...ormation or generalize the learned concepts to other areas? The practices within our professional experience do not indicate this to be so. The outcomes of special education programs seem to indicate that they are not working. Children served in special education programs have not made the expected progress in academic, social, or vocational areas (Rogers, 1993).

Which Delivery Model Works for You?

Here are two questions that we believe both general and special educators should ask:

1. How do kids learn best?
2. Does specialized instruction really work to the extent we had hoped it would?

Our goal is not to set up a program that is accommodating for us as teachers, but which is best for students' long-term needs. What we do know is that a pull-out program is easier for all teachers involved to schedule and implement; but we do not feel it is in the best interest of the students.

Before researching and choosing approaches to inclusion, determine what attitudes individual staff members have about students with special needs. Ultimately, a school's approach to inclusion depends on staff beliefs. Because negative attitudes tend to inhibit the potential of inclusion, it is important to address these attitudes in the form of different delivery models. Ideally, we would like to see a school adhere to one belief and thus one model of inclusion. Realistically, we find that teachers, just like students, work in an environment that accommodates their needs.

According to current research (Berres & Knoblock, 1987; Rogers, 1993), several approaches are effective in including students with special needs in the general classroom setting. These include consultation, team teaching, aide services, and limited pullout services.

Team teaching approaches can involve both general and special education teachers instructing the entire class or working with small groups to make classroom experiences successful.

planning meetings. General and special educators use special time allotments to meet and discuss student needs and services, and they make adaptations and modifications, as needed. The special education teacher may also provide additional instructional materials based on individual needs.

In this model, we suggest modifying the student's environment to meet attention, vision, hearing, and behavior needs. We also suggest reductions and modifications of classroom assignments. Teachers may provide materials to help students with spatial or organizational difficulties and may supply different writing tools, paper, assignment format, or a word processor.

Consultation requires a strong trust and communication system between the two teachers, as well as parents. It is imperative that the inclusion belief is intact before attempting this model. Since this is the *least* restrictive model, we consider it ideal in theory, but general education teachers may find it the most difficult to buy into. They may have concerns that other children in the classroom may be neglected because of the needs of the students with disabilities. Teachers may feel ineffective and taken advantage of by the special education teacher. Other, less inclusive models, such as team teaching, may work for some teachers.

Benefits and Challenges of Inclusion

Benefits •••••••••

- Cooperative learning allows diverse groups of students to succeed.
- Performance-based assessments involve both general and special education teachers in setting goals and evaluating students' progress.
- In a middle school, inclusionary practices are essential to students' self-esteem.

Challenges •••••••••

- Training and funding of professional personnel are essential for success.
- Programming for students with multiple disabilities and emotional disturbance must be carefully considered.
- Teachers must provide instruction for all without slowing the pace of the curriculum.

Consultation

Consultation involves no direct services to students in the classroom setting, except for assessment, observation, and

Team Teaching

Team teaching can be done in a variety of ways, but involves both general and special education teachers working to-

gether in the classroom and instructing the entire class. The least restrictive approach is co-teaching, where both teachers teach together at the same time, or switch subjects or days teaching. Other team-teaching approaches

Team Teaching

Consultation

involve small-group work, as well as individual tutorial or assistance to make classroom experiences successful. This approach lends itself to flexibility in delivery, depending on the lesson and students' daily needs. The advantage of team teaching over consultation is the ability to modify and adapt, as needed, on the spot.

When in a co-teaching model, we may work alongside the classroom teacher or deliver instruction independently to the entire class. The amount of time spent in this role depends highly on the number of students and the degree of need in that particular classroom. If a special education teacher possesses a strength or interest in a particular area, he or she will typically be more comfortable teaching this subject. Or if the student is in great need in one area, the general education teacher may plan for the special education teacher to teach that lesson.

Once again, while this is less restrictive in delivery and practice, one or both teachers may not be comfortable with it. We have found ourselves in situations where the co-teachers do not hold the same belief systems. In this case, it is not a comfortable work environment for the teachers or students. However, compatible teams have found this approach to be successful and positive.

Aide Services

One way to avoid tracking students by ability is to use instructional aides in the classroom, as we have done in our district. Realistically, special education teachers cannot meet the needs of students placed in several different classrooms at different grade levels without the use of instructional assistance or ownership by the general education

teacher. The success of this approach depends on the professional abilities of the aides and on a district's willingness to budget sufficiently. We recommend that the special education teacher have at least monthly contact with the students in their classrooms, to observe and assess progress.

Our aides typically go into a classroom where one to four students with disabilities are placed. Their job is to check the students' progress, provide individual or small-group tutorial assistance, assist the classroom teacher, and report back to the special education teacher. Occasionally, to avoid distractions, the aide may take a small group of students out of the classroom to work on a test or project.

In our experience, most classroom teachers are willing to work with this delivery system as long as the aides are well trained and helpful to them. The problem with this model is the inconsistency with funding and personnel from year to year.

Limited Pullout Service

When most people think of the job of a special education teacher, they think of a pullout program. It is more traditional, and it relieves the general education teacher from a lot of responsibility involving students with disabilities. The special education teacher does not need to plan or collaborate as frequently with

the general education teacher; therefore, both teachers can independently direct their curriculum and classroom.

A pullout program often allows for more individualized instruction. However, it breaks apart the student's day, as well as the student's learning. Students must leave their general classroom at specific times and travel to and from the resource room. Thus, time is wasted gathering supplies and traveling the halls. Most of the lessons learned are not transferred to the general education class because what is learned in the resource room is sometimes out of context. It is almost impossible to coordinate and align curriculum on a daily basis and expect students to transfer this learning. Students often don't feel part of their general class because they are not "smart enough" to remain in there the whole day. Thus, there is a stigma attached to pullout programs, with negative implications.

An example of the need for pullout services is in the case of students with more severe disabilities. For instance, we have pulled students out to work on skills that are extremely low for their grade placement and cannot realistically be adapted or taught within the general classroom. Another case is when the disability creates a distraction that prevents other students from learning or the teacher from teaching.

A pullout option is available only in a limited capacity within an inclusion model. Students should be pulled out

Learners with disabilities work alongside those without to benefit both learners in life skills and academics.

only during noninstructional times, as needed. It is our goal to pull students out only when there is no way for them to succeed in the classroom without the more individualized instruction and tutoring. It is clearly the most restrictive model within our program.

Cooperative learning is essential in an inclusive environment since students of varying abilities are placed together and need to function as a whole unit.

Advantages of Inclusion in an Intermediate School

Allows for Best Teaching Practices

Cooperative learning appears to be effective and practical within the classroom. Learners with disabilities work alongside those without to benefit both learners in life skills and academics. Cooperative learning is essential in an inclusive environment since students of varying abilities are placed together and need to function as a whole unit. Diversity among students is accepted and appreciated. We have found that students of lower abilities benefit greatly from working cooperatively with students of higher abilities. Cooperative learning, developing independent life skills, and improving academics is a common goal among general education and special education. Thus, this practice is accepted and beneficial.

Allows for Active Assessment Practices

Inclusion allows for more realistic assessment of what students can and cannot do, based on performance rather than individually administered tests. IEP goals and objectives in an inclusive model became more practical for the teacher and the student. The classroom teacher also becomes more involved in writing and reviewing the IEP, allowing them to take more ownership for the student. Our purpose of assessment is

learning, along with assessment for accountability.

Allows for Personal Growth

Self-esteem and a strong, trusting relationship with a classroom teacher are critical to a student's success through the intermediate grades. To be segregated from age-level peers, work with different curriculum and materials, and be excluded from activities and discussion can in no conceivable way strengthen a student's self-confidence and bonding with a teacher. Students need a self-contained, heterogeneous setting to nurture development at this stage in their lives (Merenbloom, 1988).

Challenges with Inclusion

Successful inclusion programs involve trained personnel. To prevent tracking, more teachers are required than with a pullout program. Funding for inclusion is costly, and many question if this is cost prohibitive. Without adequate funding, inclusion is likely to fall short as a means of servicing learners with disabilities.

There are concerns regarding the inclusion of learners with multiple disabilities, or emotional disturbances, in the classroom all day. Adaptive equipment, the extra personnel required to meet needs of students with more severe needs, and extreme behavioral occurrences are concerns of teachers, parents, and administrators. Our program primarily focuses on students with learning disabilities. However, our school includes students with multiple disabilities and behavioral challenges as much as possible.

Some teachers and administrators worry that to accommodate students with disabilities, the curriculum pace is slowed or altered in a way that is detrimental to students in the classroom. Is this fair to the other students? Is this true, or is it a misconception? We believe these concerns are valid, but they can be dealt with proactively without adverse affects on classroom learning.

Inclusion and Civil Rights

In our intermediate school setting, we have used all the approaches to inclusion we described here. The size of our district warrants several classrooms per grade; therefore, the issue of placing students each year may cause a lack of continuity in our inclusion program. Our

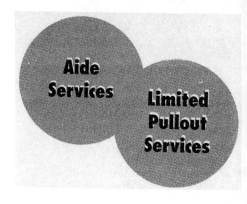

administrators would like to see all classroom teachers, Grades 4–6, involved in inclusion. However, this has not happened. We study and evaluate local issues, such as classroom size, beliefs of current teachers on staff, and funding for special education as we continue to develop and improve our inclusive model.

Inclusion, or the integration of students with special needs into the general classroom, is not going to fade away. The focus on civil rights in the United States is more predominant than ever, and inclusion is quite simply an extension of the fight for human equality.

Although the pendulum tends to swing in education, many educators have broken new ground regarding the rights of students with disabilities, and it cannot be covered up. This process of breaking new ground brings unspoken beliefs and feelings to the surface. Many people have concerns that are difficult to deal with. In developing a new educational approach, we meet obstacles that must be dealt with proactively and with an open mind, instead of impeding program development. The positive affects of inclusion have been proven; and

Ultimately, a school's approach to inclusion depends on staff beliefs.

it is clearly in the best interest of our nation that we continue to consider and develop inclusive programs in our schools. Success and failures within inclusion programs are evident and compelling; thus, we are becoming more realistic and practical in our expectations and practices.

*H*ere are two questions that we believe both general and special educators should ask: (1) How do kids learn best? (2) Does specialized instruction really work to the extent we had hoped it would?

Resources

Angle, B. (1996). 5 steps in collaborative teaching and enrichment remediation. *TEACHING Exceptional Children, 29*(1), 8–10.

Biklen, D. (1985). *The complete school: Integrating special and regular education.* New York: Columbia University, Teacher's College Press.

Chalmers, L., & Fairede, T. (1996). Successful inclusion of students with mild/moderate disabilities in rural school settings. *TEACHING Exceptional Children, 29*(1), 22–25.

Dieker, L., & Barnett, C. (1996). Effective co-teaching. *TEACHING Exceptional Children, 29*(1), 5–7.

Eichhorn, D. (1983). Focus on the learner leads to a clearer middle school picture. *NASSP Bulletin, 67*(463), 45–48.

Fuchs, D., Fernstrom, P., Scott, S., Fuchs, L., & Vandermeer, L. (1994). Classroom ecological inventory: A process for mainstreaming. *TEACHING Exceptional Children, 26*(3), 11–15.

Kluwin, T., Gonsher, W., & Samuels, J. (1996). The E. T. class: Education together. *TEACHING Exceptional Children, 29*(1), 11–15.

Stainback, W., & Stainback, S. (1987). Educating all students in regular education. *Association for Severely Handicapped Newsletter, 13*(4), 1–7.

Wang, M., & Zollers, N. (1990). Adaptive instruction: An alternative service delivery approach. *Remedial and Special Education, 11*(1), 7–21.

References

Berres, M., & Knoblock, P. (1987). *Program models for mainstreaming.* Rockville, MD: Aspen.

Merenbloom, E. (1988). *Developing effective middle schools through faculty participation.* Columbus, OH: National Middle School Association.

Rogers, J. (1993). The inclusion revolution. *Research Bulletin, 1*(11), 1–6.

Stainback, W., Stainback, S., & Bunch, G. (1989). Introduction and historical background. In Stainback, Stainback, and Forest (Eds.) *Educating all students in the mainstream of regular education,* (pp. 3–14 and 15–26). Baltimore, MD: Paul H. Brooks.

Dori Elliott *fifth-grade teacher, and* **Merry McKenney,** *fourth- and fifth-grade special education teacher, Belgrade Intermediate School, Belgrade, Montana.*

Address correspondence to Dori Elliott, 702 Hoffman, Belgrade, MT 59714 (e-mail: jelliott@ imt.com).

Unit 2

Key Points to Consider

❖ How can early childhood educators merge developmentally appropriate practices with special education strategies in inclusive preschool programs?

❖ How can a preschool teacher set up a classroom and offer choices to children with a variety of types of disabilities so that all students can learn together?

❖ How can preschool "Buddy Skills" training procedures enhance the interactions and friendships among children with and without disabilities?

❖ What is peer coaching? Describe two methods of peer coaching used in early childhood education.

 **Links**

www.dushkin.com/online/

These sites are annotated on pages 4 and 5.

The 1986 amendment to the Individuals with Disabilities Education Act (IDEA) provided for intervention for young children with disabilities much earlier than elementary school. This amendment, Public Law 99-457, calls for early childhood special education and family-child intervention at home. All services to be provided for any infant, toddler, or preschooler with a disability, and for his or her family, are to be articulated in an individualized family service plan (IFSP). The IFSP is to be written and implemented as soon as the infant or young child is determined to be at risk of developmental delay. At-risk conditions may be problems associated with prematurity, low birth weight, birth injuries, and early environmental trauma. In addition, all children diagnosed with early disabling conditions must be provided with early intervention services. IFSPs specify what these services will be for the parents, for the diagnosed child, for siblings, and for all significant caregivers. Children with autism, traumatic brain injuries, blindness, deafness, orthopedic impairments, health impairments, or multiple disabilities may require extensive and very expensive early childhood interventions. A great deal more money is being spent on early diagnosis and treatment since the enactment of P.L. 99-457.

IFSPs are written in collaboration with parents, experts in the area of the child's exceptional condition, teachers, home-service providers, and other significant providers. They are updated every 6 months until the child enters public school and receives an IEP. A case manager is assigned to oversee each individual child with an IFSP to assure high quality and continuous intervention services.

In the United States, an association called Child Find has the responsibility for locating and identifying infants, toddlers, and young children who qualify for early childhood special education and family services. Infants and children are viewed as qualifying for special services if they are at risk for delayed development. An actual diagnosis, or label of condition of exceptionality, is not required. Assessment is usually accomplished in a multidisciplinary fashion. It can be very difficult. As much as possible, it is conducted in the child's home in a nonthreatening fashion. Diagnosis of exceptionalities in children who cannot yet answer questions is complicated. Personal observations are used as well as parent reports. Most of the experts involved in the multidisciplinary assessment want to see the child more than once to help compensate for the fact that all children have good days and bad days. Despite the care taken, many children who qualify for, and would benefit from, early intervention services are missed.

A challenge to all professionals providing early childhood special services is how to work with diverse parents. Some parents welcome any and all intervention, even if it is not merited. Other parents resist any labeling of their child as "disabled" and refuse services. Professionals must make allowances for cultural, economic, and educational diversity, multiple caregivers, and single parents. Regardless of the situation, parental participation is the sine qua non of early childhood intervention.

At-home services may include instruction in the use of any aids (wheelchair, hearing aid, cane), ways of meeting the educational goals of the IFSP, and basic skills such as discipline, behavior management, nutritional goals, and health maintenance. At-home services usually also include counseling for parents, siblings, and significant others to help them deal with their fears, anger, and anxiety and to help them understand how to accept, love, and challenge their special child to become all he or she is capable of being. The case manager helps ensure that there is cooperation and coordination of services by all team and family members.

Most children receiving early childhood services have some center-based or combined center- and home-based special education. Center care introduces children to peers and introduces the family to other families with similar concerns. It is easier to ensure quality education and evaluate progress when a child spends at least a part of his or her time in a well-equipped educational setting.

The first selection for this unit on early childhood takes the reader on a journey from the philosophical roots of programs for young children to the practice of special education in early childhood education inclusion programs for children with disabilities. The authors believe that research supported special education practices should not be excluded from inclusive preschool curricula. Rather there should be a merging of developmentally appropriate practices for serving young children with intervention practices focused on special education goals and services.

The second article in this unit provides specific tips on how to include children with various types of disabilities in a preschool program. Jane Russell-Fox, a preschool teacher, has had success working in inclusive classrooms and writes about her tried-and-true techniques enthusiastically. She gives lists of specific suggestions for children with a variety of needs: communication, health, hearing, learning, physical, vision. She pays particular attention to the facilitation of social skills in all children.

The third article in this section presents an 11-step program, called "Buddy Skills," which facilitates social interaction between preschool children with disabilities and their nondisabled peers. This program has been pretested and has won approval from teachers. It encourages children to work and play together as friends.

The subject matter of the last article in this unit is peer collaboration. Many early childhood teachers do not have any coursework in special education. How can they meet the needs of very young children with disabilities? One way to help struggling teachers provide more appropriate services is peer coaching. Two accounts of teachers using peer coaching (observing and giving feedback to each other) are presented in this selection: combination expert/reciprocal coaching and an expert model. Peer coaching has benefits for everyone in an inclusive preschool program.

From Philosophy to Practice in Inclusive Early Childhood Programs

Tom Udell
Joyce Peters
Torry Piazza Templeman

Two 4-year-olds are playing at the water table. Their teacher observes that Michelle splashes her hand on the surface repeatedly, chortling with delight. Carlos is busy pouring water from a large container into several smaller ones and then arranging them in a pattern to his liking.

These children of the same age are at different developmental points in their lives. How can a teacher or a child care provider allow Michelle to do all the splashing she needs to do, teach her social skills in water play, and also encourage Carlos to continue his absorption in measuring and artistic design—as well as learn the social skills of playing with Michelle? A simple water table activity is more complicated than it seems. Why is this play activity important? How can an inclusive program meet the needs of both children?

The Individuals with Disabilities Education Act has challenged all providers of service to young children with disabilities to provide services in natural community settings where young children without disabilities participate. Educators are looking for ways to merge developmentally appropriate practices with practices found effective in the field of early childhood special education. Although these two sets of practices converge at certain points, professionals agree that differences remain (Bredekamp & Rosegrant, 1992).

The Teaching Research Early Childhood Program has developed a conceptual framework to meet the challenge of blending developmentally appropriate practices with early childhood special education recommended practices. This blended approach has resulted in the delivery of quality services within an inclusive preschool/child care setting.

Elements of an Inclusive Program

In the context of early childhood education, what are the differences among practices known as *mainstreaming, reverse mainstreaming, integration,* and *inclusion*? All these terms denote the introduction of children with disabilities into a "typical" environment for some portion of the day, or in the case of reverse mainstreaming, the introduction of some typically developing peers into what is essentially a special education program.

Inclusion goes further in that no one is introduced into anyone else's program. All children attend the same program, all of the time. Each child is given the support he or she needs to be successful in the setting. For children age 3 to school age, these settings are most often public and private community preschool and child care programs.

The most comprehensive and widely disseminated guidelines defining quality services in these settings are *developmentally appropriate practices,* as defined by the National Association for the Education of Young Children (NAEYC).

Research in early childhood special education indicates that those using these developmental guidelines as the *sole* principles for providing services to young children with disabilities would fall short of providing the full range of services these children need. Carta, Schwartz, Atwater, and McConnell (1991) warned against the adoption of these guidelines to the potential exclusion of principles and practices that we know are effective for children with disabilities, but also suggest that educators not overlook developmentally appropriate practices in providing inclusive services for these children. Indeed, Bredekamp and Rosegrant stated in a 1992 NAEYC publication:

> Experiences with mainstreaming over the past two decades suggest a conclusion that probably will be made concerning the guidelines . . . and children with special needs 20 years from now: The guidelines are the context in which appropriate early education of children with spe-

From *Teaching Exceptional Children,* January/February 1998, pp. 44–49. © 1998 by The Council for Exceptional Children. Reprinted by permission.

PRINCIPLES OF EARLY CHILDHOOD SPECIAL EDUCATION
- **Intervention focused on functional goals**
- **Family-centered services**
- **Regular monitoring and adjustment of intervention**
- **Transition planning**
- **Multidisciplinary services**

cial needs should occur; however, a program based on the guidelines alone is not likely to be sufficient for many children with special needs. (p. 106)

Let's look at both recommended practices—developmentally appropriate practices and early childhood special education practices—and find points where educators, children, families, and communities can work together to make inclusive programs successful.

Developmentally Appropriate Practice

NAEYC published a widely used position statement about developmentally appropriate practices for serving young children from birth to age 8 in early childhood programs (Bredekamp, 1987). The association compiled and published this statement in reaction to the concern of early childhood educators with the increasing academic demands made of young children in early childhood programs and general misconceptions about how teachers should provide instruction to young children.

This position statement became the most widely recognized guideline in the field of early childhood education. In 1997 NAEYC published the revised *Developmentally Appropriate Practice in Early Childhood Programs* (Bredekamp & Copple, 1997), clarifying the misunderstandings and misinterpretations that arose from a decade of extensive dissemination of the original position statement.

Based on the developmental theories of Piaget and Vygotsky, the NAEYC guidelines convey the primary message that *learning occurs through exploratory play activities* and that formal instruction beyond the child's current developmental level will result in nonfunctional, rote learning at best. Developmentally appropriate practice suggests that teachers should not attempt to direct or tightly structure learning experi-

ences and that formal academic instruction at the preschool level should not occur.

These guidelines have three dimensions, as follows:

1. *Age appropriateness.* According to child development knowledge and research, all children grow and change in a universal, predictable sequence during the first 9 years of life. This knowledge about typical child development allows teachers to plan appropriate environments and experiences.
2. *Individual appropriateness.* Each child has his or her own unique pattern of growth, strengths, interests, experiences, and backgrounds. Both the curriculum and adults' interactions with children should be responsive to these individual differences.
3. *Cultural appropriateness.* To truly understand each child, teachers and child care providers must recognize and respect the social and cultural context in which the child lives. When teachers understand the cultural context in which children live, they can better plan meaningful experiences that are relevant for each child (Bredekamp & Copple, 1997).

Teachers should use knowledge of child development to identify the range of appropriate behaviors, activities, and materials for a specific age group. As well, they should use this knowledge in conjunction with an understanding of each child in the classroom and his or her unique personalities, backgrounds, and abilities to design the most appropriate learning environment.

NAEYC recommends that instructional practices emphasize child-initiated, child-directed play activities, based on the assumption that young children are intrinsically motivated to learn by their desire to understand their environment. Teaching strategies include hands-on exploratory activities with emphases on the use of concrete, real, and relevant activities.

Rationale of Early Childhood Special Education

Early childhood special education is based on the premise that early and comprehensive intervention maximizes the developmental potential of infants and children with disabilities. Such intervention produces child outcomes that would likely not occur in the absence of such intervention (McDonnell & Hardman, 1988).

Since the initiation of publicly supported services for preschool children with disabilities in the mid-1970s, professionals in early childhood special education have developed a body of practices. This body of practice has evolved from research, model demonstration, and evaluation ef-

forts and is currently referred to as *early childhood special education recommended practices*. Researchers have documented syntheses of desired characteristics, or recommended practices, of exemplary, early childhood special education models (DEC, 1993; McDonnell & Hardman, 1988; Wolery, Strain & Bailey, 1992; Wolery & Wilbers, 1994). We have selected components of these models and practices that researchers have shown to be essential, effective, and compatible with the NAEYC guidelines (see Carta et al., 1991, for evaluation criteria). These components include setting functional goals and monitoring children's progress toward these goals, planning for transitions, and working closely with families.

Intervention Focused on Functional Goals

Intervention for children with disabilities should focus on producing specific and measurable child goals. To make meaningful changes in children's behavior, these goals need to be functional for each child and for the environments in which the child participates. A *functional* skill is one that is essential to participation within a variety of integrated environments. In early childhood settings, functional skills are those that assist children to interact more independently and positively with their physical and social environments.

For example, it is probably more functional for a child to be able to carry out his or her own toileting functions independently than to be able to name 10 farm animals. Shouldn't we give preference to skills that will enable the child to participate more fully in an integrated setting, as

Effective early childhood instructional practices emphasize child-initiated, child-directed play activities, based on the assumption that young children are intrinsically motivated to learn by their desire to understand their environment.

opposed to those skills that would be indicated in the developmental hierarchy or sequence? If our answer is yes, these goals then become the focus for providing individualized intervention. Teachers or care providers design services and instruction to produce a specific outcome—like independent toileting—and this outcome becomes the standard against which the success of an intervention is measured.

Family-Centered Services

The family is the heart of all early childhood programs. Families participate in planning and decision making in all aspects of their children's program.

A good school-family partnership includes a system for a child's family to have regular communication with the classroom staff and have frequent opportunities to participate in their child's program. Quality programs also include procedures for helping families link into existing community resources.

Regular Monitoring and Adjustment of Intervention

Educators and care providers should systematically monitor the effects of specific interventions. Researchers have shown the effectiveness of using *formative* assessment data to monitor children's progress toward their individual goals and objectives. (McDonnell & Hardman, 1988).

We know that such data must be gathered frequently enough to monitor the subtleties of progress or failure. Data-collection systems must measure child progress toward the acquisition of predetermined goals, including the application of skills in a variety of settings.

Transition Planning

Educators and care providers of all children—and particularly children with disabilities—must plan for transition from one school or child care setting to the next one. Early childhood special educators are particularly concerned with transition from preschool to kindergarten because this move signals a major change for the child and the family from familiar and secure surroundings to a new, unknown setting.

This is a time of considerable stress, and teachers and child care providers must engage in careful, timely planning to smooth the process. Many people are involved in the transition planning process: the child's family, the sending teacher, the early intervention specialist, support personnel, and the future receiving teacher. An effective transition plan often begins 1–2 years before the actual move. This preliminary planning enables the sending teachers to identify skills needed in the future environment. These skills are included in the child's curriculum during the last preschool years.

Key Aspects of Developmentally Appropriate Practices

- **Developmental evaluation of children for program planning and implementation**
- **High staff qualifications**
- **High ratio of adults to children**
- **Strong relationship between home and program**

Multidisciplinary Services

Professionals from many disciplines need to participate in the planning of comprehensive services for children with disabilities and their families. Because many of these children and their families have complex needs, no single professional and no one discipline can provide a full range of services.

The specific needs of each child and family determine what disciplines should be involved in assessing, planning, implementing, and monitoring services. The following disciplines are commonly involved in early childhood special education:

- Speech and language therapy.
- Occupational and physical therapy.
- Health and medical services.
- Audiology.
- Disability-specific specialists, such as a vision specialist or autism specialist.

Professionals in these disciplines provide services in an integrated manner: They share knowledge and methods across disciplines, and the entire team develops and implements one comprehensive plan. Following this plan, team members provide consultation services within the early childhood environment.

Merging Programs Through Developmentally Appropriate Practices

The first step to merging these approaches is to recognize the advantages a program adhering to developmentally appropriate practices offers for the successful inclusion of children with disabilities. Such a program will have high-quality components, many of which facilitate the inclusion process.

Facilitating Inclusion

The nature of developmentally appropriate practices allows for the inclusion of children with great variation in development within the same setting. Even in a group

of young children without disabilities, of the same age, children can be as much as 2 years apart developmentally.

Thus, planning developmentally appropriate activities and providing equipment and materials for the preschool setting already accommodates children in a wide development range. This allowance in planning and material selection makes it possible to include children with mild and moderate disabilities without additional adaptation.

This developmental approach to planning creates an ideal environment for embedding instruction on individually targeted skills. The developmental emphasis on learning as a process rather than a product also facilitates targeting a variety of individualized objectives. To illustrate the process-versus-product approach, let's look at ways teachers might provide art experiences—and individualized instruction—for children.

The *process* approach to art allows children to explore available materials, experiment, and create individual designs with little regard for the end product. This approach also allows for intervention on a variety of instructional objectives for children with disabilities while all children are involved in the same activity. For example, all children are involved in a finger-painting activity; one child may be working on requesting objects, another on identifying colors, and yet another on staying with the group.

Providing Quality Indicators

Developmentally appropriate practices are not a curriculum, nor do they dictate a rigid set of standards. Developmental programs will not all look the same, but they will have a similar framework that pays careful attention to child development knowledge and will assist educators in providing quality services for children. The use of developmentally appropriate practices ensures quality in programs in many ways, such as developmental evaluation of children for program planning and implementation, high staff qualifications, a high ratio of adults to children, and strong relationship between home and program.

- *Developmental evaluation.* Decisions about enrollment and placement have a major effect on children. Educators and care providers base these decisions on multiple assessment data emphasizing observations by teachers and parents. Teachers use developmental assessment of child progress and achievement to adapt curriculum, communicate with families, and evaluate program effectiveness. Developmental evaluations of children use valid instruments developed for use with young children; these assessment tools are gender, culture, and socioeconomically appropriate (Bredekamp, 1987).

Children of the same age can be as much as 2 years apart developmentally.

- *Staff qualifications.* The NAEYC guidelines for developmentally appropriate practice emphasize the need for staff with preparation and supervised experiences specific to working with young children. Early childhood teachers should have college-level preparation in early childhood education and child development.
- *High adult/student ratios.* A key to implementing developmentally appropriate practices is to have a small number of children per classroom and a high ratio of adults to children. Ratios suggested in the NAEYC position statement are higher than those required for licensing in most states. NAEYC recommended standards describe a ratio of 2 adults to 20 children ages 4–5, with younger children requiring smaller groups with higher adult-to-child ratios.
- *Home-to-program relationship.* NAEYC guidelines recommend parent involvement in all decision making, regular communication between parents and teacher, and encouragement of parent involvement in the day-to-day happenings of the program. These practices help in building a strong relationship between home and the child's community program.

Developing a Conceptual Base

We have developed a conceptual base, recognizing the two sets of practice, that will allow both developmentally appropriate practices and special education principles to exist within the same setting. The Teaching Research Early Childhood Program has developed a philosophy that views developmentally appropriate practices as the

foundation on which individualized programs are built, adding special education instruction when needed for individual children. We believe that the two approaches to early childhood are not mutually exclusive.

Figure 1 illustrates this dilemma. The builder has two sets of clearly different materials and cannot decide which to use. The key to moving beyond this dilemma is to recognize that these practices serve distinctively different purposes—and we can view them as different types of resources.

- *Developmentally appropriate practices* are used to design an age-appropriate, stimulating environment supportive of all children's needs. These practices, however, were not developed to reflect or address specific individual needs of children with disabilities and offer little information about specific intervention strategies needed to serve these children.
- *Early childhood special education* practices are used to complement the basic program for children with exceptional developmental needs and to emphasize individualized strategies to maximize children's learning opportunities. These practices, however, do not provide guidelines for designing a quality early childhood learning environment.

When educators recognize these practices as being different, but compatible, they can then plan a single comprehensive program, as shown in Figure 2. The completed school uses developmentally appropriate practices as the material from which the foundation is built and special education practices as the material that completes the structure.

Implementing Both Practices Within the Same Setting

Let's look more closely at how this merger might work. A well-designed early childhood education program, following developmentally appropriate practices, uses a planned, well-organized environment where children interact with materials, other children, and adults. Here the NAEYC guidelines are apparent: Young children are intrinsically motivated to learn by their desire to understand their environment; the program is set up to allow children to self-select activities from a variety of interest centers.

When children show they need further support, educators use special education strategies that are made available in the program. These strategies include the following:

- *Directly prompting practice* on individually targeted skills, based on functional behavioral outcomes.
- *Reinforcing* children's responses.
- *Collecting data* to monitor children's progress and make intervention changes.

Some educators view these strategies as conflicting with developmentally appropriate practices. Some people liken this direct prompting to the formal instruction that NAEYC deplored for use with young children. We believe that this view is a misinterpretation of NAEYC's position statement and the guidelines for developmentally appropriate practices.

As we mentioned earlier, however, NAEYC guidelines do not exclude intervention strategies for children with identified special needs (Bredekamp & Rosegrant 1993). We hope that by clarifying this misinterpretation, we might encourage teach-

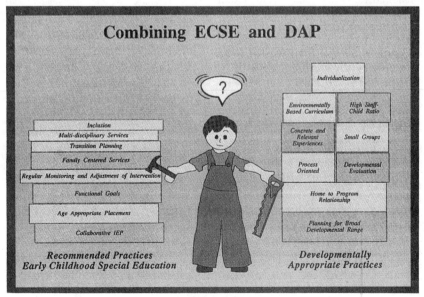

Combining ECSE and DAP

Inclusion
Multi-disciplinary Services
Transition Planning
Family Centered Services
Regular Monitoring and Adjustment of Intervention
Functional Goals
Age Appropriate Placement
Collaborative IEP

Individualization
Environmentally Based Curriculum
High Staff-Child Ratio
Concrete and Relevant Experiences
Small Groups
Process Oriented
Developmental Evaluation
Home to Program Relationship
Planning for Broad Developmental Range

Recommended Practices Early Childhood Special Education

Developmentally Appropriate Practices

Figure 1

ers to view these intervention strategies as individually appropriate for some children.

As educators begin to merge these two approaches to early childhood education, we will find all children participating in the same well-organized, systematically planned environment—with direct instruction being provided to children who need this type of intervention. This direct instruction is blended into naturally occurring opportunities throughout the ongoing daily routine, such as play at the water table or learning independent toileting. An early childhood program adhering to developmentally appropriate practices provides a strong foundation for the provision of consultation services from professionals across different disciplines.

Consider transition services—an area of special education services that some educators believe conflicts with a child-centered developmental program. The transition planning process has an apparent conflict with developmentally appropriate practice because it presumes that the needs of some future environment should drive the child's curriculum at present. Guidelines for developmentally appropriate practices reject the idea of current curriculums being driven by the needs of a future environment.

To resolve this conflict we can look to the *foundation* concept. In developmentally appropriate practice, we find children participating in an environment planned to fit their current developmental demands and individual backgrounds and interests. Within this environment, children with special needs receive instruction on specific skills that will assist them to be successful in their next setting. Teachers have selected these specific skills or objectives with direct regard to the child's current needs and level of functioning, with some, but not predominant, focus on transition skills needs as dictated by future environments. Skills selected because of the demands of a future environment are ones that can be facilitated without disruption in the current environment. These skills are also within the boundaries of being developmentally appropriate in the future environment.

Mutually Beneficial, Not Mutually Exclusive

In inclusive early childhood education programs, we must caution against adopting developmentally appropriate practices to the exclusion of research-supported special education practices. Similarly, we must not fail to recognize the benefits offered by placing children with disabilities in developmentally appropriate programs. We need

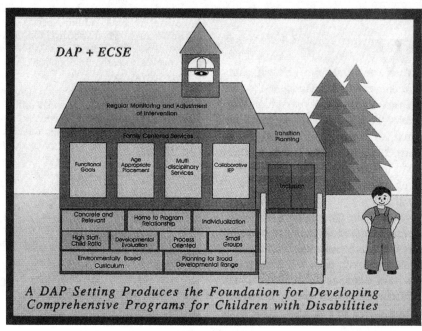

A DAP Setting Produces the Foundation for Developing Comprehensive Programs for Children with Disabilities

Figure 2

to develop an understanding of both sets of practices and to develop a program, from philosophy to practice, that merges practices.

References

Bredekamp, S. (Ed.). (1987). *Developmentally Appropriate Practices in Early Childhood Programs Serving Children from Birth Through Age 8* (Exp. ed.). Washington, DC: National Association for the Education of Young Children.

Bredekamp, S., & Copple, C. (Eds.). (1997). *Developmentally Appropriate Practices in Early Childhood Programs* (Rev. ed.) Washington, DC: National Association for the Education of Young Children.*

Bredekamp, S., & Rosegrant, T. (Eds.). (1992). *Reaching potentials: Appropriate curriculum and assessment for young children* (Vol. 1, pp. 92–112). Washington, DC: National Association for the Education of Young Children.

Carta, J. J., Schwartz, I. S., Atwater, J. B., & McConnell, S. R. (1991). Developmentally appropriate practice: Appraising its usefulness for young children with disabilities. *Topics In Early Childhood Special Education* 11(1), 1–20.

DEC Task Force on Recommended Practices. (1993). *DEC recommended practices: Indicators of quality in programs for infants and young children with special needs and their families.* Reston, VA: The Council for Exceptional Children, Division of Early Childhood Education. (ERIC Document Reproduction Service No. ED 370 253)

McDonnell, A., & Hardman, M. (1988). A synthesis of "best practice" guidelines for early childhood services. *Journal of the Division of Early Childhood, 12,* 328–337.

Wolery, M., Strain, P. S., & Bailey, D. B. (1992). Reaching potentials of children with special needs. In S. Bredekamp & T. Rosegrant (Eds.), *Reaching potentials: Appropriate curriculum and assessment for young children* (Vol. 1, pp. 92–112). Washington, DC: National Association for the Education of Young Children.*

Wolery, M., & Wilbers, J. S. (Eds.). (1994). *Including children with special needs in early childhood programs.* Washington, DC: National Association for the Education of Young Children.*

Books Now

To order books marked by an asterisk (*), please call 24 hrs/365 days: 1–800–BOOKS–NOW (266–5766) or (702) 258–3338 ask for ext. 1212 or visit them on the web at http://www.BooksNow. com/TeachingExceptional.htm. Use Visa, M/C, or AMEX or send check or money order + $4.95 S&H ($2.50 each add'l item) to: Books Now, 660 W. Charleston Blvd., Las Vegas, NV 89102.

Tom Udell, *Assistant Research Professor;* **Joyce Peters,** *(CEC Oregon Federation), Associate Research Professor;* **Torry Piazza Templeman,** *(CEC Oregon Federation), Associate Director, Teaching Research Division, Western Oregon University, Monmouth.*

Address correspondence to Tom Udell, Teaching Research Division, Western Oregon University, 345 N. Monmouth Ave., Monmouth, OR 97361 (e-mail:udellt@wou.edu).

We would like to thank Kathy Haydon for her illustrations.

Together Is Better:

Specific Tips on How to Include Children with Various Types of Disabilities

Develop a professional relationship with the child's parents. Keep communication lines open among all involved—parents, physicians, special education teachers, and other relevant people.

Jane Russell-Fox

My experiences with both inclusive and noninclusive environments has led me to conclude that "together is better." I believe that early childhood professionals who are including children with special needs in their classrooms can set up the environment so that it accommodates these children as well as typically developing children. In doing this the professional takes the first steps toward successful inclusion.

While working in several different self-contained settings, I spent most of my time negotiating with

Jane Russell-Fox, M.Ed., is a preschool teacher for the inclusive "Wee Wildcat" program for the Eastmont School District in East Wenatchee, Washington.

Photographs © The Growth Program.

my peers and administrators to plan for inclusion of the special needs children in my group. Usually my plan was for inclusion that would operate 15 to 20 minutes of the school day to give my children a chance at least to hear others model language, involve themselves in cooperative play, and establish friendships.

Staff members who knew I was a strong supporter of inclusive classrooms tended continually to say to me, "That sounds like a good idea; we should try that next week." Next week always came, and we were no closer to the beginning of an inclusive environment than we were the week before.

After my experiences in inclusive environments, I know now that everyone has to be sold on inclusion before it can work successfully. After one is sold on inclusion, it's the job

of the team to set up the environment and offer choices to all children at a variety of levels so that all can learn together in the same room.

It is also the job of the team to continue updating skills and working to improve the effectiveness of the program. Children with special needs do need specialized services based on individual needs, including predictable routines, accurate record keeping of goals, effective teaching strategies, all performed in a developmentally appropriate environment. There is no blueprint to follow—each person is an individual.

The following ideas are only a way to get you started. A range of services needs to be provided to most children with special needs. You can't do it all by yourself. Expect your team members to be there for you. Team members can include everyone from a child care provider to an occupational therapist.

The following processes are adaptations that are easy and use many commonsense ideas and readily available materials. For example, Jennifer has a vision impairment and is not able to see some of the books you read during circle time. What can you do? Try storytelling, enlarging the books, using flannelboard characters, or giving Jennifer a designated spot toward the front during circle time.

Working with a child who has exceptional health needs

• Develop a professional relationship with the child's parents and physician, and in some cases with other care providers who may come in contact with the child.

• Keep communication lines open among all.

• Get informed about the child's health needs, including medicine and diet.

• Invite the school nurse to become a part of the team.

• Develop a program plan for the child who may be out of the classroom for long periods of time. Home visits, telephone calls, classmate phone lists, and care packages from classmates or activity packets from the teacher can assist the child and his or her family in continuing to be a part of the classroom.*

Working with a child who has exceptional hearing needs

• Develop a professional relationship with the child's parents, audiologist, hearing specialist, sign language interpreter, and speech and language therapist.

• Keep communication lines open with them.

• Learn to change a hearing aid battery and cord.

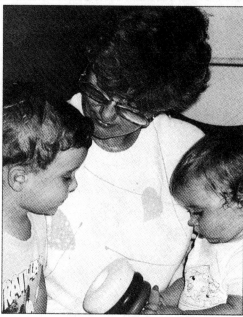

Facilitating social skills is an essential part of facilitating true inclusion. Teachers will want to keep groups relatively small so children can interact as children typically do.

• Use visual and tactile aids as much as you can.

• Use the child's name when seeking the child's attention.

• Make sure you have the child's attention before beginning the activity, giving directions, or introducing additional material.

• Speak at normal speed and volume without exaggerating lip movements.

• Make certain the child sits up close for good visibility of the teacher, activity, and other children.

• Encourage language in group activities by allowing time for the child to start and finish speaking.*

Working with a child who has exceptional learning needs

• Concentrate on the child's strengths, not weaknesses.

• Present content in short segments using a multisensory approach (audio, visual, manipulative).

Provide for as much overlearning or repeated practice as necessary.

• Praise the child's progress.

• Use task analysis.

• Be patient when it is necessary to show a child how to do something many times.

• Give directions one at a time until a child can handle more than one.

• Help parents to recognize their children's small successes.

• Plan for modeling and imitation.

• Provide clear transitions; try to avoid abrupt changes in activities.

• Present developmental-level challenges.

• Allow time and opportunity to practice new skills needed for activities.

Specific intervention strategies for working with a child with visual impairments

• Consult with the child's parents and vision specialists to determine what the child can see and what play materials would be most appropriate.

• Orient the child to the classroom layout and locations of materials. Give a new orientation whenever changes are made.

• Provide the child with a rich variety of tactile, manipulative, and auditory experiences.

• Encourage independent both by your actions and in the way the room is arranged.

• Be alert to the need for physical prompts.

• Before beginning a new activity explain what is going to happen.*

Working with a child who has exceptional communication needs

• Be a good listener.

• Use parallel talk. Broadcasting play-by-play action of the child's activity helps to stimulate the acquisi-

*Source: Adapted by permission, from R. E. Cook, A. Tessier, and M. D. Klein, Adapting Early Childhood Curricula for Children with Special Needs, 3d ed. New York: Merrill/Macmillan, 1992. 206–07, 209.

tion of language (e.g., "You're putting the ball in the basket").

• Use alternative communications as needed (e.g., sign language, augmentative communication).

• Have everyone in the classroom model good language by talking about and labeling what they are doing.

• Promote specific reasons for expressing language (i.e., giving information, requesting and getting attention, protesting, and commenting).

Working with a child who has exceptional physical needs

• Get input from the physical therapist on the proper handling and positioning of the child. Get specific directions on the length of time the child should be in a given position. Seek suggestions from the occupational therapist on adapting fine-motor materials so that the child participates in all of the classroom projects. (Of course parents must be included in all planning for the child.)

• Make sure materials and toys are accessible to the child.

• Remember that physical delays don't always have an accompanying mental disability.

• Become familiar with adaptive equipment and know how to use and care for it.

• Arrange the environment to accommodate adaptive equipment.

• Allow extra time for making transitions.

• Support and encourage that which the child can do physically.

• Foster independence by focusing on the child's nonphysical abilities.

◦✦◦

Facilitating social skills is an essential part of facilitating true inclusion. Teachers will want to keep groups relatively small so children can interact as children typically do. Rewarding remarks reinforce specific desired behaviors. Materials appropriate to the skills of interaction desired need to be provided. For example, if your desired outcome is cooperation, set up situations in the classroom to encourage teamwork—"After we pick up the blocks, then we can get ready for snack." Making sufficient materials available helps promote cooperation and imitation.

With each new child with special needs, a few accommodations can be made to a classroom environment and the instruction to allow these children to be included. Placing children with special needs in a learning environment with their typical peers offers many challenges for families and staff, but the rewards reaped and the teamwork accomplished are well worth the effort.

Coming into a work environment that is already sold on inclusion and is *practicing* it has been one of the greatest rewards of my professional career. I strongly urge you to develop inclusive classrooms in *your* setting!

For further reading

Allen, K.E. 1980. *Mainstreaming in early childhood education.* Albany, NY: Delmar.

Barnes, E., C. Berrigan, & D. Biklen. 1978. *What's the difference: Teaching positive attitudes toward people with disabilities.* Syracuse, NY: Human Policy Press.

Buscaglia, L. 1983. *The disabled and their parents: A counseling challenge.* New York: Holt, Rinehart, & Winston.

Chandler, P.A. 1994. *A place for me: Including children with special needs in early care and education settings.* Washington, DC: NAEYC.

Cook, R.E., A. Tessier, & M.D. Klein. 1987. *Adapting early childhood curricula for children with special needs.* 3d ed. New York: Harcourt Brace Jovanovich.

Deiner, P.L. 1983. *Resources for teaching young children with special needs.* New York: Harcourt Brace Jovanovich.

Debelak, M., J. Herr, & M. Jacobson. 1981. *Creative innovative classroom materials for teaching young children.* New York: Harcourt Brace Jovanovich.

Froschl, M., L. Colon, E. Rubin, & B. Sprung. 1984. *Including all of us—An early childhood curriculum about disabilities.* New York: Project Educational Equity Concepts.

Fullwood, D. 1990. *Chances and choices: Making integration work.* Baltimore: Paul H. Brookes.

Trainer, M. 1991. *Differences in common. Straight talk on mental retardation, Down syndrome and life.* Bethesda, MD: Woodbine House.

"Buddy Skills" for Preschoolers

Kris English
Howard Goldstein
Louise Kaczmarek
Karin Shafer

Kris English, *Project Coordinator;* **Howard Goldstein** *(CEC Chapter #184), Professor; and* **Louise Kaczmarek** *CEC Chapter #961, Assistant Professor, Child Language Intervention Program;* **Karin Shafer,** *Research Specialist, Alliance for Infants, University of Pittsburgh, Pennsylvania.*

You have an inclusive preschool. You have children with a wide range of abilities, including children with disabilities. You want the children to work and play together—to be friends. One way many teachers encourage positive social relationships is by using the buddy system.

This article describes a buddy system that helps children work—and play—together more cooperatively throughout the day. It is child-tested and teacher-approved. Follow these 11 steps to "preschooler peer 'preciation."

Figure 1 summarizes the sequence of the 11 steps of the "Buddy Skills" training procedure. An explanation of each step follows.

Step 1. Initial Assessment

Before you conduct Buddy Skills training, make an inventory of the potential buddies in your classroom, weighing factors like the maturity of the children without disabilities, the social and communicative levels of the children with disabilities, and any shared interests in particular activities (e.g., playing similar games, or using similar materials.) We recommend matching genders when possible. We also recommend that the pairing be considered a long-term match (although not necessarily exclusive); ex-

tended time is needed for friendships to develop in any situation.

Step 2. Pretraining/ Sensitization

Children without disabilities often fail to notice or sometimes misinterpret the communicative or play attempts of a child with a disability (Goldstein & Kaczmarek, 1991; Goldstein, Kaczmarek, Pennington, & Shafer, 1992). The goal of the first 20-min pretraining session is to sensitize children to these communicative attempts.

In a small group, lead a discussion with peers without disabilities about different ways children in their class might communicate: with voices, signs, or gestures, or with varying response times and sometimes unclear intent. The use of videotaped samples of classmates at play can be used to help peers focus on, recognize, and interpret the intended meaning of subtle or ambiguous communicative acts.

Because it is difficult to generalize about children's unique communication strategies, we recommend that you use videotapes of actual classmates rather than unknown children. For example, the teachers and peers might view a 2-min videotape of a 4-year-old girl sitting on a chair at a table. They observe that three times she tries to get the attention of children walking by, but is unintelligible and therefore is ignored. Finally, she gets up and pulls on the hand of an adult, leading her to the table. She points to a disassembled puzzle on the table.

The teacher discusses with the peers:
• What did the girl want?

During the "Buddy Skills" training procedure, stickers can be used at the end of a session to reinforce success. These reinforcers will be eliminated as social reinforcers (friendship) take over.

- How did she try to get what she wanted?
- How did she tell other children?
- Why didn't other children answer her?
- How did she tell the adult what she wanted without using words?

The teacher and peers might go on to view another video segment of a classmate who throws a toy after trying unsuccessfully to participate in a play interaction. Each segment is discussed in the same manner.

If videotaping is not an option, demonstrate with role-playing some of the communicative and play behaviors observed in the classroom, and conduct the same type of discussion.

Learning how children use different abilities and strategies to communicate will help generate discussion on how to respond to those behaviors. Here are some questions for discussion:

- What should we do if we can't understand what our classmate is saying?
- What does it mean if he or she points or reaches for a toy?
- Will questions help, such as "Do you want this truck? Do you want to share this book with me?"

Explain to the children that responses to such questions from a child with a disability may be delayed or unclear. Discuss the need to take extra time to understand. During this pretraining session, take time to discuss what the concepts of "friendship" and "being a buddy" mean to the peers.

Step 3. Peer Training

Follow the sensitization session with two 20-min training sessions for children without disabilities, on two consecutive days, if possible. The training sessions will teach three Buddy Skills: to *STAY*, *PLAY*, and *TALK* with their buddy (a child with a disability). After the peers have learned the Buddy steps, show them how to apply the three steps with in-class guided practice. The following is a format for the two sessions.

Session 1. STAY and PLAY with Your Buddy

Teach the peers to maintain proximity with their buddy during free play, sit with them during snack and group ac-

tivities, and participate in play activities with their buddy.

Teach the peers that to STAY with their buddy means to "stick close." When approaching a buddy for the first time, the peer is asked to get the buddy's attention by saying hello, using the buddy's name, tapping on the arm, and asking the buddy to play with them. If during free play their buddy moves from one activity to another, they are to follow.

Then show the peers that to STAY and PLAY with a buddy means: While "sticking close" to their buddy, they can

join in the activity in which their buddy is participating, bring a toy over if the buddy is not playing, or ask the buddy to join in an ongoing activity. If the first suggestions do not appeal to the buddy, encourage the peer to think of other play activities, while maintaining proximity. During Buddy Skills training in our preschool classrooms, the peers practiced these steps with adult modeling, and received token reinforcement (e.g., stickers or stamps on a chart) for demonstrating competency. These may be replaced with whatever reinforcement

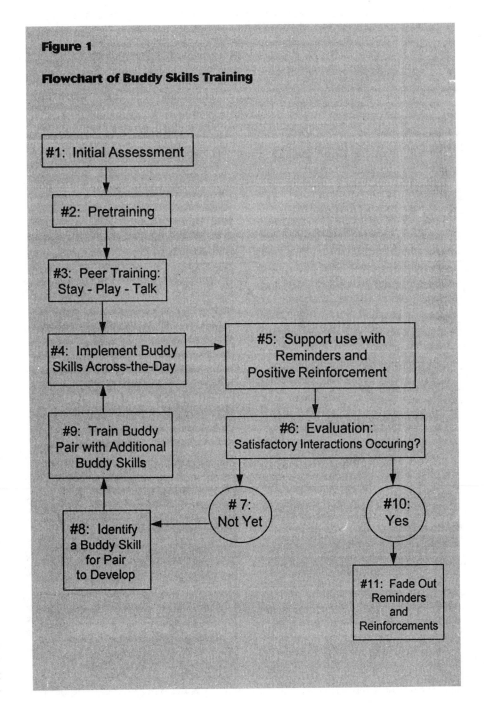

Figure 1

Flowchart of Buddy Skills Training

- #1: Initial Assessment
- #2: Pretraining
- #3: Peer Training: Stay - Play - Talk
- #4: Implement Buddy Skills Across-the-Day
- #5: Support use with Reminders and Positive Reinforcement
- #6: Evaluation: Satisfactory Interactions Occuring?
- #7: Not Yet
- #10: Yes
- #8: Identify a Buddy Skill for Pair to Develop
- #9: Train Buddy Pair with Additional Buddy Skills
- #11: Fade Out Reminders and Reinforcements

What Does the Research Say About "Peer Interactions"?

As preschool programs continue to include children with disabilities, many educators contemplate how to promote friendships in their classrooms. Uditsky (1993) discussed the normative pathway to childhood friendship:

For children, the normative pathways of childhood support and encourage opportunities to play together informally and formally . . . sharing in the celebration of milestones, making discoveries together, and following each other's leads. These are the pathways that adults clearly need to support. (p. 94)

Physical placement in an integrated program alone, however, may not sufficiently *"encourage opportunities to play together."* Without direction and support, children with disabilities are more likely to interact with adults and not with other children. In addition, children without disabilities are more likely to play together and not interact with children with disabilities (Beckman, 1983; Goldstein & Gallagher, 1992; Strain, 1984).

Educators have designed peer-mediated interventions that teach preschoolers a *set of initiation strategies* (Day, Powell, Dy-Lin, & Stowitschek, 1982; Odom, Hoyson, Jamieson, & Strain, 1985). Although research has been promising, there has been concern for the lack of generalization—that is, the inability of the peers to generalize the use of these strategies in activities across the classroom.

---

systems are most successful within different classrooms and with different children.

Session 2. STAY, PLAY and TALK with Your Buddy

Teach the peers to add a new step to "stay and play." STAY, PLAY, and TALK with a buddy involves additional interaction and communication, such as talking about the ongoing actions of the buddy or themselves, the toys (their colors, shapes, names, parts, or other attributes), or the actions and uses of the toys, as well as watching and responding to the communicative attempts of their buddy. In our classrooms, the peers again practiced all three steps with adult modeling, and received token reinforcement when mastery was demonstrated.

This phase of training ends when the peers are able to use these three steps in a chain without being told what to do, for at least two consecutive role-playing episodes. For some children, more than two training sessions may be required.

In-class Guided Practice

Allow the children without disabilities to try these Buddy Skills in class with a peer who has a disability. This practice serves as a transition activity from the controlled training situation to the classroom environment. During this time, help the peer stay on task and apply the steps to new situations.

Step 4. Implement Across the Day

Decide on three activities across the day (e.g., free play, snack time, and a structured activity) where the peer can be a buddy. To *keep "costs" at a minimum,* ask the peer to be a buddy for only a portion (4–5 min) of the activity, or share the role with other peers. This should reduce the possibility of peers losing interest or becoming anxious during interactions.

Step 5. Support Use with Reminders and Positive Reinforcement

You may find it useful to have a hierarchy of reminders or prompts. Friendships among children with and without disabilities may require a great deal of support and encouragement. Simply teaching Buddy Skills will usually not ensure mutually satisfying interactions. *Reminders and reinforcements ("rewards") to help children try new social skills* with a friend or in a new activity.

Initially, you may give a combination of verbal and visual prompts. Examples of verbal prompts include: "Tell me the Buddy Skills. Show me how to use them with Erica," or "Remember to talk to your buddy when you're playing." Examples of visual prompts include: a "thumbs-up" signal, or the sign for "friend." In our pro-

gram, peers were positively reinforced with verbal praise or tokens for the way they "stayed, played, and talked" with their buddies during classroom activities across the day.

Step 6. Evaluation: Is Satisfactory Interaction Occurring?

Observe and evaluate the quality of the interaction resulting from the peers' use of the Buddy Skills. The first attempts at "being a buddy" usually do not result in social or communicative reciprocity. Following are typical early buddy behaviors, illustrated by Jacob (a child with disability) and Erik (a peer without disabilities):

• Erik asks a question, but Jacob does not respond.
• Jacob asks for help, but Erik doesn't pay attention. Jacob does not repeat the request.

Through observations of these kinds, you may determine either that satisfactory interactions are "not yet" occurring (Step 7), or that the training has resulted in a relationship that is mutually enjoyable (proceed to Step 10).

Step 7. Not Yet

If you observe that mutually enjoyable interactions are not happening, make the determination that satisfactory interactions are "Not Yet" occurring, which leads to the beginning of a Buddy Pair training cycle (Steps 8 and 9, and repeating Steps 4, 5, and 6).

Step 8. Identify a Buddy Skill for the Pair to Develop

Choose a skill that will improve the give-and-take of the interaction between the buddies, based on your observation of the pair's interactions ("following each other's leads," Uditsky, 1993, p. 94). These skills may include using attention-getters (e.g., arm taps or verbalizations), responding to questions, and taking turns.

For example, in the Jacob-and-Erik example:

• If Jacob does not respond to a request from Erik, his new Buddy Skill will be to look when his arm is tapped, or look when his name is called. Erik in turn will be taught to respond with a smile, eye contact, and repetition of the request when Jacob responds to the arm-tap or the use of his name.

• If Erik doesn't pay attention to a request, Jacob's new Buddy Skill is to get Erik's attention with an arm touch or other attention-getter, and to "ask again" and point to the item of interest. Erik, in turn, is taught to look in the direction of the item, and ask questions to find out Jacob's intent.

The cycle of Buddy Training should convey to both members of the Buddy Pair that they have *mutual responsibility* in the interaction and that both are expected to understand and respond to each other.

One strategy that will improve communication between buddy partners is eye contact and a friendly smile.

Step 9. Teach Buddy Pair a New Buddy Skill

When you have identified the new Buddy Skill, teach the pair *together* so that both partners learn the new skill. This will help support a growing mutual investment in the developing relationship. Conduct this training across the day in various activities, and continue it over several days, until both children use the new skill.

Repeat Steps 4 and 5: Implement New Buddy Skill Across-the-Day
Once each member of the pair demonstrates the new skill, implement buddy interaction again across the school day.

Continue to support the use of the Buddy Skills with the use of *reminders* and *reinforcers.*

Repeat Step 6: Evaluation: Is Satisfactory Interaction Occurring?
Again, observe the children to evaluate the effects of prior training. Initially, there may be room for much improvement, so it is likely that after one Buddy Skill is mastered by the Buddy Pair, another developmentally appropriate Buddy Skill may suggest itself. For example, after Jacob learns to look when his name is called, and Erik learns to respond with eye contact and a smile and a request to play, Jacob's next step is to provide a verbal or nonverbal response (such as a head nod or a verbal acknowledgment).

Typically, the peer may need to develop a new skill in response to the skill recently mastered by the child with a disability, and vice versa. If so, repeat the training cycle. Through these training cycles, both children can add to their repertoire of Buddy Skills. These common repertoires and shared experiences should facilitate social interactions.

Step 10. Yes

At some point, your observations may confirm that the quality of the interaction resulting from the use of the Buddy Skills has resulted in a fairly balanced,

---

What Are "Buddy Skills"?

We developed "Buddy Skills" to promote generalization of peer relationships across the day. The Buddy Skills program is an application of "social exchange theory" (Kelly & Thibaut, 1978), which states that the rewards of a potential relationship must outweigh the cost for each participant if the relationship is to be mutually satisfying.

• **Rewards** are the factors that reinforce behaviors, such as enjoyment, satisfaction, or task completion.

• **Costs** are factors that inhibit behaviors, such as embarrassment, anxiety, or excessive effort.

The Buddy Skills intervention attempts to *reduce the costs* and *increase the rewards* of relationship development between preschoolers with and without disabilities by teaching social-communication skills to both partners in a Buddy Pair. Each partner is asked to share responsibility for the relationship by developing a reciprocity in their social exchanges (Gaylord-Ross, Haring, Breen, & Pitts-Conway, 1984).

The Buddy Skills program was tested in three integrated preschool classrooms composed of one-third children without disabilities and two-thirds children with mild-to-moderate disabilities. Positive effects were noted in the relationships between each Buddy Pair, and teachers indicated that the training procedures were appropriate for class use. Anecdotal observations by teachers indicated that some generalization of the learned Buddy Skills occurred (e.g., Buddy Pairs held hands while walking to other activities, saved seats for the buddy partner for snack and calendar, and extended invitations to play without prompting). The program also was found to be socially valid by three panels of objective evaluators, who viewed randomly ordered videotapes and rated postintervention videos as displaying more and better interactions between Buddy Pairs.

reciprocal relationship—a friendship is developing. Reduce adult intervention by proceeding to Step 11.

Step 11. Fade Out Reminders and Reinforcement

Decrease reminders and reinforcements. For example, if you have initially awarded stickers at the end of each session that the Buddy Skills are practiced (three times a day), you may delay these tokens and replace them with praise. Say, "Good job, you two! I like the way you're playing together. Keep up the good work—I'll hold on to these stickers now until the end of the day." Postpone the stickers until the end of the school day, and soon you will be able to delay them for 2 to 3 days, until you "extinguish" the use of stickers as social reinforcers take over. Friendship becomes its own reward.

During Step 2, students without disabilities observe a videotape to help them understand subtle or ambiguous communicative acts of students with disabilities.

References

Beckman, P. (1983). The relationship between behavioral characteristics of children and social interaction in an integrated setting. *Journal of the Division of Early Childhood, 7,* 69–77.

Day, R., Powell, T., Dy-Lin, E., & Stowitschek, J. (1982). An evaluation of a social interaction training package on mentally handicapped preschool children. *Education and Training of the Mentally Retarded, 17,* 125–130.

Gaylord-Ross, R., Haring, T., Breen, C., & Pitts-Conway, V. (1984). The training and generalization of social interaction skills with autistic youth. *Journal of Applied Behavior Analysis, 17,* 229–247.

Goldstein, H., & Gallagher, T. (1992). Strategies for promoting the social-communicative competence of young children with specific language impairments. In S. Odom, S. McConnell, & M. McEvoy (Eds.), *Social competence of young children with disabilities: Nature, development, and intervention* (pp. 189–213). Baltimore: Paul H. Brookes.

Goldstein, H., & Kaczmarek, L. (1991). Promoting communicative interaction among children in integrated intervention settings. In S. Warren & J. Reichle (Eds.), *Causes and effects in communication and language intervention* (pp. 81–111). Baltimore: Paul H. Brookes.

Goldstein, H., Kaczmarek, L., Pennington, R., & Shafer, K. (1992). Peer-mediated intervention: Attending to, commenting on, and acknowledging the behavior of preschoolers with autism. *Journal of Applied Behavior Analysis, 25,* 289–306.

Kelly, H., & Thibaut, J. (1978). *Interpersonal relations: A theory of interdependence.* New York: John Wiley.

Odom, S., Hoyson, M., Jamieson, B., & Strain, P. (1985). Increasing handicapped preschoolers' peer social interactions: Cross-setting and component analysis. *Journal of Applied Behavior Analysis, 18,* 3–16.

Strain, P. (1984). Social behavior patterns of non-handicapped-developmentally disabled friend pairs in mainstream preschools. *Analysis and Intervention in Developmental Disabilities, 4,* 15–28.

Uditsky, B. (1993). Natural pathways to friendships. In A. Amando (Ed.), *Friendships and community connections between people with and without development disabilities* (pp. 85–95). Baltimore: Paul H. Brookes.

Preparation of this article was supported by U.S. Department of Education, Office of Special Education and Rehabilitative Services Grant #H023C10167 awarded to the University of Pittsburgh.

We thank Holly Polatas for her technical assistance in the development of this manuscript.

Address correspondence to Kris English, Child Language Intervention Program, 3600 Forbes, #500, Pittsburgh, PA 15213 (e-mail: english + @pitt.edu).

DYADS AND DATA IN
PEER COACHING

Cynthia O. Vail
Jennifer M. Tschantz
Alicia Bevill

■

Early Childhood Educators in Action

Private preschools
Day care
Head Start
Public preschools

The world of early childhood education includes programs in many settings, and more and more of these community-based programs include young children both with and without disabilities.

In these inclusive programs, early childhood special educators collaborate and consult with other professionals with varied backgrounds. The minimal educational and experience requirements for early childhood teachers range from a high school education with no experience to a teaching certificate based on undergraduate or graduate coursework. Given this variability in teacher preparation, many teachers need collaborative support from early childhood special educators to meet the needs of their students with disabilities.

In this article, we share how we used peer coaching, a collaborative way to meet teachers' needs, in two different communities (see box "What Is Peer Coaching?"). One account by Jennifer Tschantz, describes a *combination expert/reciprocal peer coaching*

method used by an early childhood special educator with Head Start teachers. The second account (pp. 14–15), by Alicia Bevill, describes an *expert model* that is currently being field-tested by an early childhood special educator who is working with teachers in private and public preschool programs.

Discussion

You may face barriers and challenges when trying to put peer coaching in action. A primary challenge is working with professionals or paraprofessionals with various levels of training and experience. They may operate from a philosophical position much different from your own. Because of these differences, individuals may view problems or situations from disparate perspectives. This challenge may be viewed as an advantage if professionals can collaborate and truly learn from one another. For example, a preschool teacher may bring a great wealth of expertise to a situation regarding the use of play as a context for learning from a Developmentally Appropriate Practice perspective (Bredekamp & Copple, 1997). The early childhood special educator can provide information related to how to embed individual objectives and evaluate progress within play. As these professionals work together they can become more knowledgeable and able to view situations from multiple perspectives. This will enhance their ability to provide constructive feedback to each other during the coaching process.

From *Teaching Exceptional Children,* November/December 1997, pp. 11-15. © 1997 by The Council for Exceptional Children. Reprinted by permission.

PEER COACHING

WHAT IS PEER COACHING?

According to Joyce and Showers (1982), peer coaching involves teachers observing one another and giving specific feedback on teaching behaviors that need enhancement. Peer coaching can serve as a framework to guide the collaborative consultation process to bridge gaps in knowledge and skill among both professionals and paraprofessionals. Coaching by experts and reciprocal peer coaching are two coaching models (Ackland, 1991).
• Coaching by experts is more of a consultative model whereby professionals with specific expertise observe teachers and give them feedback and recommendations.
• Reciprocal peer coaching differs in that teachers observe one another in a collaborative manner, providing joint feedback.

Educators have successfully used both types of peer coaching models for both preservice and inservice teachers. (For more information on peer coaching, see Fishbaugh, 1997; Hendrickson, Gardner, Kaiser, & Riley, 1993; Kohler, McCullough, & Buchan, 1995; Miller, Harris, & Watanabe, 1991; Morgan, Gustafson, Hudson, & Salzberg, 1992; Morgan, Menlove, Salzberg, & Hudson, 1994.)

COMBINATION EXPERT/RECIPROCAL PEER COACHING MODEL

The final task in fulfilling requirements for a master's degree in early childhood special education is conducting a research study. As I approached this task, I wanted my study to be practical—one that would not only add to the field of early childhood special education research but that would help me on a day-to-day basis.

Child-Directed Play—Facilitation Issues

As an early childhood special education teacher, I served children with special needs using a community-based model. Ten children with varying needs were spread across three Head Start classrooms. I spent approximately 3 hours per week in each of the classrooms working with the children during child-directed activities. I began to notice that during these periods, the Head Start teachers did not facilitate the children's play; rather, they interacted with the children on a limited basis (when children were arguing over a toy, answering children's questions, or praising work when brought to them).

I soon realized that the Head Start teachers had received limited training on child-directed/initiated instruction. My role as a consultant and collaborator was to share information about the students with special needs, answer questions, and help develop plans to embed individualized education program (IEP) goals and objectives into play. Before we could concentrate on embedding specific objectives, the teachers needed to facilitate play with all students.

A Nonthreatening Approach

To avoid the "turf" issues that arise whenever an outsider comes into a classroom, I decided to develop a nonthreatening method of imparting information about facilitative play to the Head Start teachers. Peer coaching was the perfect solution. My research question became, "Would peer coaching increase

the rate of responsive teacher statements during a child-directed period in an inclusive preschool setting?"

The model I developed was both expert and reciprocal. I had expertise in specific teaching strategies to share with the Head Start teachers. However, rather than directly giving them advice, I wanted to foster an exchange of information through reciprocal observation and joint feedback. The focus was not specifically geared toward meeting the needs of children with disabilities only, but improving instructional strategies that are appropriate for all young children (Tschantz, 1995).

Dyads, Observations, and Discussions

We formed three peer coaching dyads, including myself and each of the Head Start teachers. Each Head start teacher and I would observe each other for 15 minutes daily during the child-directed period. In addition, during individual peer-coaching sessions held twice a week, we would discuss the observations and target specific teaching strategies we wanted to improve.

During the initial peer-coaching sessions, I shared a list of effective teaching strategies. I provided definitions and examples and encouraged discussions to obtain common understanding. This list included responsive statements, defined as the use of specific activity-related questions/comments or reflective statements made in the context of ongoing play. Other strategies included giving specific praise statements, giving reminders before transitioning, giving choices, stating rules in the positive, following through on directions, and embedding objectives. During these first sessions, I also introduced the teaching behavior plan forms (Figure 1), which included behaviors to improve or increase, examples of these behaviors, and space for anecdotal information from observations. Each of us completed the forms reciprocally. Each of us chose at least two behaviors to improve and together generated exam-

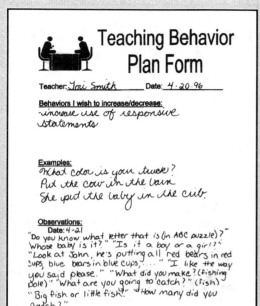

Figure 1
Teaching behavior plan form

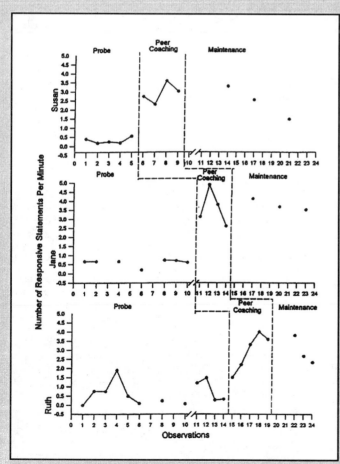

Figure 2
Rate of responsive teacher statements
during a child-directed period

ples. Behaviors selected came from the teaching strategy list or were self-generated.

Follow-Up and Decisions

During subsequent observations, each of us took anecdotal data on the behaviors selected during the peer-coaching sessions. For example, if the teacher selected "giving choices" as a teaching behavior to enhance, the observing teacher noted specific examples of when this behavior occurred or could have occurred. I also collected data on the Head Start teachers' rate of responsive statements.

After the initial session, each peer-coaching session consisted on the following:
• I verbally outlined what would occur during the session.
• The Head Start teacher reviewed her observation of me. With the Head Start teacher's input, I decided whether to continue working on the same behaviors or choose new ones. I always chose "increasing responsive statements" as one of my targeted behaviors because I wanted to model this behavior for them. I then developed a plan for improving my behaviors and documented it on the plan form, again defining the behavior, providing examples, and so forth.
• We switched roles. I gave anecdotal feedback on the Head Start teacher's chosen behaviors. I always offered specific feedback on responsive statements (e.g., defined responsive statements, gave examples, and reported rate observed).
• The Head Start teacher followed the same steps in developing her plan for improving teaching behaviors and documented it on the plan form.

To maintain a natural, comfortable dialogue, we followed a flexible sequence of these steps in each session.

Results? Positive!

The results of my study indicated that peer coaching was effective in increasing the rate of responsive statements made by all three teachers during a child-directed period (see Figure 2). This was wonderful news for the completion of my degree; but the positive feedback I received from the Head Start teachers on questionnaires was more important to me as a collaborative teacher. Teachers reported that peer coaching increased communication with the special educator, improved their effective teaching strategies, and was not too time-consuming. One teacher stated that peer coaching was "very beneficial" in a nonintrusive manner, and it made her aware of the importance of "exactly what I say to the children." Most important, all three teachers indicated that they wished to continue peer-coaching sessions on at least a bimonthly basis.

The results of this study document the effectiveness of peer coaching on improving teaching behaviors. Peer coaching was also demonstrated as practical in that the entire study was conducted over a 8-week period. It was efficient in increasing effective teaching behaviors.

> [Peer coaching] helped me to look at and evaluate my strengths and weaknesses. It helped me deal with and avoid behavior problems by actually sitting down with a peer teacher and figuring out positive solutions.

PEER COACHING

EXPERT MODEL

As a preschool special education resource teacher, my role is to support students with significant developmental delays who are served in general preschool classrooms. Teachers in these community-based settings have a range of training and experience; but none have had formal training in the field of early childhood special education, and few have experience working with children with special needs. The support services I provide range from consultation with classroom teachers to direct service with students for a few hours each week. The 1996–97 school year was unusual, because several children who were previously served in self-contained special education preschool classes would now be included in regular preschool settings.

Inclusive Meetings for Adults

Before the school year began, I arranged individual meetings for four children on my caseload who would be served in a general preschool classroom. I invited all the adults who might be involved in serving the child, including teachers, therapists, paraprofessionals, parents, and administrators. The meetings took place during the first week of school, each lasting 30 minutes to an hour, with full attendance by all invited.

We all had concerns about how we could meet the needs of children with developmental delays, as well as their peers, in a preschool classroom. The recurring theme at every meeting was how we would address developmental concerns—the cognitive, language, motor, and social goals of the students with developmental delays. We discussed adaptations and purchased special materials and equipment. We scheduled support staff to serve children during times that we anticipated would be challenging for them, based on their delays.

Day 1 Arrives

By the first day of school, I felt that we had planned adequately for each child and that the groundwork had been laid for a successful school year. In some ways, I was correct in this assumption. The preschool service providers appeared to be comfortable including the students with special needs in their classrooms. They modified activities and tasks to allow successful participation and asked me for assistance when needed.

> The preschool service providers appeared to be comfortable including the students with special needs in their classrooms.

Issues of Fairness and Time

Within 2 weeks, however, the situation in some settings took a turn for the worse. Classroom teachers and administrators began to contact me with concerns about whether the children we'd placed in their programs "belonged" there. They raised the issue of whether it was fair to the other children in the classroom for one child to "to take too much of the teacher's time." I was stunned—the adaptations and plans we'd made had seemed to be working.

I made visits to the sites to observe students and speak directly with the teachers. I discovered that it was not the cognitive, language, or motor delays addressed on the students' IEPs that were causing such problems. In every case, it was students' troublesome behavior. The preschool classroom teachers were unprepared to work with students with challenging behavior. After observing and videotaping in the classrooms in question, I found that several students without identified delays were also exhibiting behaviors that interfered with learning.

Behavior Management Issues

In speaking with each of the preschool teachers, I discovered that none had experience in analyzing behavior or in behavior management beyond a basic "time out" procedure. It was clear that training in these areas would benefit not only the students with special needs but the classroom as a whole.

We discussed several options, including inservice training on a teacher workday. Eventually, we decided that ongoing training and support in dealing with challenging behaviors was the best solution.

> Classroom teachers and administrators began to contact me with concerns about whether the children we'd placed in their programs "belonged" there.

Planning Peer Coaching

We designed a plan of action that involved peer coaching between myself and each of the preschool teachers having difficulty with student behavior. This plan will be implemented over the course of the next several months to determine whether peer coaching between special and general educators will result in substantial changes in student behavior. Future research is also planned to examine whether teacher behavior will generalize to other students and whether changes in student behavior endure over time. Here are the steps of the model:

- The first step is pinpointing the target behavior. This step will be completed collaboratively between the special and preschool teacher and will yield a specific, observable definition of the behavior in question.
- The special educator will then guide the preschool teacher in conducting a functional analysis of the behavior.
- Once it has been determined that environmental factors are not causing or reinforcing the behavior, the special educator will use information from the functional analysis to suggest possible interventions.
- The final decision on which intervention to implement in the classroom will be left to the preschool teacher because

he or she will ultimately be responsible for carrying out the plan.

• The preschool teacher will have the opportunity to role play and to observe the early childhood special educator carrying out the behavior management plan before implementing it on his or her own.

• Ongoing data will be collected to ensure that the preschool teacher is following the intervention plan as written, and feedback will be provided as necessary. The primary measure of this project will be the change in student behavior as a result of the intervention designed through peer coaching. Such information is needed to fill gaps in the literature, which has been primarily concerned with changes in teacher behavior and has examined the resulting change in student behavior as a secondary measure, if at all.

Peer coaching can be adapted to meet a variety of teacher needs in various settings. With the movement toward more inclusive environments and the changing roles of special educators, peer coaching could become a practical and powerful tool in increasing the communication and collaboration between general and special educators.

Another challenge inherent in peer coaching is the collaborative process. Many personnel preparation programs focus on teaching skill and content needed to work with children and spend little time on skills required for effective adult collaboration. Understanding various communication styles, how to overcome turf issues, and role release are a few of the critical variables related to successful collaboration and coaching. Staff development may help fill in training gaps regarding effective collaboration and facilitate successful peer coaching.

Finally, in order for the peer coaching process to work, time set aside to collaborate is essential. This requires administrative support and creative scheduling. This becomes more challenging when working across settings such as child care, private preschool, and Head Start. Within child care settings there may be frequent staff turnover and schedule changes. We have faced these issues with the second model we described. Given the administrative support we have for our peer coaching project, we hope that persistence, ongoing communication, and flexibility will help us overcome these staffing and scheduling barriers.

References and Resources

Ackland, R. (1991). A review of the peer coaching literature. *Journal of Staff Development, 12,* 22–27.

Bredekamp, S., & Copple, C. (Eds.). (1997). *Developmentally appropriate practice in early childhood programs.* Washington, DC: National Association for the Education of Young Children.

Fishbaugh, M. S. E. (1997). *Models of Collaboration.* Boston: Allyn & Bacon.

Hendrickson, J. M., Gardner, N., Kaiser, A., & Riley, A. (1993). Evaluation of social integration coaching program in an integrated daycare setting. *Journal of Applied Behavioral Analysis, 26,* 213–225.

Joyce, B., & Showers, B. (1982). The coaching of teaching. *Educational Leadership, 40,* 4–8.

Kohler, F. W., McCullough, K. M., & Buchan, K. A. (1995). Using peer coaching to enhance preschool teachers' development and refinement of classroom activities. *Early Education and Development, 6,* 215–239.

Miller, S. P., Harris, C., & Watanabe, A. (1991). Professional coaching: A method for increasing effective and decreasing ineffective teaching behavior. *Teacher Education and Special Education, 14,* 183–191.

Morgan, R. L., Gustafson, K. J., Hudson, P. J., & Salzberg, C. L. (1992). Peer coaching in a preservice special education program. *Teacher Education and Special Education, 15,* 249–258.

Morgan, R. L., Menlove, R., Salzberg, C. L., & Hudson, P. J. (1994). Effects of peer coaching on the acquisition of direct instruction skills with low-performing preservice teachers. *The Journal of Special Education, 28,* 59–76.

Tschantz, J. M. (1995). *The effects of peer coaching on the rate of facilitative teacher statements during a child-directed period in an inclusive preschool setting.* Unpublished master's thesis, University of Georgia, Athens.

Cynthia O. Vail *(CEC Georgia Federation), Associate Professor, Department of Special Education, University of Georgia, Athens.* **Jennifer M. Tschantz,** *Preschool Special Education Teacher, Madison County Schools, Danielsville, Georgia.* **Alicia Bevill,** *Preschool Special Education Teacher, Jackson County Schools, Jefferson, Georgia.*

Address correspondence to Cynthia O. Vail, Department of Special Education, 537 Aderhold Hall, University of Georgia, Athens, GA 30602 (e-mail: cvail@sage.coe.uga.edu).

Unit 3

Key Points to Consider

❖ Can ensuring that students succeed in learning in the early grades prevent the assessments and special educational remediations needed later for students with LD in public schools? What are the dollar costs of allowing students to experience learning disabilities that might have been prevented?

❖ How is the concept "pyramid power" applied to the education of students with learning disabilities?

❖ What does research say about 18 common teaching strategies used for students with learning disabilities? Which strategies seem to work best? Which ones do not seem to work as well?

 **Links** # www.dushkin.com/online/

These sites are annotated on pages 4 and 5.

Since the passage of PL 94-142 in 1975, the ways in which students with learning disabilities (LDs) are identified and educated has been transformed almost 180 degrees. Today it is the largest and most controversial area of exceptionality served by IDEA (Individuals with Disabilities Education Act). New assessment methods have made the identification of students with LDs easier and more common. However, many educators feel that students who are behavior problems, students with poor learning histories, and students from dysfunctional families are erroneously being diagnosed with LDs. Amendments to PL 94-142 in 1986 and 1990 mandated earlier diagnoses and provision of services (birth to public school admission), and later provision of education and transitional services (public school through age 21). The reauthorization of PL 94-142 required states to place students with disabilities in regular classrooms as much as possible or lose their federal funding. A landmark U.S. Supreme Court case in 1993 (Carter v. Florence Co. SC) ruled that public schools must give appropriate educational services to students with LDs or pay the tuition for private schools to do so.

Learning disabilities encompass a wide range of difficulties. There is no one accepted definition of an LD. To a large extent, exclusionary definitions help clarify the nature of LDs. They are not mental retardation. They are not deficiencies in any of the sensory systems (vision, hearing, taste, touch, smell, kinesthetics, vestibular sensation). They are not problems associated with health or physical mobility. They are not emotional or behavioral disorders. They are not disabilities of speech or language. They can be assessed as true LDs if there is a discrepancy between the child's ability to learn and his or her actual learning.

IDEA's strong emphasis on a free and appropriate educational placement for every child with a disability has forced schools to be more cautious about all assessments and labeling. Increasing numbers of children are now being assessed as LD who once might have been labeled mentally retarded or disabled by speech, language, emotions, behavior, or one of the senses. A child with an LD may concurrently have a disability in any of these other areas, but if this occurs, both the LD and the other disability/ies must be addressed in an individualized education program (IEP) designed especially for that unique child with multiple disabilities.

The 1990s have seen a persistent annual increase in the number of children assessed as LD. They now account for about one-half of all children with exceptionalities, or about 5 percent of the total school enrollment. Recent research suggests that reading disabilities may affect about 15 percent of elementary school-aged children. If this is accurate, many LD children are not yet being identified and serviced. The question about where to draw the line in assessing LDs, especially reading disabilities, is currently problematic.

Learning disabilities are identified in many diverse disciplines outside of education, adding to the diagnostic difficulties. The American Psychiatric Association's *Diagnostic and Statistical Manual of Mental Disorders* (4th edition) divides LDs into academic skills disorders (reading, mathematics, written expression) and attention deficit hyperactive disorder (ADHD). The National Joint Committee for Learning Disabilities (NJCLD) stresses that LDs are heterogeneous. It separates LDs into specific problems related to the acquisition and use of listening, speaking, reading, writing, reasoning, or mathematical abilities. Attention deficit hyperactive disorder (ADHD), if not accompanied by any specific learning problem or any specific behavioral/emotional disorder, is assessed as a health disability, especially when it can be ameliorated with medication.

The causes of LDs are unknown. Usually some central nervous system dysfunctions are believed to underlie the disabilities, even if their existence cannot be demonstrated with current diagnostic equipment. Other suspected causes include genetic inheritance and environmental factors such as poor nutrition or exposure to toxic agents. The NJCLD definition of LD states a presumption of biological causation and lifetime chronicity.

The education of students with LDs remains controversial. About two out of every five students assessed as having a learning disability leaves school before graduation. Frequently the school failure begins early, with delayed reading. Special education directed at reading frequently chooses either a phonic or a whole language strategy. Phonics seems to work better for children who do not automatically grasp what reading is about, while whole language seems to work better for students who grasp reading and writing but have difficulty accomplishing them. The need for individualized strategies for individual LD students is paramount.

This unit on learning disabilities addresses both the successes and frustrations of assessing and educating children with LDs. The first article in the section speaks to the prevention of LDs. The author compares waiting for children to develop LDs with putting an ambulance at the bottom of a cliff in case anyone should fall off the cliff. Robert Slavin believes that prevention and powerful early intervention programs could ensure that every child would learn without difficulty in the first place.

The topic of the second essay for this unit on learning disabilities is collaborative planning for appropriate individualized education for students with learning differences. The authors of this selection recommend degrees of learning for students in classes where not all individuals will learn all of the content covered.

The results of research analyses of various techniques used to intervene in the education of students with LDs is given in the last section article. What works well and what does not work as well are presented with meta-analyses of effect size (ES). The authors caution that while ESs are suggestive of more helpful strategies, some students respond better than others to each intervention and some strategies with negligible ESs work well for some students.

Learning Disabilities

G. Reid Lyon

Abstract

G. Reid Lyon, Ph.D., is a psychologist and director of extramural research in learning disabilities, language disorders, and disorders of attention at the National Institute of Child Health and Human Development at the National Institutes of Health, Bethesda, MD.

Approximately 5% of all public school students are identified as having a learning disability (LD). LD is not a single disorder, but includes disabilities in any of seven areas related to reading, language, and mathematics. These separate types of learning disabilities frequently co-occur with one another and with social skill deficits and emotional or behavioral disorders. Most of the available information concerning learning disabilities relates to reading disabilities, and the majority of children with learning disabilities have their primary deficits in basic reading skills.

An important part of the definition of LD is its exclusions: learning disabilities cannot be attributed primarily to mental retardation, emotional disturbance, cultural difference, or disadvantage. Thus, the concept of LD focuses on the notion of a *discrepancy* between a child's academic achievement and his or her apparent capacity to learn.

Recent research indicates, however, that disability in basic reading skills is primarily caused by deficits in phonological awareness, which is independent of any achievement-capacity discrepancy. Deficits in phonological awareness can be identified in late kindergarten and first grade using inexpensive, straightforward testing protocol. Interventions have varying effectiveness, depending largely on the severity of the individual child's disability.

The prevalence of learning disability identification has increased dramatically in the past 20 years. The "real" prevalence of LD is subject to much dispute because of the lack of an agreed-upon definition of LD with objective identification criteria. Some researchers have argued that the currently recognized 5% prevalence rate is inflated; others argue that LD is still underidentified. In fact, it appears that there are both sound and unsound reasons for the increase in identification rates.

Sound reasons for the increase include better research, a broader definition of disability in reading, focusing on phonological awareness, and greater identification of girls with learning disabilities. Unsound reasons for the increase include broad and vague definitions of learning disability, financial incentives to identify students for special education, and inadequate preparation of teachers by colleges of education, leading to overreferral of students with any type of special need.

There is no clear demarcation between students with normal reading abilities and those with mild reading disability. The majority of children with reading disabilities have relatively mild reading disabilities, with a smaller number having extreme reading disabilities. The longer children with disability in basic reading skills, at any level of severity, go without identification and intervention, the more difficult the task of remediation and the lower the rate of success.

Children with extreme deficits in basic reading skills are much more difficult to remediate than children with mild or moderate deficits. It is unclear whether children in the most severe range can achieve age- and grade-approximate reading skills, even with normal intelligence and with intense, informed intervention provided over a protracted period of time. Children with severe learning disabilities are likely to manifest an increased number of and increased severity of social and behavioral deficits. When children with disabilities in reading also manifest attention deficit disorder, their reading deficits are typically exacerbated, more severe, and more resistant to intervention.

While severe reading disorders are clearly a major concern, even mild deficits in reading skills are likely to portend significant difficulties in academic learning. These deficits, too, are worthy of early identification and intervention. Even children with relatively subtle linguistic and reading deficits require the expertise of a teacher who is well trained and informed about the relationships between language development and reading development. Unfortunately, such teachers are in short supply, primarily because of a lack of professional certification programs providing this training.

This article focuses primarily on deficits in basic reading skills, both because of their critical importance to academic success and because relatively more is known about these deficiencies. However, other academic, social, and behavioral manifestations of learning disability are also important and cannot be assumed to be adequately addressed by programs to improve basic reading skills. While early intervention is necessary, it should not be assumed to be sufficient to address the multiple manifestations of learning disability.

Approximately one-half of all children receiving special education services nationally, or about 5% of the total public school population, are identified as having a learning disability (LD) when the federal definition of LD is used by schools to formulate identification criteria.[1] At the same time, LD remains one of the least understood and most debated disabling conditions that affect children. Indeed, the field continues to be beset by pervasive, and occasionally contentious, disagreements about the definition of the disorder, diagnostic criteria, assessment practices, treatment procedures, and educational policies.[2–6]

Learning disability is not a single disorder, but is a general category of special education composed of disabilities in any of seven specific areas: (1) receptive language (listening), (2) expressive language (speaking), (3) basic reading skills, (4) reading comprehension, (5) written expression, (6) mathematics calculation, and (7) mathematical reasoning. These separate types of learning disabilities frequently co-occur with one another and also with certain social skill deficits and emotional or behavioral disorders such as attention deficit disorder. LD is not synonymous with reading disability or dyslexia although it is frequently misinterpreted as such.[7,8] However, most of the available information concerning learning disabilities relates to reading disabilities, and the majority of children with LD have their primary deficits in reading.[2]

Box 1 shows the statutory definition of learning disabilities contained in the Individuals with Disabilities Education Act (IDEA). An important part of the definition of learning disabilities under the IDEA is the exclusionary language: learning disabilities cannot be attributed primarily to mental retardation, emotional disturbance, cultural difference, or environmental or economic disadvantage. Thus, the concept of learning disabilities embedded in federal law focuses on the notion of a discrepancy between a child's academic achievement and his or her apparent capacity and opportunity to learn. More succinctly, Zigmond notes that "learning disabilities reflect unexpected learning problems in a seemingly capable child."[9]

Although poverty and disability are often found together and each tends to exacerbate the other (see the article by Wagner and Blackorby in The Future of Children, Spring 1996), Congress has established separate programs to serve children with disabilities (the IDEA) and children in poverty (Title 1). Title 1 of the Elementary and Secondary Education Act provides funding for supplemental programs in schools serving large numbers of economically disadvantaged children. Because individual children with disabilities have strong entitlements to services under the IDEA, Congress's intent was that the IDEA serve only children with "true disabilities" and that the IDEA specifically exclude those students whose underperformance is primarily attributable to poverty. However, in the category of learning disability, and perhaps also in the category of mental retardation, this distinction is difficult or impossible to draw, and no empirical data exist to support this exclusionary practice.

While there is some agreement about these general concepts, there is continued disagreement in the field about diagnostic criteria, assessment

Definition of Learning Disability Under the Individuals with Disabilities Education Act

"Specific learning disability" means a disorder in one or more basic psychological processes involved in understanding or in using language, spoken or written, that may manifest itself in an imperfect ability to listen, speak, read, write, spell, or to do mathematical calculations. The term includes such conditions as perceptual disabilities, brain injury, minimal brain dysfunction, dyslexia, and developmental aphasia. The term does not apply to children who have learning problems that are primarily the result of visual, hearing, or motor disabilities, of mental retardation, of emotional disturbance, or of environmental, cultural, or economic disadvantage.

Source: Code of Federal Regulations, Title 34, Subtitle B, Chapter III, Section 300.7(b)(10).

practices, treatment procedures, and educational policies for learning disabilities. A number of influences have contributed to these disagreements which, in turn, have made it difficult to build a generalizable body of scientific and clinical knowledge about learning disabilities and to establish reliable and valid diagnostic criteria.[4,5] While some progress has been made during the past decade in establishing more precise definitions and a theoretically based classification system for LD,[8–10] it is useful to understand these historical influences because of their continuing impact on diagnostic and treatment practices for children with learning disabilities.

The next section of this article reviews briefly the historical events that have molded the field of learning disabilities into its present form. Subsequent sections address issues related to the prevalence of learning disabilities, the validity of current prevalence estimates, impediments to the identification and teaching of the child with LD, advances in identification, classification, intervention practices in the area of reading disability, comorbidity of types of learning disabilities (reading, written expression, mathematics disabilities) with disorders of attention and social skills deficits, outcomes for individuals with learning disabilities, and the implications for teacher preparation and school policies.

Historical Influences

The study of learning disabilities was initiated in response to the need (1) to understand individual differences among children and adults who displayed *specific* deficits in spoken or written language while maintaining integrity in *general* intellectual functioning and (2) to provide services to these students who were not being adequately served by the general educational system.[6,9,10] Overall, the field of learning disabilities emerged primarily from a social and educa-

tional need and currently remains a diagnostic practice that is more rooted in clinical practice, law, and policy than in science. Advocates for children with learning disabilities have successfully negotiated a special education category as a means to educational protection at the same time that the schools have seen an increase in the identification of LD.[6]

The unexpected pattern of *general* strengths and *specific* weaknesses in learning was first noted and studied by physicians during the early twentieth century, thus giving the field its historical biomedical orientation.[10] Doctors noted that children with learning disabilities were similar to adults and children with focal brain damage in that specific impairments in some areas of learning could occur without diminishing strengths in general cognitive ability.

Although the clinical work conducted during the first half of the twentieth century recognized the existence of learning disabilities, such information had little influence on public school policies until the mid-1960s. At this time, behavioral scientists, educators,[11] and parents expressed concern that some children had learning handicaps that were not being served effectively by general educational practices.[9] At the same time, these children were ineligible for special education services because their characteristics did not correspond to any recognized categories of disability. This disenfranchisement stimulated an advocacy movement to provide special educational services to students with learning disabilities,[4,6,9] leading many states to establish a special education category for LD during the late 1960s and 1970s.

Prevalence

The influence of advocacy has, in turn, contributed to a substantial proliferation in the number of children who have been identified with learning disabilities relative to other handicapping conditions (see Figure 1). Clearly, the prevalence of LD identification has increased dramatically.

The "real" prevalence of learning disabilities is subject to much dispute because of the lack of an agreed-upon definition of LD and objective diagnostic criteria.[4,8,12] Some have argued that the currently recognized 5% prevalence rate is excessive and is based on vague definitions, leading to inaccurate identification. On the other hand, research efforts to identify objective early indicators of LD in basic reading skills have concluded that virtually all children scoring below the 25th percentile on standardized reading tests can meet the criteria for having a reading disorder.[12] While less is known about LD in written expression, researchers estimate its true prevalence at between 8% and 15% of the school population.[13] Research also indicates that approximately 6% of the school population has difficulties in mathematics which cannot be attributed to low intelligence, sensory deficits, or economic deprivation.[14]

Increase in Identification

The substantial increase in the identification of children with learning disabilities shown in Figure 1 has led many to question the validity and reliability of LD as a diagnostic category or its "realness" as a handicapping condition.[15] In fact, it appears likely that there are both sound and unsound reasons for the increase, as is discussed later.

It should be made clear that difficulties in the identification of children with learning disabilities do not make the disabilities any less "real" to the student who cannot learn to read, write, or understand mathematics despite good intelligence, an adequate opportunity to learn, and ostensibly good teaching. However, such an anecdotal understanding of learning disability and its prevalence seems inadequate now, given the increase in diagnoses of LD, the consequences of learning failure in children, and the tremendous financial resources that are applied to the identification and teaching of children with learning disabilities. Given what is at stake, it is critical that the construct of learning disability and procedures for identifying children and adults with LD be valid and accepted by the scientific and clinical communities.

The question remains, however, of how to go about increasing the ability to identify individuals with LD accurately. Valid prevalence estimates depend upon a set of criteria for identification that are clear, observable, measurable, and agreed upon.

The Discrepancy Standard

There is currently no universally accepted test, test battery, or standard for identifying children with LD. While a discrepancy between intelligence quotient (IQ) and achievement has been a widely accepted criterion for the identification of LD and still serves as the driving clinical force in the diagnosis of LD, there is considerable variation in how the discrepancy is derived and quantified.[9,16] Federal regulations and extant clinical criteria[17] do not specify particular formulas or numerical values to assess discrepancy objectively. The effect of this lack of specification on both clinical and research practices is substantial. From a clinical standpoint, a child can be identified as having a learning disability in one school district but not in a neighboring district because of differences in the measure of discrepancy used. From a research perspective, different approaches to the discrepancy measurement lead to substantially different sample characteristics and different prevalence estimates, which undermine the ability to replicate and generalize findings.[5,6,8,9]

For the individual child, use of the discrepancy standard clearly promotes a wait-to-fail policy because a significant discrepancy between IQ and achievement generally cannot be detected until about age eight or nine. In fact, most school districts do not identify children with learning disabilities until a child is reading well below grade level, generally in third or fourth grade.[18] By this time the child has already experienced at least a few years of school failure and probably has experienced the common attendant problems of low self-esteem, diminished motivation, and inadequate acquisition of the academic material covered by his classmates during the previous few years.

It is clear that the longer children with learning disabilities, at any level of severity, go without identification and intervention, the more difficult the task of remediation becomes and the harder it is for the children to respond. Specifically, the data strongly suggest that children at risk for reading failure should be identified before the age of nine if successful intervention results are to be anticipated.[13] For example, a longitudinal investigation of 407 students[19] found that 74% of the children whose disability in reading was first identified at nine years of age or older continued to read in the lowest quintile throughout their middle and high school years. In addition, the longer children, at all severity levels, are faced with failure in reading in the classroom setting, the greater the probability that comorbid learning and behavioral difficulties will arise, further complicating the remediation task.

Figure 1

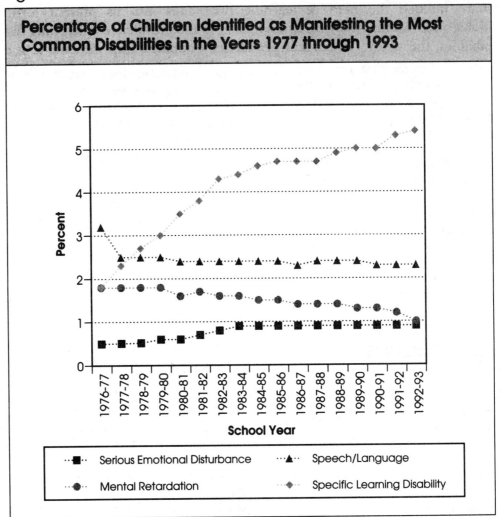

Percentage of Children Identified as Manifesting the Most Common Disabilities in the Years 1977 through 1993

Source: Office of Special Education Programs. *Implementation of the Individuals with Disabilities Education Act: Fifteenth Annual Report to Congress.* Washington, DC: U.S. Department of Education, 1993.

Developing a Diagnostic Standard

If current definitions of learning disability are not useful and if the discrepancy standard is a poor one, why have schools not adopted other means of defining and identifying LD? There are a number of conceptual and methodological barriers to the accurate identification of learning disabilities, and these impediments lead to confusion about definitions, diagnostic issues, and rising prevalence rates.

Multidisciplinary Nature of the Field

Opinions about what constitutes a learning disability vary[6,10] in part because LD is the concern of many disciplines and professions, including education, psychology, neurology, neuropsychology, optometry, psychiatry, and speech and language pathology, to name a few. Each of these disciplines has traditionally focused on different aspects of the child or adult with learning dis-

ability, so divergent ideas and contentious disagreements exist about the importance of etiology, diagnostic methods, intervention methods, and professional roles and responsibilities.[10] It is not surprising that so many children are identified because each professional may view the child through his or her own idiosyncratic clinical lens. For example, optometrists may identify a child as having a learning disability if the youngster displays difficulties in visual tracking. Speech and language pathologists, on the other hand, become concerned if the child's vocabulary and syntactic development are not commensurate with expectations. Educators become concerned primarily when development in reading, writing, and mathematics is deficient.

Lack of Specific Identification Criteria

Probably the most significant and persistent problem in the field is the lack of a precise definition and a theoretically based classification system that would allow (1) the identification of different types of learning disabilities and (2) a means of recognizing distinctions and interrelationships between types of learning disabilities and other learning disorders such as mental retardation, attention deficit disorder, speech and language difficulties, and general academic underachievement.[20] At present, the field continues to construct and use vague and ambiguous definitions that rely heavily on the exclusion of alternative diagnoses, such as the IDEA definition shown in Box 1.

Overly Broad Label

Some observers argue that the term "learning disability" is too broad to be of any diagnostic value. Stanovich,[16] a leading proponent of this view, proposes that the general term learning disabilities be abandoned and that definitional and research efforts focus on the specific types of disabilities that are now identified in ambiguous terms.

As noted earlier, the generic term learning disabilities encompasses disabilities in seven categories: (1) listening, (2) speaking, (3) basic reading skills, (4) reading comprehension, (5) written expression, (6) mathematical calculation, and (7) mathematical reasoning. Given the complexity and heterogeneity of each of these disabilities, it seems unrealistic to expect that any definitional clarity can be achieved by grouping them together under one label. To do so only obscures the critical features of each disability and makes research findings difficult to interpret.

Definitions of specific learning disabilities can be more easily and successfully operationalized than generic definitions, as the research on disabilities in basic reading skills shows.[8] To establish valid prevalence estimates for the number of individuals with learning disabilities, the first step should be to establish explicit diagnostic criteria for *each* of the seven specific disability domains. At present, the greatest progress toward this goal has been in the area of disability in basic reading skills.[8]

LD as a Sociological Phenomenon

The simplest explanation for the increasing numbers of children identified with learning disabilities and for the difficulty in understanding and defining LD is that "LD" is not a distinct disability, but an invented category created for social purposes. Some argue that the majority of students identified as having learning disabilities are not intrinsically disabled but have learning problems because of poor teaching, lack of educational opportunity, or limited educational resources.[15] In addition, because the label of LD is not a stigma-

tizing one, parents and teachers may be more comfortable with a diagnosis of LD than with labels such as slow learner, minimal brain dysfunction, or perceptual handicap. A diagnosis of LD does not imply low intelligence, emotional or behavioral difficulties, sensory handicaps, or cultural disadvantage. Thus, more positive outcomes are expected for children with learning disabilities than for those with mental retardation or emotional disturbance.

Reasons for Increase in Identification of LD

As pointed out, the substantial increase in the identification of LD, as shown in Figure 1, has caused many researchers to question the validity of the data. No doubt, the failure to develop an agreed-upon, objective, operational definition of learning disability gives credence to the concern about the validity of the identification process. Thus, it seems reasonable to assume that at least some of the increase in prevalence can be linked to conceptual, methodological, social, and political factors that spuriously inflate the identification of children with learning disabilities.[5] However, despite the conceptual and methodological shortcomings that have plagued the field with respect to definition and identification practices, there exist a number of possible sound reasons that could account for an increase in the number of children identified with LD.

Some Sound Reasons

As knowledge about learning disabilities grows, some academic difficulties not previously recognized as LD can be identified as such. Greater knowledge also affects the behavior and practices of teachers and parents. Sound reasons for the increase in identification rates are described and discussed in the sections that follow.

■ *Better Research.* Research in the past decade measures underachievement in reading as it occurs naturally in large population-based samples[12,13] rather than as identified by schools, which use widely varying criteria. In addition, much of this new research is longitudinal and has been replicated, providing the necessary foundation for epidemiological studies.[2,12,13,19,21–24] Finally, many of these studies have been specific to LD in reading, rather than LD in general, allowing greater precision.

■ *Broader Definitions.* Prevalence is directly linked to definition. LD in reading has been defined in recent research as *significant difficulties in reading single words accurately and fluently, in combination with deficits in phonological awareness.*[8] Using this definition and stronger longitudinal research methods outlined above, the prevalence for reading disability alone has increased from estimates of less than 5% in 1976 to approximately 17% in 1994.[12]

Both market and legal forces can stimulate the development of new professional specialties whose members have financial incentives to diagnose students with learning disabilities.

Phonological awareness is a critical attribute in learning to read, and children who lack this awareness can be identified in late kindergarten and early first grade. Typical diagnostic questions for kindergartners or first graders involve rhyming skills (for example, "Tell me three words that rhyme with 'cat'") and phoneme deletion skills (for example, "Say 'cat' without the /t/ sound"). The majority of children pick up phonological awareness skills easily by six to seven years of age, but a large minority of children (about 17%) have significant difficulty with these skills and will have great difficulty learning to read, regardless of their intelligence, unless these skills are acquired.

■ *Identification of LD in Girls.* A substantial portion of this increase can be attributed to the fact that females have been found to manifest reading disabilities at rates equal to males, in contrast to previous reports that males with reading disabilities outnumbered females with reading disabilities at a ratio of four to one.[25] This finding necessarily increases the prevalence rate.

■ *Increased Awareness.* Information disseminated in the past decade, particularly concerning the characteristics of reading disability, has increased the number of children referred for assessment of a learning disability.[6]

■ *Understanding of the Impact.* There has been an increase in the recognition that even "mild" deficits in reading skills are likely to portend significant difficulties in academic learning and are, therefore, worthy of early identification, diagnosis, and intervention.[26,27]

Some Unsound Reasons

There is no shortage of horror stories about the misidentification of LD and reports that the category serves as a "catch all" for any youngster who is not meeting the expectations of parents and teachers. Are there legitimate reasons for these criticisms? The answer appears to be yes. Examples are described and discussed in the sections that follow.

■ *Ambiguous Definitions.* The ambiguity inherent in the general definitions of LD (see Box 1) leaves the identification process open for wide interpretation and misinterpretation. Flexible identification decision making allows some children to be identified as having learning disabilities when they do not, while others with learning disabilities may be overlooked.[5] This latitude can be manipulated to increase prevalence rates in response to financial incentives (for example, to qualify for increased state funding), to decrease prevalence rates in response to political movements (for example, inclusion), or to abandon programs that appear too costly.[28]

■ *Social and Political Factors.* Social and political factors also contribute to the inflation of prevalence rates for learning disabilities. In 1976–77, the first year of full implementation of Public Law 94-142, 2.16% of all school-children were served in programs for children with mental retardation (MR) and 1.80% in programs for children with learning disabilities (Figure 1). By the 1992–93 school year, placements for children with MR had decreased to 1.1% while placements for children with LD had increased to 5.4% of the total school population (Figure 1). While these reversed trends mask substantial variations among states, the dramatic changes in identification rates of the two types of disability suggest that attempts to apply less stigmatizing labels may be influencing the identification process.

■ *Number of Professional Specialties Involved.* The large number of professional specialties involved in the identification process provides fertile ground for the overidentification of LD because each specialty brings its own set of diagnostic assumptions, theories, and measures to the assessment task. Inconsistent identification practices allow prevalence rates to escalate. This is a significant problem when there are financial incentives to encourage identification (see the article by Parrish and Chambers in *The Future of Children,* Spring 1996). Both market and legal forces can stimulate the development of new professional specialties (such as language/learning disorder specialist) whose members have financial incentives to diagnose students with learning disabilities, which the specialists will often be employed to treat. Although it may be uncomfortable to mention these factors, they exist and play some role in the increase of prevalence of LD. At the same time, the majority of professionals serving children with learning disabilities appear well intentioned and well informed.

■ *Inadequate Preparation of Teachers.*
Unfortunately, a major factor contributing to invalid prevalence estimates may be the inadequate preparation of teachers by colleges of education. Recent studies have found that a majority of regular classroom teachers feel that they are not prepared to address individual differences in learning abilities within classroom settings.[29] Even more alarming, research suggests that special educators themselves do not possess sufficient content knowledge to address the language and reading needs of children with learning disabilities.[30] Without adequate preparation, teachers have a tendency to overrefer children for specialized assistance because they feel ill-equipped to provide the necessary services.[31]

Interpreting Prevalence Rates

The prevalence of learning disabilities is completely dependent upon the definition used. In most areas, the identification of LD is based largely upon the discrepancy standard and, thus, provides a count of the number of older elementary students (third grade and above) who are achieving significantly below expectations based on IQ. This is, at best, an incomplete definition of LD and one that, for the majority of students with learning disabilities, is based upon an invalid criterion, namely, the discrepancy standard.

Clearly, current definitions allow both overidentification and underidentification of L.D. Depending upon the magnitude of financial incentives and upon unrelated factors (for example, class size, goals for increasing test scores) that often shape the decisions of classroom teachers to refer students with special needs, an individual school district may drastically overidentify or underidentify students with learning disabilities. Therefore, local or national statistics on identification rates for students with LD must be interpreted with caution.

Efforts to Improve Identification

To improve the diagnosis and remediation of learning disabilities, a classification system is needed to identify different types of learning disabilities as well as the distinctions and interrelationships among types of LD and other childhood disorders.[2,20,32] Prospective longitudinal studies are one of the most powerful means to study the different types of LD and their relationships to other disorders and to obtain data for a focused and succinct definition.

Approximately 80% of children identified as having learning disabilities have their primary difficulties in learning to read.

Prospective, longitudinal studies of LD can serve as a platform to (1) identify critical learning and behavioral characteristics that may be manifested in different ways at different developmental periods, (2) develop early predictors of underachievement for different academic domains (for example, reading, written language, math), (3) map the developmental course of different types of learning disabilities, (4) identify commonly co-occurring disorders and secondary behavioral consequences and develop in response to failure in school, and (5) assess the efficacy of different treatment and teaching methods for different types of learning disabilities.

To address this compelling need to establish a valid classification system and definition for LD, Congress enacted the Health Research Extension Act of 1985 (Public Law 99-158). This act called for the development of an Interagency Committee on Learning Disabilities (ICLD), under the lead of the National Institute of Child Health and Human Development (NICHD), to identify critical research needs in LD and to implement comprehensive studies to address issues relevant to identification, prevention, etiology, and treatment.

New Knowledge of Reading Disabilities

Since the inauguration of the NICHD Learning Disability Research Network in 1987, researchers have learned the most about learning disabilities that affect linguistic, reading, and spelling abilities and the least about learning disabilities in mathematics.[2] A number of new findings have also been obtained in the area of attention deficit disorder (ADD) and its relationship to different types of LD, particularly disorders in reading.[12] For brevity, the major discoveries made during the past several years are presented in Table 1. Selected findings are reviewed here. The reader should note that many findings have been replicated by multiple research groups, as cited in Table 1, and that the findings are primarily based on large longitudinal samples. Finally, readers should note that studies being conducted in Canada by Stanovich and Siegel at the Ontario Institute for Studies in Education are included in Table 1 because of their impact on the field and because Stanovich and Siegel serve as consultants to the Yale Learning Disability Research Center (LDRC).

Interventions applied after a child has failed in reading for two or three years may not be effective for several reasons, including the student's declining motivation and impaired self-concept.

As Table 1 shows, a majority of discoveries made during the past decade have been in the area of reading disabilities. This is appropriate. As Lerner pointed out from her analysis of public school referral data in 1989,[33] approximately 80% of children identified as having learning disabilities have their primary difficulties in learning to read. This high rate of occurrence of reading difficulties among youngsters with LD has also been reported by Kavale in his meta-analytic studies.[34] More recent longitudinal and cross-sectional studies have supported the high rate of reading difficulty among children with learning disabilities, but have also found that reading deficits frequently co-occur with other academic and attentional difficulties. For example, Fletcher and his associates at the Yale Center for the Study of Learning and Attention have, as part of a larger classification effort, studied 216 children, 7.5 to 9.5 years of age, who were identified as normal readers, reading disabled, math disabled, both reading and math disabled, normal reading with ADD, and reading disabled with ADD.[21,35] From this sample of children with a variety of learning disabilities, only 25 youngsters were reading at age-appropriate levels.

Research indicates that reading disorders reflected in deficient decoding and word-recognition skills are primarily caused by deficiencies in the ability to segment syllables and words into constituent sound units called phonemes.[16,22,36–38] For example, in a large study of 199 seven- to nine-year-old children who had significant difficulties in decoding and word recognition, more than 85% of the youngsters manifested deficits on measures of phonological awareness. In this investigation, children with and without IQ-reading-achievement discrepancies appeared equally impaired on both the phonological and reading measures.[21] This extremely high frequency of phonological awareness deficits in children with reading disabilities has led Share and Stanovich to conclude: "We know unequivocally that less-skilled readers have difficulty turning spellings into sounds. . . . This relationship is so strong that it deserves to be identified as one, if not the defining, feature of reading disability."[39]

Biological Bases

Several NICHD investigations have indicated that these phonologically based reading disabilities are linked to neurobiological and genetic factors.[2,8,13,40] Functional and structural neuroimaging studies indicate that the poor phonological skills which limit the development of basic reading abilities, are highly related to aberrant neurophysiological processing.[22,40] Moreover, there is increasing evidence from behavioral and molecular genetic studies that the phonological deficits observed in reading disability are heritable.[41,42] Taken together, longitudinal studies of the linguistic, neurobiological, and genetic factors in reading disabilities provide strong and converging evidence that reading disability is primarily caused by deficits in phonological processing and, more specifically, phonological awareness.[8,13,30,37,38,40]

Likewise, the data derived from genetic and neurobiological studies suggest that some reading disabilities are associated with subtle chromosomal[42] and neurological differences,[22,40] indicating that such disabilities are biologically "real" rather than sociopolitically created.

Discrepancy Standard

In addition to the previously discussed problems of the discrepancy standard, Table 1 indicates that the use of a discrepancy formula, which calculates differences between IQ reading scores, is not a valid indicator of reading disability; that is, children with reading disabilities both with and without such discrepancies have similar deficits in phonological awareness and similar genetic and neurophysiological characteristics.[36] At this time, it is not clear whether children with higher IQs respond more favorably to intervention.[7]

Persistent Deficit

Unfortunately, as Table 1 indicates, reading disabilities appear to reflect a persistent deficit rather than a developmental lag. That is, children with

Table 1

Major Findings from Research Programs Supported by the National Institute of Child Health and Human Development		
Research Domain	**Findings**	**Research Group***
Definition of learning disabilities	Definitions that measure the discrepancy between IQ and achievement do not adequately identify learning disabilities, particularly in the area of basic reading skills.	Yale Ontario
Reading processes	Disabled readers with and without an IQ-achievement discrepancy show similar information processing, genetic, and neurophysiological profiles. This indicates that the existence of a discrepancy is not a valid indicator of disability in basic reading skills.	Colorado Bowman Gray Yale Ontario
Reading processes	Epidemiological studies indicate that as many females as males manifest dyslexia; however, schools identify three to four times more boys than girls.	Bowman Gray Colorado Yale
Reading processes	Reading disabilities reflect a persistent deficit rather than a developmental lag. Longitudinal studies show that, of those children who are reading disabled in the third grade, approximately 74% continue to read significantly below grade level in the ninth grade.	Yale Ontario
Reading processes	Children with reading disability differ from one another *and* from other readers along a continuous distribution. They *do not* aggregate together to form a distinct "hump" separate from the normal distribution.	Yale Bowman Gray Colorado Ontario
Reading processes	The ability to read and comprehend depends upon rapid and automatic recognition and decoding of single words. Slow and inaccurate decoding are the best predictors of deficits in reading comprehension.	Yale Bowman Gray Colorado Johns Hopkins Florida Houston
Reading processes	The ability to decode single words accurately and fluently is dependent upon the ability to segment words and syllables into phonemes. Deficits in phonological awareness reflect the core deficit in dyslexia.	Yale Colorado Bowman Gray Miami Johns Hopkins Florida Houston
Reading processes	The best predictor of reading ability from kindergarten and first-grade performance is phoneme segmentation ability.	Bowman Gray Yale Florida Houston
Attention	A precise classification of disorders of attention is not yet available; however, operational definitions are emerging.	Yale
Attention	Approximately 15% of students with reading disability also have a disorder of attention. Approximately 35% of students with disorders of attention also have reading disability. However, the two disorders are distinct and separable.	Bowman Gray Yale

*See the related endnote at the end of this article for a detailed description of research groups.

Table 1 (continued)

Major Findings from Research Programs Supported by the National Institute of Child Health and Human Development		
Research Domain	**Findings**	**Research Group***
Attention	Disorders of attention exacerbate the severity of reading disability.	Bowman Gray Miami
Genetics	There is strong evidence for a genetic basis for reading disabilities, with deficits in phonological awareness reflecting the greatest degree of heritability.	Colorado Bowman Gray
Neurology	Regional blood studies indicate that deficient word recognition skills are associated with less than normal activation in the left temporal region.	Bowman Gray
Neurology	PET studies indicate that dyslexic adults have greater than normal activation in the occipital and prefrontal regions of the cortex.	Miami
Intervention	Disabled readers do not readily acquire the alphabetic code because of deficits in phonological processing. Thus, disabled readers must be provided highly structured programs that explicitly teach application of phonological rules to print.	Bowman Gray Florida Houston
Intervention	Longitudinal data indicate that systematic phonics instruction results in more favorable outcomes for disabled readers than does a context-emphasis (whole language) approach.	Bowman Gray Florida Houston

*See the related endnote at the end of this article for a detailed description of research groups.

delays in understanding phonological concepts in first grade are unlikely to catch up later without explicit and informed teaching. Longitudinal studies show that, of the youngsters who are identified in the third grade, approximately 74% remain reading disabled through the ninth grade.[19,43] This appears to be true even when special education has been provided. It should be made clear, however, that interventions applied *after* a child has failed in reading for two or three years may not be effective for several reasons, including the student's declining motivation and impaired self-concept. Instructional difficulties in later intervention abound. For example, the teacher carrying out the interventions may not be properly trained, the interventions may not include explicit and informed instruction in the development of phonological awareness and sound-symbol relationships, the interventions may not be consistently applied and/or may be limited in intensity and duration, and there may be insufficient follow-up or explicit instruction to enable the student to generalize the specific concepts learned to material presented in regular classroom settings.

Distribution of Severity

A significant finding from the Yale LDRC is that reading disability represents the extreme of a normal distribution of reading ability so that there is an unbroken continuum from reading ability to reading disability.[43] The finding that reading disability is part of continuum now places the disorder in the context of other biologically based disorders such as hypertension and obesity.[43] The discovery that reading disability is best conceptualized as occurring along a normal distribution of reading skills underscores the fact that children will vary in their level of severity of the disorder running along a mild-to-severe spectrum, with the majority of children with reading disabilities falling at the mild end. This finding has significant implications. For example, what are the criteria for identifying a child as having a *severe* reading disability, and does this degree of disability warrant entitlement to a greater intensity and duration of specialized interventions?

To answer such questions, the NICHD is embarking on a series of studies to identify the most valid points along the distribution of reading scores that distinguish levels of severity. In part, the validity of different cutoff points for mild, moderate, and severe reading disability is being determined by how children in each severity group respond to different types and intensities of intervention. At this writing, some initial results derived from the Florida State Intervention Project show that children with scores at the extreme lower end of the distributions for both phonological awareness skills and basic reading skills are much more difficult to remediate than children who fall along the distribution in the mild and moderate ranges.[44–46] It is as yet unclear whether children in the more severe range can achieve age- and grade-approximate reading skills, even with intense, informed intervention provided over a protracted period of time.

While children with severe reading disabilities will most likely require a greater amount of time in high-impact intervention programs than children with less severe deficits, as discussed earlier, it is clear that the longer children *at any level of severity* go without proper identification and intervention, the more difficult the task of remediation and the harder it becomes for the children to respond. It is also clear that even children with relatively subtle linguistic and reading deficits require the expertise of a teacher who is well trained and informed about the relationships between language development and reading development.[30] Unfortunately, such teachers are in short supply, primarily because of a lack of programs providing this training.[31]

Co-occurring Disorders

As noted, most children with learning disabilities have more than one of the seven subtypes of learning disabilities. It is also not unusual to find LD co-occurring with certain behavioral or emotional disorders. The most common co-occurring combinations are discussed briefly below.

Reading and Attention Disorders

Attention deficit disorder (ADD) is an increasingly common diagnosis recognized in medicine[47] and psychology[17] although it is not a category of disability recognized under the IDEA. Like LD, ADD is the subject of considerable controversy, and diagnostic criteria for ADD continue to evolve. There is no litmus test for ADD, which is diagnosed on the basis of persistent and maladaptive behavior patterns (inattention, impulsivity, and hyperactivity) that are inappropriate for the child's age. The number of diagnoses of ADD has increased dramatically in the past decade,[48] and

one study[12] found 7% of a survey sample of 445 kindergarten students qualifying as "inattentive" on the Multigrade Inventory for Teachers.

Even children with relatively subtle linguistic and reading deficits require the expertise of a teacher who is well trained.

Figure 2[12] indicates that a child identified with reading disabilities is twice as likely as a member of the general population to also meet the diagnostic criteria for inattention (15% versus 7%). Similarly, an individual diagnosed with ADD is at higher risk than a member of the general population of having a reading disability/phonological awareness deficit (36% versus 17%). Despite this co-occurrence, recent studies have indicated that reading disabilities and ADD are distinct and separable disorders.[12,22,49]

Instruction in phonological awareness at the kindergarten level has significant positive effects on reading development during the first grade.

Unfortunately, when children with disabilities in reading also manifest ADD, their reading deficits are typically exacerbated, more severe, and more resistant to intervention.[22] In contrast to reading disabilities, ADD is more prevalent in males. Given the frequent co-occurrence of ADD with reading disabilities and given the tendency of boys with ADD to attract considerable attention from teachers, this combination may make boys with disabilities in reading much more likely than girls with disabilities in reading to come to the attention of teachers and to be referred for testing.

Social Adjustment Problems

In a broad sense, data indicate that learning disability, no matter what the specific type, has a tendency to co-occur with social adjustment problems.[50] Bruck,[51] in her review of the literature related to social and emotional adjustment, concluded that children with learning disabilities are more likely to exhibit increased levels of anxi-

Figure 2

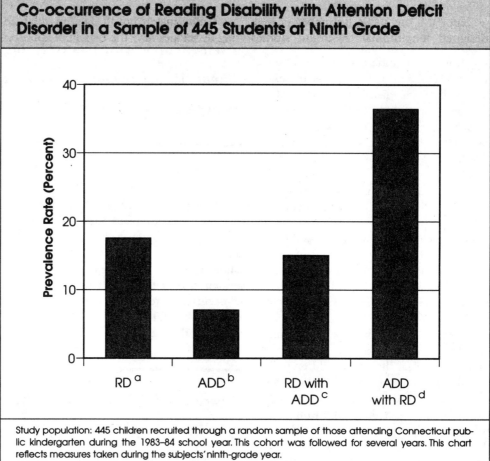

Co-occurrence of Reading Disability with Attention Deficit Disorder in a Sample of 445 Students at Ninth Grade

Study population: 445 children recruited through a random sample of those attending Connecticut public kindergarten during the 1983–84 school year. This cohort was followed for several years. This chart reflects measures taken during the subjects' ninth-grade year.

a **RD** is defined as either an ability-achievement discrepancy (based on a regression formula) or a reading standard score below the 25th percentile.

b **ADD** is defined as a score of greater than or equal to 1.5 above the mean on the inattention scale of the Multigrade Inventory for Teachers.

c **RD with ADD** is the percentage of all students meeting the criteria for RD in this study who also met the criteria for ADD.

d **ADD with RD** is the percentage of all students meeting the criteria for ADD in this study who also met the criteria for RD.

Source: Adapted with permission from Shaywitz, S.E., Fletcher, J.M., and Shaywitz, B.A. Issues in the definition and classification of attention deficit disorder. *Topics in Language Disorders* (1994) 14:1–25.

ety, withdrawal, depression, and low self-esteem compared with their nondisabled peers. This co-morbidity is persistent. For example, Johnson and Blalock[52] found that, of the 93 adults studied in an LD clinic sample, 36% continued to receive counseling or psychotherapy for low self-esteem, social isolation, anxiety, depression, and frustration. In many instances, it appears that such emotional problems reflect adjustment difficulties resulting from academic failure.[13] Deficits in social skills have also been found to exist at significantly high rates among children with learning disabilities.[53] In general, social skill deficits include difficulties interacting with people in an ap-propriate fashion (for example, lack of knowledge of how to greet people, how to make friends, and how to engage in playground games or a failure to use knowledge of such skills in these situations). While not all children with learning disabilities exhibit deficits in social skills, there are certain common characteristics among those who do. For example, Bruck[51] reported that children with more severe manifestations of LD are likely to manifest both an increased number of and increased severity of social skills deficits. Moreover, the gender of the child appears to be a factor, with evidence suggesting that girls with LD are more likely to have social adjustment problems.[51]

Reading Disorders with Other Learning Disabilities

There is abundant evidence that it is rare for a child with learning disabilities to manifest only one specific type of learning disability.[3,53] The co-occurrence of learning disorders should be expected given the developmental relationships between listening, speaking, reading, spelling, writing, and mathematics. For example, it is clear that deficits in phonological awareness lead to difficulties in decoding and word recognition which, in turn, lead to deficits in reading comprehension.[16,37,38] Likewise, children with disabilities in reading frequently experience persistent difficulties in solving word problems in math for the obvious reason that the printed word is difficult for them to comprehend.[14]

An important conclusion to draw from the literature on co-occurring disorders is that any intervention or remediation effort must take into account the range of deficits a child may have. More specifically, while an intensive reading intervention may consist of explicit instruction in phonological awareness, sound-symbol relationships, and contextual reading skills, the child may also require elements essential to bolstering self-esteem, and to fostering reading in other content areas such as mathematics, social studies, and science. One cannot expect the intervention for the reading deficit to generalize serendipitously to other domains of difficulty.

LD in Written Expression

Typically, children who display LD in written expression have difficulties in spelling, formulation and expression of ideas, handwriting, and knowledge of grammar and syntax. Unfortunately, well-designed research investigating disorders of written expression is relatively meager. Definitions for disorders of written expression remain vague.[54] Therefore it is not surprising that estimates of the prevalence of such disorders range from 8% to 15%.[13] What is known is that boys and girls display written language deficits at relatively equal rates.[54] Despite the lack of objective and detailed identification criteria, a number of excellent studies have been conducted to identify effective assessment and intervention programs for problems in written expression.[55-57]

The most successful programs tend to ensure that clear linkages are drawn between oral language, reading, and written language. Successful programs also ensure that basic skills development in spelling and writing (graphomotor production) are explicitly taught and/or accommodated and that the student is also taught how to employ strategies to guide the formulation of ideas for writing and the organization of these ideas in writing. These elements are common to many writing programs; however, successful instruction for students with disabilities in written expression depends upon their intensity and explicitness.

LD in Mathematics

Children identified as manifesting LD in mathematics can demonstrate deficits in arithmetic calculation, mathematics reasoning, or both. In general, authorities agree that approximately 6% of the school population have difficulties in mathematics that cannot be attributed to low intelligence, sensory deficits, or economic deprivation.[14,58] While the data are sparse at this time, it appears that deficits in arithmetic calculation skills are more frequently identified than deficits in arithmetic reasoning.[14] However, common sense would suggest that attempts to reason mathematically would be constrained by limitations in calculations skills. Unfortunately, a major difficulty in identifying math learning disabilities accurately is that, like learning to read, learning mathematics concepts is dependent upon the teacher's knowledge of the concepts and ability to present them.[13]

Interventions for Learning Disabilities

Space does not permit an extended review of research on intervention methods for different types of learning disabilities. However, high-quality prospective longitudinal research methods are now being applied to the study of treatment methods for reading disabilities, and that research is summarized here.

Research attempting to identify effective treatment methods for different types and severity levels of reading deficits has been enormously difficult. This is because typical treatment studies have not been able to reliably determine whether the outcomes seen were attributable to the treatment method, the child's general development, the child's previous instruction, the concurrent instruction being provided in the regular classroom, or combinations of these factors. In addition, a majority of treatment studies have been hampered by not having control over teacher expertise and training. Thus, if a treatment method does or does not work effectively, one does not know if it is because of the characteristics of the method, the characteristics of the teacher, or the characteristics of the child.

Since the late 1980s, a number of well-designed longitudinal treatment studies have been conducted. Because these studies have the capability to intervene with children early on and follow them over time, many of the methodological problems described above have been addressed. These intervention studies have provided information about how to prevent reading disabilities as well as how to address reading disabilities once they are detected at later ages.

For example, Blachman and her colleagues[59–61] have shown that instruction in phonological awareness at the kindergarten level has significant positive effects on reading development during the first grade. Within this context, research has demonstrated that proper instruction carried out by informed teachers can prevent reading failure both for children with inherent LD in basic reading skills and for children whose lack of exposure to "language rich" environments and language development activities during the first five years of life places them at risk for reading deficits. For instance, in a series of studies, Blachman[60,61] provided 84 low-income, inner-city children with 11 weeks of intensive instruction, 20 minutes per day, with one teacher instructing a small group of four to five students in several aspects of phonological awareness. Prior to instruction, classroom teachers also received 14 hours of intensive training. At the end of the 11 weeks, children receiving the interventions significantly (p < 0.0001) outperformed control children at reading phonetically regular words and at related tasks. A follow-up study conducted in February and May of the first-grade year showed that the gains were maintained if the first-grade curriculum continued the same emphasis on phonological skill development. Similar studies of kindergarten and first-grade children conducted by other researchers[62–64] have yielded similar results.

Unfortunately, not all children with reading disabilities have the benefit of appropriate early interventions. As discussed earlier, most children whose reading disability is not recognized until third grade or later and who receive standard interventions fail to show noticeable improvement. However, intensive instruction of appropriate duration provided by trained teachers can remediate the deficient reading skills of many children. For example, in one study, Alexander and her colleagues[65] provided 65 severely dyslexic children with 65 hours of individual instruction in addition to group instruction in phonemic awareness and synthetic and analytic skills. This intensive treatment approach improved the reading skills of the children from an initial reading score of 77 to an average of 98.4 (mean = 100) on a measure of alphabetic reading skills. Longitudinal studies continue to demonstrate the efficacy of intensive and informed multidimensional treatment programs.[64,66]

Several additional findings have emerged from these longitudinal treatment studies. It is clear that children with severe phonological deficits, leading to poor decoding and word recognition skills, respond to treatment at slower rates than youngsters with mild to moderate deficits.[44,67] In addition, instruction and interventions for reading failure, which focus primarily on context and reading comprehension without commensurate attention paid to phonological awareness, decoding, and word recognition, show limited results.[67–69] Finally, the success of even the best-designed reading intervention program is highly dependent upon the training and skills of the teacher.[22,29–31,38]

Disability in basic reading skills has been a prime candidate for treatment studies because it is the most common form of LD, it is the most objectively identifiable, and more knowledge is available concerning its causes and developmental course. Interventions for other types of learning disabilities have been developed but not studied as extensively and not studied in prospective, longitudinal research. There is as yet no solid indication whether early, effective interventions for disability in basic reading skills will affect the developmental course of other forms of learning disability.

Outcomes

Learning disabilities, sometimes inappropriately conceptualized as a "mild" disorder, may be anything but—they may be persistent and may not respond to general instruction or to inappropriate (for example, whole language) instruction. Unless identified early on and taught by expert teachers using detailed and intensive approaches emphasizing teaching both in phonological awareness and phonics instruction, children who learn poorly in the third grade can be expected to learn poorly throughout middle- and high-school grades. Unfortunately, the majority of children with learning disabilities are still not identified until the third or fourth grade and do not receive appropriate and timely reading instruction. In turn, those students with learning disabilities who graduate from high school are destined for few postschool opportunities. The minority of children with LD who received appropriate early intervention have not been identified for long-term follow-up so their long-term outcomes are speculative, but there is reason for optimism in their significantly improved short-term outcomes.

At present, the long-term outcomes for the majority of individuals with learning disabilities who did not receive appropriate early reading instruction are frequently bleak. It is known from the epidemiological data cited earlier that 75% of the children with disabilities in reading who are not identified until the third grade continue to have reading disabilities in the ninth grade.[24] In a recent review, Martin[70] reported that a considerable percentage (26.7%) of high school students identified as having learning disabilities drop out of school prior to graduation. Another 16% of students with learning disabilities exit school for "unknown" reasons without a diploma. Equally disturbing, Fairweather and Shaver[71] found that only 17.1% of the individuals with learning disabilities whom they followed for three to five years after high school were enrolled in any post-secondary course, including vocational courses. Only 6.7% of the students with learning disabilities participated in two-year higher education programs, and only 1.8% participated in four-year programs.

While these data suggest that individuals with learning disabilities do not markedly improve their academic skills (particularly reading skills) and face limited educational and vocational opportunities, it should not be concluded that individuals with LD cannot be taught. They can, but, as stated throughout this paper, interventions are most likely to be successful if applied early and carried out by expert teachers.

Conclusions

The past decade has witnessed a significant improvement in the quality of research on learning disabilities. Much of this recent research has been longitudinal in nature, thus opening the door to the identification of better predictors of different types of LD, their prevalence, their developmental course, and their response to intervention. Specifically,

■ The definitional issues addressed in this article continue to be the single greatest impediment to understanding learning disabilities and how to help children and adults with LD.

■ Maintaining the term "learning disabilities" makes little sense for scientific purposes, clinical purposes, or school policy purposes. Instead, the field must grapple with the clear need to address each type of learning disability individually to arrive at clear definitional statements and a coherent understanding of etiology, developmental course, identification, prevention, and treatment.

■ Reading disability in the form of deficits in phonological awareness is the most prevalent type of learning disability and affects approximately 17% of school-age children to some degree.

■ While other factors will, no doubt, be identified as contributing to reading disability, deficits in phonological awareness will most likely be found to be the core deficit. Research during the past decade has shown that deficits in phonological awareness can be identified in late kindergarten and first grade using inexpensive, straightforward testing protocols, and the presence of these deficits is a strong indicator that reading disability will follow.

■ Although it is now possible to identify children who are at-risk for reading failure, and some of the instructional conditions that must be in place from the beginning of formal schooling are understood, it is still true that the majority of LD children are not identified until the third grade. Therefore, policy initiatives should focus on the dissemination of existing early identification and early intervention programs.

■ Interventions for reading disability must consist of explicit instructional procedures in phonological awareness, sound-symbol relationships, and meaning and reading comprehension, and should be provided by expert teachers in the kindergarten and first-grade years.

■ In general, teachers remain seriously unprepared to address individual differences in many academic skills but particularly in reading. However, teachers cannot be expected to know what they have not been taught, and clearly colleges of education have let students down. Regrettably, being unprepared takes a toll on teachers. Many teachers worry about their failures with hard-to-teach students, become frustrated, lose confidence, and leave the profession, or discontinue attempting to teach children with special needs. This cycle of events calls for honest and aggressive reform in higher education.

■ While early intervention is *necessary*, it should not be assumed to be *sufficient* to address the multiple manifestations of learning disability. Even those students who receive appropriate phonological instruction at a young age may require continuous and intensive support to deal with other co-occurring disorders.

■ When policymakers consider "inclusionary" models of instruction, they must consider carefully whether those models can provide the critical elements of intensity and the appropriate duration of instruction, along with teacher expertise in multiple teaching methods and in accommodating individual learning differences.

1. Office of Special Education Programs. *Implementation of the Education of the Handicapped Act: Eleventh annual report to Congress.* Washington, DC: U.S.Department of Education, 1989.

2. Lyon, G. R. Research initiatives and discoveries in learning disabilities. *Journal of Child Neurology* (1995) 10: 120–26.

3. Lyon, G. R., ed. *Frames of reference for the assessment of learning disabilities: New views on measurement issues.* Baltimore: Paul H. Brookes, 1994.

4. Lyon, G. R., and Moats, L. C. An examination of research in learning disabilities: Past practices and future directions. In *Better understanding learning disabilities: New views from research and their implications for education and public policies.* G. R. Lyon, D. B. Gray, J. F. Kavanaugh, and N. A. Krasnegor, eds. Baltimore: Paul H. Brookes, 1993, pp. 1–14.

5. Lyon, G. R. Learning disabilities research: False starts and broken promises. In *Research in learning disabilities: Issues and future directions.* S. Vaughn and C. Bos, eds. San Diego, CA: College-Hill Press, 1987, pp. 69–85.

6. Moats, L. C., and Lyon, G. R. Learning disabilities in the United States: Advocacy, science, and the future of the field. *Journal of Learning Disabilities* (1993) 26:282–94.

7. Lyon, G. R. IQ is irrelevant to the definition of learning disabilities: A position in search of logic and data. *Journal of Learning Disabilities* (1989) 22:504–19.

8. Lyon, G. R. Toward a definition of dyslexia. *Annals of dyslexia* (1995) 45:3–27.

9. Zigmond, N. Learning disabilities from an educational perspective. In *Better understanding learning disabilities: New views from research and their implications for education and public policies.* G. R. Lyon, D. B. Gray, J. F. Kavanagh, and N. A. Krasnegor, eds. Baltimore: Paul H. Brookes, 1993, pp. 251–72.

10. Torgesen, J. K. Learning disabilities: Historical and conceptual issues. In *Learning about learning disabilities.* B. Y. L. Wong, ed. New York: Academic Press, 1991, pp. 3–29.

11. Kirk, S.A. Behavioral diagnosis and remediation of learning disabilities. In *Conference on the Exploration of the Perceptually Handicapped Child.* Evanston, IL: Fund for Perceptually Handicapped Children, 1963, pp. 1–7.

12. Shaywitz, S. E., Fletcher, J. M., and Shaywitz, S. E. Issues in the definition and classification of attention deficit disorder. *Topics on Language Disorders* (1994) 14:1–25.

13. Lyon, G. R. Learning disabilities. In *Child psychopathology.* E. Marsh and R. Barkley, eds. New York: Guilford Press, 1996, pp. 390–434.

14. Fleishner, J. E. Diagnosis and assessment of mathematics learning disabilities. In *Frames of reference for the assessment of learning disabilities: New views on measurement issues.* G. R. Lyon, ed. Baltimore: Paul H. Brookes, 1994, pp. 441–58.

15. Coles, G. *The learning mystique: A critical look at learning disabilities.* New York: Pantheon Press, 1987.

16. Stanovich, K. E. The construct validity of discrepancy definitions of reading disability. In *Better understanding learning disabilities: New views on research and their implications for education and public policies.* G. R. Lyon, D. B. Gray, J. F. Kavanaugh, and N. A. Krasnegor, eds. Baltimore: Paul H. Brookes, 1993, pp. 273–307.

17. American Psychiatric Association. *Diagnostic and statistical manual of mental disorders.* 4th ed. rev. Washington, DC: APA, 1994.

18. Foorman, B. R., Francis, D. J., Shaywitz, S. E., et al. The case for early reading intervention. In *Cognitive and linguistic foundations of reading acquisition: Implications for intervention.* B. Blachman, ed. Mahwah, NJ: Erlbaum. In press.

19. Francis, D. J., Shaywitz, S. E., Steubing, K. K., et al. Measurement of change: Assessing behavior over time and within a developmental context. In *Frames of reference for the assessment of learning disabilities: New views on measurement issues.* G. R. Lyon, ed. Baltimore: Paul H. Brookes, 1994, pp. 29–58.

20. Fletcher, J. M., Francis, D. J., Rourke, B. P., et al. Classification of learning disabilities: Relationships with other childhood disorders. In *Better understanding learning disabilities: New views on research and their implications for education and public policies.* G. R. Lyon, D. B. Gray, J. F. Kavanagh, and N. A. Krasnegor, eds. Baltimore: Paul H. Brookes, 1993, pp. 27–56.

21. Fletcher, J. M., Shaywitz, S. E., Shankweiler, D. P., et al. Cognitive profiles of reading disability: Comparisons of discrepancy and low achievement definitions. *Journal of Educational Psychology* (1994) 95:1–18.

22. Wood, F., Felton, R., Flowers, L., and Naylor, C. Neurobehavioral definition of dyslexia. In *The reading brain: The biological basis of dyslexia.* D. D. Duane and D. B. Gray, eds. Parkton, MD: York Press, 1991, pp. 1–26.

23. Lyon, G. R., Gray, D. B., Kavanagh, J. F., and Krasnegor, N. A., eds. *Better understanding learning disabilities: New views from research and their implications for education and public policies.* Baltimore: Paul H. Brookes, 1993.

24. Shaywitz, B. A., and Shaywitz, S. E. Measuring and analyzing change. In *Frames of reference for the assessment of learning disabilities: New views on measurement issues.* G. R. Lyon, ed. Baltimore: Paul H. Brookes, 1994, pp. 29–58.

25. Shaywitz, B. A., and Shaywitz, S. E., Fletcher, J. M., and Escobar, M. D. Prevalence of reading disability in boys and girls: Results of the Connecticut longitudinal study. *Journal of the American Medical Association* (1990) 264:998–1002.

26. Fletcher, J. M., and Foorman, B. R. Issues in definition and measurement of learning disabilities: The need for early identification. In *Frames of reference for the assessment of learning disabilities: New views on measurement issues.* G. R. Lyon, ed. Baltimore; Paul H. Brookes, 1994, pp. 185–200.

27. Blachman, B. A. Getting ready to read: Learning how print maps to speech. In *The language continuum: From infancy to literacy.* J. F. Kavanagh, ed. Parkton, MD: York Press, 1991, pp. 41–62.

28. Senf, G. Learning disabilities as a sociological sponge: Wiping up life's spills. In *Research in learning disabilities: Issue and future directions.* S. Vaughn and C. Bos, eds. Boston: College-Hill Press, 1987, pp. 87–101.

29. Lyon, G. R., Vaasen, M., and Toomey, F. Teachers' perceptions of their undergraduate and graduate

preparation. *Teacher Education and Special Education* (1989) 12:164–69.

30. Moats, L. C. The missing foundation in teacher education: Knowledge of the structure of spoken and written language. *Annals of Dyslexia* (1994) 44:81–102.

31. Moats, L. C., and Lyon, G. R. Wanted: Teachers with knowledge of language. *Topics in Language Disorders* (1996) 16, 2:73–86.

32. Interagency Committee on Learning Disabilities. *A report to Congress.* Bethesda, MD: The National Institutes of Health, 1987.

33. Lerner, J. W. Educational interventions in learning disabilities. *Journal of the American Academy of Child and Adolescent Psychiatry* (1989) 28:326–31.

34. Kavale, K. A. Potential advantages of the meta-analysis technique for special education. *Journal of Special Education* (1984) 18:61–72.

35. Fletcher, J., Morris, R., Lyon, G.R., et al. Sub-types of dyslexia: An old problem revisited. In *Cognitive and linguistic foundations of reading acquisition: Implications for intervention research.* B. Blachman, ed. Mahwah, NJ: Erlbaum. In press.

36. Stanovich, E. E., and Siegel, L. S. Phenotypic performance profile of children with reading disabilities: A regression-based test of the phonological-core variable-difference model. *Journal of Educational Psychology* (1994) 86:24–53.

37. Adams, M. J. *Beginning to read: Thinking and learning about print.* Cambridge, MA: Cambridge University Press, 1990.

38. Adams, M. J., Bruck, M. Resolving the great debate. *American Educator* (1995) 19:7–10.

39. Share, D. L., and Stanovich, K. E. Cognitive processes in early reading development: Accommodating individual differences into a mode of acquisition. *Education: Contributions for Educational Psychology* (1995) 1:34–36.

40. Lyon, G. R., and Rumsey, J., eds. *Neuroimaging: A window to the neurological foundations of learning and behavior in children.* Baltimore: Paul H. Brookes. In press.

41. DeFries, J. C., and Gillis, J. J. Etiology of reading deficits in learning disabilities: Quantitative genetic analyses. In *Neuropsychological foundations of learning disabilities: A handbook of issues, methods, and practice.* J. E. Obrzut and G. W. Hynd, eds. San Diego: Academic Press, 1991, pp. 29–48.

42. Pennington, B. F. Genetics of learning disabilities. *Journal of Child Neurology* (1995) 10:69–77.

43. Shaywitz, S. E., Escobar, M. D., Shaywitz, B. A., et al. Evidence that dyslexia may represent the lower tail of a normal distribution of reading ability. *New England Journal of Medicine* (1992) 326:145–50.

44. Torgesen, J. K. A model of memory from an information processing perspective: The special case of phonological memory. In *Attention, memory, and executive function.* G. R. Lyon and N. A. Krasnegor, eds. Baltimore: Paul H. Brookes, 1996, pp. 157–84.

45. Torgesen, J. K., and Davis, C. Individual difference variables that predict response to training in phonological awareness. Unpublished manuscript. Florida State University, 1994.

46. Wagner, R. From simple structure to complex function: Major trends in the development of theories, models, and measurements of memory. In *Attention, memory, and executive function.* G. R. Lyon

and N. A. Krasnegor, eds. Baltimore: Paul H. Brookes, 1996, pp. 139–56.

47. Dalton, R., and Forman, M. Attention deficit hyperactivity disorder (ADHD). In *Nelson textbook of pediatrics.* 15th ed. R. Behrman, R. Kliegman, and A. Arvin, eds. Philadelphia: W. B. Saunders, 1996, pp. 91–93.

48. Barkley, R. *Attention deficit hyperactivity disorder: A handbook for diagnosis and treatment.* New York: Guilford, 1990.

49. Gilger, J. W., Pennington, B. P., and DeFries, J. D. A twin study of the etiology of comorbidity: Attention-deficit hyperactivity disorder and dyslexia. *Journal of the Academy of Child and Adolescent Psychiatry* (1992) 31:343–48.

50. Bryan, T. Social problems in learning disabilities. In *Learning about learning disabilities,* B. Y. L. Wong, ed. New York: Academic Press, 1991, p. 195–226.

51. Bruck, M. Social and emotional adjustments of learning disabled children: A review of the issues. In *Handbook of cognitive, social, and neuropsychological aspects of learning disabilities.* S. J. Cedi, ed., Hillsdale, NJ: Erlbaum, 1986, pp. 230–50.

52. Johnson, D. J., and Blalock, J., eds. *Adults with learning disabilities: Clinical studies.* New York: Grune & Stratton, 1987.

53. Gresham, F. M. Conceptual issues in the assessment of social competence in children. In *Children's social behavior: Development, assessment, and modification.* P. Strain, M. Guralink, and H. Walker, eds. New York: Academic Press, 1986, pp. 143–86.

54. Hooper, S. R., Montgomery, J., Swartz, C., et al. Measurement of written language expression. In *Frames of reference for the assessment of learning disabilities: New views on measurement issues.* G. R. Lyon, ed. Baltimore: Paul H. Brookes, 1994, pp. 375–418.

55. Beringer, V. W. *Reading and writing acquisition: A developmental neuropsychological perspective.* Madison, WI: Brown and Benchmark, 1994.

56. Graham, S., Harris, K., MacArthur, C., and Schwartz, S. Writing and writing instruction with students with learning disabilities: A review of a program of research. *Learning Disability Quarterly* (1991) 14:89–114.

57. Gregg, N. Disorders of written expression. In *Written language disorders: Theory into practice.* A. Bain, L. Bailet, and L. Moats, eds. Austin, TX: PRO-ED, 1991, pp. 65–97.

58. Norman, C. A., and Zigmond, N. Characteristics of children labeled and served as learning disabled in school systems affiliated with Child Service Demonstration Centers. *Journal of Learning Disabilities* (1980) 13:542–47.

59. Blachman, B. A., ed. *Cognitive and linguistic foundations of reading acquisition: Implications for intervention research.* Mahwah, NJ: Erlbaum. In press.

60. Blachman, B. A., Ball, E., Black, R., and Tangel, D. Kindergarten teachers develop phoneme awareness in low-income inner-city classrooms: Does it make a difference? *Reading and Writing: An Interdisciplinary Journal* (1994) 6:1–17.

61. Tangel, D. M., and Blachman, B. A. Effect of phoneme awareness instruction on the invented spelling of first grade children: A one year follow-up. *Journal of Reading Behavior* (June 1995) 27,2:153–85.

62. Torgesen, J. K., Wagner, R. K., and Rashotte, C. A. Approaches to the prevention and remediation of phonologically based reading disabilities. In *Cognitive and linguistic foundations of reading acquisition: Implications for intervention research*. B. A. Blachman, ed. Mahwah, NJ: Erlbaum. In press.

63. Torgeson, J. K., Morgan, S., and Davis, C. The effects of two types of phonological awareness training on word learning in kindergarten children. *Journal of Educational Psychology* (1992) 84:364–70.

64. Foorman, B. R. *Early interventions for children with reading problems*. Progress Report. NICHD Grant HD 30995. Bethesda, MD: The National Institute of Child Health and Human Development, December 1995.

65. Alexander, A., Anderson, H., Heilman, P. C., et al. Phonological awareness training and remediation of analytic decoding deficits in a group of severe dyslexics. *Annals of Dyslexia* (1991) 41:193–206.

66. Torgesen, J. D. *Prevention and remediation of reading disabilities*. Progress Report. NICHD Grant HD 30988. Bethesda, MD: The National Institute of Child Health and Human Development, December 1995.

67. Torgesen, J. K., Wagner, R. K., and Rashotte, C. A. Longitudinal studies of phonological processing and reading. *Journal of Learning Disabilities* (1994) 27:276–86.

68. Iversen, S., and Tunmer, W. E. Phonological processing skills and the Reading Recovery Program. *Journal of Educational Psychology* (1993) 85:112–26.

69. Foorman, B. R. Research on the great debate: Code-oriented versus whole-language approaches to reading instruction. *School Psychology Review* (1995) 24:376–92.

70. Martin, E. W. Learning disabilities and public policy: Myths and outcomes. In *Better understanding learning disabilities: New views from research and their implications for education and public policy*. G. R. Lyon, D. B. Gray., J. F. Kavanagh, and N. A. Krasnegor, eds. Baltimore: Paul H. Brookes, 1993, pp. 325–42.

71. Fairweather, J. S., and Shaver, D. M. Making a transition to postsecondary education and training. *Exceptional Children* (1990) 57:264–70.

Sources for Table 1:

The Yale Research Group

The principal investigator for the Yale Learning Disability Research Center is Dr. Bennett Shaywitz, professor of pediatrics and professor and chief of pediatric neurology, the Yale University School of Medicine, 333 Cedar Street, New Haven, CT 06510. The Yale Group also consists of Drs. Sally Shaywitz, John Gore, Pawel Skudlarski, Robert Fulbright, Todd Constable, Richard Bronen, and Cheryl Lacadie from Yale University; Drs. Alvin Liberman, Kenneth Pugh, Donald Shankweiler, Carol Fowler, Ann Fowler, and Leonard Katz from the Haskins Laboratories; Drs. Jack Fletcher and Karla Steubing from the University of Texas Medical School; Drs. David Francis and Barbara Foorman form the University of Houston; Dr. Dorothy Aram from Emerson College; Dr. Benita Blachman from Syracuse University; Dr. Keith Stanovich and Linda Siegel from the Ontario Institute for Studies in Education; Dr. Rafael Kloorman from the University of Rochester; and Dr. Irwen Kirsch from the Educational Testing Service.

The Ontario Research Group

Drs. Keith Stanovich and Linda Siegel are professors of psychology and special education at the Ontario Institute for Studies in Education (OISE), Department of Special Education, Toronto, Ontario, Canada M5S 1V6 Canada. They are affiliated with the Yale University Learning Disability Research Center funded by the NICHD, as well as senior level scientists at OISE where funding is obtained primarily through the Canadian Research Council.

The University of Colorado Research Group

The principal investigator for the University of Colorado Learning Disability Research Center is Dr. John DeFries, professor and director of the Institute for Behavioral Genetics, the University of Colorado, Campus Box 447, Boulder, CO 80309-0447. The Colorado research team consists of Drs. Richard Olson, Barbara Wise, David Fulker, and Helen Forsberg from the University of Colorado, Boulder; Dr. Bruce Pennington from the University of Denver; Drs. Shelly Smith and William Kimberling from the Boys Town National Research Hospital in Omaha; Dr. Pauline Filipek from the University of California, Irvine; and Drs. David Kennedy and Albert Galaburda from Harvard University.

The Bowman Gray School of Medicine Research Group

The principal investigator for the Center for Neurobehavioral Studies of Learning Disorders is Dr. Frank Wood, professor of neurology and neuropsychology, Bowman Gray School of Medicine, 300 S. Hawthorne Road, Winston-Salem, NC 27103. Also from the Center are Drs. Rebecca Felton, Cecille Naylor, Mary McFarlane, John Keyes, Mark Espeland, Dale Dagenbach, and John Absher from the Bowman Gray School of Medicine; Dr. Raquel Gur from the University of Pennsylvania; Dr. Connie Juel from the University of Virginia; and Dr. Jan Loney from the State University of New York at Stony Brook.

The Johns Hopkins Research Group

The principal investigator for the Johns Hopkins Learning Disability Research Center is Dr. Martha Denckla, professor of neurology, pediatrics, and psychiatry, Johns Hopkins University School of Medicine, 707 North Broadway, Suite 501, Baltimore MD 21205. The Hopkins research team consists of Drs. Allan Reiss, Harvey Singer, Linda Schuerholz, Lisa Freund, Michelle Mazzocco, and Mark Reader from the Kennedy-Kriger Research Institute at Johns Hopkins; Drs. Frank Vallutino and Donna Scanlon at the State University of New York at Albany; Dr. Mark Appelbaum from Vanderbilt University; and Dr. Gary Chase from Georgetown University.

The Florida State University Research Group

The principal investigator of the Florida State University Learning Disabilities Intervention Project is Dr. Joseph Torgesen, professor of psychology, Florida State University, Tallahassee, FL 33124-2040. Members of the Florida State Research Group are Drs. Richard Wagner and Carol Rashotte from Florida State University; Drs. Ann Alexander and Kytja Voeller from the University of Florida, and Ms. Patricia Lindamood from Lindamood-Bell Learning Processes.

The University of Houston Research Group

The principal investigator for the University of Houston Learning Disabilities Intervention Project is Dr. Barbara Foorman, professor of educational psychology, University of Houston, 4800 Calhoun, Houston, TX 77204. The Houston group also consists of Drs. David Francis and Dorothy Haskell from the University of Houston; Drs. Jack Fletcher and Karla Steubing from the University of Texas Medical School; and Drs. Bennett and Sally Shaywitz from Yale University.

The University of Miami Research Group

The principal investigator for the University of Miami Learning Disabilities Program Project is Dr. Herbert Lubs, professor of pediatrics and genetics, University of Miami School of Medicine, MCCD, P.O. Box 18620, Miami, FL 33101. The Miami group also consists of Dr. Ranjan Dura, Bonnie Levin, Bonnie Jallad, Marie-Louis Lubs, Mark Rabin, Alex Kushch, and Karen Gross-Glenn, all from the University of Miami.

PYRAMID POWER FOR COLLABORATIVE PLANNING

Manny teaches 10th-grade world history to more than 200 students a day, including 12 students with learning disabilities. He is constantly frustrated because he cannot finish the textbook, as mandated by the school district. As he puts it, "I have 38 chapters to finish in 36 weeks. It's impossible."

Tiffany is a first-year 5th-grade teacher with a self-contained classroom. She has three students with learning disabilities in her classroom for social studies. Her concern is that she doesn't know how to incorporate planning for individual differences within her planning for the whole class.

Jeanne Shay Schumm
Sharon Vaughn
Judy Harris
■

Gina (a general education teacher) and Alyssa (a special education teacher) co-teach in a 3rd-grade inclusion classroom. They are anxious to make their co-teaching model work, but are in the process of defining their new roles and responsibilities. They want to coordinate their work so they can meet the needs of all students in their classroom.

This article describes a planning tool that can help both special and general educators with "covering the curriculum." This tool, the Planning Pyramid (Schumm, Vaughn, & Leavell, 1994), is designed to facilitate inclusion and collaboration.

Planning Pyramid

The Planning Pyramid is a framework for planning instruction to enhance learning for all students. The pyramid is particularly helpful in subject areas like science and social studies, which introduce concepts and vocabulary that are new to many students. It is a flexible tool that teachers can adjust to their personal styles of planning and teaching (Figure 1).

Degrees of Learning

The Planning Pyramid has three layers, the Degrees of Learning. The layer at the base of the pyramid—the largest volume—represents "what all students will learn." The middle layer represents "what most, but not all, students will learn"; and the smaller layer at the top represents "what some students will learn." The Degrees of Learning are based on the premise that although all students are capable of learning, not all students will learn all the content covered. To guide their instruction, teachers might ask three questions:

- "What do I want *all* students to learn?" This content is represented by the large volume at the base.

From *Teaching Exceptional Children*, July/August 1997, pp. 62-66. © 1997 by The Council for Exceptional Children. Reprinted by permission.

- "What do I want *most* students to learn?" Shown by the middle layer, this is information that most students are expected to learn or grasp: supplementary facts and information about ideas and concepts presented at the base of the pyramid.

- "What information will a *few* students learn?" The top of the pyramid represents information that enhances the basic concepts and facts. For example, some students may decide to pursue a topic that he or she has read about in the text or that the teacher has mentioned or briefly discussed in class.

The Planning Pyramid is designed to help teachers prioritize curricular components and to help students focus on those critical components. Here are some important cautions:

- The pyramid is not meant to limit expectations for students or to limit student opportunities to learn. All students should have equal access to information that represents all levels of the pyramid.

- All students should have the opportunity to be exposed to the same information, although presentation of the information may vary somewhat according to the student's needs.

- Activities at the base of the pyramid should not consist of tasks of activities that are less stimulating (e.g., dittos, worksheets), nor should the upper levels be viewed as the place for creative and fun activities.

- Students *must not* be assigned to a particular level of the pyramid based on their academic ability. Students who learn at the middle and top levels do so based on their interests, prior knowledge, personal experience, or need for prerequisite skills.

Points of Entry

The second component of the Planning Pyramid is called the Points of Entry. Each axis, or point, of the pyramid represents one aspect of instruction: teacher, topic, content, student, and instructional practices. Each Point of Entry is guided by questions that help teachers plan lessons and courses (Figure 2). For example, two questions that pertain to students are "Will a language difference make comprehension of a particular concept difficult for a student?" and "Will there be students with high interest in or prior knowledge of these concepts?"

Using the Planning Pyramid in Collaborative Planning

We offer the following suggestions for special educators who collaboratively plan with general education colleagues using the Planning Pyramid:

1 Identify one general education teacher with whom you will pilot the planning procedure in your school. Ask this teacher to make a commitment to planning at least two or three lessons.

2 During the first meeting, explain the basic premise and components of the Planning Pyramid and plan one lesson. Start by discussing the lesson, using the questions from the Points of Entry as a guideline. Use the questions related to topic, teacher, students, and context to guide the initial discussion.

3 Identify concepts for each of the Degrees of Learning and record the concepts on the lesson planning form (see Figure 3). Use textbook objectives, state or district curricular

Collaboration Today

With the national trend toward inclusion of students with disabilities into general education classrooms, classroom teachers must plan lessons to meet the varying needs of students with disabilities, as well as academically talented or gifted students, students with limited English proficiency, and students who do not qualify for special services.

Although special educators have long served as consultants for their general education colleagues, more and more special educators are being asked—indeed, required—to work closely with general classroom teachers as collaborators. The realities of most general education classrooms can be daunting.

For example, most classroom teachers feel great pressure to complete state and district mandated curricular objectives by the end of the school year (Schumm et al., 1995; Vaughn & Schumm, 1994). Teachers are expected to *cover the content* at a steady pace, without enough time to ensure understanding or learning by all students. General education teachers often feel that they have no choice but to "water down" the curriculum and reduce the quality or quantity of content coverage.

guidelines, and personal judgment about the content to determine and prioritize content. As a special educator you can help your general education colleague identify areas of potential difficulty for students with disabilities

Figure 1. The Planning Pyramid

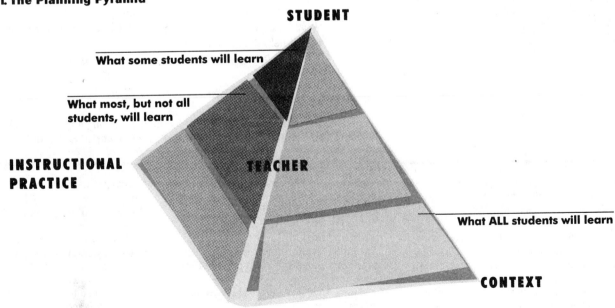

STUDENT

What some students will learn

What most, but not all students, will learn

INSTRUCTIONAL PRACTICE

TEACHER

What ALL students will learn

CONTEXT

TOPIC

Figure 2. Questions Related to Each Point of Entry

1. **Questions pertaining to the Topic:**

Is the material new or review?
What prior knowledge do students have of this topic?
How interesting is the topic?
How many new concepts are introduced?
How clearly are concepts presented in the textbook?
How important is this topic in the overall curriculum?

2. **Questions pertaining to the Teacher:**

What prior knowledge do I have of this topic?
How interesting is the topic to me?
How much time do I have to plan for the lesson?
What resources do I have available to me for this unit?

3. **Questions pertaining to Students:**

Will a language difference make comprehension of a particular concept difficult for a student?
Is there some way to relate this concept to the cultural and linguistic backgrounds of my students?
Will students with reading difficulties be able to function independently in learning the concepts from text?
Will a student with behavior or attention problems be able to concentrate on this material?
Will there be students with high interest in or prior knowledge of these concepts?
Will my students have the vocabulary they need to understand the concepts to be taught?
What experiences have my students had that will relate to this concept?

4. **Questions pertaining to Context:**

Are there any holidays or special events that are likely to distract students or alter instructional time?
How will the class size affect my teaching of this concept?
How well do my students work in small groups or pairs?

5. **Questions pertaining to Instructional Strategies:**

What methods will I use to motivate students and to set a purpose for learning?
What grouping pattern is most appropriate?
What instructional strategies can I implement?
What learning strategies do my students know or need to learn that will help them master these concepts?
What in-class and homework assignments are appropriate for this lesson?
Do some assignments need to be adapted for children with disabilities?
How will I monitor student learning on an ongoing, informal basis?
How will I assess student learning at the end of the lesson?

and think about prerequisite skills or advance organizers they may need to be successful in learning key concepts.

4 Identify instructional strategies using the questions in Figure 2. At this stage, the special education teacher can be of most help. Often classroom teachers are unsure about how to teach students with disabilities and what adaptations can be made for them.

You will need to be prepared to offer suggestions for instructional strategies and adaptations related to the following:

• Grouping (cooperative learning groups, student pairing).
• Presenting information (using advance organizers, modifications in pacing of instruction).
• Learning strategies (notetaking, reading comprehension strategies).

• Reading assignments (study guides, audiotapes of textbooks).

Be prepared to provide additional resources for teachers who may be unfamiliar with instructional strategies and adaptations for students with disabilities (Bos & Vaughn, 1994; Mercer & Mercer 1989; Schumm & Strickler, 1991; Vaughn, Bos, & Schumm, 1997). If you co-teach, decide together who will teach what and how you will coordinate instruction and monitoring of students during the lesson.

5 List the sequence of activities or instructional procedures to implement the lesson plan on the "agenda" section of the lesson planning form. Keep in mind that this is the agenda for the lesson for all students and for all levels of the degrees of learning. Also list materials to be gathered and identify in-class and homework assignments. Finally, identify what method will be used to assess student learning. At this point, you may offer suggestions for the following lesson elements:

- Adaptations in assignments (reducing the length of assignments, completing assignments orally rather than in writing).
- Tests (reading tests aloud to students, providing extended testing time).
- Informal monitoring of student understanding (asking questions, learning journals or logs).

6 Meet again for reflection after the lesson. Discuss how concepts at all Degrees of Learning were presented. Discuss what instructional strategies and adaptations worked well and what didn't work in respect to both academic and social outcomes. You may find it helpful to talk about students' reactions to the strategies and adaptations. Conclude the reflection session by thinking about how the lesson might be taught differently and about what lessons were learned that might affect future planning and instruction.

7 Evaluate the Planning Pyramid procedure after completing two or three lessons. Discuss improvements that you can make and possible new directions for using the pyramid with other colleagues in the school.

Implicit Planning Made Explicit

The Planning Pyramid may assist teachers with the new impetus toward collaborative instruction in inclusive classrooms. Directives and mandates about consultation and collaboration may seem vague, but we have found that the Planning Pyramid enables teachers to become more *explicit* about what they want students to learn and more proficient in planning instructional lessons that promote learning for *all* students.

References

Box, C. S., & Vaughn, S. (1994). *Strategies for teaching students with learning and behavior problems* (3rd ed.). Boston: Allyn & Bacon.

Mercer, C. D., & Mercer, A. R. (1989). *Teaching students with learning problems* (3rd ed.). Columbus, OH: Merrill.

Schumm, J. S., & Strickler, K. (1991). Guidelines for adapting content area textbooks: Keeping the teachers and students content. *Intervention, 27,* 79–84.

Schumm, J. S., Vaughn, S., Haager, D., McDowell, J., Rothlein, L., & Saumell, L. (1995). General education teacher planning: What can students with learning disabilities expect? *Exceptional Children, 61,* 335–352.

Schumm, J. S., Vaughn, S., & Leavell, A. (1994). Planning pyramid: A framework for planning for diverse student needs during content area instruction. *The Reading Teacher, 47,* 608–615.

Vaughn, S., Box, C. S., & Schumm, J. S. (1997). *Teaching mainstreamed, diverse, and at-risk learners in the general education classroom.* Boston: Allyn & Bacon.

Vaughn, S., & Schumm, J. S. (1994). Middle school teachers' planning for students with learning disabilities. *Remedial and Special Education, 15,* 152–161.

Jeanne Shay Schumm *(CEC Chapter #121), Professor;* **Sharon Vaughn** *(CEC Chapter #121), Professor, School-Based Research Project;* **Judy Harris,** *Research Associate, Department of Teaching and Learning, University of Miami, Florida.*

Address correspondence to Jeanne Shay Schumm at the School of Education, University of Miami, P.O. Box 246065, Coral Gables, FL 33124 (E-mail: jjschumm@aol.com).

We gratefully acknowledge partial support for this project from the U.S. Department of Education, Office of Special Education and Rehabilitative Services.

We also wish to acknowledge the expert assistance of Maria Elena Arguelles, Special Education Teacher, W. R. Thomas Middle School, Dade County, Florida, who helped us field-test the Planning Pyramid as a collaborative planning tool.

Figure 3. Lesson Planning Form

Date: _____ Class Period: _____ Unit: _____

Lesson Objective (s): _____

Materials	Evaluation
In Class Assigments	**Homework Assignments**

LESSON PLANNING FORM

Pyramid	Agenda
What some students will learn.	_____
What most students will learn.	_____
What ALL students should learn.	_____

MEGA-ANALYSIS of META-ANALYSES

What **Works** in **Special Education** and **Related Services**

Steven R. Forness
Kenneth A. Kavale
Ilaina M. Blum
John W. Lloyd

What does the research say about:

Ritalin
Perceptual-motor training
Social skills instruction
Peer tutoring
Behavior modification
Special class placement
Mnemonics
Direct instruction
Antidepressants
Ongoing assessment
Learning styles
Visual organizers

Conflicting reports on the effectiveness of these approaches abound—but *meta-analysis* can help sort out overall benefits and weaknesses of these and other educational practices. This article reports on some of these broad studies of research that seem to indicate effective—and noneffective—teaching strategies. But as special educators all know, the most important consideration

is a knowledge of what works with your individual student, as well as a compelling curiosity that leads you to read the meta-analyses for yourself.

In meta-analysis, a researcher examines many studies on a particular strategy and derives a numerical indicator of the relative effectiveness of the strategy, averaged across all studies. This indicator is called an *effect size* (ES) (see box, "How Meta-analysis Works"). Such an analysis of research not only provides a numerical indicator of the relative effect of a particular intervention, but the effect size also allows comparison with other approaches used in special education or related services.

Comparing Meta-analyses Available to Date

We have summarized the results of 18 meta-analyses on special education or its related services that have been done to date (but see

our cautions about how some of these studies are "dated"). We also depict these studies in relation to one another so you can see which strategies are most (or least) effective. This "mega-analysis" provides a summary of the relative power of a variety of special education and related interventions, at least those to which meta-analysis has been applied thus far.

Table 1 shows the overall mean effect sizes and number of studies used for each of these 18 meta-analyses. The table shows various strategies and instructional approaches in rank order, from most to least effective, as found by the meta-analyses.

We begin at the bottom of this table with interventions in which meta-analysis produced ineffective or very modest effect sizes. We then describe those with relatively good ESs and finish with those at the top of the table, in which effect sizes were quite convincing as to the effectiveness of the interventions in question. In this summary, we also point out certain ESs within each meta-analysis that suggest circumstances in which the intervention seems to work best.

Interventions with Modest Effect Sizes

In this table, the bottom five interventions are those in which meta-analysis produced relatively modest ESs. As a matter of fact, the 50 efficacy studies on special class placement produced a negative ES, suggesting a potentially harmful effect. It should be noted, however, that most ESs in these meta-analyses were from studies on special class placement of children with mild mental retardation. In those few studies on placement of children with learning disabilities or emotional and behavioral disorders, the mean ES was .29, suggesting an improvement of 11 percentile ranks (i.e., an unplaced child with learning disabilities or behavioral disorders would be at the 50th percentile, and an ES of .29 would move that child to the 61st percentile). It is also interesting to note that the overall ES of −.12 was equivalent to a loss of only about 1 or 2 months in academic achievement during an average special class placement of about 2 years. Although this meta-analysis was done 17 years ago (1980), relatively few well-controlled efficacy studies have been conducted since then.

Both perceptual-motor training and its counterpart, in which children with so-called visual-perceptual deficits are placed in linguistic-based interventions or vice-versa (modality instruction or learning styles) produced negligible ESs. Despite the popularity of the latter approach with teachers, it did not have much empirical support.

The Feingold diet, in which foods containing certain synthetic additives are restricted in an attempt to reduce hyperactivity, also produced a negligible ES. This ES was even smaller when only double-blind or challenge studies were included.

Somewhat of a surprise, the social skills training literature also produced only a modest effect, though there were mild differences when *teachers* rated improvement as opposed to when target *students* measured their own progress (ESs were .16 and .24, respectively). Note that this particular meta-analysis was done primarily on children with learning disabilities. A forthcoming meta-analysis on children with emotional disorders by the same authors and other collaborators produced an even smaller mean ES of .20 (Kavale, Mathur, Forness, Rutherford, & Quinn, 1997).

Interventions with Good Effect Sizes

Although mean ESs of some of the next six meta-analyses were in the .30s, some components of treatment produced ESs that ranged into the .40s or higher. Psychotropic drugs for severe behavior disorders, for example, had a mean ES of .30; but, interestingly, the ES for effect on cognitive measures was .74, as compared to the ES of .28 on observed behavior. Psychotropics include primarily drugs such as antipsychotics and antidepressants, as opposed to stimulants, which we discuss later. Note that research on the newer generations of these drugs such as the antidepressant, Prozac, or the antipsychotic, Risperdal, has all been done in the past 5 years so that this meta-analysis might be considerably different if repeated now.

The meta-analysis on reducing class size, in which most of the studies were on students without disabilities, had an overall ES of .31. When outcome measures of attitudes toward school were parceled out from those of general academic increases, however, the ES was .47. Some studies of students in special settings were included, and a relatively significant increase in ES seemed to be associated with class sizes below 20 pupils.

As opposed to perceptual-motor training noted previously, psycholinguistic training produced an ES of .39 with a range of ESs for selected outcomes (e.g., receptive language ES = .21, expressive language ES = .63). Psycholinguistic training is based on the assumption that language should be broken into its individual components such as sound blending, grammatic usage, listening skills, and the like and that each isolated component should be individually trained as a remedial strategy.

In the next meta-analysis in the table, peer tutoring appears to produce nearly half a standard deviation increase (ES = .48), although only 19 studies were available at the time. In this meta-analysis, peer tutors seemed to gain from the experience in some areas at almost the same rate as tutees.

Likewise, computer-assisted instruction (CAI) produced a similar ES; but the ES for CAI for students with mild disabilities was somewhat lower than that for students with severe disabilities. Note, however, that more sophisticated studies have been done since original publication of these meta-analyses.

The meta-analysis for stimulant drugs, such as methylphenidate (Ritalin) or dextroamphetamine (Dexadrine), produced an ES of .58. The ES on behavioral outcomes was considerably higher than that for academic or cognitive measures (.80 and .38, respectively). Although somewhat dated, these findings reflect much of the current concern around use of stimulants with some children with attention-deficit disorders, in which behavior may be controlled but classroom learning may not be improved.

Interventions with Convincing Effect Sizes

The top seven meta-analyses in the table produced ESs that led to increases of at least two-thirds of a standard deviation or higher as compared to controls. In this category was early intervention although, interestingly, the ES for studies of home-based interventions was somewhat lower than the ES for interventions that were center based. The ESs for interventions begun after 30 months was higher than ESs for interventions begun earlier. These findings nonetheless reflect available evidence and suggest that sufficient attention to certain early intervention components in some studies may have been lacking.

The next four meta-analyses are somewhat interrelated in that direct instruction is often associated with formative evaluation (charting or graphing of discrete units of progress, such as number of words read correctly each day) and with reinforcement of effort or accomplishment (cognitive and behavior modification). Although the mean ES for formative evaluation is .70, studies in this meta-analysis in which *positive reinforcement was combined with systematic, ongoing assessment* produced an ES of 1.12. The meta-analysis for direct instruction produced an ES of .85 for reading but only .50 for math.

Interestingly, the ESs in the meta-analysis for behavior modification were .61 and 1.57, respectively, in behavioral versus academic improvement. Note that most studies in behavior modification, however, are not group-design studies but single-subject designs; thus, this meta-analysis might not accurately reflect the research in this area. Although there are meta-analytic techniques for single-subject studies, these have not been widely used. The ES in the meta-analysis for cognitive behavior modification indicated that these interventions produced better outcomes for controlling hyperactivity than for managing aggression.

Finally, meta-analyses for techniques of systemically enhancing reading comprehension (e.g., strategy training, visual representations, or organizational cues) and for the use of mnemonics (e.g. keyword, pegword, or acoustic representations) produced mean ESs *above* one standard deviation. In the former, it was of interest that, when authors or researchers provided the classroom instruction themselves, the ESs were higher than when classroom teachers were trained to do so. It is also a testament to the reliability of meta-analysis that another meta-analysis recently published on reading comprehension also produced similar findings (Mastropieri, Scruggs, Bakkeu, & Whedon, 1996). In the latter meta-analysis on mnemonics, 21 of the 24 meta-analyses were done on the authors' own research studies; but unlike the Feingold meta-analysis discussed previously, ESs from the outside studies were generally as high or higher.

How Meta-analysis WORKS

Meta-analysis aggregates findings across a particular area of research by converting data in each study to a common metric or effect size (ES). The ES is computed by subtracting the obtained mean of the untreated subjects from the mean of the treated subjects and dividing the difference by a measure of the variance in the sample, usually the standard deviation of the controls. An alternative ES uses pretest and posttest data, when no control group has been used. Note that one or several ESs may be obtained from each study, depending on the following:

Different variations of the intervention studied.

Number of outcome measures used.

Types of children serving as subjects in each study.

ESs may range from zero (meaning no observable effect) to one or greater and may be thought of as a z score or standard deviation unit, and negative ESs are possible. ESs from each study are then aggregated together to arrive at a mean ES across all studies. This overall mean ES can be correlated with related study variables or subjected to statistical analyses designed to tease out differences or trends.

While a particular ES possesses no inherent value, ESs approaching the range of .40 or greater conventionally tend to be considered significant. The collection and analysis of related study variables ultimately depend on research questions generated in previous research or in literature reviews. These may involve age, diagnosis, intelligence, duration of treatment, and quality of research. Meta-analysis is a deceptively simple technique, and a growing body of statistical or related procedures is available to guard against misinterpretation of obtained ESs (Cooper & Hedges, 1994; Forness & Kavale, 1994; Mostert, 1996). It should be noted, however, that an overall mean ES (an average of all ESs across all studies in a research area) is usually reported as a way to capture the "power" of the procedure or intervention being studied.

Cautions and Recommendations for Further Study

Any meta-analysis—and, particularly, a mega-analysis of meta-analyses such as this one should be labeled "Caution: Students Are All Different." Although mean ESs provide an *estimate* of the relative power of an intervention or procedure, we have shown how considerable variability occurs within each meta-analysis. Some types of pupils may be shown to respond even when the mean ES is negligible, or some procedures may produce only modest effects on certain outcome measures even when the overall mean ES is compelling; for example, the greater effects of antidepressants or antipsychotics on learning ability than on observed

Table 1

Summary of Meta-analyses

INTERVENTIONS THAT WORK

ES	ES	ES	ES	ES	ES	ES
1.62 Mnemonic Strategies, (Mastropieri & Scruggs, 1989)	**1.13 Enhancing Reading Comprehension** (Talbot, Lloyd, & Tankersley, 1994)	**.93 Behavior Modification** (Skiba & Casey, 1985)	**.84 Direct Instruction** (White, 1988)	**.71 Cognitive Behavior Modification** (Robinson, Brownell, Smith, & Miller, in press)	**.70 Formative Evaluation** (Fuchs & Fuchs, 1986)	**.68 Early Intervention** (Casto & Mastropieri, 1986)

INTERVENTIONS THAT SHOW PROMISE

ES	ES	ES	ES	ES	ES
.58 Stimulant Drugs (Kavale, 1982)	**.52 Computer-Assisted Instruction** (Schmidt, Weinstein, Niemic, & Walberg, 1985–1986)	**.46 Peer Tutoring** (Cook, Scruggs, Mastropieri, & Casto, 1985–1986)	**.39 Psycholinguistic Training** (Kavale, 1981)	**.31 Reduced Class Size** (Glass & Smith, 1979)	**.30 Psychotropic Drugs** (Kavale & Nye, 1984)

INTERVENTIONS THAT WORK

ES	ES	ES	ES	ES
.21 Social Skills Training (Forness & Kavale, 1996)	**.15 Modality Instruction** (Kavale & Forness, 1987)	**.12 Feingold Diet** (Kavale & Forness, 1983)	**.08 Perceptual Training** (Kavale & Mattson, 1983)	**−.12 Special Class Placement** (Carlberg & Kavale, 1980)

behavior. The same is true for certain identifiable components of treatment or for characteristics of persons carrying out the intervention.

Note, too, that many of these meta-analyses are becoming dated and that, in some instances (e.g., psychotropic drugs, computer-assisted instruction, peer tutoring), pertinent research has taken place since their publication. In many cases, we were unable to discuss many other significant ESs in this brief article. We encourage you to read the original meta-analyses for more complete information on uses with particular children or on particular components of the intervention that seemed most effective.

Nonetheless, we may conclude from these studies that some interventions or procedures, such as formative evaluation and direct instruction, are relatively well- established as effective and should be encouraged in practice. In other cases, such as peer tutoring, reducing class size, the efficacy is promising and at least remains open to further research. In yet others (most likely perceptual-motor training, Feingold diet, modality, or learning-styles instruction), there seems little evidence to endorse practice or to continue further study.

Finally, effect size for this mega-analysis (the mean of all 18 ESs in Table 1) is .535, or an increase from an average percentile rank of .50 for the untreated group to a percentile rank of .70 for groups that received the various special education or related service interventions. For those critics who decry the cost of special education or its effectiveness, such an increase seems a substantial refutation.

References

Carlberg, C., & Kavale, K. A. (1980). The efficacy of special versus regular class placement for exceptional children: a meta-analysis. *Journal of Special Education, 14,* 296–309.

Casto, G., & Mastropieri, M. A. (1986). The efficacy of early intervention programs: A meta-analysis. *Exceptional Children, 52,* 417–424.

Cook, S. B., Scruggs, T. E., Mastropieri, M. A., & Casto, G. C. (1985–1986). Handicapped students as tutors. *Journal of Special Education, 19,* 486–492.

Cooper, H. M., & Hedges, L. V. (1994). *Handbook of research synthesis.* New York: Russell Sage Foundation.

Forness, S. R., & Kavale, K. A. (1994). Meta-analysis in intervention research: Methods and implications. In J. Rothman & J. Thomas (Eds.), *Intervention research: Effective methods of professional practice* (pp. 117–131). Chicago: Haworth Press.

Forness, S. R., & Kavale, K. A. (1996). Treating social skill deficits in children with learning disabilities: A meta-analysis of the research. *Learning Disability Quarterly, 19,* 2–13.

Fuchs, L. A., & Fuchs, D. (1986). Effects of systematic formative evaluation: A meta-analysis. *Exceptional Children, 53,* 199–208.

Glass, G. V., & Smith, M. L. (1979). Meta-analysis of research on class size and achievement. *Education Evaluation and Policy Analysis, 1,* 2–16.

Kavale, K. A. (1981). Functions of the Illinois Test of Psycho Linguistic Abilities (ITPA): Are they trainable? *Exceptional Children, 47,* 496–510.

Kavale, K. A. (1982). The efficacy of stimulant drug treatment for hyperactivity: A meta-analysis. *Journal of Learning Disabilities, 15,* 280–289.

Kavale, K. A., & Forness, S. R. (1987). Substance over style: A quantitative synthesis assessing the efficacy of modality testing and teaching. *Exceptional Children, 54,* 228–234.

Kavale, K. A., & Forness, S. R. (1983). Hyperactivity and diet treatment: A meta-analysis of the Feingold hypothesis. *Journal of Learning Disabilities, 16,* 324–330.

Kavale, K. A., Mathur, S. R., Forness, S. R., Rutherford, R. B., & Quinn, M. M. (1997). Effectiveness of social skills training for students with behavior disorders: A meta-analysis. In T. Scruggs & M. Mastropieri (Eds.), *Advances in learning and behavioral disabilities, Vol. 11* (pp. 293–312). Greenwich, CT: JAI Press.

Kavale, K. A., & Mattson, P. D. (1983). "One jumped off the balance beam":Meta-analysis of perceptual-motor training. *Journal of Learning Disabilities, 16,* 165–173.

Kavale, K. A., & Nye, C. (1984). The effectiveness of drug treatment for severe behavioral disorders: A meta-analysis. *Behavioral Disorders, 9,* 117–130.

Mastropieri, M. A., & Scruggs, T. E. (1989). Constructing more meaningful relations: Mnemonic instruction for special populations. *Educational Psychology Review, 1*(2), 83–111.

Mastropieri, M. A., Scruggs, T. E., Bakkeu, J. P., & Whedon, C. (1996). Reading comprehension: A synthesis of research in learning disabilities. In T. Scruggs & M. Mastropieri (Eds.), *Advances in learning and behavioral disabilities, Vol. 10* (pp. 277–303). Greenwich, CT: JAI Press.

Mostert, M. P. (1996). Reporting meta-analysis in learning disabilities. *Learning Disabilities Research and Practice, 11,* 2–14.

Robinson, T. R., Brownell, M. T., Smith, S. W., & Miller, M. D. (in press). Cognitive behavior modification of hyperactivity/impulsivity and aggression: A meta-analysis. *Behavioral Disorders.*

Schmidt, M., Weinstein, T., Niemic, R., & Walberg, H. J. (1985–1986). Computer-assisted instruction with exceptional children. *Journal of Special Education, 19,* 497–509.

Skiba, R., & Casey, A. (1985). Interventions for behavior disordered students: A quantitative review and methodological critique. *Behavioral Disorders, 10,* 239–252.

Talbott, E., Lloyd, J. W., & Tankersley, M. (1994). Effects of reading comprehension interventions for students with learning disabilities. *Learning Disability Quarterly, 17,* 223–232.

White, W. A. T. (1988). A meta-analysis of effects of direct instruction in special education. *Education and Treatment of Children, 11,* 364–374.

Steven R. Forness *(CEC Chapter #520), Professor, Psychiatry and Biobehavioral Sciences, University of California, Los Angeles.* **Kenneth A. Kavale,** *Professor of Special Education, University of Iowa, Iowa City.* **Ilaina M. Blum** *Assessment Teacher, Neuropsychiatric Hospital, University of California, Los Angeles.* **John W. Lloyd** *(CEC Chapter #383), Professor of Special Education, University of Virginia, Charlottesville.*

Address correspondence to Steven R. Forness at UCLA Neuropsychiatric Hospital, 760 Westwood Plaza, Los Angeles, CA 90024. (e-mail: johnl @ virginia.edu).

Unit Selections

Key Points to Consider

❖ How can a culturally sensitive educator decide if language used by a child is dialectally different speech or a language-speech disorder?

❖ What kinds of verbal interactions are most helpful to young children learning language?

 **Links**   **www.dushkin.com/online/**

These sites are annotated on pages 4 and 5.

The terms *communication, language,* and *speech* are not synonymous. Communication refers to an exchange of information between sender and receiver. It may be through language. However, the exchange may be a movement, a nonlanguage vocal noise, or a symbolized marking in a nonlanguage medium (for example, art, scent, sculpture). Both human and nonhuman species can communicate without language. Language refers to the use of voice sounds (or writing that represents these voice sounds) in combinations and patterns that follow rules that are accepted by the users of the language. Speech refers simply to the vocal utterances of language. The three terms are subsumed in descending order. Communication includes language and speech. Language includes speech. The opposite is not accurate. Communication disorders, as they affect children with disabilities, are usually separated into the subcategories of speech and language.

Speech, the vocal utterance of language, is considered disordered in three underlying ways: voice, articulation, and fluency. Voice involves coordinated effects by the lungs, larynx, vocal cords, and nasal passages to produce recognizable sounds. Voice can be considered disordered if it is incorrectly phonated through the lungs, larynx, and vocal cords (breathy, strained, husky, hoarse) or if it is incorrectly resonated through the nose (hypernasality, hyponasality). Articulation involves the use of the tongue, lips, teeth, and mouth to produce recognizable sounds. Articulation can be considered disordered if sounds are added, omitted, substituted, or distorted. Fluency involves appropriate pauses and hesitations to keep speech sounds recognizable. Fluency can be considered disordered if sounds are very rapid with extra sounds (cluttered) or if sounds are blocked and/or repeated, especially at the beginning of words (stuttered). Language problems refer to the use of voice sounds in combinations and patterns that fail to follow the arbitrary rules for that language or to a delay in the use of voice sounds relative to normal development in other areas (physical, cognitive, social). Language delays can also be diagnosed in conjunction with other developmental delays (health, sensory, motoric, mental, personal, social). Delays in language are fairly common and can usually be resolved with proper treatment.

Disordered language is usually more difficult to remedy than delayed language. Disordered language may be due to a receptive problem (difficulty understanding voice sounds), an expressive problem (difficulty producing the voice sounds that follow the arbitrary rules for that language), or to both. Language disorders include aphasia (no language) and dysphasia (difficulty producing language). Many language disorders are the result of a difficulty in understanding the syntactical rules and structural principles of the language (form), or are the result of a difficulty perceiving the semantic meanings of the words of the language (content). Many language disorders are also due to a difficulty using the language pragmatically, in a practical context (function).

All children with language and/or speech disorders are entitled to assessment as early in life as the problem is realized, and to remediation under the auspices of the Individuals with Disabilities Education Act (IDEA) and its amendments. In addition, they are entitled to a free and appropriate education in the least restrictive environment possible and to transitional help into the world of work, if needed, after their education is completed.

Most speech and language impairments occur in younger children (preschool and primary school) and have been remediated by high school. An exception to this is speech problems that persist due to physical impairments such as damage or dysfunction of lungs, larynx, vocal cords, nasal passages, tongue, lips, or teeth. Another exception is language problems that persist due to concurrent disabilities such as deafness, autism, compromised mentation, traumatic brain injuries, and/or some emotional and behavioral disorders.

The prevalence rates of speech and language disorders are higher than the rates for any other condition of disability in primary school. However, the exact extent of the problem has been questioned because assessment of communication takes a variety of forms. Shy children may be diagnosed with delayed language. Bilingual or multilingual children are often mislabeled as having a language disorder when they simply have different language because they come from linguistically and culturally diverse backgrounds. Many bilingual children do not need the special services provided by speech-language clinicians but do benefit from English as a second language instruction, bilingual education, or sheltered English.

Speech-language clinicians usually provide special services to children with speech and language impairments in pull-out sessions in resource rooms. Computer technology is also frequently used to assist these children in both their regular education classes and in pull-out therapy sessions.

The first unit article has been included in this edition of *Annual Editions: Educating Exceptional Children* to stimulate discussion about the sticky problems associated with assessing and diagnosing language disorders. Language differences are not language disorders. The American Speech-Language-Hearing Association (ASHA) has clearly articulated the view that regional, social, or ethnic variations in symbol systems (dialects) should not be considered disorders of language or speech. While a dialect difference is just a difference, disorders existing within a dialectally different language must not be overlooked. A child may have limited English proficiency, but a delay or disorder in the mother tongue or in learning English must not be ignored.

The second article included in this unit is a research-based treatise on how to prevent language delays in infancy and early childhood, especially in children who, historically, have been at risk for language disorders. William Fowler presents data from a series of research projects. He articulates the principles of language development as they are currently known. Fowler also presents several methods that he and his colleagues have devised to increase language stimulation in infant day care and preschool settings.

Speech and Language Impairments

Distinguishing Language Differences

from

Language Disorders

in

Linguistically and Culturally

Diverse Students

Celeste Roseberry-McKibbin

Celeste Roseberry-McKibbin is an associate professor in the Department of Communicative Sciences and Disorders, California State University, Fresno.

Introduction

Many educators today view bilingualism as a great linguistic and social advantage (Cummins, 1994; Wong Fillmore, 1993). However, sometimes educators are confronted with linguistically and culturally diverse (LCD) students who appear to be struggling in school. When this happens, one of the first questions usually asked is: "Does this LCD student have a language difference or a language disorder?" In other words, can the problems be traced to cultural differences and/or the student's lack of facility with English, or is there an underlying disability that requires special education intervention? The question of distinguishing a language difference from a language disorder is a very challenging one. (The terms "language disorder" and "language-learning disability" are used interchangeably in this article.)

The "diagnostic pie" is a simple conceptual framework that can help educators begin to distinguish language differences from language disorders. The diagnostic pie paradigm assumes that LCD students speak their primary language and are in the process of learning English as a second language. Bloom and Lahey's (1978) definition of language is central here:

> Language is a system of symbols used to represent concepts that are formed through exposure and experience.

There are practical ramifications of this definition. I am assuming that exposure and

From *Multicultural Education*, Summer 1995, pp. 12–16. © 1995 by the National Association for Multicultural Education. Reprinted by permission.

experience refer to exposure to good language models, to a variety of "mainstream" experiences (that are consistent with schools' expectations), to literacy, and to environmental and linguistic stimulation. For example, when students come to kindergarten, some educators assume that the children have looked at books; that they have been read to; that they know how to listen in groups; that they have used scissors, crayons, and pencils before. The educators may further assume that children have been taken to stores, zoos, libraries, and other places in the community; that the children have had literacy experiences which prepare them to learn the alphabet, print their names, etc.

Some LCD students come from backgrounds where they have had all these experiences. Some LCD students, especially older ones, may even have a broader experience base than many monolingual English-speaking students who are born and raised in the United States. These LCD students may be bilingual or even trilingual, have traveled in different countries, and be bicultural. These students have a great deal to offer to mainstream American students. Mainstream American students can be enriched and learn many things from these sophisticated LCD students.

Other LCD students come from non-literate backgrounds. They and their families may be non-literate for one or more reasons. Perhaps family members have not had educational opportunities; these opportunities are extremely limited in some countries, especially if the family is of refugee status. Others come from backgrounds where the language is oral only and has not been put in written form. Van Deusen-Scholl (1992) gives the example of a number of Morrocan children in the Netherlands who come from isolated rural areas where no formal education is available; they struggle in the Netherlands' school system. Some of these children speak Berber languages which do not have a tradition of print literacy. Other linguistic groups, such as some Native Americans and speakers of Haitian Creole, have predominantly oral traditions and no written language.

Some educators do not stop to ask themselves whether or not students have had some or any of the usual mainstream experiences that are inherently assumed, like exposure to literacy. And this is often where deficits in students are created: when students' exposure and experiences are different than those expected in the mainstream school environment, then educators may assume that there are deficits inherent in the students themselves.

A centrally important idea in this article is that before educators even begin to ask whether or not a student manifests a language disorder, they must stop and remind themselves of what language really is: a system of symbols that represents concepts formed through **exposure** and **experience.** If a student's background experiences and exposure to life situations and linguistic models are different than those expected by schools, then it follows that their language will represent *their unique backgrounds,* which are not necessarily consistent with those expected by the school.

This difference in students' backgrounds and schools' expectations can lead to misdiagnosis of students and consequent inappropriate placement into special education. Many experts point out that historically in United States schools, disproportionate numbers of LCD children have been placed in to special education unnecessarily (Ruiz & Figueroa, 1993). The "diagnostic pie" (see page 89) can help educators begin to conceptualize students' backgrounds and current status, and see that there are various alternatives to special education.

normal underlying ability to learn language. They come from backgrounds that may be rich in stimulation and general experiences, but the backgrounds have not been consistent with expectations in mainstream United States schools. Some older immigrant students are good examples of this: they had schooling in their country of origin, and generally have a good enough conceptual foundation to succeed academically. If these students are dominant in their primary language and thus are having some difficulty in all-English classrooms, their needs can usually be served best through placement into good bilingual classrooms where both English and the primary language can be developed. If bilingual education is not available, then these students can benefit from Sheltered English or, barring this, English as a second language teaching. Again, if these students are given time, attention, and help, they will generally succeed in school.

Diagnostic Pie Quadrant 1

Students who fall into this quadrant of the pie are those LCD students who have

Diagnostic Pie Quadrant 2

These students have normal underlying ability to learn language. However, they

---

Student Behaviors to Observe when Distinguishing a Language Difference from a Language Disorder

Teachers can tell when an LCD student might need special education services for a language-learning disability when some of the following behaviors are manifested in comparison to similar peers:

1. Nonverbal aspects of language are culturally inappropriate.
2. Student does not express basic needs adequately.
3. Student rarely initiates verbal interaction with peers.
4. When peers initiate interaction, student responds sporadically/inappropriately.
5. Student replaces speech with gestures, communicates nonverbally when talking would be appropriate and expected.
6. Peers give indications that they have difficulty understanding the student.
7. Student often gives inappropriate responses.
8. Student has difficulty conveying thoughts in an organized, sequential manner that is understandable to listeners.
9. Student shows poor topic maintenance ('skips around').
10. Student has word-finding difficulties that go beyond normal second language acquisition patterns.
11. Student fails to provide significant information to the listener, leaving the listener confused.
12. Student has difficulty with conversational turn-taking skills (may be too passive, or may interrupt inappropriately).
13. Student perseverates (remains too long) on a topic even after the topic has changed.
14. Student fails to ask and answer questions appropriately.
15. Student needs to hear things repeated, even when they are stated simply and comprehensibly.
16. Student often echoes what she or he hears.

If an LCD student manifests a number of the above behaviors, even in comparison to similar peers, then their is a good chance that the student has an underlying language-learning disability and will need a referral to special education.

come from backgrounds where they may have experienced some limitations or differences in environmental stimulation and linguistic exposure. These students may come from backgrounds where society has placed them and their families at profound economic disadvantage. I have worked with many children like this: they have good ability to learn, but life circumstances have curtailed their opportunities to learn and be exposed to various experiences before they come to school. These students often perform poorly on standardized tests, many of which are based on mainstream, White middle-class expectations. If these students have not been exposed to certain experiences and thus developed the conceptual background assumed by these tests, they will often appear "language disordered" simply because the tests do not adequately tap into their unique and individual backgrounds.

Several years ago, I had the experience of taking the WAIS (Wechsler Adult Intelligence Scale) and being penalized for lack of knowledge of items on the "General Knowledge" subtest. Because I grew up in the Philippines (ages 6–17 years), I had not had the exposure to facts that the WAIS assumed everyone had—and my overall IQ score was lowered because of it! Although I was taking the WAIS mostly out of personal interest, I was poignantly reminded of how often our standardized tests penalize LCD students for not having life experiences consistent with test writers' expectations.

Students in Quadrant 2 will usually show good gains in school if they can receive adequate quantities of input, exposure, and stimulation that may have been unavailable in their homes. These students will benefit from good bilingual education, ESL, and/or Sheltered English programs that enhance both the primary language and English. These students often also need extra stimulation which can be provided through tutoring and participation in school enrichment programs. Unfortunately, these students often are placed into special education programs. Special education is usually unnecessary for students whose underlying language-learning ability is intact. If extra programs outside of special education are provided and the student can attend school consistently enough to benefit from them, usually good academic gains can be made without special education assistance.

Diagnostic Pie Quadrant 3

Quadrant 3 students come from backgrounds where they have had adequate exposure and language stimulation. Their life experiences are often consistent with those assumed by mainstream schools. Often, their

parents have given them as much help as possible in the home, and the students still do not succeed in school. Many of them have a history of academic failure. Often, school personnel have given these students opportunities such as extra tutoring and participation in school programs designed to foster academic growth. Despite these measures, however, the students still do not learn and make adequate academic gains. These students have underlying language-learning disabilities that prevent them from learning and using any language adequately despite backgrounds that have attempted to provide environmental and linguistic stimulation.

These students need to be placed into special education so that their unique disabilities can be appropriately addressed. No matter how hard schools and parents try to use traditional methods to assist these students, the students will still struggle because they have underlying language- learning disabilities. As one speech-language pathologist puts it, "These students have a glitch in the computer." Students with these needs will benefit from (ideally) bilingual special education where the primary language is used. Because this ideal option is often not available, these students may be served by special education in English with as much primary language support as possible. Students with disabilities still benefit greatly from being taught concepts initially in their primary language.

Diagnostic Pie Quadrant 4

Students in Quadrant 4 come from backgrounds where there are differences and/or limitations of environmental experience and exposure. These students are very similar to those described in Quadrant 2, except that the students in Quadrant 4 also have underlying language-learning disabilities. These students are very difficult to assess because educators can never be sure whether the students' low test scores are due to background/environment, an underlying disability, or both.

Most educators wrestle with the issue of whether to place these students into Quadrant 2 or Quadrant 4. On the one hand, educators do not want to place into special education a Quadrant 2 student who would be adequately served through additional school enrichment programs such as ESL. On the other hand, educators do not want to deprive Quadrant 4 students of the opportunity to receive special education help because that is what they need. According to Ortiz (1994), we are so afraid of mislabeling LCD students unnecessarily that the pendulum has swung in the other direction: some LCD students who genuinely need special education assistance are not

receiving it, and are failing in school year after year.

Quadrant 4 students ideally need bilingual special education with additional enrichment experiences to compensate for limitations/differences of linguistic and environmental experience and stimulation. Barring the provision of these ideal services, Quadrant 4 students may be served by English special education with as much primary language support as possible. They can also benefit from participating in whatever additional enrichment experiences are available.

What to Look For

Comparing LCD students to monolingual English-speaking peers is very biased and provides a poor point of reference from which to make decisions. It is critical to analyze student behaviors in interactions in natural settings with peers from similar cultural and linguistic backgrounds. For example, I recently evaluated a 15-year old Russian immigrant ("Viktor") who was having learning difficulties. A major question I asked was: "How does Viktor perform/interact in comparison to other newcomer Russian students who have been in the United States the same length of time that he has?" When we compare students to their linguistic and cultural peers, our decisions will be much more fair and accurate.

I have found that interpreters who work regularly with LCD students are wonderful sources of information in this regard, because they have a great deal of experience with certain populations and thus can validly (albeit subjectively) compare the student in question with other students from the same cultural and linguistic background. I have also found that educators—especially general education classroom teachers—can serve as excellent resources for referral of LCD students who need special services.

Some teachers are fluent in the student's primary language, and can thus make judgments about delays or deviancies in the student's primary language assessment and comprehension. Other teachers, while not speaking a particular student's primary language, have many years of experience working with ESL students. These teachers may have worked, for example, with many Filipino students in the past and may have a number of Filipino students in their current classes. The teachers frequently have a frame of reference for what is "normal" behavior for Filipino learners of English as a second language, and can tell when a particular student is not performing as his/her peers are. While the teachers cannot make the judgment as to whether there is an actual language-learning disability, they can

The Diagnostic Pie

1 — Normal Language Learning Ability

Adequate Background

May need one or more of the following:
1. Bilingual education
2. Sheltered English
3. English as a second language instruction

2 — Normal Language Learning Ability

Differences and/or limitations of linguistic exposure & environmental experience

May need:
1. Bilingual education Sheltered English, English as a second language
2. Aditional enrichment experiences (e.g. tutoring, etc.)

3 — Language-Learning Disability

Adequate Background

May need:
1. Bilingual special education
2. English special education with as much primary language input and teaching as possible

4 — Language-Learning Disability

Differences and/or limitations of linguistic exposure & environmental experience

May need:
1. Bilingual special education, English special education with primary language support
2. Additional enrichment experiences

languages of Tagalog and Ilocano. In this case, the experienced teacher's insight turned out to be accurate.

Summary

Educators can provide appropriate services to LCD students who may show difficulties in the classroom. Using the "diagnostic pie" as a starting point can help educators to classify students appropriately and thus provide services commensurate with students' background and abilities. When educators suspect that a student may have an underlying language-learning disability that requires special education assistance, they can use the above list as a guideline to assist in differential diagnosis. It is imperative not only to avoid "false positives" in identifying LCD students with special needs, but to avoid "false negatives" that deprive these students of assistance which they need and deserve.

References

Bloom, L., & Lahey, M. (1978). *Language development and language disorders*. New York: John Wiley & Sons, Inc.

Cummins, J. (1994, March). Accelerating second language and literacy development. Paper presented at the California Elementary Education Association, Sacramento, CA.

Ortiz, A. (1994, June). Keynote address. Symposium on Second Language Learners in Regular and Special Education, Sacramento, CA.

Ruiz, N., & Figueroa, R. (1993). Why special education does not work for minority children. Paper presented at National Association for Multicultural Education, Los Angeles, CA.

Wong Fillmore, L. (1993). Educating citizens for a multicultural 21st century. *Multicultural Education Magazine*, 1(1), 10–37.

refer the student to personnel who have access to Filipino interpreters and who have the resources and background to make this type of diagnosis.

The classroom teacher, then, frequently serves as the "first layer" of the referral process. For example, an African American monolingual English-speaking teacher referred a Filipino kindergartener to me for language testing. In her opinion, his classroom performance was less than optimal and she was concerned that he might have

a language-learning disability. This teacher had 15 years of teaching experience. When I asked her how the child compared to other ESL students in her experience, especially Filipino students, she replied "I have never seen a child like this one." She went on to describe some of the student's deviant academic and linguistic behaviors. When I and a Filipino interpreter (who also knew the family) tested the student, it turned out that he had a learning disability that was manifested even in his Filipino

Language interaction techniques for stimulating the development of at risk children in infant and preschool day care

WILLIAM FOWLER

Center for Early Learning and Child Care, Inc., 29 Buckingham St., Cambridge, MA 02138, USA

It is often assumed that children's language will develop normally in the average, "good" day care and home environments. In fact teachers and parents from all social backgrounds vary widely in the quality of language interaction they furnish to children in the early years. These variations, moreover, are highly correlated with how well children develop language and other skills. Over a series of research projects in both day care and the home, principles and methods have been devised that have been shown to enable both normal and at risk young children to develop high and long-lasting competencies in language and other cognitive and social skills. The approach centers on engaging the whole child to interact with language informally in play and the ordinary routines of child care, both individually and in small groups, and emphasizing both the social, communicative and cognitive functions of language. A variety of specific techniques for use in day care are described and illustrated with several successful cases with at risk children.

Key words: Language, delay, enrichment

When a child of two or three comes into day care saying nothing at all or at best only a few words we say her language is delayed. We are then likely to ask why and begin to think about what to do to help her learn to talk. Yet in a "normal" day care program we almost expect children will learn to talk as a matter of course. Many people assume that a good, average environment furnishes all the language experiences young children need to foster speech development.

Actually, it turns out that both teachers in day care and parents in the home vary enormously in the quality of language they provide for young children. And these large differences have important effects on how children develop, not only in their verbal skills, but also in their overall cognitive development. McCartney (1984), for example, found that the varying quality of language day care teachers used in different day care centers in Bermuda in infants from 19 months on made highly significant differences in the children's language and intellectual development between 3 and 5½ years. Carew (1980) reported that the cognitive experiences guided by language interaction with adults, in both day care and the home, in children between 18 and 34 months, were the chief factors relating to language and cognitive development at age 3. Of special interest is the fact that the children's own experimentation in play activities during infancy showed no effect on later development.

It is important to note that in these and other studies, these differences were true in families and day care centers of all social backgrounds, from the lowest to the highest socioeconomic and educational levels. Huttenlocher and her associates (1991) in a longitudinal study measured the actual range of difference in the amount of parent verbalization and vocabulary development in children in two-parent, well-educated families. The most talkative mothers used vocabularies of 33 more words

From *Early Childhood Development and Care*, Volume 3, 1995, pp. 35-48. © 1995 by Gordon and Breach Science Publishers, Inc. Reprinted by permission.

than the least talkative, which resulted in vocabulary differences between the extremes of 131 words at 20 months and 295 words at 24 months.

It seems clear that the traditional view that what are often considered "good" homes and "good" day care centers typically produce well skilled, verbal children is far from universally true, as these and other studies show (see Fowler, *et al.*, 1992). Given the variation, many programs must be falling short in the quality of attention to language needed to ensure children develop their full potential. Our concerns here are with day care, of course, though effective teachers are likely to express concerns to parents when they feel the child may not be getting enough attention at home.

The Dilemma

But if many ordinary children are not experiencing the kind of interactions they need to foster good verbal skills, how can busy teachers also manage to tend to the special needs of the delayed or at risk child? Is there a way out of this dilemma? If we are going to have millions of the nation's children enrolled in group care from an early age, and to mainstream delayed children as well, can teachers be expected to pay more attention to the language needs of the average child and still take care of the child with special needs? It is one thing to ask parents and child care providers in the home to devote more attention to talking activities with one or two children. It is quite another for teachers in day care to furnish the same high quality to groups of infants, toddlers and preschoolers who often vary widely in skills they bring to group care.

SOME ANSWERS FROM RESEARCH

Some years ago I undertook a series of research projects with infants and preschoolers in group day care and in homes with parents. While two major longitudinal projects in day care (Fowler, 1972; Fowler, 1978) embraced a broad curriculum designed to foster high quality language, cognitive and social development, curriculum goals in the home centered for the most part on guiding parents to enrich the child's language experiences. In all studies, however, the quality of language was a major focus in all daily activities. The day care children came from a wide spectrum of social, ethnic and educational backgrounds, many of them single parent families and all with working mothers, cob pared to home-reared control families of two parents with non-working mothers. One day care center included a group of high risk infants from largely single-parent families on welfare with less than a high school education. Another included a large number of children from immigrant families with less than a complete high school education. Children entered with widely different levels of developmental compe-

tence, including children with various forms of risk and delay and some with bilingual/non-English-speaking backgrounds. It proved possible, nevertheless, to resolve the apparent dilemma of tending to the needs of both the "average" and the "special" child.

Out of that original research has come an approach (since applied in all later projects) to infant and child care or enriching language through play and the informal routines of basic care. The approach is really a whole child, developmental strategy in which language communication is embedded in the activities of daily care. These methods have recently been discussed at length in a recent book and illustrated in a companion videotape, both entitled, *Talking from Infancy: How to Nurture and Cultivate Early Language Development*, (Fowler, 1990a and 1990b). The book includes a chapter on working with language-delayed children.

In these and successive projects children have typically progressed in speech development easily months ahead of norms and no child has failed to develop well in social and general cognitive skills. Both in the projects with infants reared at home (Fowler, 1983; Fowler and Swenson, 1979; Ogston, 1983; Roberts, 1983; Swenson, 1983) and in the day care studies (Fowler, 1972, 1978), children have developed as well and sometimes better than randomized controls (home studies) or comparison groups (day care studies).

In follow-up studies of day care children at ages 4 and 5 (Fowler and Khan, 1974), and as late as age 9 in a study in progress, the day care children scored above average or higher in IQ, language and social skills, as high or higher than children in the home reared comparison group, despite the higher proportion of single parents and the working-mother status of the day care families.

In follow-up studies through high school of infants enriched through guiding parents in the home, most children have developed high competence in multiple skills, including verbal, math and science, are well balanced socially, active in sports and independently motivated intellectually (Fowler, Ogston, Roberts-Fiati and Swenson, 1992, 1993a, b, and c). Over half are creative writers. Throughout our collected studies, ensuring mastery of verbal skills in the early years appears to be central to promoting children's development in cognitive and social skills and later school learning. Further follow-up studies are now in process on the long-term development of these subjects, now approaching early adulthood.

METHODS OF LANGUAGE AND CARE ENRICHMENT

Principles for Stimulating Language Learning

The methods themselves embraced certain core principles and a variety of supporting ones that can easily be applied in virtually any kind of language activity with children. Language is in fact such a convenient educational tool that it requires only the human voice to implement. No external aids are needed, leaving the hands and eyes free to conduct other tasks freely, including the care of the child. Among the most important principles are to:

1. Interact with the child, taking turns in any activity: respond to the child as much as taking initiative.
2. Use language as a tool of social communication, engaging the child in the give and take about personal wants, feelings and interests.
3. Use language to guide the child in understanding how words represent meanings—the world and our ideas about it.
4. Engage the child in a warm and friendly manner, encouraging and personalizing according to the child's style.

Of all these principles, interacting with the child in a balanced way, seems to have an especially critical role. Yet it is apparently the one easiest to overlook. Thus, in the follow-up studies of our original early home intervention studies, turn-taking in language play during infancy proved to be the most powerful predictor of the later language competencies during both early and later development (Fowler, Ogston, Roberts-Fiati, and Swenson, 1993b). How well parents took turns in the language play with their infants turned out to correlate with the children's later SAT scores in high school, significantly with TSWE (Test of Standard Written English) and Reading Comprehension scores.

No doubt many teachers (and parents) use language games with young children to some degree in this way without thinking about it. But in fact adults vary widely in how well they apply them, as the research cited above on teacher differences and how children develop shows. Moreover, the fact that parents furnished with special guidance in our early language intervention research could still vary significantly in the quality of their interacting, underscores the need for special focus on this principle.

Care and consistency in using them becomes of special importance, of course, in the case of children who already have or are moving out of infancy with fewer communication or other cognitive skills than the average child. The complete set of principles is outlined in my book, *Talking from Infancy*.

Applying the Principles in Practice

Principles may sound impressive, and may have worked with parents in the home and with specially structured research programs in day care, but how will they work in the practice of the ordinary day care center? Actually, the research in both the day care and home settings in-

cluded a substantial number of at risk children, and in any case, these principles have been applied successfully in other group programs and home settings.

Let us consider a variety of situations, drawing on experience in various projects and paying special attention to situations involving a language delayed child in some way. Keep in mind that the focus is on infants at risk or preschoolers with mild to moderate problems of delay or difficulties in verbal communication. Children with severe communication disorders or delays will usually require referral to specialized therapy of some kind. (See especially, Harris, 1990.) Marked hearing loss, organic involvement or severe emotional difficulties are often implicated in such cases.

The delayed or slow-learning child alone

Let us suppose a teacher has some free time to work with a delayed child for a few minutes in some secluded corner of the play room, while the rest of a group of two year olds are otherwise engaged. What to do?

The first thing to keep in mind is to identify the stage of language development, in very general terms, the child has attained. . . .

To a large extent, use language according to how well the child can talk, regardless of the child's age. With many delayed children, a few words and perhaps a phrase or two that functions as a hold phrase (a phrase serving as a unit, such as "go bye-bye", in which the individual component words have no separate meaning for the child), is all that some delayed children use. This means that, whereas the average child is well on the way to building a good vocabulary by 20 months and the enriched child as early as about 10 months, the slow child may hardly have gotten any start with words at all by age two. . . . In any case, even if the child is as old as three or more, the focus in language play needs to be on using single words.

Here are some things to do:

1. *Prepare a set of toys in advance,* choosing items likely to appeal to the child's interests and small objects with frequently used common names (e.g., block, doll, car, truck, ball, clock, spoon). Keep objects in a box or other container, ready to bring them out from time to time to involve the child in repeated sessions. Substitute new toys when the child tires of the toys or new items are needed to expand the child's vocabulary.
2. Engage the child in *play with the toys,* introducing one or two at time and letting the child explore and use them in play spontaneously.
3. *Label each toy as the child handles it.* Be sure to time your naming of the item to the child's attention to the object.

4. *Keep the language simple:* start with the names of small, interesting toys and common objects—nouns, and concrete actions like run, walk, jump, kiss, hug—verbs. Prepositions (up, down, in and out) also function as action terms in the early stages.

5. Keep the play interesting by *introducing variations* of an activity. Engage the child in *sociodramatic play* by pretending that any of the objects are "live" and have them do different social activities (e.g., walk, run, jump, eat, drink, etc.). Social play can often be combined with construction activities with blocks and other building toys.

6. Try to fit in *a series of mini sessions* of 2 or 3 minutes or so several times a day or even only once or twice a day. Such a pattern will quickly start to yield real progress in the delayed child's mastery of verbal skills. Brief time slots of this kind have some realistic chance of being fitted into busy teaching schedules. Should schedules occasionally permit, longer spans of as much as 15 minutes are also productive, as long as the child remains interested.

Avoid Withholding and Correcting Errors

Some teachers withhold opportunities for a child to play with some toy, until the child says a word or phrase. Although sometimes recommended by behaviorist philosophies, in our studies we have found that such withholding strategies are likely to arouse a child's resentment and resistance. Although withholding techniques can be effective in the hands of skilled therapists, too often they lead to subtle or not-so-subtle battles of negative social interaction. The delayed child, especially, often has underlying feelings of failure that lead to the passive resistance of not talking, which is only reinforced by adult withholding. *Warmth, support and encouragement of effort are the most important ingredients to foster learning.*

A better strategy is simply to engage children, including the passive resisters, in the play, letting them start to say words and progress at their own speed in their own way. By the same token, avoid correcting errors (saying the wrong word or choosing a "block" when the teacher has asked the child to put a "ball" in a container). It is particularly important to spare children who have already felt a sense of failure in learning to talk, from meeting another failure experience. A better method is for the teacher simply to label the missed object correctly by making another demonstration in a play task, without referring to the child's "error", and the teacher should continue to do so over a series of play sessions, along with labeling various other objects. In this manner even the slow learning children will gradually understand and eventually say more and more words as they develop confidence.

Avoid Correcting Pronunciation and Grammar

There is also little need to stress correct pronunciation, following some model of standard English or even some dialect. Adequate pronunciation and adequate mastery of grammatical forms (e.g., pronouns, plurals, tenses, and sentence structures) will gradually be shaped as teachers demonstrate the correct or useful forms while interacting with the child. The same is true when the child uses the wrong label, mispronounces a word, uses "you" when "I" is meant, or uses present tense when past tense is called for. All these errors will be most easily corrected sooner or later by the children themselves as they come to grasp the relevant concept.

Teachers need only to label objects and actions correctly themselves, to use correct pronominal designations, and to employ tenses properly for the child gradually to understand and correct his or her own errors. Giving multiple, varied and accurate examples in the course of play furnishes all the material a child needs to make cognitive inferences of various rules for correct usage. At the same time, modeling in the course of play keeps the activity lots of fun for the child, without the burden of being labeled "wrong". The advantage of this focused language activity, anchored in manipulating objects directly, over the ordinary adult speech of everyday life, which is too often much of what children have to make inferences from, is that the language is simplified, relevant and more accessible in helping the child make useful inferences.

OTHER DEVICES AND SITUATIONS

Many programs and teaching situations may not allow much room for scheduled play time alone with any child on a regular basis. But even if they do, what about the rest of the day, the 6 to 7 or more hours of the day spent in working with groups of children? Actually, the routines of child care for children under two, and often up to 2½ or more, typically require individualized care for a number of activities, especially, changing diapers and beginning toileting routines, dressing and undressing on departure and arrival or even movement to and from the playground in inclement weather, feeding and eating routines, and washing and bathing activities. If nothing else, such activities represent large blocks of otherwise lost learning time and they are in fact ideal settings for engaging the child in language learning. Indeed, some infant-toddler enrichment projects have been based on embedding cognitive and language interactions in just such routines (Lally, Mangione and Honig, 1986).

Basic care routines

Think about the routines of getting dressed or washing hands. Activities repeated several times a day become demanding tasks to be gotten through with each child in turn, hopefully with sensitivity and warmth—but in any case executed with despatch to get on to the main "business" of care, activities of some kind in the play room or on the playground. But what if such routines involved a teaching goal, in which one could see progress in the child's development, almost day to day, from one's efforts?

Language interaction is just such an activity. A few well-timed words said during each routine, repeated every time, will in a matter of days bring about noticeable progress. Use vocabulary of the names of clothes—shirt, sock, diaper, pants, and the concrete actions performed each time—sit, stand, lie, up, down. These terms are used so often that the prespeech infant is soon showing evidence of understanding, then imitating here and there and finally saying them. In the same way, the delayed child will begin to make up for time lost.

The same flexible, informal style, *timing* the saying of each key word to your or the child's action, will engage the child's interest in language, in the same way individual play sessions do. Equally important, the tasks become rewarding to the teacher and the child is also involved in gradually learning about the steps to master her or his own self-care.

Small group activities

But can caregivers use language effectively in the same focused manner with groups of infants and preschoolers? Two-to-five year olds in most centers are of course regularly assembled into groups of different sizes around a table for eating or on the floor for singing, story time, and circle activities, or to observe plants, frogs or other phenomena for "science" learning. Much of the time, however, the flow of words may not relate closely to the item talked about. If the pace is not too fast, and some children are not left on the periphery in an oversized group, language and understanding will be far enough along in the average child for them to learn something about the activity. For infants under two, however, and even many two-year-olds, and especially the child with very little language, little understanding may get through—certainly not in understanding words, parts of speech and syntax. Keep in mind that the so-called "average" child is a mathematical myth. In any group of children of the same age, language skills often vary widely. For example, the skills of a group of two-year-olds may range from the child who spouts sentences to the one who only occasionally stumbles through two or three words. What to do?

How about breaking up main groups of 8 two-year-olds or 12 three-year-olds into more manageable groups of 3 and 4 each? But how can this be done when there is only a single teacher for each set of 8 or 12 children? One way to accomplish this is to find a relatively quiet corner to engage 3 or 4 children at a time in a separate language activity for a few minutes while the rest of the children are engaged in free play. If there is no such corner, set up one. Arrange an area with a small table and chairs. Just a throw rug will do sometimes. Give the activity additional focus and shield the group from intrusions from other children by placing two toy shelves to form an angle. Leave only a small entry way, blocked by a small chair that can quickly be removed for teacher exit in an emergency.

Groups of 3 or 4 little ones in a close circle are small enough so that every child can see every block, truck, or nose on a doll, at the exact moment the toy is labeled by the teacher. The teacher can also easily go from child to child, asking each one in turn to "put a block in a box" or "make the doll walk", without a long waiting period in between. Small groups thus combine the advantage of children learning in groups with highly focused individual attention. Extended discussions of engaging small groups of children in interactive play in language and concept learning activities may be found in my text, *Infant and Child Care* (Fowler, 1980).

It is also easy to keep track of each child's individual needs in small circle groups. Tailor your comments and requests according to the child's level. For example, with one child it may be important to stick to the simplest nouns—ball, car and bell. With another, use verbs—roll, walk and jump; and with still another a few more abstract terms like adjectives—round, big and little, can be woven in. When there are wide gaps between levels, then hesitant and slower children sometimes become intimidated and the fast and confident ones become bored. Some of these problems can be handled by involving the fast learners in leadership roles. It is vital to ensure that even the slowest child gets turns in performing tasks. Another alternative is to organize groups on the basis of skill levels instead of age. On this basis a group might consist of 4 children, all of whom are only beginning to say their first few words, yet range in age from 12 to 20 months or even more.

By rotating the small subgroups, every child gets a turn with this relatively individualized form of language play with toys. It is often useful to make up different combinations of children from time to time to vary the kind of stimulation and play interests children provide for one another. But little ones sometimes feel more secure if they can count on a familiar friend in their group.

Parent and other teacher assistants

Teacher assistants can add a great deal to a program, but too often they are not used for much more than setting out and putting away toys and art materials and moving groups of children from activity to activity. When aides are assigned to watch over children in free play, at least for short periods, the teacher can be free to engage a small group in language play, or even occasionally an individual child with special learning needs. Taking time to guide an assistant (or parent assistant) in techniques of handling and guiding children multiplies the amount of individual teacher attention for children. Many assistants can readily learn to work effectively in the language interactions activities, certainly individually in toy play and the child care routines, if not so easily in groups.

KEEPING TRACK OF EACH CHILD'S PROGRESS

Perhaps the most pleasant reward for a teacher is observing children's progress in development. Language growth is one of the easiest areas in which to chart a child's progress. Such charting takes more time and the changes are often difficult to perceive in the development of such concepts as number or size. But language development follows a highly visible course from sounds, to words, phrases, sentences, and sequential telling about things in a string of phrases and sentences. It is true that the first understandings of words are some times tricky to verify, and documenting progress in the different parts of speech and forming sentences (syntax) can be more technical. But even here, rather simple day-to-day (or perhaps every other day or so) records will shed light on a child's learning in these areas, at least enough to ascertain that a child is actually progressing. Especially, for the delayed or slow learner, written records will supply information to reassure teachers of progress that casual memory may overlook.

The child's first understanding of words is easily verified by asking a child to give you the [toy] dog or cow, when three or four toys to choose from are placed in front of him or her. In this way, if children can repeatedly pick the right one, you can judge they understand a given word. They show *word recognition*. Varying the setting broadens the child's experience and gives evidence of how generalized the child's understanding is. But don't press the child with repeated requests and usually avoid asking, "What is this?" This task requires the child to *recall* a word, a much more abstract task, which will come spontaneously with practice in play.

Written records or charts need consist only of a single page in a notebook or chart posted on the wall, one page for each child, with two columns, one for the date and a second for the sound, word or phrase a child is heard to use that day. A third column could also describe the circumstances when the child said something, such as "imitating the teacher" or "in response [to] looking at a picture of a duck." This additional information, while furnishing more insights on how the child is learning, may not be necessary except for a child with special difficulties.

Perhaps the *most important value of recording progress in language is to guide teachers on what to do next with a child*, especially with the slower children or those with special difficulties in pronunciation, use of adjectives, or forms of syntax. Checking over a child's record for the past week or two, for example, will reveal not only whether a certain child is learning much slower than others of a similar age, but that this child is learning no verbs, only the simplest nouns, or forms no phrases except occasional rote imitations (e.g., "big truck" or "go out") without ever applying them alone to new situations. A teacher can then zero in on desirable steps—using more examples with simple verbs or applying the same simple phrase to slightly varying situations, such as "more cars," "more blocks," etc.

Because time demands are of the essence of all teaching, jotting down any new term when a teacher has an odd moment free or at the end of the day, will probably serve very well. Don't give up if some term is missed or two or three days go by with no notations. Even spotty records can furnish valuable information on how well a child's language is progressing. This is particularly true in the early stages for infants up to 18 months or age two, and above all for the delayed and slow learning child.

Early records are the easiest to keep, because new sounds for the typical 6 months old, new words for the typical 12 months old and new phrases for the typical 20 months old start out slowly—one or two for the first week or two or even for several weeks. Gradually, the rates for most children accelerate at each stage, however. At some point in each successive stage, children grasp the concept of how to make new sounds, then that words have meaning—that they stand for things, and then that words can be put together (in phrases, later sentences) to describe actions and events of and about things. It is when these shifts occur that children learn new terms more and more rapidly and it becomes both increasingly difficult and relatively unimportant to keep track of the new terms. Just move on to recording progress for the next stage, from the now rapidly expanding vocabulary to the first halting, occasional phrases, or the rapid production of two word phrases to the beginning of constructing 3 or more word sentences.

SOME EXAMPLES

John[1]

John came from a well-off, college-educated family. When he entered our program at one year, it was almost immediately evident to everyone that he had a strange way of relating to people, and that there were none of the usual signs that he responded in any way to what a teacher said. Although lack of words is hardly surprising at one year, lack of any response to the human voice through smiling or gesture is. John usually totally ignored the speaker or looked very blank, and quite often looked right past the speaker, though tests given before

---

[1]All names of children are pseudonyms to preserve privacy.

entering day care had established that he had no hearing loss. In fact, John never made any rapport at all with adults or other children. It was quite evident that communication of any kind, gestural, vocal, or verbal, was out of the question with John. Yet, curiously, when the psychologist (myself) attempted to engage him in play with toys to diagnose his patterns, he did interact in manipulating the toys, though maintaining his usual stance of avoiding vocal communication and all except furtive eye contact. There was a distinct paranoid quality of complete mistrust and emotional blockage of relations with others. Later it was revealed that the mother could not stand infants, John included.

Because the center had a training program for students, we were able to assign an interested student, who soon formed a close attachment to John, as his main caregiver. With staff guidance she engaged John daily in toy play and frequently cared for him in basic routines. Gradually, she added more and more language into her play with him and involved him with the other children and teachers, with whom he was initially quite distant. Over the course of the 18 months he attended the program, John formed a close attachment to this student and gradually expanded relations to other caregivers and the children in play. By the time he was 2½, at graduation, he was speaking well in sentences and he was admitted to another pre-school program, where he adapted well, despite being the youngest child attending by several months. Especially interesting were changes in the mother's perceptions of John as an interesting, verbal little boy she came to accept and love, no longer the dependent infant she initially could not abide.

Terry and Mary

Two infants from a poor, inner city English Canadian single parent family on welfare, Terry was only 13 months older than his younger sister, Mary. The mother had only an 8th grade education and a much below average IQ. Terry's developmental test scores were also extremely low when he entered day care at 3½ months. Over the course of 14 months in the program his language skills blossomed and his test scores rose to very high average levels, which were maintained through the last follow-up with him at age 4½.

By the time his sister entered day care at 4 months, the mother had been engaged in a year of parent education and Mary had enjoyed the daily undivided attention of her mother during her early months while Terry attended day care. Mary's test scores were about average at entry. Her language and other test scores also rose to very high average like Terry's while she was in the program, but were found to have receded to average levels over the course of her final follow up at just over age 3. Given her circumstances, the mother could apparently sustain the care and stimulation of one child, the older

boy, but not two, once the children no longer attended day care.

Ed

The language focus of our day care program was particularly important for Ed. Despite his college-educated family background, when he enrolled at 14 months Ed could neither imitate nor say any words, though he had good perceptual-motor skills. By the time he left the program 16 months later, his language and other skills were all at the superior level and remained this high when last followed up at age 4½. Had he been in a program where nothing but free play prevailed without much teacher-child interaction and attention to language, his mild language delay might have expanded to become serious, since he was also getting little attention to his language at home. The mother was working at two jobs and the father was chronically ill.

CONCLUSION

Children having a wide range of language and other skills, including children from high risk backgrounds, can be accommodated in day care for infants and preschoolers, just as children with a wide range of other learning problems and emotional styles are regularly fit into the ordinary environment. The "average" or "ordinary" child is in fact an extraordinarily varying individual, who because of different backgrounds, varies in both the pace of development and the variety of courses followed. Within the average environment, a teacher strategy of bringing language into special focus, and anchoring it in the child's "natural" world of play to enhance accessibility, will enable the fast, the moderate, the slow and the different child all to progress in their own ways to acquire language and related cognitive skills at minimal acceptable levels of competence.

References

Bzoch, K. R. and League, R. (1971) *Receptive Expressive Emergent Language Scale.* Tallahassee, FL: Tree of Life Press.

Carew, J. V. (1980) Experience and the development of Intelligence in young children at home and in day care. *Monographs of the Society for Research in Child Development,* **45,** Serial no. 187.

Fowler, W. (1972) A developmental learning approach to infant care in a group setting. *Merrill-Palmer Quarterly,* **18,** 145–175.

Fowler, W. (1978) *Day Care and Its Effects on Early Development: A Study of Group and Home Care in Multi-Ethnic Working Class Families.* Toronto: Ontario Institute for Studies in Education.

Fowler, W. (1980) *Infant and Child Care: A Guide to Education in Group Settings.* Boston: Allyn and Bacon.

Fowler, W. (1983) *Potentials of Childhood.* Vol. 2: *Studies in Early Developmental Learning.* Lexington, MA: Lexington Books.

Fowler, W. (1990a) *Talking from Infancy: How to Nurture and Cultivate Early Language Development.* Cambridge, MA: Brookline Books.

Fowler, W. (1990b) (same title) Cambridge, MA: Center for Early Learning and Child Care.

Fowler, W. and Khan, N. (1974) *The Later Effects of Enfant Group Care: A Follow-up Study.* Toronto: Ontario Institute for Studies In Education.

Fowler, W. and Swenson, A. (1979) The influence of early language stimulation on development. *Genetic Psychology Monographs,* **100,** 73–109.

Fowler, W., Ogston, K., Roberts-Fiati, G. and Swenson, A. (1992) *The influence of early language term development of abilities: Identifying exceptional abilities through educational intervention.* Paper presented at the 1992 Esther Katz Rosen Symposium on the Psychological Development of Gifted Children: Developmental Approaches to Identifying Exceptional Ability. (To be published in Proceedings by the American Psychological Association).

Fowler, W., Ogston, K., Roberts-Fiati, G. and Swenson, A. (1993a) Accelerating Language Acquisition. In K. Ackrill (ed.) *The Origins and Development of High Ability.* Chichester, UK: Wiley.

Fowler, W., Ogston, K., Roberts-Fiati, G. and Swenson, A. (1993b) Increasing societal talent pools through early enrichment. Paper presented at A Gifted Globe: Tenth World Congress on Gifted and Talented Education. Toronto, Ontario, Canada, August 8 to 18, 1993. Submitted for publication in Proceedings.

Fowler, W., Ogston, K., Roberts-Fiati, G. and Swenson, A. (1993c) *The longterm development of giftedness and high competencies in children enriched in language during infancy.* Paper presented at the 1993 Esther Katz Rosen Symposium on the Psychosocial Development of Gifted Children: Relating Life Span Research to the Development of Gifted Children (To be published in Proceedings by the American Psychological Association).

Griffiths, R. (1970) The *Abilities of Young Children.* London: Child Development Research Centre.

Harris, J. (1990) *Early Language Development: Implications for Clinical and Educational Practice.* London: Routledge.

Huttenlocher, J., Height, W., Bryk, A., Seltzer, M. and Lyons, T. (1991) Early vocabulary growth: Relation to language input and gender. *Developmental Psychology,* **27,** 236–248.

Lally, J. R., Mangione, P. L. and Honig, A. S. (1986) Syracuse University Family Development Research Project: Long-Range Impact of Early Intervention on Low Income Children and Their Families. In D. R. Powell (Ed). *Parent Education as Early Childhood Intervention: Emerging Directions in Theory Research, and Practise* (pp. 79–104), Norwood, NJ: Ablex.

McCartney, K. (1984) Effect of quality day care environment on children's language development. *Developmental Psychology,* **20,** 244–260.

Menyuk, P. (1977) *Language and Maturation.* Cambridge, MA: MIT Press.

Ogston, K. (1983) The effects of gross motor and language stimulation on infant development. In W. Fowler (ed.) *Potentials of Childhood.* Vol. 2. Lexington, MA: Lexington Books.

Roberts, G. (1983) The effects of a program of stimulation in language and problem solving on the development of infants from lower-income, black Caribbean immigrant families. In W. Fowler (ed.) *Potentials of Childhood.* Vol. 2. Lexington, MA: Lexington Books.

Swenson, A. (1983) Toward an ecological approach to theory and research in child language acquisition. In W. Fowler (ed.) *Potentials of Childhood.* Vol. 2. Lexington, MA: Lexington Books.

Unit 5

Key Points to Consider

❖ What are the benefits of specifying intensities of support for children with developmental delays and mental challenges? Why is classification by level of mental retardation being encouraged?

❖ What strategies can make transition from special education in primary school to regularized education in middle school easier for a child who is mentally challenged?

❖ How can children with autism, who have minimal language and nonproductive social skills, be helped to socialize with other children?

❖ Can students who have sustained traumatic brain injuries return successfully to their school classes? What strategies assist their reintegration?

 **Links** www.dushkin.com/online/

These sites are annotated on pages 4 and 5.

Children with disabilities of mentation have been the focus of much of the attention of the changes to a kinder, gentler, more "politically correct" vocabulary in the 1990s. Children who have cognitive skills falling two standard deviations below the norm for their age may be considered mentally challenged or developmentally delayed. They may also be described as having mental retardation. However, while technically children who have autism or children who have sustained brain damage through traumatic brain injury may fall two standard deviations below the intellectual norms for their age, the preferred terms in use for their conditions are autism and traumatic brain injury, not mental retardation. Each are recognized as separate disability categories by IDEA.

Children with significantly subnormal intelligence, mental challenges, or mental retardation (MR) were once classified as "educable," "trainable," or "custodial" for purposes of placement. These terms are strongly discouraged today. Even severely retarded children are educable and can benefit from some schooling. The current preferred categorical terms for children who are mentally challenged are "intermittent," "limited," "extensive," and "pervasive." These terms refer to how much support the individuals need to function as capably as possible.

The U.S. Individuals with Disabilities Education Act (IDEA) mandates free and appropriate public school education for every child, regardless of mental ability. While the U.S. legal windows on education are from ages 6 to 16, individuals with disabilities are entitled to a free and appropriate education from age of assessment (birth, early childhood) to age 21. This encompasses parent-child education programs and preschool programs early in life and transitional services into the community and world of work after the public school education is completed.

A child with MR who is in the "intermittent" classification needs support at school, at times when special needs arise, and at times of life transitions. This terminology is generally used for children whose MR does not create an obvious and continual problem. These children have slower mentation but also have many abilities. The level of support classified as "limited" is usually used for children whose MR creates daily limitations on their abilities, but who can achieve a degree of self-sufficiency after an appropriate education. Limited refers to the period of time from diagnosis (infancy, early childhood) until adulthood (age 21). The "extensive" support classification extends the support throughout the lifespan for individuals whose MR prohibits them from living independently. The "pervasive" support classification is used infrequently. It is only for those individuals whose MR prevents them from most self-help activities. Pervasive support is intensive and life-sustaining in nature.

The majority of children with MR can be placed in the intermittent support classification. To casual observers, they often do not appear to have any disabilities. However, their ability to process, store, and retrieve information is limited. In the past, this group of children was given IQ measurements between two and three standard deviations below the mean (usually an IQ below 70 but above 55). Intelligence testing is an inexact science with problems of both validity and reliability. The current definition of MR endorsed by the American Association on Mental Deficiency (AAMD) does not include any IQ scoring results other than to use the phrase "subaverage intellectual functioning." It emphasizes the problems individuals with MR have with adaptive skills such as communication, self-care, home living, social skills, community use, self-direction, health and safety, functional academics, leisure, and work.

The causes of mental retardation are unclear. About one-half of all individuals with MR are suspected of having sustained some brain damage prenatally, neonatally, or in childhood. (Brain damage after age 18 that results in impaired mentation is not referred to as MR.) Several hundred factors have been identified that can singly or in combination alter brain functioning or destroy neurons. Most of these factors are silent killers. We lack the technology to even detect small areas of brain damage, much less to determine what caused them. Among the better-known factors that damage brain tissue are very early birth and/or very low birth weight, anoxia, malnutrition, drugs, viruses, radiation, trauma, and tumors. Children with more severe functional disabilities (those classified in the limited, extensive, and pervasive categories) usually have other symptoms of neurological damage and are entitled to special services under the category of multiple disabilities.

The first article in this unit addresses the changed terminology recommended by the American Association on Mental Retardation (AAMR). Functional labels (for example, intermittent support, limited support) have been urged as replacements for the more handicapping and often incorrect diagnoses such as "educable" or "trainable." This recommendation, referred to as the 1992 system, has engendered considerable resistance among some professionals working with individuals with mental retardation. The article's authors defend the 1992 system and answer some of the questions of critics.

The second unit essay depicts the transition of a boy with autism, developmental delays, and mental challenges from special education in primary school to regular education in middle school. The authors emphasize the collaborative efforts of the school staff, how they shared leadership roles, and how they attended to due process. Both problems encountered and factors that contributed to success are presented.

The third article addresses the need for early intervention and preschool programming for children with autism. Short case studies of two autistic children help the reader understand how challenging their symptoms and unusual behaviors are. Mark Brown and Jackie Kalbli provide many suggestions on how to make life a little easier for the children, their preschool peers, and the adults working with them.

The unit's last article, on traumatic brain injury, suggests ways to help students who were functioning at a much higher level to reenter school successfully after their brain injury.

The 1992 AAMR Definition and Preschool Children: Response From the Committee on Terminology and Classification

Ruth Luckasson, Robert L. Schalock, Martha E. Snell, and Deborah M. Spitalnik

As members of the American Association on Mental Retardation (AAMR) Committee on Terminology and Classification, we are pleased to have the opportunity to engage in dialogue on the AAMR 1992 *Definition, Classification, and Systems of Supports*—hereafter called the 1992 System (Luckasson et al., 1992) and its relation to the needs of preschool children. Vig and Jedrysek (1996) presented several arguments against the 1992 System. They urged application of the label of mental retardation (rather than developmental delays) to young children and retention of the old IQ-based classification system for these children. Vig and Jedrysek also questioned the relevance of the 1992 delineation of 10 adaptive skill areas and further suggested that specifying intensities of supports for young children is almost impossible and, even if possible, will lead to the expenditure of scarce resources on young children with the most intense needs for supports. In this response we have attempted to address each of these concerns and clarify other issues of a general nature.

Since the publication of the 1992 System, we have seen considerable movement toward its incorporation into state rules and regulations, legal opinions, the 4th edition of the *Diagnostic and Statistical Manual* (American Psychiatric Association, 1994), and education and habilitation practices. (For those interested in the general application of the definition, AAMR, in its newsletter, *News and Notes*,

regularly updates its readers on the implementation of the 1992 System.) However, the introduction of the 1992 System has not been without criticism. This system has brought to the forefront of the field of mental retardation a number of long-simmering issues, and valued colleagues have raised psychometric concerns and offered differing conceptual analyses of the nature of intelligence. It is our hope that the response presented here will contribute to these ongoing discussions. Our reply to the concerns expressed by Vig and Jedrysek regarding young children is divided into five sections: applying the concept of supports, incorporating developmentally based labels, determining intensities of supports, analyzing impact on services, and suggesting research implications.

Applying the Concept of Supports to Young Children

Vig and Jedrysek (1996) argued that young children with and without disabilities "need maximum adult support in all aspects of their lives because of their young age" (p. 246), and any attempt to specify support functions and kinds or intensities of supports for this age group are artificial or subjective. Yet current law (Part H of P.L. 99–457, Early Intervention, 1986) requires that multidisciplinary teams develop Individualized Family Service Plans (IFSPs) to "identify and organize formal and

From *Mental Retardation*, August 1996, pp. 247–253. © 1996 by the American Association on Mental Retardation. Reprinted by permission.

informal resources to facilitate the family's goals for the children and themselves" (Raver, 1991, p. 363; Johnson, McGonigel, & Kaufmann, 1989). The overriding premise of the IFSP is that when provided with the right kinds of resources (i.e., supports), a family can support the development of their child with special needs. Thus, services support and assist rather than replace or supplant the family, and professionals do not intrude into families' lives but provide services in ways consistent with the children's characteristics and the family's values, strengths, needs, and daily routines. The concept of an IFSP is highly compatible with the systems of supports core of the 1992 definition of mental retardation.

Incorporating Developmentally Based Labels

When children are very young and being considered for early intervention and/or special education services due to a failure to accomplish developmental milestones, they are typically found to have general developmental delay (e.g., 25% delay in two or more developmental areas on tests such as the Bayley Scales of Infant Development [Bayley, 1969] for which there is no identified diagnosis. The labels of "developmental delay," "developmental disabilities," or even "pervasive developmental delay" are used in place of more specific labels such as mental retardation, learning disabilities, emotional disorders, or autism. Physicians are currently unable to make a specific diagnosis in at least half of very young children with significant developmental delays. Also, labels of "at risk" are applied to young children whose environmental conditions (e.g., poverty and malnutrition) threaten regular development. Such children typically also show developmental delays. Because many individual characteristics in such at-risk children are resilient, including their cognitive skills (Campbell & Ramey, 1995; Garmezy, 1991; Werner & Smith, 1989), many children who experience multiple risks and developmental delays grow up to become competent adults. For example, Werner (1990) estimated that 33% of children at-risk "escape" successfully. Therefore, the use of more specific labels such as mental retardation is regarded as troublesome and inaccurate and frequently elicits the "self-fulfilling prophecy" phenomenon.

There are several reasons for using developmentally based labels rather than the level of mental retardation as proposed by Vig and Jedrysek, during the preschool years: (a) Most reliable measures for young children are developmentally organized and, thus, it is not unusual to determine whether a child is ahead or behind in various areas of development (e.g., Bayley Scales of Infant Development); (b) other disability labels are typically associated with failure in school and are applied only after a child is in the elementary grades when school achievement, measures of adaptive skills, and intelligence are more meaningful and reliable guides; and (c) the primary cause of the child's developmental delay may be environmental, which can be overcome by family support and early intervention (Hanson & Carta, 1995; Trivette, Dunst, Boyd, & Hamby, 1995). Obviously, there are some exceptions to these practices of using nonspecific disability labels. Examples include identifiable chromosomal, motor, and sensory disabilities such as Down syndrome, cerebral palsy, blindness, and deafness.

Determining Intensities of Supports

The recognition in the 1992 Manual (Luckasson et al., 1992) that "the support functions and activities may need to be modified slightly to accommodate individuals of different ages" (p. 104) reflects a sensitivity to the concerns raised by Vig and Jedrysek (1996) about the applicability of the existing typology to the needs of young children. However, by emphasizing classification and labeling, Vig and Jedrysek appear to lose sight of the utility of the support paradigm in addressing the needs of preschool children with disabilities and their families or caregivers, particularly families coping with other stresses, such as poverty, and the needs of children in foster and other out-of-home placements. The world view expressed by Vig and Jedrysek where labeling and classifying by IQ is given more primacy than intervention belies a lack of understanding of the support dimensions inherent in part H of the Individuals with Disabilities Education Act (IDEA)—P.L. 101–476 (Individuals With Disabilities, 1990).

The developmental nature of supports and the additional supports needed by families or other caregivers raising preschool children with disabilities in contrast to children without interference in their development is not recognized by Vig and Jedrysek (1996). They contended that

> During the preschool years, all children need maximum adult support in all aspects of their lives because of their young age. Attempting to specify support functions, or kinds and intensities of supports, for this age group is apt to be subjective or artificial. (p. 246)

Their contention indicates that they do not recognize either the supports needed by families to enable them to raise their children with disabilities or the needs recognized in the IFSP component of Part H of IDEA (Johnson et al., 1989). They characterized supports as "subjective" and cited MacMillan et al. (1995) about reliability of measures of support. This mistakenly conceptualizes supports as statistically measured commodities and reflects a lack of understanding of the support paradigm. A more accurate description of supports than "subjective" would be personalized, individualized, and tailored to the needs of the child and/or the family. This view of supports is more in keeping with the trends toward family-centered care and family support for children with disabilities (Brewer, McPherson, Magrab, & Hutchins, 1989) rather than a psychometric conceptualization of "service needs."

Vig and Jedrysek (1996) are also incorrect in stating that only three of the eight support functions described by Luckasson et al. (1992) and elsewhere (Schalock et al., 1994) can be applied to children. All eight support functions apply to preschool-age children, but the language in the matrix in the Manual (Table 9.1, p. 104) is not as elucidating as it could be, relying more on service system terminology rather than encompassing terminology that embraces natural supports as well as supports across the age-span. We also assert that their contention that using intensities of supports in times of scarce resources will disadvantage children with milder disabilities confuses social policy about access to services and rationing of services with questions of diagnostic and predictive accuracy and limitations, particularly about the benefit derived from services.

Continuing conceptual work has been done since the publication of the 1992 System operationalizing the intensities of needed supports. However, if the supports paradigm is to be effective, we will need to persist in our work in this area and, more specifically, de-

velop a technology of supports regarding the determination of support intensities.

Once the specific needed supports are identified, through the use of the Supports Planning Matrix found in the Manual, one then needs to determine their intensity. Since 1992, a technique that will assist teams in determining the appropriate intensity of needed support has been developed. This work has led to the Supports Intensity Decision Grid (Figure 1). The four levels of support intensity are listed across the top of the matrix: intermittent, limited, extensive, and pervasive. Five factors that affect the intensity are listed down the side: time (duration), time (frequency), settings (living, work, recreation, leisure, health, and community), resources (professionals and technological assistance), and intrusiveness. The matrix is used by the interdisciplinary team to determine the intensity of each of the identified needed supports.

We note that the Grid has been used primarily to determine the intensity of needed supports and not the cost of those supports. A number of questions about the Grid remain. For example, are the cells orthogonal or interdependent? Can the pattern of intensities be averaged? What type of clustering is most appropriate? Are support functions and intensities age dependent?

Analyzing Impact on Services

Vig and Jedrysek's (1996) concern (as well as that of others, cf. MacMillan, Gresham, & Siperstein, 1993, 1995) about the impact of the 1992 System on service eligibility and prevalence rates is understandable but should be interpreted in light of the current trend toward using a functional limitations criterion for defining a disability and determining its prevalence rate (Ficke, 1992; Institute of Medicine, 1991; La Plante, 1990; Schalock, 1995; Zola, 1993). Consistent with this trend, the 1992 definition includes both a cognitive and a functional limitations component. The Committee on Terminology and Classification was (and is) acutely aware of the significant need to develop better measures of adaptive skills across age and culturally and linguistically diverse groups. To that end, AAMR has worked with the publishers of the AAMR Adaptive Behavior Scales to develop scoring templates for each of the 10 adaptive skill areas included in the 1992 definition (Bryant, Taylor, & Rivera, 1996) and supported the work of the

	INTERMITTENT	LIMITED	EXTENSIVE	PERVASIVE
TIME duration	As needed	Time limited occasionally ongoing	Usually ongoing	Possibly lifelong
TIME frequency	Infrequent low occurrence	Regular, anticipated, could be high frequency		High rate, continuous, constant
SETTINGS LIVING WORK RECREATION LEISURE HEALTH COMMUNITY ETC.	Few settings, typically one or two settings	Across several settings, typically not all settings		All or nearly all settings
RESOURCES PROFESSIONAL/ TECHNOLOGICAL ASSISTANCE	Occasional consultation or discussion, ordinary appointment schedule, occasional monitoring	Occasional contact, or time limited but frequent regular contact	Regular, ongoing contact or monitoring by professionals typically at least weekly	Constant contact and monitoring by professionals
INTRUSIVENESS	Predominantly all natural supports, high degree of choice and autonomy	Mixture of natural and service-based supports, lesser degree of choice and autonomy		Predominantly service-based supports, controlled by others

Figure 1. Supports Intensity Decision Grid.

AAMR Ad Hoc Task Force on the cross-cultural measurement of adaptive behavior. We encourage and invite others to join in these and similar efforts.

The Committee also studied the potential impact of the 1992 System. One area of concern was any impact on estimated prevalence rates of using the dual component (IQ and adaptive skills) criterion for defining mental retardation. As discussed previously (Schalock et al., 1994), across a number of studies the estimated prevalence rates average 1.26%, which is consistent with the U.S. Department of Education (1993) service prevalence rate of 1.15% for the school-age population. A second concern was whether the 1992 System reflected the emerging understanding of mental retardation and its acceptance and use by the field. In the final field survey, preparatory to the finalization of the 1992 System, we collected utilization data from respondents in service agencies, universities, and government agencies. The responses generally were very favorable, and many people submitted suggestions that were incorporated into the fi-

nal work. In addition, when asked whether they foresaw any significant problems with the content of the definition, 63% of the respondents answered no and 95% stated that the definition reflected the emerging trends in the field of mental retardation and developmental disabilities. The classification system, however, generated less strong support at that time: 79% stated that they foresaw significant problems with the system, although 74% stated that the classification system reflected the emerging trend in the field. Since then, additional conceptual and practical work has been done to operationalize the system, particularly the Supports Intensity Decision Grid (Figure 1).

Suggesting Research Implications

In his landmark book *The Structure of Scientific Revolutions*, Kuhn (1970) suggested that in a paradigm shift such as the one we are currently experiencing in our field, major works serve to define the legitimate problems and methods of a research field for succeeding generations of practitioners. Thus, rather than addressing the research implications of eliminating the four levels of mental retardation mentioned by Vig and Jedrysek (1996), which we have already discussed extensively in Luckasson et al. (1992) and Schalock et al. (1994), we suggest a research agenda regarding the conceptualization and measurement of mental retardation for the next decade. Two critical aspects of that agenda include further defining the concept of intelligence and validating the general dimensions of adaptive behavior.

Further Defining the Concept of Intelligence

What is intelligence and what role should intelligence play in the definition and diagnosis of mental retardation? Today, a reduction in reliance on intelligence tests is clearly underway, and we are seeing many school districts shift from such tests to achievement and aptitude tests (Snyderman & Rothman, 1987). As the emphasis on measurement of academic intelligence decreases, we are beginning to see individuals (Greenspan, 1979, 1981; Greenspan, Switzky, & Granfield, in press; Sternberg, 1984, 1994; Sternberg, Wagner, Williams, & Horvath, 1995) advocating for not just the assessment of specific mental abilities but also for further defining the concept of intelligence to include at least three types of "intelligence": social, practical, and academic.

From a research perspective, there are at least six implications of this (potentially) broader conception of intelligence, including integrating a tripartite model of intelligence with a primary mental abilities approach to understanding intelligence, developing psychometrically sound measures of social and practical intelligence, determining whether social and practical intelligence are conceptually pragmatically different, determining what role social and practical intelligence should play in the definition of mental retardation, validating the role of observations, self-report, and professional judgment in assessing social and practical intelligence; and distinguishing how social and practical intelligence are different from adaptive behavior. Anastasi (1986), for example, made the statement that "intelligent behavior is essentially adaptive, insofar as it represents ways of meeting the demands of a changing environment" (pp. 19–20).

Validating General Dimensions Comprising Adaptive Behavior

The concept of adaptive skills found in the 1992 System is a continuation of the historic attention given to social competence in the diagnosis of mental retardation. The major purposes of adaptive behavior assessment include diagnosis and intervention planning, program evaluation and management, and population description and research (Bruininks, McGrew, & Maruyama, 1988; Horn & Fuchs, 1987; McGrew & Bruininks, 1989; Reschly, 1982). Research to date suggests the presence of a number of domains comprising adaptive behavior, including self-help skills, physical development, communication skills, cognitive functioning, domestic and occupational activities, self-direction and responsibility, socialization, personal independence, and personal and social responsibility (see Bruininks, Thurlow, & Gilman, 1987; Gresham & Elliott, 1987; Harrison, 1987; McGrew & Bruininks, 1989, 1990; Meyers, Nihira, & Zetlin, 1979; Widaman, Borthwick-Duffy, & Little, 1991; Widaman, Stacy, & Borthwick-Duffy, 1993, for excellent reviews).

Despite the studies just listed, results to date on the factor structure of adaptive behavior is equivocal. Recent reviews suggest the following needed research areas: resolving the unifactorial versus multifactorial positions on the factor structure of adaptive behavior, including a broader range of samples, instruments, and constructs; exploring adaptive behavior in the context of other constructs, such as personal competence; studying the contextual and crosscultural basis of adaptive behavior; and identifying critical behavioral skills that reflect the construct of adaptive behavior and that emphasize the acquisition of daily living skills and the achievement of personal independence and social adaptation.

Conclusion

In summary, in this response we have addressed the application of the AAMR 1992 *Definition, Classification, and Systems of Supports* and have concluded that the supports paradigm is not only applicable but is routinely applied through such mechanisms as the IFSP required by P.L. 99–457. We have also argued that developmentally based labels such as developmental delay are appropriate for many preschool children and that intensities of supports have more utility than do IQ-based levels. We have introduced the Supports Intensity Decision Grid (Figure 1) to assist in determining intensities and concluded that the classification system based on support needs is consistent with emerging trends in the field and will not dramatically affect prevalence rates.

We continue to encourage ongoing discourse regarding the 1992 System. Today, the field is experiencing not just a significant paradigm shift in the conceptualization of mental retardation but also fundamental questions about what we know and do not know about intelligence (Neisser et al., 1996) and the viability of the diagnosis of mental retardation (MacMillan, Siperstein, & Gresham, 1996). It is an exciting and challenging time in the field, and we welcome continuing discourse and research as AAMR further develops the *Definition, Classification, and Systems of Supports.*

References

American Psychiatric Association. (1994). *Diagnostic and statistical manual on mental disorders* (4th ed.). Washington, DC: Author.

Anastasi, A. (1986). Intelligence as a quality of behavior. In R. J. Sternberg & D. K. Detterman (Eds.), *What is intelligence? Contemporary viewpoints on its nature and definition* (pp. 19–22). Norwood, NJ: Ablex.

Bayley, N. (1969). *Bayley Scales of Infant Development.* New York: Psychological Corp.

Brewer E. J., McPherson, M., Magrab, P. R., & Hutchins, V. I. (1989). Family-centered, community-based, coordinated care for children with special health care needs. *Pediatrics, 83*(6), 1055–1061.

Bruininks, B., McGrew, K., & Maruyama, G. (1988). Structure of adaptive behavior in samples with and without mental retardation. *American Journal on Mental Retardation, 93,* 265–272.

Bruininks, R. H., Thurlow, M., & Gilman, C. J. (1987). Adaptive behavior and mental retardation. *Journal of Special Education, 21,* 69–88.

Bryant, B. R., Taylor, R. L., & Rivera, D. P. (1996). *Assessment of adaptive areas: A method for obtaining scores that correspond to the American Association on Mental Retardation's adaptive areas.* Austin, TX: Pro-Ed.

Campbell, F. A., & Ramey, C. T. (1995). Cognitive and school outcomes for high risk African-American students in middle adolescence: Positive effects of early intervention. *American Educational Research Journal, 32,* 743–772.

Early Intervention Program for Infants and Toddlers with Disabilities, Education of the Handicapped Act Amendments of 1986, Pub. L. 99–457, 20 U.S.C. § 1471–1485 (1986).

Faver, S. A. (1991). The Individualized Family Service Plan process. In S. A. Faver (Ed.), *Strategies for teaching at-risk and handicapped infants and toddlers* (pp. 363–399). New York: Merrill.

Ficke, R. C. (1992). *Digest of data on persons with disabilities.* Washington, DC: National Institute on Disability and Rehabilitation Research.

Garmezy, N. (1991). Resilience and vulnerability to adverse developmental outcomes associated with poverty. *American Behavioral Scientists, 24,* 416–430.

Greenspan, S. (1979). Social intelligence in the retarded. In N. R. Ellis (Ed.), *Handbook of mental deficiency: Psychological theory and research* (2nd ed., pp. 483–531). Hillsdale, NJ: Erlbaum.

Greenspan, S. (1981). Social competence and handicapped individuals: Implications of a proposed model. *Advances in Special Education, 3,* 41–82.

Greenspan, S., Switzky, H., & Granfield, J. (in press). Everyday intelligence and adaptive behavior. A theoretical framework. In J. Jacobson & J. Mulick (Eds.), *Manual on diagnosis and professional practice in mental retardation.* Washington, DC: American Psychological Association.

Gresham, F. M., & Elliott, S. N. (1987). The relationship between adaptive behavior and social skills: Issues in definition and assessment. *Journal of Special Education, 21,* 167–181.

Hanson, M. J., & Carta, J. J. (1995). Addressing the challenges of families with multiple risks. *Exceptional Children, 62,* 201–212.

Harrison, P. L. (1987). Research with adaptive behavior scales. *Journal of Special Education, 21,* 37–68.

Horn, E., & Fuchs, D. (1987). Using adaptive behavior in assessment and intervention. An overview. *Journal of Special Education, 21,* 11–26.

Individuals With Disabilities Education Act. 20 U.S.C. § 1400 *et seq.*, P.L. 101–476 (1990).

Institute of Medicine. (1991). *Disability in America: Toward a national agenda for prevention.* Washington, DC: National Reading Press.

Johnson, B., McGonigel, M., & Kaufmann, R. (1989). *Guidelines and recommended practices for the Individualized Family Service Plan.* Washington, DC: American Association for the Care of Children's Health.

Kuhn, T. W. (1970). *The structure of scientific revolution* (2nd ed.). Chicago: The University of Chicago Press.

La Plante, M. P. (1990). Who counts as having a disability? Musing on the meaning and prevalence of disability. *Disability Studies Quarterly, 10*(3), 15–17.

Luckasson, R., Coulter, D. A., Polloway, E. A., Reiss, S., Schalock, R. L., Snell, M. E., Stark, J. A., & Spitalnik, D. M. (1992). *Mental retardation: Definition, classification, and systems of supports.* Washington, DC: American Association on Mental Retardation.

McGrew, K., & Bruininks, R. (1989). The factor structure of adaptive behavior. *School Psychology Review, 18,* 64–81.

McGrew, K., & Bruininks, R. (1990). Defining adaptive and maladaptive behavior within a model of personal competence. *School Psychology Review, 19,* 53–73.

MacMillan, D. L., Gresham, F. M., & Siperstein, G. N. (1993). Conceptual and psychometric concerns about the 1992 AAMR definition of mental retardation. *American Journal on Mental Retardation, 98,* 325–335.

MacMillan, D. L., Gresham, F. M., & Siperstein, G. N. (1995). Heightened concerns over the 1992 AAMR definition: Advocacy vs. precision. *American Journal on Mental Retardation, 100,* 87–97.

MacMillan, D. L., Siperstein, G. N., & Gresham, F. M. (1996). A challenge to the viability of mild mental retardation as a diagnostic category. *Exceptional Children, 62,* 356–371.

Meyers, C., Nihira, K., & Zetlin, A. (1979). The measurement of adaptive behavior. In N. R. Ellis (Ed.), *Handbook of mental deficiency: Psychological theory and research* (2nd ed., pp. 431–481). Hillsdale, NJ: Erlbaum.

Neisser, U., Boodoo, G., Bouchard, T. J., Boykin, A. W., Brody, N., Ceci, S. J., Halpern, D. F., Loehlin, J. C., Perloff, R., Sternberg, R. J., & Urbina, S. (1996). Intelligence: Knowns and unknowns. *American Psychologist, 51,* 77–101.

Reschly, D. J. (1982). Assessing mild mental retardation. The influence of adaptive behavior, sociocultural status, and prospects for nonbiased assessment. In C. R. Reynolds & T. B. Gutkin (Eds.), *The handbook of school psychology.* New York: Wiley Interscience.

Schalock, R. L. (1995). *Outcome-based evaluation.* New York: Plenum.

Schalock, R. L., Stark, J. A., Snell, M. E., Coulter, D. A., Polloway, D. L., Luckasson, R., Reiss, S., & Spitalnik, D. M. (1994). The changing conception of mental retardation: Implications for the field. *Mental Retardation, 32,* 181–193.

Snyderman, M., & Rothman, S. (1987). Survey of expert opinion on intelligence and aptitude testing. *American Psychologist, 42,* 137–144.

Sternberg, R. J. (1984). Macrocomponents and microcomponents of intelligence: Some proposed loci of mental retardation. In P. H. Brooks, R. Sperber, & C. McCauley (Eds.), *Learning and cognition in the mentally retarded* (pp. 89–114). Hillsdale, NJ: Erlbaum.

Sternberg, R. J. (1994). The triarchic theory of intelligence. In R. J. Sternberg (Ed.), *Encyclopedia of human intelligence* (pp. 1090–1091). New York: MacMillan.

Sternberg, R. J., Wagner, R. K., Williams, W. M., & Horvath, J. A. (1995). Testing common sense. *American Psychologist, 50,* 912–927.

Trivette, C. M., Dunst, C. L., Boyd, K., & Hamby, D. W. (1995). Family oriented program models, helpgiving practices, and parental control appraisals. *Exceptional Children, 62,* 237–248.

U.S. Department of Education. (1993). *Fifteenth annual report to Congress on the implementation of the Individuals With Disabilities Education Act.* Washington, DC: Author.

Vig, S., & Jedrysek, E. (1996). Application of the 1992 AAMR Definition: Issues for preschool children. *Mental Retardation, 34,* 244–246.

Werner, E. E. (1990). Protective factors and individual resilience. In S. J. Meisels & J. P. Shonkoff (Eds.), *Handbook of early childhood intervention* (pp. 97–116). Cambridge: Cambridge University Press.

Werner, E. E., & Smith, R. S. (1989). *Vulnerable but invincible: A longitudinal study of resilient children and youth.* New York: Adams Bannister Cox.

Widaman, K. F., Borthwick-Duffy, S., & Little, T. D. (1991). The structure and development of adaptive behavior. In N. W. Bray (Ed.) *International review of research in mental retardation* (Vol. 17, pp. 1–54). New York: Academic Press.

Widaman, K. F., Stacy, A. W., & Borthwick-Duffy, S. A. (1993). Construct validity of dimensions of adaptive behavior: A multitrait-multimethod evaluation. *American Journal on Mental Retardation, 98,* 219–234.

Zola, I. K. (1993). Disability statistics, what we count and what it tells us: A personal and political analysis. *Journal of Disability Policy Studies, 4*(2), 9–39.

The authors thank Paul Kolstoe, Harold Kleinert, and Steven Eckert, who assisted with the development of the grid, and Charlie Silva, who helped analyze the field survey data. We also thank the other members of the Committee on Terminology and Classification: David Coulter, Edward Polloway, Steven Reiss, and Jack Stark.

Authors: **RUTH LUCKASSON, JD,** Chair, AAMR Committee on Terminology and Classification, Regents' Professor and Professor of Special Education, College of Education, University of New Mexico, Albuquerque, NM 87106. **ROBERT L. SCHALOCK, PhD,** Professor and Chair, Department of Psychology, Hastings College, Hastings, NE 68901, and Program Consultant, Mid Nebraska Individual Services. **MARTHA E. SNELL, PhD,** Professor, Curry School of Education, Department of Curriculum, Instruction, and Special Education, University of Virginia, Charlottesville, VA 22903. **DEBORAH M. SPITALNIK, PhD,** Executive Director, University Affiliated Program of New Jersey, Associate Professor Clinical Pediatrics, University of Medicine and Dentistry of New Jersey, Robert Wood Johnson Medical School, Piscataway, NJ 08855.

Collaborative Planning for Inclusion of a Student with Developmental Disabilities

Jane E. Doelling, Suzanne Bryde, Judy Brunner & Barbara Martin

It appears that many education professionals in both general and special education are experiencing confusion regarding the concept of inclusion. There is a misconception regarding corresponding legal mandates pertaining to provision of services to students with disabilities. In a recent position statement, The Council for Exceptional Children (1993) cites the need for increased collaboration and greater emphasis on inclusive practices. Inclusion in itself is not a legal mandate; however, implementing the Individual Educational Plan (IEP) in the least restrictive environment is a component of the Individuals with Disabilities Act (IDEA) of 1990. Full inclusion programs typically offer students with disabilities services in the general education classroom with little or no time in special education settings. IDEA mandates that placement decisions be made by a multidisciplinary team and that a continuum of service delivery options be maintained.

The setting in which educational services for students with disabilities are provided remains a major issue, particularly in middle level and secondary education where students are expected to spend a great deal of time in content classes. Nolet and Tindal (1993) suggest that demands for response in content classes may directly affect students' ability to use content information and that low performing students benefit from accommodative instruction that includes modeling of problem solving solutions and rich contextual clues. Most general educators agree that inclusion is a positive practice, but do not feel prepared to serve students with disabilities. A support system with shared involvement is necessary for successful inclusion (Simpson, & Myles, 1993).

The current paradigm shift to less restrictive models for educating students with disabilities requires collaborative planning, routine modification of instructional materials, and the inclusion of parents and peers as important components of the educational process (Bradley & Fisher 1995). The following discussion will focus on clarifying issues surrounding inclusion, as well as a description of specific action taken to implement an appropriate educational program for Matt, an 11-year-old student with autism, entering a middle school program. Emphasis is placed on the collaborative efforts of school staff, the importance of shared leadership roles, adherence to appropriate due process, and analysis of the instructional environment in planning and implementing an inclusive educational program appropriate to individual needs.

History

Matt had previously received educational services in a self-contained language development classroom with limited integration in general education classes at the elementary level. The greatest concerns expressed by Matt's family and the school team were social interaction and severely delayed communication. Matt was functioning at approximately an eight-year-old level with the exception of expressive language which fell below other areas. He rarely initiated interaction with peers and had developed limited interest in age-appropriate leisure activities. Previous success with implementing behavioral change

Jane E. Doelling, Suzanne Bryde, and Barbara Martin teach at Southwest Missouri State University in Springfield. Judy Brunner is a middle school principal in the Springfield Public Schools in Missouri.

From *Middle School Journal,* January 1998, pp. 34-39. © 1998 by the National Middle School Association (NMSA). Reprinted by permission.

Figure 1

Functional Behavioral Analysis and Interventions

		Intervention	Implementor
A. Setting Task Hall transition to music	**Antecedent** Student transition to music with limited supervision from teachers posted at each end of the hall.	Modeling and guided practice of appropriate hall behavior and increased adult proximity to Matt. Fade proximity with practice.	All educators collaborate.
Behavior(s) Matt followed behind peer in line. Touched peer on shoulder 5 times in 2 minutes.	**Consequence(s)** Peer tolerant of first two touches. Turns to Matt and shouts "stop" for the last three touches. Matt smiles.	Direct instruction in appropriate interaction skills. Generalization sessions implemented in natural contexts (luncheon, hall, classroom).	Special Educators
	Function Request for interaction/attention. Difficulty with self monitoring.	Develop monitoring/ cueing system. (Card that reads "Hands down" and "Act like a teenager.")	Special Educators
		Monitoring and check for appropriate behavior.	All educators collaborate
B. Setting/Task General Education Classroom—social studies class discussion on protection of natural resources.	**Antecedent** Teacher asked student to open social studies text, survey the passage, and brainstorm information gleaned from survey.	**Intervention** Develop prior knowledge for lesson through vocabulary lessons, survey of pictures, participation in hands on activities.	**Implementor** Special educators.
Behavior(s) Walked to the back of the room. Repeatedly stacked and unstacked library books for duration of 15 minute discussion. Did not comply to verbal directive to re turn to seat.	Consequence Matt told to return to seat. Teacher ignored behavior since Matt's activity was not disruptive.	Include structured, parallel lesson to be implemented independently on a visual schedule.	Special educators
	Function Escape/avoidance. Protest of non-meaningful activity. Confusion.	Structure cooperative group activity appropriate to diverse abilities (e.g. recycling school materials, identifying community resources and how to care for them).	All educators collaborate

was credited with determining the reasons for Matt's behavior through an analysis of environmental variables and planning intervention accordingly. (See Figure 1)

The middle school Matt was to attend had implemented a collaborative teaching model that involved core teams of three content teachers in general education with one special services consultant/teacher assigned to each team. The district had no autism specialist and the middle school teachers were apprehensive about working with a student that presented such unique challenges. The family requested that the next IEP include age-appropriate tasks and specific plans for including Matt with typical peers. They expressed long range goals for Matt that included independent living and employment in a competitive or semi-supported setting; however, they noted their concern that this did not seem

---

Figure 2

Agenda for the Transition Team

1. Review the IEP and all available diagnostic and programming data in the following areas: social, behavioral, academic, health, adaptive, and cognitive to determine Present Level of Performance (PLP).

2. Determine IEP goals and objectives appropriate to meeting needs identified in the PLP.

3. Determine placement and services appropriate to implementing goals and objectives.

4. Determine accommodations necessary for implementation of goals and objectives across settings (i.e. grading alternatives, curricular and material modifications, physical arrangements, teaching and student response modes).

5. Assign a liaison/case manager to coordinate the collaborative process and implementation of the IEP.

---

possible without exposure to typical language and social models. A systematic plan of transition was developed in order to ease the movement to middle school for Matt, his family and school personnel.

Phase One: Planning the Transition

The special education director and middle school principal assumed leadership roles for initial transition planning. A meeting was arranged with the family and included elementary team members as well as the team from the receiving middle school. Due to questions regarding Matt's placement and the content of his IEP, it was essential to set an agenda for the meeting that reflected sensitivity to the family's requests and adherence to due process. Figure 2 includes the agenda for the transition team.

By reviewing major instructional goals for the district and comparing them to Matt's Present Level of Performance (PLP), the team addressed the family's wishes regarding inclusion of Matt in age-appropriate academic activities. For example, the team related district curriculum goals such as listening and reading comprehension skill development to the needs identified in Matt's diagnostic report and corresponding IEP. For the benefit of general education professionals, as well as Matt's family, it was noted in the IEP that Matt would not be expected to master all district

curriculum goals presented at his chronological age level and that modification was fair and appropriate based on diagnostic data documenting the effects of Matt's disability.

It was the decision of the team that full inclusion would not meet all specified IEP goals and objectives at that time. Matt needed specialized language, occupational therapy, and special education services to meet individual needs. However, it was also determined that many of the goals and objectives of Matt's IEP could be attained in both special and general educational settings.

In an effort to alleviate confusion regarding the district's policy on inclusion, a brief explanation had been added to both the student and faculty handbooks. A portion of the district policy is provided here:

- Decisions regarding services and educational placement will be based on a multidisciplinary evaluation and a detailed IEP developed by the family and educational team.
- Regardless of disability, students will be fully included in general education programs, when deemed appropriate by the IEP team. A full continuum of service delivery options should be maintained by the school district as full inclusion may not meet the needs of all students.
- Those students whose IEP does not include full inclusion requirements should be placed in the least restrictive environment possible based on the student's needs and the continuum of available services.

Finally, it was determined that Mr. Brown, the special education teacher assigned to one of the established middle school teams would serve as liaison, case manager, and integration specialist for Matt's program. This determination was based on the team's record of success in regard to meeting educational goals and Mr. Brown's experience with developmental disabilities.

Phase Two: Preparing for the Transition

In an effort to address programmatic barriers to collaboration, district administrators agreed to provide transitional support by providing an additional plan hour for Matt's team leader, Mr. Brown. A commitment was also made to provide an instructional aide for Matt. It was noted the support of the individual aide would be phased out as Matt progressed since the ultimate family and school goal was developing his independence. Further, Mr. Brown received specialized training in autism to serve as a consultant for the middle school, thus enhancing a site-based approach to program management. Conceptual barriers to inclusion were addressed through district supported staff development and team planning coordinated by Mr. Brown. Other team members attended various staff development activities supported by the district. To facilitate transition to the middle school setting, several ecological variables effecting Matt's performance were analyzed. Examples from the functional behavioral analysis that assisted the team in program planning are noted in Figure 1. The provision of contextual cues within a structured environment had been noted as important to behavioral control and supported in data collected and the professional literature on autism. Based on this analysis of behaviors, the team implemented a plan that included a visual schedule with clear criteria for assigned tasks and a physical arrangement that reduced frustration.

Phase Three: Implementing the Program

The majority of the goals and objectives on Matt's IEP were to be implemented across settings. Because several different implementors were involved, it was necessary to establish a system for effective collaborative planning and systematic communication. An agenda for planning sessions was established by the team with a focus on five areas: (a) instructional content, (b) methods of presentation, (c) participant roles, (d) evaluation procedures, and (e) lesson accommodations. In an effort to further improve communication and consistency of programming, Matt carried his individual schedule across settings. Mr. Brown followed a rotating instructional schedule, alternating days in inclusive settings while still providing direct instruction to students in special education settings. This system allowed him to work with students on IEP objectives as well as assist the general education teacher with inclusive programming.

Providing services in inclusive settings required each team member to share leadership roles and all team members to be consultants in their varied areas of expertise. A primary barrier expressed by general educators on

Matt's team was time involved in development of an alternate curriculum for Matt as well as concern with the appropriateness of the academic curriculum. Mr. Brown took the lead in designing a curriculum that included prevocational skills crucial to independent adult functioning yet, when possible, parallel to the general education curriculum. General educators typically took lead roles in collaborative planning sessions involving the discussion of content for future instructional units. Alternative lessons plans were maintained on disk by Mr. Brown and other building specialists to be disseminated among instructional teams so that they could be modified and appropriately implemented for diverse learners.

Providing Matt with a means to more readily communicate with individuals across settings was imperative to successful integration, socialization, and behavioral control; therefore, speech and language therapy was provided in individualized sessions, as well as the general education settings, hall transitions, and luncheon. To ensure that language programming goals were clear, each team member was provided with a data collection form containing five communication skills specific to Matt's IEP. In addition, each member kept brief records regarding progress to share in collaborative planning sessions.

Due to Matt's expressive communication problems, a small photograph album with line drawing illustrations was employed. Sight words and phrases were attached to each picture; therefore, the system could be used to enhance reading and vocabulary skills. The low technology system was chosen for its flexibility and its potential for promoting communication between Matt and his peers and adults.

With desks arranged in a format that promoted face-to-face interaction, Matt was assigned to cooperative learning groups. An additional peer mediated strategy found to contribute to positive outcomes for Matt and his peers was peer tutoring (Dettmer, Thurston, & Dyck, 1993). Mr. Brown and the general education team members discussed cooperative roles appropriate to various curricular assignments and Matt's role in these assignments. Teachers analyzed cooperative lessons and structured them to provide rich contextual cues including schedules, material organizers, and self-monitoring forms. Specific cooperative group behaviors were targeted for direct instruction in language therapy and in the special education setting.

These included passing papers, making eye contact, requesting assistance, taking turns, and listening. Peers were selected as cooperative group partners on the basis of their expressed interest in working with Matt and because they were noted to be appropriate social and academic models.

It was apparent that positive behavioral intervention could not be separated from academic and communication instruction. Priorities identified in the team planning process included expanding Matt's repertoire of leisure activities, replacing socially inappropriate behaviors with appropriate skills, and developing friendships. It was determined that serving as an office worker would provide opportunity to apply social and academic skills. Matt was paired with a peer for some office activities and conducted other jobs independently. Opportunities were structured for Matt to interact, take direction, and request assistance from secretaries, administrators, or other adults in the building in an effort to generalize targeted social behaviors.

Peer networks were expanded from the original cooperative group members by rotating a peer in and out of the cooperative group on a periodic basis. In addition, Matt was assigned to a home room group that met twenty minutes daily. Each home room group in the building choose a theme or area of interest to pursue and Matt's group met in the gymnasium due to their interest in weight lifting and physical development. Matt's occupational therapist designed a program to be implemented in daily sessions and appropriate to Matt's physical ability and sensory integration needs. In addition to meeting social and motor development goals, mathematics goals were implemented by having Matt and a peer monitor physical progress.

Summary

Support for collaborative efforts to provide services to students with disabilities in inclusive settings became a district priority. Some faculty meetings and district inservice days were reserved for team meetings as educators schedules were organized to promote collaborative planning. District policies and philosophy clearly reflected inclusive educational practices; however, programming decisions continued to be based on individual student needs, attributes of the school, and the expertise of building professionals.

It is important to note that variables and processes noted to contribute to success for Matt may not generalize to all students with disabilities; and, of course, problems with implementation did occur. Although there is a need for further research that validates effective collaborative and inclusive practices, the existing literature does support many of the practices implemented in Matt's educational program. These include the use of cooperative learning techniques; analysis of the instructional environment to determine variables affecting learning; problem solving strategies; and the shared leadership and consultative roles demonstrated by administrators, instructional team members, and ancillary staff (Dettmer, Thurston, & Dyck, 1993; Ysseldyke, Christenson, & Kovaleski, 1994). Matt did not master all district curricular goals; however, partial inclusion in the general education setting did contribute to the increased success with language, social, and academic goals of Matt's IEP.

Programmatic collaborative barriers noted in the literature (Johnson, Pugach, & Hammitte, 1988 [as cited in Heron & Harris, 1993]; Dettmer, Thurston, & Dyck, 1993) included scheduling problems, lack of resources, and lack of shared planning time and lack of role clarification. These were primarily addressed through administrative support and as a part of district reorganization. Conceptual barriers to collaboration and inclusion also corresponded to those noted in the literature and these included philosophical differences and lack of knowledge regarding diverse populations. In Matt's case, administrative support was essential, particularly for establishing a school climate that reflected the shared responsibility of educating all students. Therefore, professional credibility and the resolve of all team members are required to alleviate any conceptual barriers that may exist.

Educators want instructionally relevant strategies for teaching students with special needs and brainstorming alone may not lead to effective intervention (Ysseldyke, Christenson, & Kovaleski, 1994). Previously, emphasis was placed on the special educator as an outside or impromptu consultant and on the operation of parallel, segregated service delivery systems. It is essential that instructional models stress collaborative planning and problem solving that address the needs of education professionals, as well as a diverse student population.

As noted in Matt's program, decisions evolved from analysis of the learning environment along with assessment of learner characteristics. This emphasis on environmental analysis may include consideration of instructional presentation, physical accommodations, teacher expectations, academic engaged time, and adaptive instruction as recommended by Ysseldyke and others (1994). In summary, the following guidelines are offered to middle level educators planning collaboratively for inclusion of children with disabilities:

1. Conduct data review and planning sessions (IEP meetings) prior to placement in inclusive settings. These team sessions should include a consideration of family, professional, and peer needs along with a review of all present-level information for the particular child to be included. Long term goals (including post graduation goals) and corresponding short term objectives must be developed with clear delineation of settings for implementation, acceptable standards of performance, evaluation procedures, accommodations, and roles of various professionals.

2. Determine training, support service, and organizational needs as deemed appropriate from review of IEPs and general instructional goals. A focus on strengthening site-based management, collaborative opportunities, and the reallocation of available resources to meet the needs of diverse learners is essential to successful inclusion. Professional development needs may include enhancement of expertise in academic or behavioral strategies while organizational restructuring may call for reassignment of personnel or the reorganization of teams, planning times, or instructional schedules.

3. At collaborative planning sessions conduct ongoing evaluation of student performance and modify classroom instruction and IEPs accordingly. Collaborative sessions should include analysis of the effectiveness of instructional content, teaching methods, classroom organization, evaluation procedures, and professional roles. Analysis must be based on measurable outcomes for *all* students in the setting and IEPs may need to be revised prior to the expected annual review.

4. In collaborative planning sessions, determine how district curriculum goals and instructional methods can be modified to meet the needs of individuals with IEPs. Partial participation, alternative grading systems, peer coaching, and reduced assignments may all be appropriate. Inclusion in general education may not mean that students with IEPs are expected to master all objectives of the inclusive setting.

5. Delineation of professional roles should be based on analysis of the needs of all students within the setting. Although the general educator is basically responsible for presentation of content, and the special educator responsible for accommodation, roles may change. In collaborative instructional partnerships, flexibility, respect for individual expertise, and equal participation are stressed.

Educators demonstrate a wide range of skills and training; therefore, no single collaborative model is likely to be successful. General education teachers must clearly identify concept and principles they view as critical and special education teachers must support this process by providing expertise in formatting content information (Nolet & Tindal, 1993). Further, a continuum of services to meet the needs of individuals with varied needs must be maintained. Placement in collaborative, integrated settings remains an individualized decision based on the specific goals and objectives targeted in the IEP by a multidisciplinary team.

References

Bradley, D.F., & Fisher, J. F. (1995). The inclusion process: Role changes at the middle level. *Middle School Journal, 26*(3), 13–19.

The Council for Exceptional Children (1993). CEC policy on inclusive schools and community settings. *Supplement to Teaching Exceptional Children, 25*(4)

Dettmer, P., Thurston, L. P., & Dyck, N. (1993). *Consultation, collaboration, and teamwork for students with special needs.* Needham Heights, MA: Allyn & Bacon.

Heron, T. E., & Harris, K. C. (1993). *The educational consultant.* Austin, TX: Pro-ed.

Nolet, V., & Tindal, G. (1993). Special education in content area classes: Development of a model and practical procedures. *Remedial and Special Education, 14*(1), 36–48.

Simpson, R. L., & Myles, B. S. (1993). General education collaboration: A model for successful mainstreaming. In E. L. Meyen, G. A. Vergason, & R. J. Whelan (Eds.), *Challenges facing special education* (pp. 63–78). Denver, CO: Love.

Ysseldyke, J. E., Christenson, S., & Kovaleski, J. F. (1994). Identifying students' instructional needs in the context of classroom and home environments. *Teaching Exceptional Children, 26*(3), 37–41.

Early Childhood Special Education

Facilitating the Socialization of Children with Autism

Mark Brown[1,3] and Jackie Kalbli[2]

INTRODUCTION

Many teachers of young children are now being asked to incorporate children who have been diagnosed as having autism within their classroom. While an inclusionary classroom with typically developing special needs children usually works very well, teachers may encounter some new challenges when autistic children are also members of the classroom.

The case study that is being presented was examined by two researchers with experience in early childhood special education and atypical child social development. The first author is a university professor who is a specialist in behavior disorders. He began his involvement with the class as a research observer studying social development. He had been assisting the teacher in finding effective strategies to work with these autistic children. The severity of their disorders range across the spectrum.

The second author is a preschool teacher with over 17 years of experience. It is her responsibility to instruct two preschool integrated classes on a daily basis. In each of the two preschool integrated classes, she enrolls eight children with disabilities and four typically developing children. The school year follows the calendar of the district in which we are housed. We function as a collaborative model involving the county Mental Retardation Developmental Disability (MRDD) board and the school district. Using a team approach, we attempt to meet the diverse needs of children with broad differences in their understanding of social behaviors. Our strategies are guided by our adherence to developmentally appropriate practices, a philosophy with sufficient elasticity to allow eclectic approaches. We view ourselves as facilitators for children. We set up an environment that indirectly teaches (Prizant & Wetherby, 1988). We also collaborate with the children on meeting their agenda. In the past year, we have been surprised by the numbers of children we are servicing with the diagnosis of PDD (i.e., pervasive developmental disorder) or autism. Of the 18 children enrolled, four now have an official diagnosis of PDD. One more is waiting to enroll. There is another one in the community with whom we have made contact. We have discovered that each autistic child has his or her way of dealing with the stress of the disorder. Adults must be very flexible in dealing with these children and they must be aware of the impact their strategies may have. Billy and Adam, two children who vary significantly in their stages of cognitive and social development, are described to illustrate this point.

BILLY

Billy is a 3-year-old who looks like an "angel" without wings. He has curly brown hair and a cherubic face. Upon enrollment, Billy had yet not spoken. His disorder was at the severe end of the spectrum. He often wandered around the room in a repetitive manner and attended to an activity for an average duration of 20 seconds (Dahlgren & Gillberg, 1989). He had limited skill in using his hands with objects and didn't seem to know the purpose of common toys or how to play with them. Frequently, he tossed plates or other objects across the preschool classroom resulting in crashes that scared the other children. He also made scary noises when he attempted to play with toy blocks (Keogel & Kern-Keogel, 1994). For his socialization to be improved, he needed to have peer modeling and take part in positive peer social interactions. Billy's interaction with other children involved sometimes staring at them when they were performing an activity at the water table (i.e., cooking/washing plates), computer station (i.e., activating

[1]Department of Education/Psychology, Miami University, Oxford, Ohio
[2]Butler County MRDD Board, Talawanda City Schools, Oxford, Ohio.
[3]Correspondence should be directed to Mark Brown, Department of Education/Psychology, 201 McGuffey Hall, Miami University, Oxford, Ohio.

a sound from the keyboard), or wooden loft area (i.e., walking up/down the stairs or fishing). Billy's interactional style consisted of making repeated ineffective attempts to join social groups. He was frequently rejected by other children who did not pick up on his nonverbal cues. For example, there were many instances when Billy would stand in proximity to his peers and watch them intently while they were playing at the water table or making "dinner" in housekeeping. The students were often unaware that Billy may have wanted to partake in that activity because Billy could not nonverbally or verbally communicate his interest. At the end of an unsuccessful interaction attempt, he would show discomfort, sometimes through vocalizations or sometimes through physical gestures and/or tears. His inability to contribute to play inhibited others from including him in their social events.

We observed in him a "movement disturbance" that caused him to shake involuntarily (Leary, 1996). When this occurred, he became flustered. Consequently, he often left that particular play area. Billy was also unable to tune out distracting noises of other children who were interacting with one another or with classroom objects during play (Bauman & Kemper, 1994). If another student splashed too much water in the water table or dropped a pot on the floor in housekeeping, for example, Billy's typical reaction was to flee the area.

Adult Direct Interaction

We also noticed that Billy made many attempts to partake in activities, but while he was able to observe his peers, he could not model their behaviors independently. Billy's attempts at social interaction were also not self-sustaining due to his delay in fine/gross motor development. This delay often precluded any possible attempts at independent object manipulation. Consequently, we attempted to be facilitators of his many attempts. When we saw him pick up pencils, we would gently move the pencil in his dominant hand so that he would become less frustrated when he attempted to move his pencil against a piece of paper. When he walked into the housekeeping area, we would ask him if he wanted to "make lunch." The teacher then might say, "Let's get some plates, forks and knives." Sometimes upon hearing our voice, he would respond. Other times he would run away from that area and move to another area. We would then leave him alone. We were uncertain whether his auditory defensiveness, or his social inhibitions were at work there.

Adult Narration

We discovered the importance of "narration" to reinforce appropriate social behaviors. Narration took place when the child was involved in a social activity. In Billy's case, stating out loud what he was attempting to do during explorations, even if for a brief period, provided support as well as information. The need to narrate for Billy, to facilitate his awareness

of cause and effect and to promote the opportunity for increased social interaction intervals is demonstrated in the following ethnographic example.

Context: Billy approaches the water table by himself.
Scenario:

Billy walks over to the water table. He places his hands into the water and picks up an eggbeater. Billy attempts to move the eggbeater through the water. The teacher sees Billy and quietly stands behind him and gently places her hands over his. She guides his hands so that he begins to turn the eggbeater.

Teacher:

"Billy's going around and around and around and around!"

April (i.e., a typical 4-year-old) and Sandy (i.e., a 4-year-old who is partially hydrocephalic) enter the area. April leaves. Sandy picks up an eggbeater and places it into the water. Billy leaves the water table and begins to walk toward the housekeeping area.

While Billy's social behaviors were very developmentally immature, he did choose to model another child with PDD, Adam. As the school year progressed, Billy's admiration for Adam became unyielding. This was demonstrated by Billy's repeated nonverbal attempts to interact with his new friend.

ADAM

Adam is a 4-year-old but looks more like a robust 5-year-old. He has blondish hair and inquisitive brown eyes, frequently lit with his impish grin. His autistic condition (PDD) is at the milder end of the spectrum. In addition, Adam, unlike Bill was able to "speak." "Speaking" as it pertains to this student was not typical communication. However, Adam used "filler statements" that were scripted and often out of context. For example, he would often say to another peer, "Where you going?" even when the other child had made no attempts to leave his present location. In addition, these statements did not grant him interaction with his preschool peers because after a statement was made, Adam could not follow it up with a linking thought (Dawson & Gallpert, 1986). Adam's peers became accustomed to this behavior and generally ignored his verbalizations. What permitted him to interact with his typical peers was his very socially appropriate nonverbal behaviors. He would often parallel play with typical and atypical students for long durations. In one instance, he was observed manipulating a "Batman" toy with Charlie, a typically developing 4-year-old. Both males were not speaking, but their nonverbal manipulation of their Batman toys paralleled one another for the entire play interval. In contrast to Billy, Adam was able to ignore "intrusive" peers, who were not directly involved with the same activity. This behavior on the part of Adam is demonstrated in the following ethnographic example.

Context: Adam and Charlie are at opposite ends of small desk. They both have Batman toys in their hands. Travis, a 4-year-old male with language delays is attempting to elicit their help to chase the "bad guys".

Travis:

(to Adam and Charlie): "Come on, come on, "Two-face" . . . "Two-face" is here in castle (wooden loft), you (Adam) got to talk to him".

Travis:

(throws a "bomb") "Guys, gonna get the bomb?".

Adam moves his Batman toy in the air. Adam makes a noise and lifts his toy in the air. Travis runs back and forth to the side of the table where Adam and Charlie are seated.

Travis attempts to place a cape on Adam who walks back to his original place and then begins to move his toy. Charles looks at his Batman toy and proceeds to move it in the air. Travis then looks at another area of the classroom.

In addition, Adam could ignore external noises with relative ease. The dropping of pots or the crashing of blocks did not seem to bother him nor did they cause him to lose his concentration. Frequently, as he engaged in solitary play or was working alone, we had difficulty knowing how much social cognition Adam was developing. We were reassured and somewhat awed when we observed a remarkable incident where Adam obtained a[n] extra gift toy from a structured incentive program in the building to promote reading. Before anyone could intervene, he sprinted over to the child in our room who is blind and presented him with the extra toy. He had apparently realized Sam could not obtain this coveted reward on his own. Adam, therefore initiated an act of kindness. We observed other acts of kindness, sympathy, and caring from this preschooler throughout the school year.

Adult Facilitation with a Preferred Peer

As Billy continued to struggle, his continuing rejection by his classroom peers was depressing to us. But, every time we tried to help, he would move quickly to another area of the classroom. One morning during an observation where he was being rejected repeatedly, we saw an opportunity to facilitate. Billy always watched Adam and initiated proximity [to] him. On this day, Adam was listening to books on tape, and was seated alone at a table in the corner. Billy walked over and Adam pushed him away. Again, Billy attempted an interaction and Adam became more aggressive. Billy was distressed, red in the face, and tears began to well up in his eyes. Before he retreated, he stood a minute just looking in Adam's direction wondering what to do. The teacher quietly walked up behind Billy and slipped a chair underneath him. Billy accepted this supportive gesture. Billy was pushed quietly into the table, next to Adam, where he sat for a long time, savoring this brief moment with his friend. Adam, unaware of what had just occurred, continued to listen to the tape.

WHAT WE LEARNED

Guidelines for facilitating the social behaviors of these atypical children may be further developed through the following reflective domains. Reflection is a process that may allow teachers to more critically examine the actions demonstrated by a child with autism. Questions that are reflected upon should pertain to contextual behaviors that are demonstrated by the child with autism.

Self-Initiated Play

1. Does the child attempt to pick up an object or toy?

2. Does the child attempt to manipulate an object or toy?

3. Does the child have gross motor skills that would allow him/her to play with an object or toy successfully?

Social Interaction Potential

1. Is the child staring at another peer or group of peers for more than 3 seconds?

2. Can the child play independently with a peer or a group?

3. Can the child tune out external distractions when making an attempt to enter into a group?

4. Can the child tune out external distractions when playing with a peer or group of peers for an extended time period?

Environmental Variables

1. Does the child prefer to play in a particular area?

2. Does the child prefer to play with a particular toy or object?

3. Do certain sounds cause the child to leave an area?

4. Are certain sounds relaxing to the child?

In summary, human interaction is often stressful for children with autism. One must watch for opportunities to facilitate their participation in nonthreatening ways. Adults can assume that even children with autism may wish for some social interaction. Therefore, it is necessary for teacher[s], to observe, persevere, and be creative when attempting to facilitate social interaction among atypical preschoolers and peers.

With Adam, the teacher's narrating of his social actions when he was engaged in parallel play with other classmates or verbally reinforcing his appropriate nonverbal behaviors offered approval and validity to his activity. From Adam's example, we learned that these children may have a social agenda and a great social awareness, as well as a need to be involved affectively in their social group. Our learning from the behavior of these two children may be useful for all teachers who wish to facilitate social development whether they are involved with at-risk, early intervention, typical, or atypical children. They are especially crucial when working with children with autism.

CONCLUSION

In retrospect, we believe it can never be assumed that, because a preschooler is nonverbal, his attempts at social interaction should be interpreted as less meaningful. Autistic children's partial attempts at social initiations serve the purpose of establishing and maintaining possible social interactions within the context of peer-relevant group events. Even if their interactions are minimum or appear nonproductive, their attempts to socialize with other children may facilitate their ability to communicate and their ability to be more successful in modeling the social and/or play behaviors demonstrated by other typical and atypical classmates.

The teacher's role, in the context of child-directed socialization, should be one of facilitation, so that preschoolers with autism can partake of the same activities as their typical peers at whatever their ability level. Billy's mother frequently expressed the concern that he needed a friend. It is interesting that he chose to admire another child (i.e., Adam), who, if the two of them could communicate, would be an understanding and empathetic companion.

In conclusion, teachers must challenge both typical and atypical preschoolers through the facilitation and narration of their many social interaction initiations and responses. Teachers must also be prepared for the child with autism to sometimes abandon an activity when an adult's interaction is perceived as intrusive. Therefore, the teacher may have to be creative when entering into the space of an autistic child. Teachers and teacher assistants have to carefully observe and document antecedent behaviors that may be linked to a child's decision to flee or stay. Finally, teachers should collaborate on possible alternative interventions when the child flees, as well as determining interventions that might sustain a child's behavior over an increased time interval. These interventions may be narrated in the presence of other children. Over time, typical peers may begin to model the teacher's discourse and/or behavior in an attempt to create more interactions with their atypical peer as well.

ACKNOWLEDGMENTS

This research was funded by a mini-grant through Miami University's School of Education Allied Professions (SEAP). Dr. Randy Flora is the director of the Institute for Educational Renewal at Miami University (Room 203 McGuffey). He can be contacted at 513–529–6926.

RESOURCES

For more information concerning children and youth with autism, please contact the following organizations.

Autism Society of America
    8601 Georgia Avenue
    Suite 503
    Silver Springs, MD 20910
Council for Exceptional Children
    1920 Association Drive
    Reston, VA 22091–1589
National Registry for Autism and Tourett's Syndrome
    Autism Training Center
    Marshall University
    Old Main, Room 316
    Huntington, WV 25755–2430
National Information Center for Handicapped Children and Youth
    1355 Wilson Boulevard
    Rosslyn, VA 22209
Special Education Parents Alliance
    Suite K–164
    305 22nd Street
    Glen Ellyn, IL 60137

REFERENCES

Bauman, M. L., & Kemper, T. L. (1994). *The neurobiology of autism.* Baltimore: The Johns Hopkins University Press.

Dahlgren, S. O., & Gillberg, C. (1989). Symptoms in the first two years of life: A preliminary population study of infantile autism. *European Archives of Psychiatric and Neurological Science, 283,* 169–174.

Dawson, G., & Gallpert, L. (1986). A developmental model for facilitating the social behaviors of autistic children. In E. Schopler & G. Mesibov (Eds.), *Social behavior in autism.* New York: Plenum Press.

Keogel, R. L., & Kern-Keogel, L. (1994). *Autism.* Baltimore: Paul H. Brooks.

Leary, M. R., & Hill, D. A. (1996). Moving on: Autism and movement disturbance. *Mental Retardation, 34*(1), 39–53.

Prizant, B. M., & Wetherby, A. M. (1988). Providing services to children with autism (ages 0 to 2 years) and their families. *Topics in Language Disorders, 9,* 1–23.

GETTING THE STUDENT WITH HEAD INJURIES BACK IN SCHOOL:

Strategies for the Classroom

Strategies for successfully returning students with head injuries to school

By Mary Steensma

In 1979, when he was 12 years old, Jamie was hit by a car while riding his bike. In the seconds it took for the car to hit his bike and his head to hit the pavement, Jamie went from being a gifted sixth-grade boy to being a student with head injuries in the special education system. There were no programs to help him, and no support groups for parents. The schools had no information or guidance for designing programs to meet Jamie's needs.

In 1989, when he was 12, Matt was hit by a car while riding his bike. He too went from being a gifted sixth-grade boy to being a head injured student in the special education system. But here Matt's story differs from Jamie's. In December 1989, after weeks of outpatient therapy and 3 months in a transitional educational program, he returned to his class in school. Matt's head injury did change his life: Things are not the way they used to be for Matt or his family. But in his case, the school and his parents had information and assistance, and Matt's transition back to school was more successful than Jamie's.

In a review of educational studies of children with head injuries, Telzrow (1987) noted that these children do not make a good educational adjustment. She cited studies showing that the majority of head injured students (56%) in special education classes are in programs for students with physical handicaps and mild to profound levels of retardation (Brink, Garrett, Hale, Woo-Sam, & Nickle, 1970). Students whose brain injuries have resulted in significant character change and difficult behavior have often been placed in behavior disorder classrooms. The less severely brain injured students are often placed in learning disability or resource rooms.

But students who suffer head trauma differ from students with emotional disturbance, learning disabilities, or mental retardation in one important way: Their disabilities are acquired suddenly and result from neurological damage to specific areas of the brain. The head injured student may retain skills and information, and IQ scores may return to within the normal range (Chadwick, Rutter, Brown, Schaffer, & Traub, 1981).

When students are released from the hospital or in-patient facility, they should be medically recovered from the injury, but they are rarely ready to return to school—and the school is rarely ready to receive them. The students still have a variety of cognitive and emotional problems that affect their educational adjustment, and typically these problems are not addressed in reintegrating them to their school. Optimally, these deficits should be addressed during a transition period of several months in a setting with a low teacher/student ratio and minimal distractions. A classroom with a 1:3 ratio and a maximum class size of six is preferable to a classroom with a ratio of 1:3 and a maximum of 12 students.

The students who have had recent head injuries often are not aware of how the injury has affected their behavior and ability to do schoolwork. Like people who have experienced the death of someone close, they may go through the stages of grief—denial, anger, bargaining, and depression. Without an effective transition program to help the students become aware of their new deficits, they may build up a wall of denial and defensive behaviors to cope with the effects of the accident. This may become as debilitating as the injury itself.

From *Intervention in School and Clinic*, March 1992, pp. 207–210. © 1992 by PRO-ED, Inc. Reprinted by permission.

Transition Program Structure

The primary goal of a transitional program is to place students back in their school districts in programs that best meet their current needs. To be successful, the transitional program should begin immediately after primary rehabilitation needs have been met. The students are given neuropsychological evaluations to isolate specific cognitive and neurobehavioral problems. During the initial months, all classroom activities should take place in a self-contained classroom with a high degree of control and a low staff-student ratio. Telzrow (1987) emphasizes the importance of this, as well as McCabe and Green's (1987) study of three severely brain injured adolescents. The adolescents showed a need for consistent, authoritative handling in a controlled structure. Without this, they exhibited a "fight or flight" reaction. Program goals in the first few months are to increase the students' awareness of how the injury has affected them, to develop coping strategies, and to build tolerance for classroom activities.

When school reintegration begins, the program enters a new phase. Teacher and staff members receive in-service training on head trauma and the special needs of the students as outlined in the Individualized Education Plan developed by the transition classroom teacher. The students are reintegrated slowly to build tolerance for larger classes, room transitions, and the variety of people with whom they must interact.

Classroom Strategies

Head injured students need to relearn how to learn. Although many skills are preserved and students' IQs may be within the normal range, the ability to draw on their knowledge and skills is impaired. Because the students do not respond well to traditional classroom strategies, teacher and students often become angry and frustrated. Six common deficits that students exhibit—and some classroom strategies for working around them—are discussed in the following paragraphs.

Problem: Structure

Head injured students have lost some of the ability to organize their work and environment. The impact on their school work is obvious in the inability to take notes or write an essay with a logical structure. But the students may also be unable to keep track of their books and assignments or to organize their morning routines. These problems are less obvious signs of an inability to organize and may be attributed instead to carelessness or resistance to school.

Strategy. The teacher must build the structure around the students and teach compensatory techniques. For example: Keep one set of books at school and one

> *"Without an effective transition program to help the students become aware of their new deficits, they may build up a wall of denial and defensive behaviors to cope with the effects of the accident. This may become as debilitating as the injury itself."*

at home to eliminate the problem of forgotten books. To reduce confusion and lost notebooks, use a five-subject notebook instead of five separate notebooks. Schedule a resource room or study hall at the end of the day to allow the students to "check in" with a staff member and make sure all assignments are recorded and understood.

Problem: Abstraction

Head injured students find it difficult to summarize, draw conclusions, and differentiate fact from opinion. This often makes essay questions on tests or assignments and higher level math concepts quite difficult.

Strategy. Initially, essay questions and reports must be avoided as methods of testing students' knowledge in content area subjects, since students are unable to effectively retrieve information using this approach. Information must be kept concrete and learned gradually in a structured manner. New information is broken down into smaller units and reinforced in writing. Progress takes time and repetition. Finding the main idea or summarizing a story must be taught with specific steps to follow, one at a time. These steps should be presented in writing and kept in the students' notebooks.

Problem: Attention and Concentration

Cognitive and physical fatigue are important factors affecting students' ability to make the transition back into school. Head injured students tire quickly and may be physically unable to sustain concentration through a full day at school and additional activities or studying at night.

Cognitively, students rapidly reach a "saturation" level where they simply stop processing information. Like a water glass that begins overflowing when you reach the top, head injured students may simply stop hearing the instructions given to them halfway through a 45-minute class period.

In addition to being unable to sustain attention and concentration, head injured students are very sensitive to distraction. Asking the students to read or take a test in a regular classroom of 12 to 20 students is equivalent to trying to compute your taxes at a Rolling Stones concert.

Strategy. Lessons initially are kept to 15 or 20 minutes and are increased gradually. Even after the student's tolerance has been increased to 30 to 40 minutes in a transitional classroom, he or she will suffer some cognitive and physical fatigue when placed back in regular classes at school. This can be compensated for by alternating content area subjects such as History and English with time spent in the resource room, lunch, gym, and so forth. This allows time for the students to "down load" information from one class before beginning another. Since students will begin to fatigue as the day goes on, classes that allow more flexibility should be scheduled for the later periods in school. In addition to alternating the content area subjects with catch-up periods and making sure that the content area subjects are not scheduled for final periods, the student's course load must be reduced to only those classes required for graduation.

Problem: Transition

For head injured students, transitions always seem to create problems. The primary focus is usually on the students' difficulties with physical transitions—from home to school, or from class to class. Equally difficult are the students' mental transitions within a specific subject, and from one format to another. For example, students may have difficulty transferring math problems from the book to paper, or switching from fraction problems to decimals while completing a worksheet.

Strategy. The physical transition of head injured students back into school must be thought of as a desensitization process. It must be taken step by step with a safety net positioned underneath.

For example: Students are ready to leave the transitional classroom and join a regular ninth-grade class.

Step 1: They visit the first class they will join, walking through the route to the class and bathrooms. This visit is kept simple and covers only the essentials. Lockers, homerooms, and other important places are introduced gradually, one at a time.

Step 2: Students are met at their bus by someone they know and are escorted to class. Initially there are no changes from class to class.

Step 3: Class changes are practiced, walked through, and added one at a time. Class changes are made with someone from the class, if possible.

Throughout the desensitization process, students continue to attend the self-contained transitional classroom. The hours in this classroom are reduced gradually as students are reintroduced to their regular classes. This continued contact with the self-contained classroom acts as a safety net to handle any problems that may occur during the transition.

Transitions within subject areas, or from one subject to the next, can be handled for head injured students much as teachers handle students with learning disabilities. Transitions on a worksheet page are reduced and clearly delineated. Pages from books or workbooks can be

copied so the students do not need to make the transition from book to paper. If possible, outlines in content area subjects should be handed out on worksheets—not placed on the board to be copied by students.

Problem: Writing

Neurological damage may cause partial paralysis in head injured students that affects the physical ability to write. It may also affect students' ability to organize or express thoughts. Students' writing speed often is reduced as well. Particularly for junior high or high school students, this makes re-entry difficult because so much of the work involves taking notes, writing reports, and answering written homework questions.

Strategies. For lectures and instructions that must be recorded, a micro-cassette recorder is effective. Students can carry it to all classes and record information inconspicuously, and the information can then be played back and repeated at the students' speed.

Often, writing must be retaught as a skill in a very structured fashion. The steps of brainstorming, organizing information, constructing topic sentences, supplying details, and summarizing must be set out in writing for reference each time students write.

As mentioned previously, teachers should hand out preprinted lecture notes, assignments, and other information given orally. Students with handwriting problems may be able to learn to use a computer effectively for outlining and word processing and should be allowed to use the computer as a compensatory strategy.

Problem: Processing Speed

Most students who have had a head injury process information more slowly. This means the students' auditory, visual, or reaction speed may be slower than before the accident. How the students process information depends on the seriousness and site of the head injury. The slowed processing speed may affect the students' ability to read assignments, listen to directions, and take notes.

Strategies. All textbooks students use in school also should be recorded on tape. This allows students to listen to the text while following it in the book.

All standard junior high and high school textbooks are available on tape through Recording for the Blind for blind, physically, and perceptually handicapped students. Recording for the Blind headquarters are located at 20 Roszel Road, Princeton, NJ 08540. This service can be reached toll free outside New Jersey by calling 1–800/221–4792. With the special-format tapes used by Recording for the Blind, students can control the playback speed.

Testing procedures must be modified so that time limits are eliminated or extended.

Conclusion

Head injured students can return to school successfully. However, it takes more time, intervention, and money than the average special education student gets. Students with head injury require a highly structured, consistent program that changes as their needs change. School staff members must understand and be trained to deal with the cognitive and psychological changes caused by the head trauma and the grieving process that follows. Students are atypical in their performance and needs, and they cannot be judged by standard test data. If the school is able to meet students' needs in the early stages of their re-entry, their chances for a successful re-entry are good. This in turn will reduce their special education needs as they continue in school.

Mary Steensma, MA, is a teacher and consultant who helps students with head injuries re-enter regular classrooms. Address: Mary Steensma, 211 Mildorf St., Rochester, NY 14609.

References

Brink, J.D., Garrett, A.L., Hale, W.R., Woo-Sam, J., & Nickle, V.L. (1970). Recovery of motor and intellectual function in children sustaining severe head injuries. *Developmental Medicine and Child Neurology, 12,* 565–571.
Chadwick, O., Rutter, M., Brown, G., Shaffer, D., & Traub, B. (1981). A prospective study of children with head injuries: II. Cognitive sequelae. *Psychological Medicine, 11,* 49–61.
McCabe, R.J.R., & Green, P. (1987). Rehabilitating severely head-injured adolescents: Three case reports. *Journal of Child Psychology, 28,* 111–125.
Telzrow, C.F. (1987, November). Management of academic and educational problems in head injuries. *Journal of Learning Disabilities, 20,* 536–545.

Unit 6

Key Points to Consider

❖ How can students with emotional and behavioral disorders learn to work together with peers and assist each other in groups? How can teachers facilitate group development?

❖ What can teachers do to prevent aggressive behavior in students with emotional and behavioral disorders?

❖ What should adults be aware of to defuse confrontational scenes in the classroom? How can a classroom environment be made more conducive to education?

 **Links** | **www.dushkin.com/online/**

These sites are annotated on pages 4 and 5.

The 1990s have given rise to a strange and tragically stilted way for children with emotional and behavioral disturbances to vent their frustrations. They take a weapon to school and engage in a shooting spree. While the actual incidence of school shootings is not large, many children with distressed lives have threatened to adopt copy-cat behaviors. What would make a young person (frequently on the cusp of puberty) think about committing such a grotesquely absurd act? An easy, often cited reason is that they are barraged with images of violence on the news, in music, on videos, on TV programs, and in movies. It is too facile: The barrage is aimed at everyone, yet only a few decide that they want to become violent and harm others. Aggressive, acting-out children tend to come from homes where they see *real* violence, anger, and insults. They often feel disconnected, rejected, and afraid. They do not know how to communicate their distress. They may appear narcissistic, even as they seek attention in negative, hurtful ways. They usually have fairly easy access to weapons, alcohol, and other substances of abuse.

The identification and assessment of students with emotional and behavioral disturbances is controversial. Labels are discouraged because of their effects on self-concept and self-esteem. A student can benefit more from an individualized profile of his or her strengths, aptitudes, and achievements, plus a characterization of the dimensions of behavior in which he or she has specific needs. This profile, on the individualized education plan (IEP), needs to be updated frequently as progress is made, and/or as new needs arise.

The Individuals with Disabilities Act (IDEA) uses the diagnosis of serious emotional disturbance as a category into which students are placed for educational and related services. The numbers of students identified as falling into this category help determine a state's eligibility for federal funding of special education each year. This categorization for statistical purposes does not necessitate the severity, or seriousness, of the emotional or behavioral disorder. This category encompasses about 9 percent of the students served by special education in the United States each year.

The 1994 revision of the *Diagnostic and Statistical Manual of Mental Disorders* (4th edition) uses the diagnosis of behavioral disorders as a category into which students are placed for identification and assessment purposes. This section is subsumed under the category of disorders usually first diagnosed in infancy, childhood, or adolescence. Among the DSM-IV disorders of childhood not reviewed elsewhere are disruptive behaviors, eating disorders, tic disorders, elimination disorders, separation anxiety disorders, and reactive attachment disorders.

For educational purposes, children with behavior disorders are usually divided into two main behavioral classifications: (1) withdrawn, shy, or anxious behaviors; and (2) aggressive, acting-out behaviors. The debate about what constitutes a behavior disorder, or an emotional disturbance, has not been fully resolved. In 1990, the U.S. Department of Education elected to remove autism from its list of emotionally disturbed behaviors and gave it a separate classification under IDEA.

An alliance of educators and psychologists then proposed that IDEA simply remove the term "serious emotional disturbances" and instead focus on behaviors that adversely affect educational performance. Conduct usually considered a sign of emotional disturbance, such as anxiety, depression, or failure of attachment, can be seen as behaviorally disordered if it interferes with academic, social, vocational, and personal accomplishment. So, also, can conduct, eating, tic, or elimination disorders, and any other responses outside the range of "acceptable" for school or other settings. Such a focus on behavior can link individualized educational program (IEP) curriculum activities to children's behavioral response styles.

Should children with chronic and severe behavior disorders, especially those that interfere with the education processes in the regular classroom, be allowed to enroll in inclusive education programs? IDEA ruled yes, both in its original form and in amendments written more recently. Although teachers, other pupils, and school staff may be greatly inconvenienced by the presence of one or more behaviorally disordered students in every classroom, the law is clear. The school must "show cause" if a child with disruptive behavior is to be moved from the regular classroom to a more restrictive environment.

Inclusive education does not translate into acceptance of disordered behaviors in the regular education classroom. Two rules of thumb for the behavior of all children, however abled or disabled, are that they conform to minimum standards of acceptable conduct and that disruptive behaviors be subject to fair and consistent disciplinary action.

The first article in this section is concerned with planning for an entire classroom of students that includes some who are uncooperative or disruptive. Group functioning is viewed through developmental stages. The authors explain the nature of group development and give stage levels. By understanding the level at which a group is behaving, teachers can use instructional and management techniques that not only correspond to current behavior but also encourage group growth and development toward the highest level of behavior possible.

The proposition of the second article of this unit on emotional and behavioral disturbances is that aggressive behavior can be prevented in a classroom setting. The authors review several things that teachers can do to intervene before verbal, nonverbal, or physical injurious behaviors occur. They describe both the characteristics of therapeutic teachers and the elements of a positive classroom climate.

The last unit essay presents defusing strategies to avoid confrontations between students with emotional/behavioral disorders and other children, youth, or adults who are in tense situations. The authors encourage readers to remember that appropriate responses can alter situations. Several steps are given that can help students control their own behavior. Teachers can learn to create an environment more conducive to education.

GROUP DEVELOPMENT FOR STUDENTS WITH EMOTIONAL/BEHAVIORAL DISORDERS

■

One of the greatest challenges facing teachers of students with emotional/behavioral disorders is the management of instructional activities with an entire classroom of students, many (or all) of whom are uncooperative or disruptive. A typical comment heard from such a teacher is, "In a one-to-one situation, I can manage both behavior and academics without any serious problems. In a classroom full of children, I can't get through a lesson without interruption."

■

Sylvia Rockwell
Eleanor Guetzloe

Planning for groups is actually not very different from planning for individuals, particularly individuals with multiple problems. The factors to be considered, however, are more complex because of the *interaction of the educational, behavioral, cultural, biophysical, and social characteristics of the various individuals within the group* and the demands of the setting. The group dynamics in a classroom for students with emotional/behavioral disorders will be directly affected by (a) the number of students in the group, (b) the severity of their individual problems, and (c) their social and academic compatibility.

Students with emotional/behavioral disorders exhibit a number of social impairments that interfere with group functioning, including the difficulty in accepting responsibility for their own behavior and the inability to establish and nurture appropriate relationships with others. *Regardless of the chronological ages or intellectual abilities of the individual students in a group, the group itself will exhibit a certain "developmental stage."* Understanding the nature of group development, being aware of the level at which a group may be functioning, and using instructional and management techniques that correspond to the developmental stage of the group itself can enable teachers to move the entire group to the highest "stage" possible.

Selman (1981) has described specific assimilative (overtly controlling) and accommodative (avoiding or appeasing) behaviors that become evident as a normal child develops an interpersonal orientation. Figure 1 shows examples of behaviors typical of each age range. Progression from one level of interpersonal orientation to

From *Teaching Exceptional Children*, September/October 1996, pp. 38–43. © 1996 by The Council for Exceptional Children. Reprinted by permission.

the next signals growth of individuals as well as the group, despite the often disturbing nature of the behaviors exhibited. For example, it is often difficult to see how lying and trickery may actually be improvements over tantrums and running away. An understanding of this "normal" progression should be reassuring to the teacher, who might view the emerging behaviors as a failure of the behavior management system when they are actually signs of progress.

Maslow (1962) has described a hierarchy of basic human needs, ranging from physiological needs to the need for self-actualization. According to Maslow, a human being must satisfy one level of need before becoming motivated to attend to the next. In many ways, the stages of group development correspond to the levels of Maslow's hierarchy, as well as the developmental stages suggested by Erikson (1963). (See Figure 2.)

During Stage 2, appropriate work by students in groups of two will lead to assigning the students to groups of four.

STAGE 1

When students with emotional/behavioral disorders begin the school year, the group is usually at Stage 1. Even if the same group had attained a higher level during the previous school year, they seem to revert to Stage 1 with the addition of new classmates or a new adult (e.g., a classroom instructional aide). Stage 1 issues include the satisfaction of physiological needs and the establishment of a sense of safety and trust.

Stage 1 group behavior is characterized by frequent tantrums, low frustration tolerance, fighting, power struggles that center around limit setting, and both verbal and physical aggression. Unless the individuals in the group feel safe and establish a sense of trust in the teacher, the group will not be able to move beyond Stage 1 functioning.

PHYSIOLOGICAL NEEDS

Teachers can address the most basic level of need—the physiological—by providing physical comfort, food, drink, adequate light and temperature control, and even clothing, if necessary. Medical care and other out-of-school needs can be provided, if not directly within the school program, through referrals to social workers and other individuals and agencies in the community.

NEED FOR SAFETY AND TRUST

How does the teacher establish the sense of safety and trust? Teachers can facilitate feelings of security in the following ways:

- Establishing well-defined, consistently executed behavior management expectations and consequences.

- Being proactive in terms of scheduling, room arrangement, and academic planning.
- Developing personal abilities to remain calm, controlled, and predictable in the face of anger and outbursts.

Figure 3 shows a variety of classroom management strategies suitable for each stage of group development.

Figure 1

Interpersonal Orientation

Assimilative	*Accommodative*
Level 0 (ages 2 to 3)	
Screaming	Fear
Tantrums	Running away
Level I (ages 4 to 6)	
Bullying, bossing, threats, verbal abuse	Acting victimized
Denial, distortion, lying	Lack of assertiveness
One-way fairness	Power-oriented obedience
Level II (ages 7 to 11)	
Pitting peers against one another	Being a follower
Trickery	Confrontation
Seeking alliances	Asking for help
Friendly persuasion	Reasoning

Level III (ages 12 to 18)
Group orientation
Expectation of consistency in self and others
Anticipation of others' reactions
Use of humor and perspective as coping mechanisms

Figure 2

Basic Needs and Corresponding Stages of Affective and Cognitive Development

Affective Stages (Krathwohl et al., 1956)	Basic Needs (Maslow, 1962)	Cognitive Stages (Bloom et al., 1956)
	Level I	
Receiving: to be aware of	Physiological	Knowledge: to know about
	Level II	
Responding: to act out of	Safety and security	Comprehension: to understand
	Level III	
Valuing: To prefer	Belonging, love, socialization	Application: to put to use
	Level IV	
Organization: to establish a value system	Self-respect Respect of others	Analysis: to break into parts Synthesis: to create
	Level V	
Characterization: to live by one's beliefs	Self-actualization	Evaluation: to judge for a purpose

A positive indication of the group's progress (and the teacher's predictability) is that the students will know what the teacher's response will be before it occurs (e.g., a typical student comment might be, "Just shut up! I know, I know—five minutes in cool-off!").

The teacher's role at Stage 1 is that of a "benevolent dictator." Rules (primarily established by the teacher) must be calmly, consistently, fairly, and firmly enforced. *No* means *no*. *Yes* means *yes*. Consequences for appropriate and inappropriate behaviors are dealt with in a matter-of-fact manner. Each member of the group has equal responsibility in making his or her choices for behavior. As a choice is made, each member of the group has equal access to corresponding predetermined consequences, whether positive or aversive. Teachers must be especially sensitive to the students' fear of favoritism, their need for protection from real or perceived dangers, and their distrust of adults.

BEGINNINGS OF "BELONGING"

Teaching strategies that facilitate group development during Stage 1 include planning and implementing academic and affective activities that bring students from a "Me" to a "We" orientation. Games that allow students to participate without interacting with each other (e.g., Bingo) are appropriate social activities for Stage 1.

An appropriate academic activity would be a social studies lesson during which each student constructs two "milk box" buildings (a home and a business) for inclusion in a "town" assembled on a large piece of cardboard (so it can be moved out of "destruction range" when necessary). The students place their buildings in the town one at a time. The "town" concept can be expanded to provide activities for the entire school year, but it is especially appropriate at Stage 1.

Other group activities that would promote movement from "Me" to "We," and that would not overstimulate a group that is not developmentally ready for much student-to-student interaction, would be the production of a class book or newspaper, the construction of a class bulletin board, or a cooking activity that requires each student to do one part. For example, preparing a fruit salad is a great activity for a Stage 1 group. Each student can dice a piece of fruit with a plastic knife; the fruit can be combined, tossed, and stirred by the teacher; and the entire group can enjoy something that each helped to make.

Other measures a teacher can employ at Stage 1 have been discussed by Bryngelson (1992), Hobbs (1982), Rockwell (1993, 1995), and others. All these authors advocate the development of an integrated, thematic approach that incorporates students' ideas and interests. Figure 4 shows group activities suitable for each stage, with approximate time periods a group spends in each stage and the teacher's role.

STAGE 2

Stage 2 begins when most of the group (e.g., 7 students out of 10) is responding appropriately most of the time to the classroom management plan. A shift of thinking becomes evident in group interactions from "It's me against the world" to "It's us against the world." Major acts of physical aggression rarely occur during Stage 2, and members of the group begin to offer assistance to each other spontaneously.

NEED FOR BELONGING AND SOCIALIZATION

In terms of Maslow's hierarchy (see middle column of Figure 2), the group has moved to the level of need related to belonging or affiliation. Sharing and working in groups of two now become possible; but tattling, teasing, and other behaviors typical of normal 4- and 5-year-old youngsters begin to emerge (again, regardless of the actual chronological ages of the students).

As Figure 4 shows, the teacher's role at Stage 2 shifts from "benevolent dictator" to "director." Verbal intimidation within the group may increase as the group begins to settle on one or more peer leaders. Students now need to learn effective communication skills, and teachers must provide time in the schedule for practicing those skills—not only during a "social skills period," but also as opportunities arise during other lessons. For example, Canfield (1986) suggested teaching students to use "I" statements. Goldstein's (1988) *Prepare Curriculum* provides a comprehensive program of instruction in social skills, anger reduction, and moral reasoning. These and other commercially available social skills curricula are appropriate for use at this stage.

At Stage 2, teachers can successfully teach cooperative learning activities (Johnson & Johnson, 1987; Slavin,

may assign them to groups of four. Groups of three should be avoided, because two students may join forces to exclude or torment the other. Card games, board games, dot-to-dot tasks, construction projects, and cooking activities are appropriate activities for Stage 2. Students can also be taught to assist one another in peer tutoring sessions, using flash cards with spelling words, reading words, or math facts.

STAGE 3

As the group moves toward Stage 3 functioning, fewer and fewer conflicts occur. Students become increasingly able to stay calm enough to go through problem-solving steps and will often initiate the process on their own. Students who are not as advanced as the majority of the group are usually either assisted or tolerated, and one or two disgruntled students will not sabotage the whole group. The teacher's role now shifts from "director" to "arbitrator" as students take increasing responsibility for their own choices.

NEED FOR SELF-RESPECT AND RESPECT FOR OTHERS

Peer confrontation strategies, as suggested by Salend, Jantzen, and Giek (1992) are appropriate for Stage 3. The teacher describes the target behavior for each student. Peers provide feedback and support for one another. During the process, the teacher rewards students for encouraging others, as well as for exhibiting the desired target behaviors.

Stage 3 functioning is characterized by social behaviors typical of youngsters in the intermediate grades (roughly ages 8–10).The teacher must still be present, alert, aware, and actively involved in planning and implementing academic and social activities. The teacher, however, can now provide opportunities for students to settle some of their differences without jumping in to rescue the students.

Because students in special education settings are monitored more closely than are other students, they often have fewer opportunities to practice communication and conflict resolution skills on their own. Students with emotional/behavioral disorders, in particular, often become so isolated and insulated by well-meaning adults that they fail to benefit from the "normal" conflicts their peers experience. Expecting too little of these students can do as much damage as expecting too

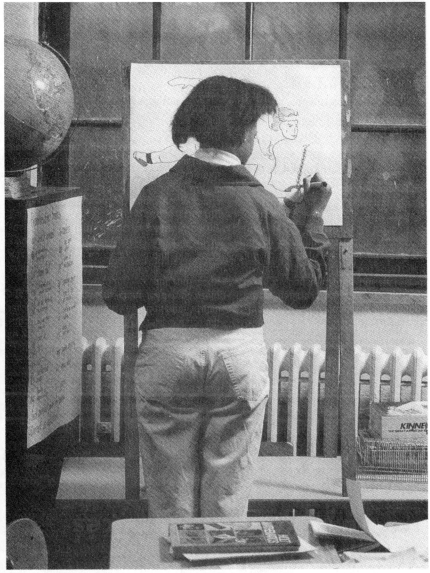

During Stage 1, individual student contributions are combined into a group effort.

1990). Groups of two can now work together, but the group is not yet ready to function as a whole. To guard against overstimulation, the teacher must constantly monitor the schedule and the work of the student dyads during cooperative learning activities. The group is also now ready to learn problem-solving and group decision-making techniques, with the teacher directing the discussions. A major focus at this stage is "making appropriate choices."

The teacher may begin to include the group in both academic and behavioral goal-setting and planning of activities. The group is now allowed to assist in refinement of preestablished rules and consequences. For example, a rule in a class for students with emotional/behavioral disorders was that all reward activities must be earned;

but as soon as the criteria for earning the rewards were set, the students became oppositional. They stated that they did not want the teacher to "tell them" the criteria or to issue reminders. A classroom meeting (Glasser, 1985) was held for purposes of determining both the criteria and the process for communicating those criteria. The group decided that the teacher should type the criteria, place them in an envelope, and leave the envelope on the counter (without talking). The students would accept responsibility for reading the criteria and signing the sheet if they agreed to participate. This procedure proved to be effective.

BEGINNINGS OF RESPECT

As students become able to work productively in groups of two, the teacher

Figure 3

Management Strategies for Each Stage of Group Development

Stage 1

Behavior management	Behavior modification
Academic instruction	Precision teaching Technology-assisted programmed instruction
Affective Instruction	Relaxation Enhancement of self-esteem
Enrichment	Activities that require individual efforts to be combined into a whole group effort or product such as Bingo, Jeopardy, class anthology of creative writing, class newspaper, class photograph album, simple cooking activities (fruit salad), craft activities (town), seasonal bulletin boards

Stage 2

Behavior management	Redl's Life-Space Interview Cognitive behavioral strategies
Academic instruction	Prerequisite skills for cooperative learning Peer tutoring Application of content knowledge
Affective instruction	Social skills Problem-solving

Stage 3

Behavior management	Cooperative discipline
Academic instruction	Cooperative learning
Affective instruction	Transfer of social skills
Enrichment	Any age-appropriate activity

much. Valuable learning experiences can be missed.

Students without disabilities normally begin to join official organizations as well as informal, loosely defined "clubs," during the intermediate grades. Sports, popular music, clothing styles, and collecting things become important topics of interest to a group at Stage 3.

NEED FOR SELF-ACTUALIZATION

The need for recognition, the next level of need on Maslow's hierarchy, combined with the feeling of belonging that was established during Stage 2,

launches individuals toward new levels of self-esteem during Stage 3. Activities related specifically to the further development of self-understanding, self-esteem, and self-management are particularly appropriate at this stage.

At Stage 3, the group is able to work together in the selection and attainment of both academic and social goals, and individuals within the group should be ready to begin the transition to a less restrictive environment. The teacher will allow students to initiate and manage group projects. It should be noted, however, that the group may be capable of carrying out these activities with their own teacher but still be unable to transfer these behaviors to other settings and with other people.

Group activities at Stage 3 could include dramatics, planting a garden, constructing an aerobic obstacle course for the school, publishing a newspaper, tape-recording songs to be played over the school intercom, or preparing a luncheon for invited guests. A major focus at Stage 3 should be on a cooperative and supportive environment—helping others, sharing, and working for the good of the entire class, the school, and the community.

NEEDED: AWARENESS, SENSITIVITY, AND ALERTNESS

Facilitating group development through the three stages described here requires both an awareness of emerging group growth and the ability to use management and instructional strategies that are sensitive to basic needs. The teacher must be alert to changes in group functioning, willing and able to shift from one role to the next, and capable of making the necessary adjustments in the classroom to match the dynamics of the group when it is ready to move to a higher level.

REFERENCES

Bloom, B., Engelhart, M. D., Frost, E. J., Hill, W. H., & Krathwohl, D. R. (1956). *Taxonomy of educational objectives. Handbook 1: Cognitive domain.* New York: David McKay.

Bryngelson, J. (1992). *Reaching and teaching troubled kids: The orchestrated classroom.* [Available from Self-Esteem Associates, 1144 Henry Road, Billings, MT 59102].

Canfield, J. (1986). *Self-esteem in the classroom.* Culver City, CA: Canfield/Self-Esteem Seminars.

Erikson, E. (1963). *Childhood and society* (2nd ed). New York: Norton.

Glasser, W. (1985). *Control theory in the classroom.* New York: Harper & Row.

Goldstein, A. (1988). *The prepare curriculum.* Champaign, IL: Research Press.

Hobbs, N. (1982). *The troubled and troubling child.* San Francisco: Jossey-Bass.

Johnson, D. W., & Johnson, R. T. (1987). *Learning together and alone: Cooperative, competitive, and individualistic learning.* Englewood Cliffs, NJ: Prentice-Hall.

Krathwohl, D. R., Bloom, B. S., & Masia, B. B. (1956). *Taxonomy of educational objectives. Handbook II: Affective domain.* New York: David McKay.

Maslow, A. (1962). *Toward a psychology of being.* Princeton, NJ: D. Van Nostrand.

Rockwell, S. (1993). *Tough to reach: Tough to teach.* Reston, VA: The Council for Exceptional Children. (ERIC Document Reproduction Service No. ED 355 672)

Rockwell, S. (1995). *Back off, cool down, try again.* Reston, VA: The Council for Exceptional Children.

Salend, S. J., Jantzen, N. R., & Giek, K. (1992). Using a peer confrontation system in a group setting. *Behavioral Disorders, 17*(3), 211–218.

Selman, R. L. (1981). The development of interpersonal competence: The role of understanding in conduct. *Developmental Review, 1,* 419.

Slavin, R. E. (1990). *Cooperative learning: Theory, research, and practice.* Englewood Cliffs, NJ: Prentice Hall.

Sylvia Rockwell *(CEC Chapter #593), Doctoral Student, University of South Florida at St. Petersburg.*
Eleanor Guetzloe *(CEC Chapter #176), Professor, Department of Special Education, University of South Florida at St. Petersburg.*

Address correspondence to Sylvia Rockwell, 3819 Lake Shore Drive, Palm Harbor, FL 34684 (e-mail: ccbd1@aol.com).

Figure 4

Approximate Time Period Required for Each Stage

Stage 1 4 to 12 weeks	*Stage 2* 4 to 18 weeks	*Stage 3* Ongoing to Transition

Teacher's Role at Each Stage

"Benevolent Dictator"	**"Director"**	**"Arbitrator"**
1. Remain calm, fair, and consistent.	1. Provide choices in limited situations.	1. Provide less external control.
2. Set limits.	2. Establish problem-solving procedures.	2. Remain aware and available.
3. Promote safety and trust.	3. Teach students to make choices and accept majority rule.	3. Open student choices to group discussions.
4. Use ecological and behavioral interventions.	4. Model problem-solving steps.	4. Allow students to initiate and manage projects.
	5. Promote partnership activities.	

Group Activities

Photograph album.	Interviews taped on audio or video equipment.	Plays.
Anthology of stories, poems, and artwork.	Simple cooking activities.	Gardens.
Model town, Indian village or other construction project.	Peer tutoring.	Construction of aerobic obstacle course.
A paper chain that represents each individual's contribution to a group effort, through links added for star days, books read, or some other group goal.	Games requiring two people, such as Checkers or connect-the-dots.	Newspaper publishing.
	Whole group projects that can be broken down into a puppet show with scriptwriters, stage construction, etc.	Luncheon for invited guests.

DISCIPLINE Behavior Intervention

How to Prevent
Aggressive
Behavior

Kerri was in the office for the 14th time this year—13 times for harassing other girls and the 14th for pushing the teacher.

● ●

When Maury has angry outbursts and starts pushing desks over, the teacher takes the whole rest of the class out of the room and sends for help.

● ●

When Jon "loses it," he throws chairs and smashes windows. All near him scatter in terror, including the teachers. This time the police came.

Brian J. Abrams
●
Amiel Segal

It's an understatement to say that students like Jon, Kerri, and Maury have poor self-control and low frustration, or that they display maladaptive behaviors. These students and others with emotional and behavioral disorders are often disruptive to the point of threatening the safety of others and interfering with teaching. No wonder that teachers often become anxious and frustrated in their efforts to deal with such behavior.

Teachers of students with behavioral disorders work with a volatile student population. Words such as *unpredictable, confrontational,* and *displaced aggression* characterize the students they teach. Clearly, these students present a wide range of behavioral excesses and deficits, conditions that can arouse negative feelings in their teachers (Dedrick & Raschke, 1990, p. 43).

Aggressive behavior in the classroom is likely to result in increased levels of stress and frustration for the teacher and the student. The major premise of this article is that student aggression is directly related to teacher behavior, and that teachers have the ability to modify their classroom environments, greatly reducing student aggression. "Staff attitudes and behavior may be the most important factor affecting aggressive behavior" (VanAcker, 1993, p. 28).

This article reviews what teachers can do to prevent aggressive behavior in students with emotional and behavioral disorders. "Aggressive behavior refers to those behaviors—verbal, nonverbal, or physical—that injure another indirectly or directly and/or result in extraneous gains for the aggressor" (Zirpoli & Melloy, 1997, p. 332).

Preventing aggressive behavior involves, first, understanding the dynamics of aggression in students with emotional and behavioral disorders. With this understanding, then, teachers can learn how to be more therapeutic in the classroom, how to create a positive classroom climate, how to conduct functional assessments, and how to teach students alternative behaviors.

Dynamics of Aggression

Aggressive behavior is learned and maintained in a similar manner to other behaviors; three important factors are modeling, positive reinforcement, and negative reinforcement (Wehby, 1994; Zirpoli & Melloy, 1997). Teachers need to be aware if they are modeling aggressive behaviors, or if students modeling aggressive behavior are reinforced, either positively (through attention from staff or peers, or getting their way), or negatively (by escaping or avoiding aversive stimuli, such as removal from a boring or frustrating class).

Another important factor in understanding aggressive behavior is the role of frustration. According to Dollard, Miller, Doob, Mowrer, and Sears (1939), frustration does not always result in aggression, but it is always an antecedent of aggression. Students with emotional and behavioral disorders are more likely than other students to engage in aggression due to deficits in cognitive and social skills. Aggressive students often exhibit deficits in social information processing—they are likely to misinterpret social cues and misassign hostile intent to others, especially during times of stress (Akhtar & Bradley, 1991). The result is that these students often feel threatened and become defensive,

> Staff attitudes and behavior may be the most important factor affecting aggressive behavior.

even when no real threat initially existed. Social skills deficits of these students often include poor impulse control, low frustration tolerance, limited ability to generate alternative responses to stress, and limited insight into the feelings of self and others (Coleman, 1996; Hughes & Cavell, 1995; Wood & Long, 1991). These cognitive and social skills deficits result in a high level of frustration during many social interactions.

Adding to this frustration are the experiences of these students in the classroom. Sources of frustration for students with emotional and behavioral disorders in general and special education classrooms include the following (see Shores, Gunter, Denny, & Jack, 1993; Swick, 1987):

- Disorganized or inconsistent teachers.
- Failure.
- Boredom.
- Lack of positive reinforcement.
- Irrelevant curriculum.
- Overuse of punishment.

- Feelings of powerlessness.

As Kauffman stated: "Many antisocial students do not know how to do the academic tasks, and do not have the social coping skills to be successful in the typical classroom, and each failure increases the probability of future antisocial responses to problems" (1997, p. 348).

The effects of student aggression on teachers often include an increased level of frustration and stress within the classroom. Common teacher reactions to stress (including aggression) are irritability, fear, counteraggression, negative thinking, fatigue, and avoidance (Dedrick & Raschke, 1990; Swick, 1987; VanAcker, 1993). When teachers are unable to manage the stress and frustration inherent in working with such students, they are more likely to overreact to minor problems and escalate the frequency and severity of student aggression in the classroom.

The Therapeutic Teacher

The therapeutic teacher is one who is able to manage the stress of working with students with emotional and behavioral disorders and create an environment that meets the students' academic, social, and psychological needs, thereby reducing the frustration experienced by the students in the classroom (see Figure 1). According to Kauffman (1997): "To be therapeutic, teachers must listen, talk, and act in ways that communicate respect, caring, and confidence, both in themselves and in their students" (p. 519).

Therapeutic teachers possess ego strength and mental health; teachers with good mental health demonstrate a high level of self-awareness and self-confidence, realistic expectations of self, and the ability to exhibit and model self-control in managing stress and frustration (Long & Newman, 1980; Kauffman, 1997). These teachers are able to remain calm in a crisis, and they do not become defensive or confrontational.

Therapeutic teachers are able to establish trust and rapport with their students. Myles and Simpson stated:

> Such rapport does facilitate effective use of a variety of verbal and physical interventions, and other less intrusive methods. Moreover, trust-oriented relationships facilitate student learning and application of alternatives to aggression and violence. (1994, pp. 43–44).

Therapeutic teachers understand that most students exhibit low levels of frustration before becoming aggressive. Teachers should be aware of the stages of frustration

Figure 1
Characteristics of Therapeutic Teachers

- Have good mental health.
- Communicate respect, caring, and confidence in self and others.
- Exhibit and model self-control.
- Establish trust and rapport with students.
- Have an awareness of stages of frustration.
- Be able to de-escalate tension in the classroom.
- Be able to understand frustration and anxiety of students.
- Do not resort to threats or confrontations during stress. Respect students' dignity.
- Display enthusiasm and positive expectations.
- Have an awareness of individual student's needs, interests, values, and talents.
- Display effective stress-coping skills.
- Be able to create a positive classroom climate.

and intervene early before negative behavior escalates (Colvin, Ainge, & Nelson, 1997; Rutherford & Nelson, 1995). Johns and Carr (1995) identified several stages of frustration and recommend what teachers can do during each stage to help de-escalate the situation.

- During the *anxiety* stage, the student shows nonverbal behavior, such as sighs and putting his or her head down; teachers should respond by active listening and nonjudgmental talk.
- During the *stress* stage, the student often shows frustration through minor behavior problems, such as tearing paper or tapping pencil; teachers should use proximity control, boost their interest, or provide assistance with assignments.
- The *defensive (verbal aggression)* stage is characterized by students' arguing and complaining; teachers should briefly remind students of rules, use

> Teachers must listen, talk, and act in ways that communicate respect, caring, and confidence, both in themselves and in their students.

conflict resolution, and encourage students to ask for help.
- During the *physical aggression* stage, a student has lost control and begins to threaten others, throw objects, or hit others; teachers should remind the student that he or she still has choices, escort the student from class, get help from other staff, protect the safety of other students, and restrain the student if necessary.
- In the final stage, *tension reduction,* the student releases tension through crying or verbal venting; teachers show empathy and help student gain insight into feelings and behavior.

The therapeutic teacher understands the frustration and anxiety of students who may become aggressive (VanAcker, 1993). These students are often confused and frightened by their lack of self-control during stressful situations, and are often receptive to teachers who respect the students' dignity while providing assistance to the student without resorting to hostile threats or confrontations.

Teachers who are able to respect students' dignity during the initial stages of frustration, and remember that it is important to allow students to save face in front of others, will help students to feel more competent in managing stress and maintain a positive teacher-student relationship (Curwin & Mendler, 1988; Myles & Simpson, 1994). Good and Brophy (1990) discussed several characteristics of effective classroom managers that are shared by therapeutic teachers:

- Display an enthusiasm for teaching and learning.
- Are cheerful.
- Are liked by their students.
- Have positive expectations of self and students.

These teachers place a high value on personal traits and talents of students (Swick, 1987). They see students as individuals and are able to individualize the classroom environment to meet each stu-

dent's needs, values, and interests (Curwin & Mendler, 1988); they are aware of the universal needs of students—need for love, acceptance, belonging, competence, self-esteem, a sense of purposefulness, and identity (Sabatino, 1987).

Therapeutic teachers are aware of the negative effects of stress on their abilities. They place a high value on stress management and the ability to cope with the many frustrations of daily teaching. They use a variety of stress-management strategies (see Dedrick & Raschke, 1990; Swick, 1987):

- Awareness of negative attitudes.
- Realistic perception of stressors.
- Diet and exercise.
- Social support systems.
- Creative problem-solving.
- Time management.
- Healthy sense of humor.
- Personally rewarding interests.
- Engagement in professional and personal renewal activities.

A final characteristic of therapeutic teachers is that they are effective in creating a positive classroom climate where students experience success and joy rather than failure and frustration (see box, "Annotated Resources on Therapeutic Teaching").

Creating a Positive Classroom Climate

Researchers have described the environments of students with emotional and behavioral disorders as unstable, inconsistent, and chaotic (Paul & Epanchin, 1991). They need order, structure, and consistency if they are to learn and feel good about themselves (see Figure 2). Kauffman's discussion of the role of teachers of students with emotional and behavioral disorders describes a positive classroom climate: "The teacher's primary task is to structure or order the environment for the pupil in such a way that work is accomplished, play is learned, love is felt, and fun is enjoyed—by the student and the teacher" (1997, p. 516). A positive, well-organized classroom environment promotes student success, as follows:

- A well-organized and *predictable* classroom (including clear expectations, rules, routines, and schedules) helps students begin to feel safe (and less threatened). A key element of a structured environment is the consistency of the teacher—not only in terms of consequences for positive and negative behaviors, but also in attitudes and expectations.
- A positive classroom climate promotes success and *student achievement* (aca-

> ### *Figure 2*
> ### Elements of a Positive Classroom Climate
>
> - Order, structure, and consistency.
> - Well-organized and predictable environment.
> - Clear and realistic expectations.
> - Students experience success, academically and socially.
> - Curriculum stresses student interests and talents.
> - Teacher able to interpret communicative intent of students.
> - Students given choices and input into classroom decisions.
> - Students encouraged to express feelings.
> - Students able to socially interact with others.
> - Students' psychological needs (belonging, safety, competence, and self-esteem) met.
> - Positive teacher-student relationship.

demically and socially). Researchers have identified that frustration due to task difficulty (DePaepe, Shores, Jack, & Denny, 1996) or boring curriculum (Clarke, et al., 1995) is associated with increases in disruptive behavior. Attempts to improve student behavior by modifying curriculum based on students' interests (determined through discussions with student and parents, and direct observations) have been successful (Clarke et al.). Students who are actively engaged in learning are much less likely to become frustrated and aggressive.
- Curriculum that stresses *students' interests and talents* are more likely to produce more successful learners. An observation shared by many teachers working with students with emotional and behavioral disorders is that in the general or special education classroom students often appear apathetic, restless, and defensive, yet in other environments they appear confident, capable, sociable, and relaxed. These other environments may be the music room, art room, gym, a vocational class, or the lunchroom where the student feels safe, enjoys the task, and feels good about his or her abilities (and consequently exhibits much less aggressive behavior).
- Multiple intelligences theory (Armstrong, 1994; Gardner, 1993) stresses that schools should *nurture students'*

various intelligences and learning styles. Too often, schools emphasize linguistic and logical-mathematical intelligences (traditional academics) and neglect or classify students whose intelligences and strengths may lie in one of the other intelligences (spatial, musical, bodily-kinesthetic, intrapersonal, and interpersonal). Research by Dunn and Dunn (1993) also stresses that learning style variables (such as the immediate environment, students' emotionality, physiological factors, and information processing styles) do affect learning.

- Teachers who are able to implement a positive classroom climate *communicate effectively* with students. "A major factor contributing to a classroom climate where respect for students is evident is the teacher's ability to interpret the communicative intent of the youngster" (DeLuke & Knoblock, 1987, p. 18). Teachers who are able to understand and interpret the student's verbal and nonverbal behavior and communicate this with the student are more likely to develop a positive teacher-student relationship.

- Students feel more secure in classrooms where they have input into what happens there. Giving students *appropriate choices and input into decisions* regarding rules, reinforcers, and curriculum are an important component of a positive classroom climate (Curwin & Mendler, 1988; Sabatino, 1987).

- Encouraging students to *express their feelings* can help to teach them more effective methods to manage stress and understand their emotions. Affective curriculum assists students in positive emotional expression, improved self-concept, and facilitates social skill development (Morse, Ardizzone, MacDonald, & Pasick, 1980). Encouraging social interaction in the classroom through peer tutoring, cooperative learning, group projects, and games can promote social skill development and meet students' needs for belonging, competence, and self-esteem.

A positive teacher-student relationship is common to classrooms with a healthy climate. "Teachers must be skilled in using the setting, the curriculum, and most especially the relationship with the child to provide an atmosphere that promotes both academic and social development" (VanAcker, 1993, p. 31). A positive classroom climate will not eliminate classroom stress, but it will reduce it so that teachers and students can experience more daily success.

Functional Assessment

Functional assessment can be helpful in reducing aggressive behavior. Through this kind of assessment, teachers can identify specific antecedents and consequences that are associated with maladaptive behaviors. Teachers can collect individual data on each student to show time, setting, situation, antecedent, and consequences for each specific maladaptive behavior. When teachers analyze the data, they may see patterns that help in understanding the function of disruptive or aggressive behavior for a student (Foster-Johnson & Dunlap, 1993).

Common functions served by maladaptive behaviors include attention seeking (positive reinforcement), escape or avoidance (negative reinforcement), or sensory feedback and stimulation; *common antecedents* to maladaptive behaviors include frustration, boredom, models, overstimulation, and environmental expectations (Alberto & Troutman, 1995). "Identification of the functional relationships is essential to the development of interventions that not only are effective, but also are least intrusive and proactive" (Rutherford & Nelson, 1995, p. 110).

Through careful collection of data, teachers can gain insights into the specific antecedents and functions associated with a student's aggressive behavior. This will allow teachers to more effectively modify the environment so that antecedents to aggression are eliminated, and students can be taught alternative behaviors that can replace aggression as a functional behavior.

Teaching Alternative Behaviors

Modifying teacher behavior and the classroom environment will help reduce frustration and stress in the classroom; but unless students are actively taught prosocial, alternative behaviors, the benefits of such changes will be limited in their duration and lack generalization. Johns et al. (1996) stated that students with emotional and behavioral disorders need a *preventive curriculum* that includes stress management, self-control training, and social skill development.

Affective education and social skills programs address many of the deficits of students with emotional and behavioral disorders, as follows:

- Cartledge and Milburn (1995) have reviewed a number of social skills programs for preschoolers, elementary schoolchildren, and adolescents.
- Goldstein has written several books on teaching social skills, through the "Prepare" curriculum (1988), whose 10 curriculum areas address interper-

> The teacher's primary task is to structure the environment for the pupil in such a way that work is accomplished, play is learned, love is felt, and fun is enjoyed—by the student and the teacher.

sonal skills, stress management, situational perception training, and empathy training; and a curriculum for aggression replacement training (1994).

- Feindler and Ecton (1986) described a 12-session group anger-control program.
- Books on teaching conflict resolution (Johnson & Johnson, 1995) and coping skills (Forman, 1993) are also relevant and useful.
- Affective education programs that encourage student awareness of feelings, and how their feelings affect their behavior include life-space intervention (Wood & Long, 1991) and values clarification (Abrams, 1992).

One final suggestion for teachers seeking to prevent aggressive behavior is to remember the importance of differential reinforcement of incompatible behaviors (DRI). To effectively modify student aggression and teach prosocial behaviors, teachers must reinforce, or reward, students when they exhibit behaviors incompatible with aggression (coping with frustration, resolving conflicts without aggression, managing anger appropriately) (Alberto & Troutman, 1995; Webber & Scheuermann, 1991). Teachers should recognize student improvement and reinforce it; too often we fall into the trap of responding to negative behavior, and forget to recognize positive behavior.

Final Thoughts

The ideas presented here will not eliminate *all* student aggression. Teachers do not have total control over classroom environments, but by modifying those variables

> Trust-oriented
> relationships facilitate
> student learning
> and application
> of alternatives to
> aggression and
> violence.

that they can control, teachers can greatly reduce student aggression. Attempts to reduce stress, frustration, and failure in the classroom are not easy, but are well worth the effort in terms of student growth and teacher satisfaction.

References

Abrams, B. J. (1992). Values clarification for students with emotional disabilities. *TEACHING Exceptional Children, 24*(3), 28–33.

Akhtar, N., & Bradley, E. J. (1991). Social information processing deficits of aggressive children: Present findings and implications for social skills training. *Clinical Psychology Review, 11,* 621–644.

Alberto, P. A., & Troutman, A. C. (1995). *Applied behavior analysis for teachers* (4th ed.). Englewood Cliffs, NJ: Prentice Hall.

Armstrong, T. (1994). *Multiple intelligences in the classroom.* Alexandria, VA: Association for Supervision and Curriculum Development.

Cartledge, G., & Milburn, J. F. (1995). *Teaching social skills to children and youth: Innovative approaches* (3rd ed.). Needham Heights, MA: Allyn & Bacon.

Clarke, S., Dunlap, G., Foster-Johnson, L., Childs, K. E., Wilson, D., & Vera, A. (1995). Improving the conduct of students with behavioral disorders by incorporating student interests into curricular activities. *Behavioral Disorders, 20*(4), 221–237.

Coleman, M. C. (1996). *Emotional and behavioral disorders: Theory and practice* (3rd ed.). Boston: Allyn & Bacon.

Colvin, G., Ainge, D., & Nelson, R. (1997). How to defuse defiance, threats, challenges, confrontations, *TEACHING Exceptional Children, 29*(6), 47–51.

Combs, A. W., & Gonzalez, D. M. (1994). *Helping relationships: Basic concepts for the helping professions.* Boston: Allyn & Bacon.

Curwin, R. I., & Mendler, A. N. (1988). *Discipline with dignity.* Alexandria, VA: Association for Supervision and Curriculum Development. (ERIC Document Service Reproduction No. ED 302 938)

Dedrick, C. V., & Raschke, D. B. (1990). *The special educator and job stress.* Washington, DC: National Education Association. (ERIC Document Service Reproduction No. ED 323 723)

DeLuke, S. V., & Knoblock, P. (1987). Teacher behavior as preventive discipline. *TEACHING Exceptional Children, 19*(4), 18–24.

DePaepe, P. A., Shores, R. E., Jack, S. L., & Denny, R. K. (1996). Effects of task difficulty on the disruptive and on-task behavior of students with severe behavioral disorders. *Behavioral Disorders, 21*(3), 216–225.

Dollard, J., Miller, N. E., Doob, L. W., Mowrer, O. H., & Sears, R. R. (1939). *Frustration and aggression.* New Haven, CT: Yale University Press.

Dunn, R., & Dunn, K. (1993). *Teaching secondary students through their individual learning styles: Practical approaches for grades 7–12.* Boston: Allyn & Bacon.

Feindler, E. L., & Ecton, R. B. (1986). *Adolescent anger control: Cognitive-behavioral techniques.* New York: Pergamon.

Forman, S. G. (1993). *Coping skills interventions for children and adolescents.* San Francisco: Jossey-Bass.

Foster-Johnson, L., & Dunlap, G. (1993). Using functional assessment to develop effective, individualized intervention for challenging behaviors. *TEACHING Exceptional Children, 25*(3), 44–50.

Gallagher, P. A. (1997). Promoting dignity: Taking the destructive d's out of behavioral disorders. *Focus on Exceptional Children, 29*(9), 1–19.

Gardner, H. (1993). *Multiple intelligences: The theory in practice.* New York: Basic Books.

Goldstein, A. (1988). *The Prepare curriculum: Teaching prosocial competencies.* Champaign, IL: Research Press.

Goldstein, A. (1994). *Student aggression: Prevention, management, and replacement training.* New York: Longman.

Good, T. L., & Brophy, J. E. (1990). *Educational psychology: A realistic approach* (4th ed.). Reading, MA: Addison Wesley. (ERIC Document Reproduction Service No. ED 314 367)

Hughes, J. N., & Cavell, T. A. (1995). Cognitive-affective approaches: Enhancing competencies in aggressive children. In G. Cartledge & J. F. Milburn (Eds.), *Teaching social skills to children and youth: Innovative approaches* (3rd ed., pp. 199–236). Needham Heights, MA: Allyn & Bacon.

Johns, B. H., & Carr, V. G. (1995). *Techniques for managing verbally and physically aggressive students.* Denver: Love.

Johns, B. H., Guetzloe, E. C., Yell, M., Scheuermann, B., Webber, J., Carr, V. G., & Smith, R. C. (1996). *Best practices for managing adolescents with emotional/behavioral disorders within the school environment.* Reston, VA: Council for Exceptional Children. (ERIC Document Reproduction Service No. ED 391 301)

Johnson, D. W., & Johnson, R. T. (1995). *Reducing school violence through conflict resolution.* Alexandria, VA: Association for Supervision and Curriculum Development.

Kauffman, J. M. (1997). *Characteristics of emotional and behavioral disorders of children and youth* (6th ed.). Upper Saddle River, NJ: Prentice Hall.

Long, N. J., & Newman, R. G. (1980). The teacher and his mental health. In N. J. Long, W. C. Morse, & R. G. Newman (Eds.), *Conflict in the classroom: The education of emotionally disturbed children* (4th ed., pp. 207–217). Belmont, CA: Wadsworth.

Morse, W. C., Ardizzone, J., MacDonald, C., & Pasick, P. (1980). *Affective education for special children and youth.* Reston, VA: The Council for Exceptional Children. (ERIC

Annotated Resources on Therapeutic Teaching

- Combs and Gonzalez (1994) discussed the importance of perceptions, beliefs, empathy, communication, and self-concept—all key elements of the therapeutic teacher.

- Curwin and Mendler (1988) presented teachers with a useful approach to classroom management for difficult students. This book presented teacher strategies that emphasize the importance of students experiencing dignity, respect, hope, and success in the classroom.

- Gallagher (1997) discussed how teachers can promote dignity and competence in students with emotional and behavioral disorders. Important concepts include communicating caring to students, discovering students' strengths, and promoting positive teacher-student interactions.

- Johns and Carr (1995) described many useful strategies for teachers working with aggressive students—what teachers should do (in a therapeutic manner) for various types of aggressive behavior.

- Purkey and Novak (1984) focused on teacher skills related to teacher and student perceptions, and teacher-student interactions, that are critical to students' feelings about themselves as people and as students. This text described how teachers can create an inviting environment for all students.

- VanAcker (1993) described specific teacher skills needed for working with aggressive students such as de-escalating threatening situations, promoting social skill development, and understanding and monitoring teacher behavior.

Document Reproduction Service No. ED 185 795)

Myles, B. S., & Simpson, R. L. (1994). Understanding and preventing acts of aggression and violence in school-age children and youth. *Preventing School Failure, 38*(3), 40–46.

Paul, J. L., & Epanchin, B. C. (1991). *Educating emotionally disturbed children and youth: Theories and practices for teachers* (2nd ed.). New York: Merrill.[*]

Purkey, W. W., & Novak, J. M. (1984). *Inviting school success: A self-concept approach to teaching and learning* (2nd ed.). Belmont, CA: Wadsworth.[*]

Rutherford, R. B., & Nelson, C. M. (1995). Management of aggressive and violent behavior in the schools. *Focus on Exceptional Children, 26*(6), 1–15.

Sabatino, D. A. (1987). Preventive discipline as a practice in special education. *TEACHING Exceptional Children, 19*(4), 8–11.

Shores, R. E., Gunter, P. L., Denny, R. K., & Jack, S. L. (1993). Classroom influences on aggressive and disruptive behaviors of students with emotional and behavioral disorders. *Focus on Exceptional Children, 26*(2), 1–10.

Swick, J. (1987). *Student stress: A classroom management system.* Washington, DC: National Education Association. (ERIC Document Reproduction Service No. ED 307 514)

VanAcker, R. (1993). Dealing with conflict and aggression in the classroom: What skills do teachers need? *Teacher Education and Special Education, 16*(1), 23–33.

Webber, J., & Scheuermann, B. (1991). Managing behavior problems: Accentuate the positive . . . eliminate the negative. *TEACHING Exceptional Children, 24*(1), 13–19.

Wehby, J. H. (1994). Issues in the assessment of aggressive behavior. *Preventing School Failure, 38*(3), 24–28.

Wood, M., & Long, N. (1991). *Life space intervention: Talking with children and youth in crisis.* Austin, TX: Pro-Ed.[*]

Zirpoli, T. J., & Melloy, K. J. (1997). *Behavior management: Applications for teachers and parents* (2nd ed.). Columbus, OH: Merrill.[*]

Brian J. Abrams, *Special Education Teacher; and* **Amiel Segal,** *Psychologist, Nassau County BOCES, Career Development Center, Baldwin, New York.*

Address correspondence to the author at Nassau County BOCES, Career Development Center, 3250 Grand Avenue, Baldwin, NY 11510.

How to Defuse
CONFRONTATIONS

DEFIANCE THREATS CHALLENGES

A comprehensive system of behavior management has three critical components: prevention, defusion, and follow-up.

Geoff Colvin
David Ainge
Ron Nelson

■

The T-shirt attention getter...

Prohibited cookies on the bus...

Profanity in class...

Outright refusal to do classwork...

Chair-throwing...

Do some of your students engage in confrontational behavior like this? Here's a litany of such behavior: attention-getting, defiance, challenges, disrespect, limit testing, verbal abuse, blatant rule violations, threats, and intimidation. Some students test the patience of teachers who have what they thought was an effective behavior-management system. This article presents teacher-tested ways to *defuse* such behavior and allow the students to learn and participate in positive ways.

Special education teachers have always had the task of managing students who display seriously disturbing behavior. More recently, these teachers are expected to provide support and consultation to general education teachers who need assistance on managing the behavior of all students in inclusive classrooms. Special education teachers can assist other educators in a comprehensive system of behavior management composed of three critical components: prevention, defusion, and follow-up (see box, "Three Approaches to Behavior Management").

We focus here particularly on *defusion,* an approach that is helpful with students who are continually confrontational. Such behavior not only leads to class disruption, but also can readily escalate to more serious behavior—and threats to the safety of both staff and students. Let's look at some examples of confrontational behavior and then explore how we can deal with it.

Three Confrontational Students

• Joe steps onto the school bus holding a monster cookie in his hand. Above his head is a large sign that reads, "No food

on the bus." Joe looks at the driver, takes a huge bite of the cookie, and takes another step on the bus. The bus driver points to the sign and says quite emphatically, "Look, no food on the bus. You'll have to give me that cookie." Joe says equally emphatically, "No," and takes another bite. The driver looks him right in the eye and says, "If you don't give me the cookie, you will not ride the bus." Joe says, "So," takes another bite of the cookie, and begins to move toward his seat. The driver calls transportation to have the student removed from the bus.

• Sarah walks into the classroom wearing a T-shirt displaying a toilet bowl with an arrow coming up out of the bowl and a written statement underneath, "Up your AZ." Some students giggle, and another asks, "Where did you get that?" The teacher comes over and says, "Sarah, that shirt is not acceptable in a public school. You had better go to the restroom and turn it inside out." Sarah looks at the teacher and says, "I'm not gonna do that. My dad gave it to me and you can't make me turn it inside out." The teacher says that if she does not cooperate, she will be sent to the office. Sarah throws her book down and heads to the back of the room.

• Jamie is sitting at his desk, arms folded, shoulders rounded, feet firmly planted on the floor, and staring at the floor with a scowl on his face, while the rest of the class is working on an independent math assignment. The teacher eventually approaches Jamie and prompts him to start on his math. He scowls and says in a harsh tone that he can't do it. So the teacher offers to help him. He says he still can't do it. The teacher provides more detail with the explanation and directs him to make a start. He says he hates math. The teacher tells him that he needs to start or he will have to do his math during the break. He utters a profanity and storms out of the room.

From *Teaching Exceptional Children,* July/August 1997, pp. 47–51. © 1997 by The Council for Exceptional Children. Reprinted by permission.

What Happened?

In each case, the supervising staff person reacts to a problem behavior in a direct manner. There is a high likelihood that the student *expects* a response. In fact, the student not only expects a response, but he or she expects a *particular* response.

For all practical purposes, the staff person is *already set up for confrontation*. In other words, the student displays engaging behavior that is highly likely to elicit a predictable response from staff that includes a clear direction. The student refuses to follow the direction, which engages staff further, leading to ultimatums and additional problem behavior.

Moreover, if the staff person becomes confrontational at this point, there is a strong likelihood that the student will react with more serious behavior. In effect, we can see a pattern—a cycle—of successive interactions beginning with problem behavior leading to more serious behavior, such as throwing a book (Sarah), continuing to disregard requests (Joe), or profanity (Jamie). These vignettes have five common features:

1. The student displays defiant, challenging, or inappropriate behavior.

2. The supervising staff person reacts to the problem behavior and provides a direction in opposition to the student's behavior.

3. The student challenges the direction by not complying and by displaying other inappropriate behavior.

4. The staff person reacts to the non-compliance and presents an ultimatum.

5. The student takes up the challenge of the ultimatum with further defiance and exhibits hostile and explosive behavior.

What Strategies Can Help?

When students exhibit confrontational behavior, you need approaches that are likely to defuse the problem behavior, rather than lead to more serious behavior. Defusing strategies minimize the likelihood that interactions between you and the student will escalate the confrontation. We have found five defusing strategies that work—in order of least intrusive student behavior to more serious confrontational behavior. These strategies range from ignoring the behavior to delaying a response and allowing the student to calm down.

Focus on the Task to Defuse Minor Attention-Getting Behavior

Students often display minor problem behavior to secure attention: talking out in class,

moving out of their seats, starting work slowly, and pencil tapping. Once you respond to such behavior, the student may exhibit more attention-getting behavior. The basic approach for managing this level of problem behavior is to use a *continuum* of steps based on the level of attention you provide:

- Attend to the students exhibiting expected behavior, and ignore the students displaying the problem behavior.
- Redirect the student to the task at hand. Do not respond to or draw attention to the problem behavior.
- Present a choice between the expected behavior and a small negative consequence (such as a loss of privilege).

For example, Michael is out of his seat wandering around the room while other students are seated and engaged in a class activity. The teacher moves among the students who are on task, acknowledges their good work and ignores Michael. Michael continues to move around the class. The teacher approaches him and says privately, "Michael, listen, it's math time. Let's go." and points to his seat. Michael still does not return to his seat. The teacher secures his attention and says calmly and firmly, "Michael, you have been asked to sit down and start work or you will have to do the work in recess. You decide." The teacher follows through on whatever Michael chooses to do.

Present Options Privately in the Context of a Rule Violation

Sometimes students will break a rule to challenge you. They know you will react and give a direction. The student will then refuse to follow the direction. In this way, a confrontation scene is established. For example, in the cases of Joe and Sarah, the staff member gave the students a direction that the students refused to follow—the cookie was not turned in to the driver, the T-shirt was not turned inside out. Here are steps to follow in such cases:

- State the rule or expectation.
- Request explicitly for the student to "take care of the problem."
- Present options for the student on how to take care of the problem.

In this way, you lessen the chance of confrontation when you present options and focus how the student might decide to take care of the problem, rather than whether the student follows a specific direction.

For example, the bus driver might have quietly said something like this to Joe: "Look, there is no food on the bus, thank you. You had better take care of that. You

can eat it before you get on or leave it here and collect it later." Note the options the bus driver might have provided.

Or, to deal with Sarah's offensive T-shirt, the teacher might take Sarah aside and say, "Sarah, that shirt is not OK in a public school. It has a rude message. You can turn it inside out, get a shirt from the gym, or wear a jacket."

Reduce Agitation in a Demand Situation

Sometimes students are already agitated when they enter a situation. When you or other people place demands on them, their behavior will likely escalate.

First, communicate concern to the student. Then allow the student time and space. Give the student some choices or options.

For example, Jamie's body posture and tone of voice suggest he is upset. When the teacher tries to prompt him to work, even in a very reasonable manner, his behavior escalates to storming out of the room. Here, the teacher might have used agitation-reduction techniques.

Signs of Agitation. Students show agitation by either increasing distracting behavior or decreasing active, engaged behavior (Colvin, 1992). Here are common signs of increases in *distracting behavior:*

- Darting eyes
- Nonconversational language
- Busy hands
- Moving in and out of groups
- Frequent off-task and on-task behavior
- Starting and stopping activities
- Moving around the room

Paradoxically, sometimes agitation doesn't seem to live up to its name. Some students can be agitated and not show it. Watch for the following *decreases in behavior* and a lack of engagement in class activities:

- Staring into space
- Subdued language
- Contained hands
- Lack of interaction and involvement in activities
- Withdrawal from groups and activities
- Lack of responding in general
- Avoidance of eye contact

Techniques for Reducing Agitation. Once you recognize that the student's behavior is agitated, your primary goal is to use strategies to calm the student down and assist him or her to become engaged in the

The most important thing to remember is that your responses can change things.

present classroom activity. Because these strategies are supportive in nature, you need to use them *before* the behavior becomes serious; otherwise, you risk reinforcing the seemingly endless chain of inappropriate behavior. The critical issue is *timing*. Use the following techniques at the *earliest* indications of agitation:

Teacher support: Communicate concern to the student.

Space: Provide the student with an opportunity to have some isolation from the rest of the class.

Choices: Give the student some choices or options.

Preferred activities: Allow the student to engage in a preferred activity for a short period of time to help regain focus.

Teacher proximity: Move near or stand near the student.

Independent activities: Engage the student in independent activities to provide isolation.

Movement activities: Use activities and tasks that require movement, such as errands, cleaning the chalkboard, and distributing papers.

Involvement of the student: Where possible, involve the student in the plan. In this way, there is more chance of ownership and generalization to other settings.

Relaxation activities: Use audiotapes, drawing activities, breathing and relaxation techniques.

Now let's replay Jamie's situation. This time, the teacher determines that Jamie seems to be agitated—he shows a *decrease* in behavior. The teacher says, as privately as possible, "Jamie, it's time for math. Are you doing OK? Do you need some time before you start?" In this way, the teacher is recognizing the agitation, communicating concern to Jamie, and giving him time to regain his focus.

Preteach and Present Choices to Establish Limits and Defuse Noncompliance

Use this strategy to establish limits and to defuse sustained noncompliance. Essentially, the student is refusing to follow the teacher's directions.

For example, suppose that Scott has been off task and distracting other students for several minutes. The teacher has tried to provide assistance, redirect him, and give a formal direction to begin work. Scott refuses to cooperate. At this point, the teacher wants to communicate to him that "enough is enough," and to establish some classroom

limits. When the teacher tries to establish limits, however, Scott may become more hostile and aggressive.

The following steps in the preteaching strategy can establish limits without escalating the behavior. Role-playing these steps can help students learn how to use self-control.

Preteach the procedures: Carefully rehearse the procedures with the student, give explanations, model the steps, and describe the consequences. Do preteaching at a neutral time when the student is relatively calm and cooperative.

Deliver the information to the students without being confrontational:

1. Present the expected behavior and the negative consequence as a decision; place responsibility on the student.

2. Allow a few seconds for the student to decide. This small amount of time helps the student calm down, enables face saving in front of peers, enables you to pull away from the conflict, and leaves the student with the decision.

3. Withdraw from the student and attend to other students. You thus help the student focus on the decision, not attend to you.

Follow through: If the student chooses the expected behavior, briefly acknowledge the choice and continue with the lesson or activity. If the student has not chosen the expected behavior, deliver the negative consequence. Debrief with the student and problem solve.

For example, if Sarah refused to take care of the T-shirt problem, the teacher could say. "Sarah, you have been asked to take care of the shirt (expected behavior), or I will have to make an office referral (negative consequence). You have a few seconds to decide." The teacher moves away from Sarah and addresses some other students or tasks. The teacher follows through on the choice made by the student.

Disengage and Delay Responding in the Presence of Serious Threatening Behavior

Students may escalate to a point of serious confrontational behavior involving threats or intimidation. For example, the teacher may

Defusing strategies minimizes the likelihood that interactions between you and the student will escalate the confrontation.

Three Approaches to Behavior Management

Prevention. The teacher places a strong focus on teaching desirable behavior and orchestrating effective learning activities. These proactive strategies are designed to establish a positive classroom structure and climate for students to engage in productive, prosocial behavior.

Defusion. Teachers use strategies designed to address problem behavior after the behavior has commenced. The goal here is to arrest the behavior before it escalates to more serious behavior and to assist the student to resume class activities in an appropriate manner.

Follow-up. A teacher or an administrator may provide consequences for the problem behavior and endeavors to assist the student to terminate the problem behavior and to engage in appropriate behavior in the future.

The goal of these approaches is to provide information to the student on the limits of behavior and to use problem-solving strategies to enable the student to exhibit alternative appropriate behavior in subsequent events (Biggs & Moore, 1993; Colvin & Lazar, 1997; Kameenui & Darch, 1995; Myers & Myers, 1993; Sprick, Sprick & Garrison, 1993; Sugai & Tindal, 1993; Walker, Colvin, & Ramsey, 1995).

have presented options, given the student time, and provided a consequence: "Eric, you are asked to start work or you will have to stay after school. You have a few seconds to decide." Eric walks over to the teacher and says, "I know where you live."

Suppose a more serious incident occurs, such as this real incident: An administrator told a student to go to the in-school suspension area or he would call his probation officer. The student picked up a cup of coffee from the secretary's desk, moved to the administrator, held the coffee in his face, and said, "You call my P.O. and I will throw this in your f_____ face."

In each of these cases, there is a direct threat to a staff member and the danger that the student's behavior may escalate. Whether the student's behavior becomes more serious *depends on the staff member's initial response to the threat.* The primary intent of this strategy is to avoid responding directly to the student's behavior and to disengage momentarily and then to redirect the student.

We are *not* suggesting that this strategy is all you need to do. Rather, the primary purpose of this strategy is to defuse a crisis situation. Once the crisis has been avoided, you should follow up and address the previous threatening behavior so that such behavior does not arise again. Here are steps to use in disengaging and delaying:

Break the cycle of successive interactions by delaying responding: This pattern consists of successive hostile or inflammatory interactions between you and the student—the student challenges you to respond. The first step is to *delay responding,* because the student is expecting an immediate response. To delay responding, very briefly look at the student, look at the floor, look detached, and pause.

Prevent explosive behavior by making a disengaging response: Do not leave the student waiting too long; otherwise, an "extinction burst" may occur. That is, if events do not go the way the student expects them to, he or she may exhibit explosive behavior, such as throwing a chair at the wall (or staff, or another student), or throwing the coffee cup. To prevent this burst, disengage swiftly and engage in something neutral or unrelated (Lerman & Iwata, 1995). For example, say to the student, "Just a minute," and move and pick up something on your desk.

Return to the student, redirect, and withdraw: If the student has not exhibited further problem behavior and is waiting, simply return to the student and present the original choice.

For example, approach the student and say, "You still have a moment or two to decide what you wish to do," and withdraw. If the student engages in more serious behavior, implement emergency procedures and policies established by the school or district.

Follow through: If the student chooses the expected behavior, acknowledge the choice briefly and debrief later. If the student does not choose the expected behavior, deliver consequences and debrief later.

Sometimes students will break a rule to challenge you; others are already agitated when you try to correct them.

Debrief: The debriefing activity is designed to help the student problem solve by reviewing the incident and events leading up to the incident, identifying the triggers, and examining alternatives. The debriefing finishes with a focus or agreement on what the student will try to do next time that would be an appropriate response to the situation (Sugai & Colvin, in press).

Now Let's Debrief

How many Sarahs and Jamies and Erics do you know? Are you tired of throwing up your hands and sending these students to the office, or facing hostility and muttered challenges—or even threats to your own safety? Are you equally concerned that these students (and other students in your class) may be missing out on learning opportunities?

The most important thing to remember is that *your responses can change things.* Go back to the section on "Disengage and Delay Responding" and memorize it. Then follow the steps in "Preteaching," and you are on your way to helping students control their own behavior and create a better environment for learning.

References

Biggs, J. B., & Moore, P. J. (1993). *The process of learning.* New York: Prentice Hall.

Colvin, G. (1992). *Video program: Managing acting-out behavior.* Eugene, OR: Behavior Associates.

Colvin, G., & Lazar, M. (1997). *The effective elementary classroom: Managing for success.* Longmont, CO: Sopris West.

Kameenui, E. J., & Darch, C. B. (1995). *Instructional classroom management: A proactive approach to behavior management.* White Plains, NY: Longman.

Lerman, D., & Iwata, B. (1995). Prevalence of the extinction burst and its attenuation during treatment. *Journal of Applied Behavior Analysis, 28,* 93–94.

Myers, C. B., & Myers, L. K. (1993). *An introduction to teaching and schools.* Fort Worth, TX: Rinehart and Winston.

Sprick, R., Sprick, M., & Garrison, M. (1993). *Interventions: Collaborative planning for students at risk.* Longmont, CO: Sopris West.

Sugai, G., & Colvin, G. (in press). Debriefing: A proactive addition to negative consequences for problem behavior. *Education and Treatment for Children.*

Sugai, G., & Tindal, G. (1993). *Effective school consultation: An interactive approach.* Pacific Grove, CA: Brooks/Cole.

Walker, H., Colvin, G., & Ramsey, E. (1995). *Antisocial behavior in school: Strategies and best practices.* Pacific Grove, CA: Brooks/Cole.

Geoff Colvin *(Oregon Federation), Research Associate, Special Education and Community Resources, University of Oregon, Eugene.* **David Ainge,** *Senior Lecturer, Special Education Department, James Cook University, Queensland, Australia.* **Ron Nelson** *(CEC Chapter #374), Associate Professor, Applied Psychology Department, Eastern Washington University, Spokane.*

Address correspondence to Geoff Colvin, Special Education and Community Resources, University of Oregon, Eugene, OR 97405 (e-mail: geoff_colvin@ccmail.uoregon.edu).

Unit 7

Unit Selections

Key Points to Consider

❖ How early should orientation and mobility training start for infants and young children? Should a pre-cane be introduced before a long cane?

❖ How can a reserved, overwhelmed young child with a hearing loss become a confident, happy child with a hearing loss in his or her first year of school?

❖ What are multimedia stories? How can they help children with hearing impairments?

 **Links**   **www.dushkin.com/online/**

These sites are annotated on pages 4 and 5.

Blindness and deafness are uncommon, and are becoming more so as medical technology increases and infectious diseases, malnutrition, and other acquired causes of sensory loss decrease. Students with vision or hearing impairments whose disabilities can be ameliorated with assistive devices are more common in the school population. Regular education can usually meet their individualized needs appropriately. However, students with visual and/or hearing disorders whose problems cannot be resolved with technological aids need the procedural protections afforded by law. They should receive special services from birth (or age of diagnosis) through age 21, in the least restrictive environment, free of charge, with semiannually updated individualized family service plans (IFSPs) until age 6, and annually updated individualized education plans (IEPs) and eventually individualized transition plans (ITPs) through age 21. The numbers of children and youth who qualify for these intensive specialized educational programs are small.

Children with visual disabilities that cannot be corrected are the smallest group of children who qualify for special educational services through the Individuals with Disabilities Education Act (IDEA). In order to be assessed as visually disabled for purposes of receiving special educational services, a child must have low vision, which necessitates large print or magnification of print, or be blind, which necessitates use of hearing (audiotapes, records) or touch (braille, long cane) aids to be educated.

The educational definition of visual impairment focuses on what experiences a child needs in order to be able to learn. Legally, a child is considered to have low vision if acuity in the best eye, after correction, is between 20/70 and 20/180 and if the visual field extends from 20 to 180 degrees. Legally, a child is considered blind if visual acuity in the best eye, after correction, is 20/200 or less and/or if the field of vision is restricted to an area of less than 20 degrees (tunnel vision). These terms do not accurately reflect a child's ability to see or read print. One must consider the amount of visual acuity in the worst eye, the perception of light and movement, the field of vision (a person "blinded" by tunnel vision may have good visual acuity in a very small field of vision), and the efficiency with which a person uses any residual vision.

Children with visual impairments that prevent reading print are usually taught to read braille. Braille is a form of writing using raised dots that are "read" with the fingers. It takes many years to learn to read braille, and instruction should begin in preschool. In addition to braille, children who are blind are usually taught with Optacon scanners, talking books, talking handheld calculators, closed-circuit televisions, typewriters, and special computer software. In early childhood, many children with low vision or blindness are given instruction in using the long cane. Although controversial for many years, the long cane is increasingly being accepted. A long cane improves orientation and mobility and alerts persons with visual acuity that the user has a visual disability.

Hearing impairments are rare, and the extreme form, legal deafness, is rarer still. In order to be assessed as hard-of-hearing for purposes of receiving special educational services, a child needs some form of sound amplification to comprehend oral language. In order to be assessed as deaf for purposes of educational programming, a child cannot benefit from amplification. Children who are deaf are dependent on vision for language and communication.

When children are born with impaired auditory sensations, they are put into a classification of children with congenital (at or dating from birth) hearing impairments. They should be assessed as early as possible and started in early-childhood special educational programs for the hearing impaired.

When children acquire problems with their hearing after birth, they are put into a classification of children with adventitious hearing impairments. If the loss of hearing occurs before the child has learned speech and language, it is called a prelinguistic hearing impairment. If the loss occurs after the child has learned language, it is called a postlinguistic hearing impairment.

Children with hearing impairments are subsumed into etiological (causative) divisions of disability as well as being classified as hard-of-hearing or deaf and congenitally or adventitiously impaired. Children whose hearing losses involve the outer or middle ear structures are said to have conductive hearing losses. Conductive losses involve defects or impairments of the external auditory canal, the tympanic membrane, or the ossicles. Children whose hearing losses involve the inner ear are said to have sensorineural hearing impairments. They are difficult or impossible to correct with surgery, medicine, or sound amplification.

Many professionals working with individuals who are deaf feel that a community of other people who are deaf and who use sign language is less restrictive than a community of people who hear and who use oral speech. The unity of individuals who are deaf has benefits. The debate about what has come to be known as the deaf culture has not been resolved.

The first report in this unit deals with vision impairment. Susan Leong presents an extensive review of the literature on orientation and mobility (O&M) training in infants, toddlers, and preschoolers. She documents the need for services and discusses several early approaches to O&M.

The second article in this unit is a story of a child with severe hearing loss who is warmly included in a general education classroom. Harry brought a phonic ear and a cued speech transliterator with him. His teacher used a voice amplifier. The rest of Harry's classmates asked and received answers to questions about hearing loss. This story has implications for the inclusive education of all students with disabling conditions.

The material for thought in the unit's third selection is how the World Wide Web can enhance the education of children with hearing impairments. Jean Andrews and Donald Jordan review the benefits of new multimedia technology. Teachers who have used multimedia labs and CD-ROM stories relate that their students increase both their vocabularies and their enjoyment of learning.

Vision and Hearing Impairments

Preschool Orientation and Mobility: A Review of the Literature

Abstract: The past decade has witnessed the extension of orientation and mobility services to visually impaired children, aged birth to 6 years. These services have expanded rapidly despite the lack of a well-documented and thorough research base. This article presents a review of the literature on this topic, including its history and body of knowledge and research and suggests avenues for further research.

S. Leong

Susan Leong, M.A., teacher, Itinerant Teaching Service, Royal NSW Institute for Deaf & Blind Children, 361–365 North Rocks Road, North Rocks, New South Wales, 2151, Australia.

The increase in orientation and mobility (O&M) services for infants and preschool children who are visually impaired (both those with low vision and those who are blind) in the past 10 years occurred despite the lack of a well-documented and thorough research base (Ferrell, 1979; Joffee, 1988; Skellenger & Hill, 1991; Stack & Minnes, 1989; Warren, 1976). At the same time, practitioners have come to accept a broader definition of O&M for young children. As yet, no attempts have been made either to trace the history of this movement or to examine the body of knowledge in this area. This article attempts to redress this situation by presenting a comprehensive yet concise account of the background and related literature on this topic.

Need for services

O&M training for preschool children should involve activities that help young children who are visually impaired to move purposefully and safely in the environment. The importance of early O&M training for the independence and orientation of blind preschoolers to their environment has been postulated by many authors (Baird, 1979; Campbell, 1970; Cratty, Peterson, Harris & Schoner, 1968; DuBose, 1976; Eichorn & Vigaroso, 1967; Ferrell, 1979; Lord, 1969; Palazesi, 1986; Stack and Minnes, 1989; Warren, 1984; Webster, 1976). Most authors agree that this training should begin as early as possible, in most instances, before or in kindergarten (Benson, 1984; Bosbach, 1988; Pogrund & Rosen, 1989; Willoughby, 1979).

Without sight, the experiences of blind children must be channeled through the other senses, primarily hearing and touch. Without movement, the children's world is limited to the length of their arms. Therefore, any instruction in movement and mobility will extend the children's world and thus the children's knowledge about the world. Galloway (1981) described the cycle of learning that mobility training can set in motion: As children who are blind begin to master the environment and adequately move within it, they often grow cognitively and physically, their motivation to move and explore further increases; their greater motivation, in turn, ensures the continued expansion of their learning, control, and independence. In this regard, the importance of mobility and its interrelationship with other areas of learning has been noted by a number of authors, including Cratty (1970) Hapeman (1967), and Lowenfeld (1964/1981).

Studies (see, for example, Ferrell, 1979; Hill, 1970; Kephart, Kephart, & Schwarz, 1974; Mills & Adamshick, 1969) have substantiated the need of young visually impaired children for motor, concept, mastery, and body-image training. In addition, it has been observed that young blind children have motor problems, such as the lack of trunk and pelvic rotation, use of shuffling gait patterns, limited arm swing, dependence on a wide base of support for stability, and poor posture (Adelson & Fraiberg, 1976; Anthony & Gense, 1987; C. Brown & Bour, 1986; Campbell, 1970; Cratty, 1971; Eichorn & Vigaroso, 1967; Warren, 1976). If these essential elements on which walking is based are not corrected, atypical movement patterns become characteristic (C. Brown & Bour, 1986). Furthermore, as Clarke (1988) noted, many of these children do not move as independently as do their sighted peers for various reasons: nonexistent or ineffective walking patterns (Holt, 1981); fixation at a low-level mode of movement (Elonen & Zwarensteyn, 1964); anxiety (Fraiberg, Smith, & Adelson, 1969); or an inability to monitor the changing environment visually, which results in the diminished ability and motivation to move within the environment (Sonksen, Levitt, & Kitsinger, 1984).

These problems may be alleviated when visually impaired children are given appropriate auditory, tactile-kinesthetic, and proprioceptive experiences and motor stimulation (Adelson & Fraiberg, 1976; Anthony & Gense, 1987; Butler, 1986; Cratty, 1971; Pereira, 1990). Such experiences include baby massage, kindergym, and sensory integration activities. Unfortunately, only anecdotal evidence has been presented on the benefits of these specific interventions.

But movement in itself is not enough. Rather, movement that is self-initiated, not passive, is what is essential for a variety of developmental achievements in early childhood (Ferrell, 1979; Olson, 1981). As Clarke (1988) summarized, active exploration by young children has been found to be related to higher levels of spatial knowledge (Hazen, 1982), to memory for spatial locations (Herman, Kolker, & Shaw, 1982), and to the ability to orient to external objects in the environment (Acredolo, 1982). Some practical suggestions for appropriate movement activities (precluding mobility aids) were published in the 1970s (D. Brown, Simmons, & Methvin, 1978; Cratty, 1971; Drouillard & Raynor, 1977; Raynor & Drouillard, 1975).

Early approaches

Early practitioners highlighted the significance of concept development, such as an adequate body image and good spatial awareness, for successful mobility but did not touch on any other areas of O&M instruction. Hapeman (1967) was concerned about the effect of the deficiencies of concept development on the mobility of a young blind child. He described the developmental concepts that need to be mastered by this age group, including body image, the nature of objects, terrain, and sounds and odors; the position of objects in space; distance and time; turning; and moving with and against objects. The

importance of concept development to mobility, and indeed to learning in all areas, was later examined by Cratty and Sams (1968) and Lydon and McGraw (1973).

It was with the publication of two O&M assessment scales for blind children that aspects other than concept development were included. Lord (1969) used a developmental task approach to develop a scale for the appraisal of O&M skills in young blind children. The scales, field tested on 173 blind children aged 3–12 included self-help, precane O&M, movement in space, use of sensory skills, and use of directions and turns. Harley, Merbler, and Wood (1975) produced the Peabody Mobility Scale, which covers four areas: locomotion, sensory training, concept development, and mobility skills. Although targeted to blind children with additional impairments, it can be argued with some justification that these scales would be equally applicable to preschool children who are blind and have no other impairments. It is important to note that these scales were the first documents to mention the use of any mobility devices. Since then, Harley, Long, Merbler, and Wood (1986) and Hill, Dodson-Burk, and Taylor (1992) field-tested and published screening tests that are targeted specifically for this population and are being used more and more by O&M instructors.

Expanded definition

Hill, Rosen, Correa, and Langley (1984) presented an expanded definition of O&M specific to the unique training needs of infants and preschoolers. To Ferrell's (1979) definition, which included sensory skill development, concept development, motor development, and formal mobility skills, they added environmental and community awareness and formal orientation skills, such as the use of the long cane or push-toy devices.

Hill, Smith, Dodson-Burk, and Rosen (1987) presented an O&M curriculum for visually impaired children, called the Preschool O&M Project (POMP), that incorporated formal orientation skills, formal mobility skills, gross motor skills, and fine motor skills. POMP includes a special section on teaching children to use mobility devices as bumpers for clearing and negotiating obstacles.

However, it is important to note that the cane skills listed in the mobility section refer only to the diagonal technique, probably because the project's initial sample was composed solely of blind children with multiple other impairments.

Mobility devices

Finnis (1975) recommended that children with physical impairments as young as 12 months should be encouraged to use mobility devices. Clarke (1988) discussed essential considerations for evaluating and selecting mobility devices to encourage age-appropriate independent movement in children who are blind. Because every mobility device has certain enabling and hampering characteristics, she noted that instructors should choose a particular mobility device for an individual child on the basis of such factors as the child's motor skills and degree of residual vision; the device's level of social acceptance, appropriateness, safety, adaptability, and cost; and the availability of training. Clarke and others (Skellenger & Hill, 1991) suggested that a continuum of mobility aids, ranging from different push-toy devices to the long cane, may be more appropriate for this population.

Clarke's continuum of mobility devices is indeed broad and exhaustive, ranging from electronic travel aids to suspended movement devices to infant walkers to push-toys to precane instruments to the long cane. Pogrund, Fazzi, and Lampert (1992) grouped these devices in three broad categories: infant appliances, toys, and adaptive mobility devices. Both authors agreed that these devices should be used selectively with individual children at various developmental stages. A more detailed examination of the pros and cons of each category is warranted because of the increasing popularity of these devices.

Pogrund et al. (1992) urged that infant appliances should be used with caution and only after consultation with a physio-therapist to ensure that they are safe. For example, these appliances strengthen an infant's legs and provide some protection and opportunity for exploration, but they may reinforce inappropriate motor patterns and limit practice in crawling. Furthermore, some appliances may actually cause injury if an infant is not closely supervised while using them.

Toys, such as broom handles, hula hoops, shopping carts, lawn mowers, and golf clubs, are simple to use and are age-appropriate devices used by sighted children; they offer a degree of protection against obstacles and drop-offs, and some can even provide practice in centering the grip hand. On the other hand, they have a number of disadvantages; they are obtrusive and non collapsible, are not objects that children have with them all the time, and are not as tactilely sensitive as canes, and are not durable. In addition, children still need a transition period from their use to learning to use a long cane.

Adaptive mobility devices are specially designed apparatuses. Some researchers have reported the successful development and trial of various "precane" devices, including a two-pronged hooked cane (Foy, Kirchner, & Waple, 1991), a hula hoop (Bosbach, 1988; Ketterer, 1986), a swiveling wheeled cane (Kronick, 1987), and a T-bar bumper (Morse, 1980). But the positive reports of the use of these devices have been restricted to single case studies that have offered only subjective data. Adaptive mobility devices have many of the same advantages as toys, but they are more durable and tactilely sensitive. Their disadvantages are that they can be obtrusive, are not common devices used by sighted children, may make the visually impaired child look more impaired than necessary because they may be confused with devices for physically disabled children, and required a transition period before the use of a long cane.

Long cane

Some authors (Pogrund & Rosen, 1989; Schroeder, 1989; Willoughby & Duffy, 1989; Wurzburger, 1990) see no need for training with these less sophisticated mobility devices and believe that the long cane should be the primary and sole mobility device. They contend that the long cane has all the same advantages of adaptive mobility devices with the additional advantages of being durable and collapsible and of offering much tactile and auditory feedback. Furthermore, since the long cane is the most likely mobility device that blind children will use as adults, they stress that its early introduction will avoid the nec-

essary and often difficult transition period from one device to another. Finally, they note that the difficulty that older children may experience in being accepted by others will not occur if the long cane is introduced early because the children will have the opportunity to build its use into their self-image.

Pogrund and Rosen (1989) convincingly refuted the traditional arguments against introducing the long cane early. First, they claimed, using the long cane requires no more control or coordination than do skills that are usually termed "precane" skills (trailing and protective arm techniques) that are, themselves, separate and less efficient travel systems. Secondly, cane skills can be refined gradually over time with improved coordination and muscle tone as are other skills (for example, scribbling leads to writing). Third, the environment, even the preschool environment, can be unstable and unpredictable. (In this regard, Wier, 1988, suggested that the long cane promotes travel in previously off-limits areas, so its use will actually increase the need for it.) Fourth, children can learn safety rules that will ensure that they use the long cane appropriately. Finally, the long cane, acting as a probe, actually offers more opportunities for hands-on experiences than do other travel techniques.

Despite these convincing arguments, Pogrund and Rosen offered no empirical evidence in support of their claims. Nor did Willoughby and Duffy (1989) and Schroeder (1989), who made similar proposals. Instead, they presented suggestions for lesson plans and teaching ideas for early long cane-travel sessions. Although both briefly mentioned that push-toy devices are excellent for promoting children's readiness for cane travel, they did so only on the basis of their personal observations and experiences. Furthermore, the fact that a search of the literature yielded no articles that questioned or refuted these authors' arguments suggests that although a thorough and well-documented research base is still to be established, the majority of O&M instructors seem to agree that the early use of the long cane is indeed the best practice.

Both Schroeder (1989) and Pogrund and Rosen stated that the term *precane skills* is a misnomer and that the term *basic skills* is preferable when referring to these techniques. Furthermore, Schroeder argued that the issue is not so much

whether the long cane should be introduced to young children who are blind but how it should be introduced. The traditional methods of cane instruction, geared to adults who are adventitiously blind, are not sufficient for young congenitally blind children. Therefore, skilled O&M instructors will take full advantage of travel lessons to incorporate environmental awareness, sensory integration, concept development, and the technical refinement of cane skills within the same lesson.

Levels of O&M training

Two surveys (Dykes, 1992; Skellenger & Hill, 1991), limited in scope because of their small sample, were conducted in the early 1990s to determine the levels of O&M training provided to young children, as well as O&M instructors' opinions of the training. Both found that many O&M instructors were introducing the long cane to young children and that most responded favorably to this practice. Skellenger and Hill noted that, given the limitations of their survey (the small number of responses, the subjective nature of the feedback, and the small degree of consensus among respondents), the average age at which children were introduced to the long cane was 4–5 years. In addition, they found that the highest level of skill that the children attained was using an object other than a cane as a bumper (25%) and that only 13 percent of the children had learned the constant-contact technique or the touch technique.

Dykes (1992) discovered that the O&M instructors who responded to this survey favored the modified diagonal technique above all other techniques. Furthermore, the respondents agreed that teaching children all the precane skills before teaching them to use the long cane is an outdated idea. They also called for additional research to determine prerequisite skills, to develop curricula and training programs for the long cane, and to identify the developmental skills that are necessary for successful cane travel.

Pogrund et al. (1992) presented the first overview of early O&M intervention. Their compilation of ideas from various experienced practitioners offers a thorough introduction to the role and practice of O&M instructors with young children and a broad discussion of programs, goals, and strategies. It is particularly valuable for parents and practitioners who are entering the field.

In the latest published article that could be found in a literature search for this article, Clarke, Sainato, and Ward (1994) compared the effects of mobility training with a long cane and with a precane device (the Connecticut Precane; see Foy, Scheden, & Waiculonis, 1992). The results of their extremely small sample were as follows:

1. All the children used the precane more effectively than the long cane.
2. The precane was more effective than the long cane in preventing body contacts.
3. There were no differences in the speed of travel using the precane or the long cane.
4. Less intervention was necessary when the children used the precane.
5. There was no difference in the children's preferences for the precane and the long cane.

These results were probably to be expected: No one has suggested that the long cane is easier to learn to use than is any of the vast array of precane devices that are available. What was noteworthy was that all the children in the study were able to learn a modified diagonal cane technique, although some practitioners might question the priority given to this cane skill above that of the constant-contact technique. Also, Clarke et al. were correct in acknowledging that in their study, effectiveness applied to detecting obstacles and travel speed. Furthermore, since the study compared long cane travel to one specific precane device, generalizations to all precane devices should not be made.

Conclusion

This review of the literature on O&M instruction for visually impaired preschoolers has revealed many general findings. The value of O&M instruction in early intervention programs has been established. Meanwhile, the definition of O&M for young children has been expanded to include concept development; sensory development; motor skills; beginning formal skills, such as the sighted guide technique and the protective arm technique; and the use of a range of mobility devices of which the long cane is just one option. These developments have occurred more because of considerations about what is the best practice than because of the prevalence of overwhelming empirical evidence. It is hoped that the next 10 years will see the emergence of a rigorous empirical base to support these trends.

The publication of the study by Clarke et al. (1994) heralds the foundations of a solid research base and is to be welcomed. However, it leads to more questions than answers. To examine the benefits of both the use of the long cane and precane devices thoroughly, researchers need to conduct longitudinal comparison studies. However, given the difficulties of long-term projects and the low incidence of preschool children who are blind, these studies may be an unrealistic venture. Furthermore, in such studies, great care must be taken to specify both the particular long cane skill and precane device that are being used. Training methods for each device must be well documented, so that studies with small samples can be replicated.

The field of exploration is practically unlimited, for an examination of the "benefits" of early O&M instruction may include anything from better safety to improved self-esteem to increased concept development. There is still the question of whether it is valuable to introduce the precane before the long cane and whether doing so accelerates the acquisition of long cane skills, as Foy et al. (1992) discussed. Finally for all the O&M skills, teaching curricula with practical methods and successful strategies for this particular age group are urgently required. These are the directions that research must take in the future.

References

Acredolo, L. P. (1982) Spatial orientation in infancy. In J. C. Baird & A. Lutkus (Eds.). *Mind child architecture* (pp. 64–85). Hanover, NH: University Press of New England.

Adelson, E. & Fraiberg, S. (1976). Sensory deficit and motor development in infants blind from birth. In Z. S. Jastrzembska (Ed.)., *The effects of blindness and other impairments* (pp. 1–28). New York: American Foundation for the Blind.

Anthony, T. L. & Gense, D. J. (1987). Early intervention orientation and mobility programming: A developmental/habilitative approach/perspective. In *Proceedings of the Second International Symposium on Visually Handi-capped Infants and Young Children* (pp. 31–34). Aruba, West Indies: International Institute for the Visually Impaired.

Baird, A. S. (1977). Electronic aids: Can they help blind children? *Journal of Visual Impairment & Blindness, 71,* 97–101.

Benson, S. (1984). *So what about independent travel?* Chicago: Catholic Guild for the Blind.

Bosbach, S. R. (1988). Precane mobility devices. *Journal of Visual Impairment & Blindness, 82,* 338–339.

Brown, C. & Bour, B. (1986). *A resource manual for the development and evaluation of special programs for exceptional students. Volume V–K: Movement analysis and curriculum for visually impaired preschoolers.* Tallahassee, FL: Bureau of Education for the Blind.

Brown, D., Simmons, V., & Methvin, J. (1978). *Oregon project for visually impaired blind children.* Medford, OR: Jackson County Education Service.

Butler, C. (1986). Effects of powered mobility on self-initiated behaviors of very young children with locomotor disability. *Developmental Medicine & Child Neurology, 28,* 325–332.

Campbell, L. F. (1970). Mobility for young blind children. In *Selected Papers from a Look at the Child* (pp. 79–84). New Orleans: Association for the Education of the Visually Handicapped.

Clarke, K. L. (1988). Barriers or enablers? Mobility devices for visually impaired and multi-handicapped infants and preschoolers. *Education of the Visually Handicapped, 20,* 115–132.

Clarke, K. L., Sainato, D. M., & Ward, M. E. (1994). Travel performance of preschoolers: The effects of mobility training with a long cane versus a precane. *Journal of Visual Impairment & Blindness, 88,* 19–30.

Cratty, B. J. (1970). *Some educational implications of movement.* Seattle: Special Child Publications.

Cratty, B. J. (1971). *Movement and spatial awareness in blind children and youth.* Springfield, IL: Charles C. Thomas.

Cratty, B. J., Peterson, D., Harris, J., & Schoner, R. (1968). The development of perceptual-motor abilities in blind children and adolescents. *New Outlook for the Blind, 62,* 111–117.

Cratty, B. J. & Sams, T. A. (1968). *The body-image of blind children.* New York: American Foundation for the Blind.

Drouillard, R. & Raynor, S. (1977). *Move it!* Reston, VA: American Alliance for Health, Physical Education, Recreation, and Dance.

DuBose, R. F. (1976). Developmental needs in blind infants. *New Outlook for the Blind, 70,* 49–52.

Dykes, J. (1992). Opinions of O&M instructors about using the long cane with preschool age children. *RE:view, 24*(2), 85–92.

Eichorn, J. R. & Vigaroso, H. R. (1967). Orientation and mobility for preschool blind children. *International Journal for the Education of the Blind, 17*(2), 48–50.

Elonen, A. S. & Zwarensteyn, S. B. (1964). Appraisal of developmental lag in certain blind children. *Journal of Pediatrics, 65,* 599–610.

Ferrell, K. A. (1979). Orientation and mobility for preschool children: What we have and what we need. *Journal of Visual Impairment & Blindness, 73,* 147–150.

Fraiberg, S., Smith, M., & Adelson, E. (1969). An educational program for blind infants. *Journal of Special Education, 3,* 121–153.

Foy, C. J., Kirchner, D., & Waple, L. (1991). The Connecticut Precane. *Journal for Blindness & Visual Impairment, 82,* 85–86.

Foy, C. J., Scheden, M., & Waiculonis, J. (1992). The Connecticut Precane: Case study and curriculum. *Journal of Visual Impairment & Blindness, 82*(4), 178–181.

Galloway, A. (1981). Orientation and mobility readiness for the preschool deaf-blind child. *San Gabriel Valley School for Multiply-Handicapped Children,* 51–59.

Hapeman, L. B. (1967). Developmental concepts of blind children between the ages of 3 and 6 as they relate to orientation and mobility. *International Journal for the Education of the Blind, 17*(2), 41–48.

Harley, R. K., Long, R., Merbler, J. B., & Wood, T. A. (1986). The development of a program in O&M for multihandicapped blind infants. Final report. Nashville, TN: George Peabody College Press.

Harley, R. K., Merbler, J. B., & Wood, T. A. (1975). The development of a scale in orientation and mobility for multiply-impaired blind children. *Education of the Visually Handicapped, 8,* 1–5.

Hazen, N. L. (1982). Spatial exploration and spatial knowledge: Individual and developmental differences in very young children. *Child Development, 53,* 239–244.

Herman, J. F., Kolker, R. G., & Shaw, M. L. (1982). Effects of motor activity on children's intentional and incidental memory for spatial locations. *Child Development, 53,* 239–244.

Hill, E. W. (1970). The formation of concepts involved in body position in space. *Education of the Visually Handicapped, 2,* 112–115.

Hill, E. W., Dodson-Burk, B., & Taylor, C. R. (1992). The development and evaluation of an O&M screening for preschool children with visual impairments. *RE:view, 23*(4), 165–176.

Hill, E. W., Rosen, S., Correa, V. I., & Langley, M. B. (1984). Preschool O&M: An expanded definition. *Education of the Visually Handicapped, 16*(2), 58–71.

Hill, E. W., Smith, B. A., Dodson-Burk, B., & Rosen, S. (1987). O&M for preschool visually impaired children, in *AER Yearbook* (pp. 8–12). Washington, DC: Association of Education and Rehabilitation of the Blind and Visually Impaired.

Holt, K. S. (1981). Review: The assessment of walking in children with particular reference to cerebral palsy. *Child: Care, Health, and Development, 7,* 281–297.

Joffee, E. (1988). A home-based orientation and mobility program for infants and toddlers. *Journal of Visual Impairment & Blindness, 82,* 282–285.

Kephart, J. C., Kephart, C. P., & Schwarz, G. C. (1974). A journey into the world of the blind child. *Exceptional Children, 40,* 421–427.

Ketterer, H. (1986). Mobility begins at birth: An early childhood orientation and mobility readiness program. In N. Neustadt-Noy, S. Merin, & Y. Schiff (Eds.), *Orientation and mobility of the visually impaired* (pp. 101–108).

Kronick, M. K. (1987). Children and canes: An adaptive approach. *Journal of Visual Impairment & Blindness, 81,* 61–62.

Lord, E. (1969). The development of scales for the measurement of O&M of young blind children. *Exceptional Children, 36*(2), 77–81.

Lowenfeld, B. (1981). The blind child as an integral part of the family and community. In B. Lowenfeld, *Berthold Lowenfeld on blindness and blind people.* New York: *American Foundation for the Blind.* (Original work published 1964).

Lydon, W. T. & McGraw, M. L. (1973). *Concept development of visually handicapped children.* New York: American Foundation for the Blind.

Mills, R. J. & Adamshick, D. R. (1969). The effectiveness of structured sensory training experiences prior to formal orientation and mobility instruction. *Education of the Visually Handicapped, 1,* 14–21.

Morse, K. A. (1980). Modifications of the long cane for use by a multiply impaired child. *Journal of Visual Impairment & Blindness, 74,* 15–18.

Olson, M. (1981). Enhancing the exploratory behavior of visually impaired preschoolers. *Journal of Visual Impairment & Blindness, 75,* 373–377.

Palazesi, M. A., (1986). The need for motor development programs for visually impaired preschoolers. *Journal of Visual Impairment & Blindness, 80,* 573–576.

Pereira, L. M. (1990). Spatial concepts and balance performance: Motor learning of blind and visually impaired children. *Journal of Visual Impairment & Blindness, 84,* 109–110.

Pogrund, R. L., Fazzi, D. L., & Lampert, J. S. (Eds.). (1992). *Early focus: Working with young blind and visually impaired children and their families.* New York: American Foundation for the Blind.

Pogrund, R. L. & Rosen, S. J. (1989). The preschool blind child can be a cane user. *Journal of Visual Impairment & Blindness, 83,* 431–439.

Raynor, S. & Drouillard, R. (1975). *Get a wiggle on!* Reston, VA: American Alliance for Health, Physical Education, Recreation, and Dance.

Schroeder, F. (1989). A step toward equality: Cane travel for the young blind child. *Future Reflections, 8,* 3–8.

Skellenger, A. C. & Hill, E. W. (1991). Current practices and considerations regarding long cane instruction with preschool children. *Journal of Visual Impairment & Blindness, 85,* 101–104.

Sonksen, P. M., Levitt, S., & Kitsinger, M. (1984). Identification of constraints acting upon motor development in young blind children. *Child, Care, Health & Development, 10,* 273–286.

Stack, D. M. & Minnes, P. M. (1989). Aberrant motor development in three disabilities: Directions for research and practice. *Early Childhood Development, 43,* 1–14.

Warren, D. H. (1976). Blindness and early development: What is known and what needs to be studied. *New Outlook for the Blind, 70,* 5–16.

Warren, D. H. (1984). *Blindness and early childhood development* (2nd ed.). New York: American Foundation for the Blind.

Webster, R. (1976). *The road to freedom.* Jacksonville, IL: Katan Publications.

Wier, S. (1988). Cane travel and a question of when. *Journal of Visual Impairment & Blindness, 82,* 197.

Willoughby, D. M. (1979). *A resource guide for parents and educators of blind children.* Baltimore: National Federation of the Blind.

Willoughby, D. M. & Duffy, S. (1989). *Handbook for itinerant teachers of blind and visually impaired students.* Baltimore: National Federation of the Blind.

Wurzburger, B. H. (1990). *Some ideas on O&M for preschool and early elementary school-aged visually impaired children.* Paper presented at the California Transcribers and Educators of the Visually Handicapped Conference, San Diego, CA.

A Child with Severe Hearing Loss Joins Our Learning Community

Mary Jane Blasi and Lori Priestley

There was much anxiety in our first-grade classroom. The rest of the school was buzzing in its usual way. The hustle and bustle of teachers and students was abundant in the hallways, but we were in our own little world. Anxious yet focused, we were preparing a program we had never attempted before. Finally, the moment everyone anticipated—the arrival of our new class member—was here.

Harry walked in slowly, with reserve. For him, everything was new: the school, the people, the situation, the experience. His crystal blue eyes absorbed the richness of the environment around him. He appeared overwhelmed by the chatter of the people wanting him to feel welcome. Harry stared intently, smiling occasionally at the attempts to make him feel at home, but he obviously wanted to be left alone to make his own adjustment. He hurried to his seat.

Harry, with profound hearing loss, wore two hearing aids that were connected to a cassette-player-like box held by suspender straps at his waist. This apparatus is sometimes called a "phonic ear."

The classroom teacher, Mary Jane, wore a microphone that amplified her voice. Harry also had a transliterator (interpreter), Lori.

Because Harry had had difficulty in preschool with lipreading and sign language, his family had decided to supplement his learning with *cued speech*, a system of hand cues that enhance lipreading. With Lori as the facilitator of communication, cued speech was to become Harry's link with the classroom environment.

Initially, the first-graders had many questions. We addressed each concern. There were no secrets. Educating ourselves and the class was crucial. Ultimately our challenge was to educate the school as well.

We as a learning community reaped many valuable benefits. We as teachers experienced the precious rewards and dynamic power of a collaborative team. This was a turning point in our careers.

From *Young Children*, March 1998, pp. 44-49. © 1998 by the National Association for the Education of Young Children (NAEYC). Reprinted by permission.

Although our experience was with a child who could not hear speech (he hears only some sounds), we hope our observations and reflections will prove valuable to teachers of other children in inclusive classrooms.

Creating a community of learners

A general educator, a cued speech transliterator, and a class of caring, compassionate children comprised our learning community. We experienced every emotion conceivable, but our union as a community gave us the support we needed to succeed. Our community became the vehicle for exploration. The innate acceptance and uninhibited minds of the children became the true magic of our community. We grew together in a way few others were able to understand.

We wanted our classroom to be warm and inviting but, most important, our own. We labeled everything, in keeping with our goal of providing a print-rich environment, and selected songs to make everyone feel welcome.

It may be hard to imagine how a child with a hearing loss could enjoy the simplicity of a song, but Harry certainly did. In the beginning it was awkward for us all. But with wonderful song cards designed by children's musician Raffi and Lori cueing the words, "Down by the Bay" became Harry's favorite song. We soon lost our awkwardness.

We shared basic educational philosophies, which proved paramount in providing a positive and stimulating environment. We established a successful learning community by first becoming "active learners" ourselves. Open and honest communication was equally important. We developed an atmosphere of trust by valuing the importance of dialogue. The ownership our community shared was essential in establishing the bond we needed to succeed.

Many hours were spent developing an awareness of serious hearing impairment and other disabilities. The class began reading Jeanne Peterson's *I Have a Sister, My Sister Is Deaf* (1977), a beautiful story about the author's childhood experiences. Developing an awareness of cued speech also was important because our new classmate had no other mode of communication and was just beginning to learn the system. We allowed time for practicing cues as well as working on class cue projects, which created an understanding and acceptance of cued speech.

We introduced cued speech to the school community by designing a school showcase. It read, "Can you cue—Hello, how are you?" We often found people eagerly attempting to cue. The school community was very accepting and supportive of Harry and made an effort to make him feel at home. From the principal with his "Just Cue It!" shirt to the cafeteria workers who eagerly interacted with him, Harry found many people attempting to communicate with him. In an odd sort of way, we were all in the same boat: we were faced with something new and were doing our best to make it work.

We learned to appreciate the benefits of whole language in conjunction with cued speech. When experimentation is the mainstay of the daily routine, emphasis is placed on that which is truly meaningful. The most valuable experiences allow true meaningful communication. We enjoyed the simplicity of thoughts yet worked very hard at the skill of communicating.

Lori remembers her first really meaningful conversation with Harry, an experience from which we learned a great deal. The two were on their way to the computer lab for another session of cued speech and language practice when Lori saw a peculiar expression on Harry's face. She stopped and motioned for Harry to join her at a nearby table. Harry sat down and said quite simply, "I'm tired." Lori, who was tired too from a trying morning with her new puppy, started talking about her unsuccessful attempts to train the pup.

Harry's eyes lit up, he cued rapidly in response, and Lori knew he was truly understanding her every word. They sat laughing and enjoying the immense rewards of true communication. The antics of Lori's puppy were a popular discussion topic for the rest of the year.

Harry, as part of a whole language classroom, benefited from a variety of learning experiences. The

What Is Cued Speech?

Cued speech was developed by Dr. Orin Cornett, a physicist and vice president for planning at Gallaudet University in Washington, D.C. Dr. Cornett was motivated by the knowledge that most severely hearing-impaired people do not read proficiently and do not make maximum use of what should be their "window on the world"—reading. This is because children with hearing losses do not learn spoken language before learning to read (Cunningham-Walker 1987).

Cued speech is a system of hand cues that enhances lipreading. Eight different handshapes represent consonant sounds and four hand positions represent vowel sounds. The hand cues, used near the lips, match what is being said to clarify ambiguities. Spelled out are grammatical constructs and changes in language that are difficult to differentiate in sign or lipreading. Cues can be used for words without standard signs—for example, for names, funny sounds ("Yikes!"), and idioms ("Cool, man")—promoting vocabulary growth and development. Cued speech aids in increasing reading skills by corresponding exactly to the words read, allowing the child to focus on the meaning of the message.

children worked on research projects throughout the year in cooperative learning groups. Each child was responsible for a part of the work, reflective of the group as a whole. Harry's excellent reading ability helped his partners with their initial research work, and he closely watched Lori's cues to understand his responsibilities. He helped the children with the content of the readings and they helped him understand what he was to do. As we worked on these projects Harry rehearsed at home so he could report his part of his group's research project clearly at school.

The numerous "pull-out" sessions for Harry were both a necessity and a problem for us. Harry needed to learn cueing, but he did not want to leave his classroom and friends. He received speech-language services daily, for 30 minutes, and was pulled out of our classroom usually during our lengthy language arts time. Initially Lori went with him to pull-out sessions, but because of his ongoing quest for independence she eventually remained in the classroom, working with other children while he was gone.

On Mondays and Thursdays Harry met with an audiologist for another half-hour session. These two days were particularly fragmented and exhausting. Initially this was a real problem, but Harry adapted, working tirelessly to complete his assigned work before lunch and the long-awaited recess. We admired his fortitude. Lori or Mary Jane clarified

assignments and helped him with any difficulties, allowing him to complete his work along with his classmates.

Fortunately the therapists working with him were honest, open, and flexible, and we worked together to minimize Harry's time away from class. Our dialogue with the speech-language pathologist was ongoing, and she devised some creative approaches to Harry's isolation by including other children from our class in her sessions. What a hit that turned out to be! Every time she appeared at our door the children excitedly waved their hands, each wanting to be the one selected to cue with Harry that day.

Many children were picking up cues themselves, cueing to each other as well as practicing from literature during our daily Drop Everything And Read (DEAR) time. They took turns going to speech class with Harry, learning language and cues and diminishing Harry's sense of being singled out to leave our community.

During the first days of school, crucial in establishing a classroom community, many well-meaning professionals came to see Harry, anxious about his adjustment. These interruptions became a difficult issue, and in exasperation Mary Jane turned to the principal. He reinforced that Mary Jane, though not an expert in deaf education, was in charge of the classroom and her decisions regarding Harry and the class were to be respected. These procedures, established early on, helped maintain a calmer atmosphere in our environment.

The principal was an integral member of our support network, a real advocate for Harry, and our dialogue with him was continuous throughout the year. His open door, support, and honest communication proved invaluable. All teachers working in inclusive situations need to enlist the support and advocacy of their principal.

Harry's school day

Harry always had less time than everyone else. He rode the shuttle bus from his home to school and arrived just as the school day began. He settled in his seat with homework assignments and the storybooks he had previewed with his mother.

Our mornings were routine, beginning with a reading of plans for the day. During these opening exercises Lori was always near the teacher, cueing dialogue and songs for Harry. Lori's role was to provide cues for all the words as well as environmental sounds and interruptions, such as announcements on the school intercom.

Harry's sense of humor eased many initial situations and allowed us to learn about deafness, cued speech, and sound-enhancing equipment with a minimum of anxiety. One day Harry raised his hand to answer a question, came up to the front of the class to write on the board, and then looked puzzled—he had no idea what to do! He started to giggle, we started to laugh, and the class joined in. His sense of humor and willingness to take risks quickly eased Harry into our community and provided a valuable lesson for the other children: that learning is a process, not a right or wrong answer.

Henry Kisor, in *What's That Pig Outdoors?* relates a similar outlook in his schooling: "I still had that sunny good humor which helped wary hearing children to accept my deafness despite my odd, breathy speech and the necessity of facing me when they spoke to me" (1990, 56). Harry embodies the qualities that we, as teachers, are constantly striving to instill in all of our students: independence, positive self-esteem, risk-taking, curiosity, humor, expressiveness, enthusiasm, and excitement about learning and the world.

Collaboration at School

Collaboration was essential. Our collaborative efforts began with a professor from Gallaudet University who spent two days training the classroom teacher, transliterator, resource teacher, resource instructional assistant, and speech-language pathologist in the basics of cued speech. He defined our roles and offered avenues to pursue for further training in deaf education and cued speech.

Our training was compact and stressful. We were inundated with rules and procedures based on each person's role. We became active learners; after all, we had only a few days to digest all of this information before making it come together in the classroom. The professor's strongest recommendation was that we attend a cue camp weekend in Virginia.

Funded by our school, we traveled to Jamestown, Virginia, for a three-day immersion in deaf culture. Cue camps are weekend or week-long (summer) events and provide the opportunity for families and professionals to discuss common concerns, provide support for each other, and have fun. Many families attend cue camp year after year. We were impressed by the support, courage, and love they displayed for each other. These people have faced and accepted obstacles in their lives with the attitude of "Let's get on with it"—in other words, "Just cue it!"

Our days were filled with interaction with the families, workshops, and dialogues with teachers. In a workshop for beginning cuers, we watched a video that simulated deafness. We were directed to read what the speaker was saying, and we watched the film over and over until someone deciphered enough words of the Declaration of Independence that we figured out what was being recited. The task was difficult, but given a context of prior knowledge, reminiscent of our whole language background, we could figure out the words.

We were exhausted after this experience. Throughout the year we recalled our intense concentration as we thought of the tremendous and exhausting focus that was always expected of Harry.

A psychologist presented a workshop on the stages of grief. We learned about the stages of grief that parents progress through when experiencing the loss of the "perfect child" they expected at birth. We learned the importance of working through these stages to promote acceptance and mental health. A critical piece in our training was developing the understanding of loss and determining where each family might be in the grief process. It helped us develop a deeper understanding of Harry and his family and gave us ideas for helping them to keep moving forward.

Strengthened by a better understanding of deafness, we returned to our classroom. The speech-language pathologist was eager to share new ideas, and our collaboration with her was enhanced by our new learnings from cue camp. We established a caring support network for ourselves and continually reflected and reevaluated our work to appropriately serve Harry as well as the other children in our class. Not only did we share ideas and concerns but also frustrations that we experienced along the way.

Following warm-up exercises the children returned to their seats for writing in their word books and journals as well as reading in heterogeneous or skills-as-needed groups. Our early writing was based on the "key word" ideas of Sylvia Ashton-Warner, as described in her book *Teacher* (1963). She says that first words must have intense meaning for a child, for it is here that the love of reading is born. The longer this reading is "organic," the stronger it becomes. Among Harry's favorite words were Batman and Riley, his dog's name.

As the children wrote, we circulated, available to all for conferencing and nurturing their thoughts. We always met the children at eye level, kneeling by their desks to talk quietly, personally. During this time Lori focused on cueing with Harry, acting as a tutor as well as a transliterator. We found the "stretch" (phonetic) spelling we used corresponded quite naturally with cued speech. Every sound was cued, with Harry picking up the same sounds and progressing with or beyond his classmates with his writing.

We found many advantages to cued speech. We noticed that for unfamiliar words the beginning reader can see the correct number of syllables, the correct consonants and vowels for use in reading and writing.

After writing we gathered to share our stories, make comments, and ask questions. The children took turns in the Author's Chair. At times we teachers became exasperated with the children's repetitious remarks: "I like your printing," "What's your favorite part?" "Why did you write about that?" Harry's comment invariably was, "I like your picture."

We worked hard to expand the children's thinking and questioning, suspecting that somehow we were not getting them into a depth of meaningful conversation. We brainstormed other possible comments and modeled thoughtful remarks but to little avail.

Then we came upon Thomas Newkirk's *Listening In* (1992), which describes the talk of a community of first- and second-grade learners. In explaining the persistence of the same questions, Newkirk says,

> Our problem with understanding it, I believe, stems from the assumption that six and seven year olds buy into an adult model of asking questions to resolve perplexities, seek information, explore motives. But do the students in these groups feel such a compelling need to know the reader's favorite page, day after day, week after week? I doubt it. Instead they see the opportunity to ask a sanctioned question as a way of participating in the group. It is the asking that is central; the answer is of secondary importance, and they often don't listen to it. . . . The formula questions are like a free pass that allows anyone to enter a conversation. (p. 39)

We realized that Harry's "I like your picture" made him a part of our community.

After lunch we all enjoyed DEAR time, with everyone finding a cozy spot to read, alone or with a friend or two. Harry loved this time because he loved books and catalogs. He assisted friends in reading and understanding texts. His personal motivation to learn about the world through literature served as a model for the other children.

After DEAR time the children usually participated in a special area class—music, art, library, or physical education (Harry's favorite). During this time Mary Jane, sometimes with Lori's assistance, prepared for math. By this time of day we were all tired, Harry sometimes more than others. Math concepts seemed to be more difficult for him to grasp. We incorporated *Mathematics Their Way* (1976) activities, a manipulatives math program designed by Mary Baratta-Lorton to develop understanding and insight into the patterns and relationships of math through the use of patterns, blocks, geoboards, unifix cubes, graphs, and so on. Children work in collaboration, with emphasis on the learning process. In this collaborative situation Harry observed his classmates to clarify his thinking as well as his own manipulation of the materials.

During math time Harry needed Lori's assistance as a cuer and tutor. The concepts of tens and ones and of money were especially difficult for him. We conferred with his mother on this and came up with the idea of saving money at home, with Harry continually counting the amounts and paying for services, such as eating at fast-food restaurants.

After math we went outside for a much needed break. Harry excelled at sports and was always involved in a game of kickball or soccer. Communication was not a problem here with a group of peers!

Mary Jane's daughter, aware of Harry and his athletic abilities, told her about Kenny Walker, a deaf player for the Denver Broncos. Mary Jane wrote a short letter to Mr. Walker describing Harry. Within a

Collaboration with Home

Like all children, Harry carried his knowledge from school to home and from home to school. The help and dedication his home environment provided helped him achieve success. Harry's mother is a tireless advocate for him in every aspect of his life. Although we had not discussed our views of literacy, we soon realized that we shared a common view: literacy and a love of books would be Harry's "window on the world." Harry's mom especially wanted him to acquire an extensive vocabulary, the same as hearing children. His favorite story was *Knots on a Counting Rope* (1987) by Bill Martin and John Archambault, which recounts the loving relationship between an Indian boy who cannot see and his grandfather.

A major concern in deaf education is the lack of language skills and vocabulary. Throughout Harry's early years he and his mother had written multitudes of language experience stories and compiled scrapbooks with photos and stories about every family outing and vacation. As Karen Smith says, "Literature [is] a universal language that binds people together and helps them create understandings of what it means to be a member of a community of learners and of the greater community of humankind" (in Short & Pierce 1990, 16).

We had high expectations for Harry and in no way planned to "water down" the curriculum. We outlined procedures that we thought would work for home/school collaboration, then reflected, evaluated, and adapted as the year progressed. We used plastic storage bags for transport of storybooks that were to be read daily in class. When Harry's mother saw the plastic bag, she knew there was work to do at home. She reviewed the stories daily, cueing, clarifying, and elaborating on the story or vocabulary.

week Harry received a handsome autographed picture with a personal note that read, "Harry, keep up the good work and *never give up!*" We all were moved by the gesture of a strong football player who had so much in common with a strong little boy.

Implications for teachers

Although our story is based on experiences with inclusion of a child with hearing loss, we believe there are critical points for all teachers to consider when faced with including a challenged child in a regular learning environment. Most important, teachers must educate themselves— seek out information and resources that will help them understand the special challenges faced by the child. Teachers can prepare the class by reading appropriate literature and talking with the children. All questions should be answered as openly and honestly as possible.

Teachers should educate the school community, including administra-tors, support staff, other teachers, and children. Our showcase, for example, sparked a schoolwide interest in cued speech. Reach out to others. Collaborate with school staff and the parents. A trusting, working relationship with the child's parents is critical. Enlist the support of your principal or director to become an advocate for you, your special-needs child, and your class. Education at all levels and collaboration are essential components of successful inclusive programs.

Conclusion

Harry became an active participant in the learning community, always moving forward and making the best of every situation. When he visited the second-grade class at the end of the school year, he appeared secure. He no longer looked down at the floor as he walked, and he intermingled with his peers happily and confidently. The embarrassment of wearing his phonic ear and having a transliterator was gone.

The enthusiasm and accepting nature of the community helped Harry make a difficult transition. His peers, with all of their eagerness, helped Harry feel like "one of the bunch" by readily accepting his situation and becoming a part of it. They were instrumental in helping Harry begin to cue and become more comfortable with his deafness.

The children's attitude was reflected in a hallway encounter one morning. Harry and a new friend, Jeremy, were on their way to the nurse's office when another child passed them slowly, staring at Harry and his phonic ear. "What's wrong with him?" the child asked, pointing. Jeremy replied simply, "He's deaf. So what?" and he and Harry went on about their business.

As Harry's teachers we became more aware of how important it is to work with every individual child. We learned from our research, workshops, collaboration, and ongoing dialogue with professionals and the family, from our reflections with each other, and most important,

from a six-year-old boy who sometimes was tired but *never gave up!* We believe, "as Jay Lemke (1985) argues, [that] schools are not 'knowledge delivery systems' but human social institutions in which people influence one another's lives" (in Pierce & Gilles 1993, 17).

Epilogue

Today Harry is in sixth grade and doing well. His mother reports that the transition to middle school was easy and that Harry has mastered cueing.

References

Ashton-Warner, S. 1963. *Teacher.* New York: Simon & Schuster.

Baratta-Lorton, M. 1976. *Mathematics their way.* Reading, MA: Addison-Wesley.

Cunningham-Walker, J. 1987. Children who cue. *The Voice* 3: 12–17.

Kisor, H. 1990. *What's that pig outdoors? A memoir of deafness.* New York: Penguin.

Newkirk, T. 1992. *Listening in.* Portsmouth, NH: Heinemann.

Pierce, J., & C. Gilles, eds. 1993. *Cycles of meaning.* Portsmouth, NH: Heinemann.

Short, K., & K. Pierce, eds. 1990. *Talking about books.* Portsmouth, NH: Heinemann.

Resources for children

DePaola, T. 1980. *Now one foot, now the other.* New York: G. P. Putnam's Sons.

Litchfield, A. 1976. *A button in her ear.* Niles, IL: Albert Whitman.

Martin, B., & J. Archambault. 1987. *Knots on a counting rope.* New York: Henry Holt.

Peterson, J. 1977. *I have a sister, my sister is deaf.* New York: Harper & Row.

Powers, M. 1986. *Our teacher's in a wheelchair.* Niles, IL: Albert Whitman.

Simon, N. 1976. *Why am I different?* Niles, IL: Albert Whitman.

Twinn, M. 1989. *Who cares about disabled people?* Singapore: Child's Play.

For further reading

Boggs, C., ed. 1990. *The cued speech journal.* Raleigh, NC: National Cued Speech Association.

Bredekamp, S., & C. Copple, eds. 1997. *Developmentally appropriate practice in early childhood programs.* Rev. ed. Washington, DC: NAEYC.

Daisey, M., ed. 1994. *Center lines.* Raleigh, NC: National Cued Speech Association.

Derman-Sparks, L., & the A.B.C. Task Force. 1989. *Anti-bias curriculum: Tools for empowering young children.* Washington, DC: NAEYC.

Vygotsky, L. 1978. *Mind in society.* Cambridge, MA: Harvard University Press.

Multimedia Stories
for Deaf Children

Jean F. Andrews
Donald L. Jordan

It's hard to beat the feel of a book between the hands—feeling its soft cover, turning crisp pages, and smelling the ink. The low cost of books and their easy portability—carrying them to the couch, backyard, bathtub, pool, and the beach—entice us. But the whir and wonder of technology has captivated many teachers. Multimedia stories on the Web, for instance, can lead children with language and reading disabilities to read print augmented with graphics, animation, and movies.

Using Multimedia Technology

Multimedia technology allows authors to develop stories in two or more languages. Each language, then, can be accessed by the click of a button on each page. Multimedia applications are especially useful for deaf children because video dictionaries of sign language can be built right into the stories. This article describes our U.S. Department of Education-funded project and shows how teachers can use the Web to research their stories—and put these stories on the Web.

Phase 1: We set up a multimedia laboratory with state-of-the-art hardware and software.

Phase 2: Our staff (graduate students in deaf education and computer science) developed scripts and multimedia stories centering on the Mexican-American culture. These student-authors used library sources, as well as the Web, for information (see Figures 1 and 2 for Web sources). Native users of American Sign Language provided sign language translations and native-Spanish-speaking students provided the Spanish translations. Our computer science students set up a Web server to distribute our stories.

Phase 3: We provided summer workshops for teachers, teaching them to use the Web and to develop their own multimedia stories for their students. We placed teacher-authored stories on the Web.

Phase 4: We set up a research plan to follow the progress of Mexican-American deaf children over 1 year to see how they learned language using this new technology.

Designing Projects for Mexican-American Deaf Children

We developed materials and activities for Mexican-American deaf children because they are the fastest growing minority group in the U.S. school-age population of deaf children, particularly in Texas, where we work. In fact, these are more than 7,000 deaf children from Spanish-speaking homes in the United States, and this number is growing (Schildroth & Hotto, 1996). These children have difficulty learning English; and on

Stories centered on Mexican-American cultural themes written at different reading levels helped students with a wide range of hearing loss meet their language and cultural needs.

From *Teaching Exceptional Children*, May/June 1998, pp. 28-33. © 1998 by The Council for Exceptional Children. Reprinted by permission.

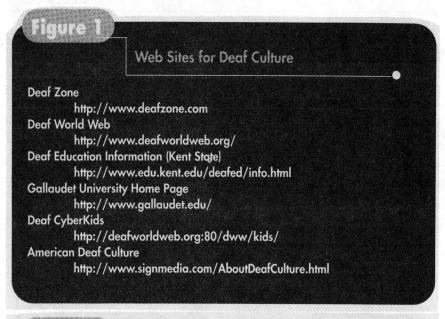

Figure 1

Web Sites for Deaf Culture

Deaf Zone
    http://www.deafzone.com
Deaf World Web
    http://www.deafworldweb.org/
Deaf Education Information (Kent State)
    http://www.edu.kent.edu/deafed/info.html
Gallaudet University Home Page
    http://www.gallaudet.edu/
Deaf CyberKids
    http://deafworldweb.org:80/dww/kids/
American Deaf Culture
    http://www.signmedia.com/AboutDeafCulture.html

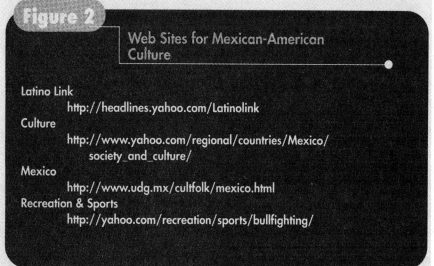

Figure 2

Web Sites for Mexican-American Culture

Latino Link
    http://headlines.yahoo.com/Latinolink
Culture
    http://www.yahoo.com/regional/countries/Mexico/
        society_and_culture/
Mexico
    http://www.udg.mx/cultfolk/mexico.html
Recreation & Sports
    http://yahoo.com/recreation/sports/bullfighting/

standardized tests that measure reading, language and mathematics, many score 2–3 years below their Anglo peers who are deaf (Allen, 1994; Gerner de Garcia, 1993).

School has been difficult for Hispanic deaf students because of cultural and linguistic differences. Cultural influences can be Spanish, Mexican, Puerto Rican, Dominican Republican, Cuban, Latin or South American origin, or mixed. These students' language learning may be fragmented. For example, children may use some spoken and written English, American Sign Language (ASL), gestures, and home signs. They may also speak and lip-read the Spanish language. In addition, they may use some spoken English and sign language, or a mixture of these. And even further, if families recently emigrated from Mexico or South America, these deaf children may use an indigenous sign language. Such a mixture of codes and languages can make learning academic subjects in English difficult for deaf Mexican-American students.

Mexican-American deaf youth must also navigate through three different cultures—Hispanic, American, and deaf cultures. Even though they might eat ethnic foods and celebrate the religious and historical holidays of their families, these cultural events have little meaning because few family members can explain these events to them in sign language. Consequently, many deaf Mexican-American children have grown up not fully understanding their home culture.

To meet their language and cultural needs, we designed a project to develop stories centered on Mexican-American cultural themes written at different reading levels—elementary, junior high, and high school. We added translations in ASL. We also provided written and spoken texts in Spanish and English because some Mexican-American deaf and hard-of-hearing children may benefit from hearing and reading Spanish words. We wanted our multimedia stories to be accessible to children with a wide range of hear-

ing losses. (See Figures 3 and 4, for other uses of multimedia stories.)

Personalizing Dictionaries and Stories

Multimedia technology lets you explore information at your own pace. It combines printed text, narration, words, sounds, music, graphics, photos, movies, and animation on one computer "page." These pages can be linked together sequentially or can branch off into new pages called *hypermedia*.

For deaf children who use ASL, printed texts can be supported with sign language video (or movie) dictionaries. These videos can include facial expressions, head tilts, eyebrow raises, and body movements, the elements that encode the grammar of ASL (Pollard, 1993). No longer must deaf students turn to the teacher or sign language interpreter to ask what a word in a story means. They can simply press a button—and a person will appear on the screen, explaining the word in sign. This person could be the teacher, thus personalizing the dictionary.

For example, one Mexican-American folktale we designed is called "The Tracks" or "Las Vias." In this story, on one page is the phrase "piled up." If the student does not know the meaning, he can click on this "hot word" (which is colored red to differentiate from the other black text). By clicking on this hot word, the student is linked to a movie clip of a deaf adult signing the concept "piled up." All pages contain hot words where the child can get a sign language translation. Students can also click on the button and have whole paragraphs signed to them (see Figure 5).

Hard-of-hearing children can choose these sign language translations or turn up the sound track volume of the story or use both. If the Hispanic child knows some Spanish words, he or she may click on a button to translate the paragraph into Spanish. Stories formatted in multiple ways pro-

Multimedia applications are especially useful for deaf children because video dictionaries of sign language can be built right into the stories.

vide options for children to choose the mode that best meets their needs. Along the way, they learn about their Mexican-American culture in stories that are motivating and entertaining to read.

Creating Mexican-American Stories

Faculty and graduate students of Mexican-American heritage decided what Mexican-American cultural themes should be used. We purchased a library of 150 books, including Hispanic history, literature, encyclopedias, and references. We bought books on holidays, food, and traditions, and we purchased videotapes and magazines. We also found Internet resources on Hispanic and deaf cultures (See Figures 1 and 2).

With Web-related information, we developed stories about folktales, animal stories, Mexican-American history, famous Hispanic Americans, holidays, crafts, foods, and entertainers. An important topic was also added—successful Hispanic-deaf persons to provide role modeling to deaf children.

Our graduate students teamed up to write short two-page scripts. They calculated a reading grade level using the Flesch-Kincaid readability formula on Microsoft Word 6.0. After stories were edited, computer-science research assistants designed a "book" using the ToolBook software. Then the computer-graphics students designed pictures for the story. We also scanned pictures from books, calendars, and magazines. Teachers who made materials for *classroom-use only* could use pictures from books and magazines. However, we wrote original stories or rewrote folktales which had been written more than 75 years ago in order to not violate copyright laws. These stories we will commercially market.

Other graduate students worked on the sign language videos of the script. Deaf students fluent in ASL signed scripts in American Sign Language. Other students used videocapturing equipment to mesh the sign language with the text of each story. One of our graduate students from Mexico who was fluent in Spanish translated our stories into written and spoken Spanish.

Other graduate students designed comprehension tests or games for each story (Pollard, 1993). The games provided the teachers with a tool to measure reading comprehension. The students could push a button to see how many points they scored after each game. For example, in one game, the student pressed a button to see a sentence signed into ASL. The student's task was to translate the ASL sentence into English. At the bottom of the screen were a group of scrambled words. The student had to drag the words and put them into the right slots that would show a grammatically correct English sentence.

Figure 3

Other Uses for Our Trilingual Multimedia Stories

* Hispanic hearing children learning English as a second language. Pictures, animation, photos, and videos can support the children's learning of home and school language.
* Anglo college and high school deaf and hearing students who are learning Spanish as a second language.
* Hearing children with language and reading difficulties. Signs support the children's learning of printed text (Vernon & Andrews, 1990).
* Hard-of-hearing Hispanic students. The stories may support their further learning of printed Spanish.
* Hearing adults (interpreters, teachers, parents) learning sign language. The multimedia stories may provide instruction in sign language.

Figure 4

Multimedia Stories Support Second-Language Learning

* Multiple translations of text (in English, Spanish, and ASL) provide students with options in learning English.
* Observing children using multimedia stories can increase our understanding of how children acquire and develop a second language.
* Trilingual multimedia materials provide "comprehensible input" (Krashen, 1996) in the child's first language.
* Trilingual stories may help the child bridge learning from one language to another (Cummins, 1988).

For example, in "The Tracks," students come upon scrambled words. They push on the "hot button" PLAY and see a video clip of a sentence signed in ASL. It is their job to unscramble the words to make a correct English sentence. If they succeed, they get a smiley face on the screen (see Figure 6).

Producing a CD-ROM and a Public Web Site

After we edited the stories, we transferred the files and pressed them to a CD-ROM disk (Andrews & Jordan, 1998). We also made copies of the CD-ROMs for the teachers participating in the research component of the project.

Mexican-American deaf children in the area were invited to the multimedia lab at our university to read the stories and comment on them. We have also loaded up some of the stories on the World Wide Web for national distribution. You can access our stories through our Web page (http://www.deafed.lamar.edu/).

Training Teachers

An important part of our project was to teach educators how to develop their own multimedia stories. During two summers, 20 teachers who worked primarily with Mexican-American deaf children attended a 2-week multimedia workshop. Some teachers had no experience with Windows applications; others had used ToolBook before. In the two summers, the teachers learned basic and advanced competencies with ToolBook software.

Skills included accessing the Internet (e-mail, newsgroups, file transfer protocol, World Wide Web). Teachers also learned how to operate a CD-ROM drive, view the internal and external components of the computer, use scanners, and create and save simple books on ToolBook. Further, they learned the basics of ToolBook software, viewed commercial CD-ROM software, and used the Internet to download and save audio and video files. Teachers created text and buttons in ToolBook; and they recorded, saved, and captured sound and video and incorporated them into their books. They com-

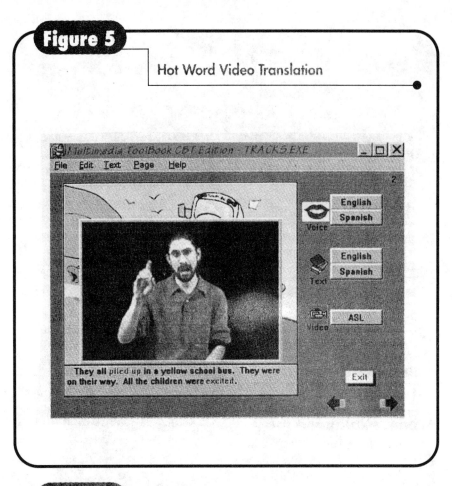

Figure 5

Hot Word Video Translation

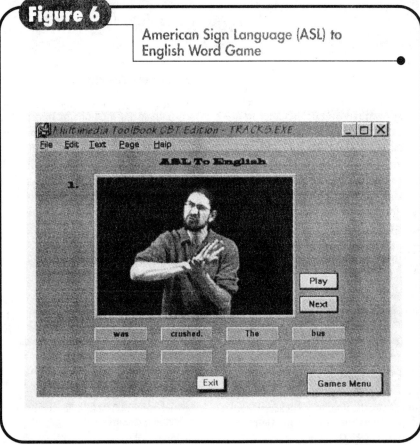

Figure 6

American Sign Language (ASL) to English Word Game

posed a story with a Mexican-American theme and storyboarded it into pages, shared files over the network, transferred files over a network, and completed a CD-ROM storybook. Teachers completed one story, and our staff pressed it to a CD-ROM so they could use it with their Mexican-American students. See our Web page for titles of stories our teachers created.

Conducting Classroom Research

Of the 20 participating teachers, 7 took multimedia computers from our university setting to their home classrooms. Teachers would use the computers with the students to create additional books using ToolBook software. These teachers worked in classrooms with at least 80% Hispanic-deaf children in McAllen, Corpus Christi, Zapata, Austin, Baytown, San Antonio, and Beaumont, Texas. These 7 teachers will study the language learning of 10 Hispanic-deaf children as they use multimedia technology during the third and final year of the project.

So far, commentary on the use of technology in the schools has been anecdotal or testimonial, rather than data on the children's performance in reading. (An exception to this is data on math score improvements using computers.) In view of this lack of data, our study will use in-depth literacy assessments to determine how deaf children learn language from reading multimedia stories in Phase 4 of our project.

The seven teachers who received computers and took them to their classrooms will follow the progress of two or three students over a full school year (September 1997—June 1998). A set of literacy measures will be given to the children. These will be standardized tests and portfolio or performance assessments.

The *literacy portfolio* is a collection of a student's work and records of progress of achievement assembled over time. In contrast to standardized tests, literacy portfolios measure students on high-quality, performance-based, meaningful tasks. These tasks include reading and discussing significant books and articles, writing reflective responses to meaningful topics, researching and writing reports, and compiling a log of books and stories read (Valencia & Calfee, 1991). Based on current reading research, we put together a battery of different tasks to measure literacy development.

Using these techniques, we can provide a detailed description of 10 Mexican-American deaf students and how they develop English literacy skills using technology, as well as other literacy activities in their curriculum over a full school year. Even though researchers have reported smaller studies of the language and communication abilities of Hispanic deaf children (Gerner de Garcia,

1993; Luetke-Stahlman & Weiner, 1984), to our knowledge, no one has examined Mexican-American deaf students' literacy development over time.

Communicating Early Results

We have started to collect data on Mexican-American deaf children using our CD-ROM multimedia stories. More detailed studies will be made in the 1998–99 school year, the final year of our project. So far, teachers report that their students enjoy using the sign language videos with the English print. This has increased vocabulary learning. One teacher reported that one of her students used the vocabulary hot words independently by pushing the ASL translation button to get the meaning in sign.

Another teacher reported that the stories with Mexican-American themes have generated class discussions about identity and customs (piñatas, 15th birthday party, immigrants, and language). For example, a Vietnamese deaf child who recognized that her skin color was the same as the Mexican-American signer in one story, asked if she was Mexican too. This started a class discussion on ethnic background and skin color. One teacher's story about the *Quinceanera*, or the 15th birthday party, an important rite of passage for young Hispanic girls, generated lots of discussion. Two students who were going through the ceremonies themselves did not understand the meaning behind it. The CD-ROM story provided explanations to these girls—for example, the meaning of the white dress, the church service, and the necklace worn by the girl in the story.

One teacher reported that her deaf students were learning Spanish words and bringing them home to show to their parents. Many of these Mexican-American deaf children came from homes where neither English nor signing was used. Thus, the CD-ROm stories raised the children's awareness of their home family's native language.

Another teacher reported that groups of her students used the CD-ROM stories independently. Students would gather around each other and take turns as the "teacher" to see if their classmates could read the text, then check the ASL translation for meaning. Our anecdotal reports are still preliminary, but we plan more comprehensive portfolio assessments of students' reading skills; and we plan to build case studies of Mexican-American deaf children and their language development.

Final Notes

The Web offers a valuable resource for researching stories. Teachers and students have access to libraries of print, graphics, and videos on the deaf culture, sign language, and the Mexican-American culture.

The Web can also be used to distribute teacher and student stories world-wide. It is easy to download our stories with the graphics, print, and Spanish translations. The sign language videos, however, may take longer to download. The technology for crisp, clear sign language videos with fast transmission rates is not here yet. But with compressed video techniques and faster computers and modems, this technology is emerging fast.

> **No longer must deaf students turn to the teacher or sign language interpreter to ask what a word in a story means. They can simply press a button—and a person will appear on the screen, explaining the word in sign.**

Schools must have computers with high-speed modems or direct lines to the Internet. Currently, the download time for our sign language translations is slow and cumbersome. We anticipate that the technology will soon allow faster transmission of sign language videos. In the meantime, we will continue our development of stories and put them on the Web for experimentation in preparation for new technology.

Our four-phase project—setting up a multimedia lab, developing stories, training teachers, and assessing the progress of deaf children as they use our CD-ROM stories—is an attempt to make a positive impact in improving literacy for deaf children from the Mexican-American heritage. With computer costs decreasing and with improvements in technology, multimedia on CD-ROMs and on the Web will continue to be excellent tools to bring deaf Mexican-American children into the 21st century.

References

Allen, T. (1994). *Who are the deaf and hard-of-hearing students leaving high school and entering postsecondary education?* Washington, DC: Office of Special Education and Rehabilitative Services, U.S. Department of Education.

Andrews, J. & Jordan, D. (1998). *The tracks and the wise stones: 2 Mexican American folktales retold in American Sign Language, English and Spanish.* A CD-ROM available now. Lamar University, Beaumont, TX 77710.

Cummins, J. (1988). Second language acquisition with bilingual education programs. In L. Beebe (Ed.), *Issues in second language acquisition* (pp. 145–166). New York: Newbury.*

Gerner de Garcia, B. (1993). *Language in use in Spanish-speaking families with deaf children.* Unpublished doctoral dissertation, Boston University.

Krashen, S. (1996). *Under attack: The case against bilingual education.* Culver City, CA: Language Education Associates.*

Luetke-Stahlman, B., & Weiner, F. (1984). Language and/or system assessment for Spanish preschoolers. In G. Delgado (Ed.), *The Hispanic deaf: Issues and challenges for bilingual special education* (pp. 106–121). Washington, DC: Gallaudet University Press.

Pollard, G. (1993). Making accessible to the deaf CD-ROM reading software. Austin, TX: Texas School for the Deaf.*

Schildroth, A., & Hotto, S. (1996). Changes in student and program characteristics. *American Annals of the Deaf, 141*(2), 68–71.

ToolBook II Assistant, Software. (1996, 1997). Published by Asymetrix Corp., Belview, WA.

Valencia, S., & Calfee, R. (1991). The development and use of literacy portfolios for students, classes, and teachers. *Applied Measurement in Education, 4*(4), 333–345.

Vernon, M., & Andrews, J. (1990). *The psychology of deafness: Understanding deaf and hard-of-hearing persons.* White Plains, NY: Longman.*

Books Now

To order books marked by an asterisk (*), please call 24 hrs/365 days: 1–800–BOOKS–NOW (266–5766) or (702) 258–3338 and ask for ext. 1212; or visit them on the Web at http://www.BooksNow.com/TeachingExceptional.htm. Use VISA, M/C, or AMEX or send check or money order + $4.95 S&H ($2.50 each add'l item) to: Books Now, 448 East 6400 South, Suite 125, Salt Lake City, UT 84107.

Jean F. Andrews *(CEC Texas Federation), Department of Communication Disorders and Deafness, Lamar University, Beaumont, Texas.*

Donald L. Jordan, *Department of Business and Management Information Systems, Lamar University, Beaumont, Texas.*

Address correspondence to Jean F. Andrews, Department of Communication Disorders and Deafness, Lamar University, P.O. Box 20076, Beaumont, TX 77710 (e-mail: JPhelan200@aol.com).

Unit 8

Unit Selections

Key Points to Consider

❖ How does team teaching benefit children with multiple disabilities? How can school-home partnerships assist children with disabilities?

❖ How many people benefit from a high school peer tutoring program? Who are they? Why do each of them reap benefits?

❖ Can teachers access state-of-the-art technology to assist in their education of students with multiple disabilities? How can research and practice be brought closer together?

 **Links** | **www.dushkin.com/online/**

These sites are annotated on pages 4 and 5.

Children and youth with multiple disabilities were kept out of the public eye until very recently. We were scarcely aware that they existed. This population of individuals was typically hidden in their parents' homes or put into institutions. A child placed in the category of multiple disabilities may have learning disabilities and speech and language impairments, and mental retardation, and autism, and traumatic brain injuries, and emotional and behavioral disorders, and visual impairments, and hearing impairments, and orthopedic impairments, and health impairments. While a child with multiple disabilities (MD) does not need to be disabled in every category set forth by the IDEA in order to be so labeled, each child with MD is very special and very needy. Most of them have more than two co-occurring areas of exceptionality.

The practice of deinstitutionalization (removing individuals from hospitals and large residential institutions and placing them in homes), and the legal initiatives requiring free and appropriate public education for all children with disabilities in the least restrictive environment, has closed some of the cracks through which these children once fell. However, the needs of many children with multiple disabilities are not yet being met.

One of the problems that looms largest in the collection of enigmas that hinder appropriate education for children with MD is lack of acceptance and preparation by society and by the school system for their inclusion. Society practices a form of discrimination against many people who are different and/or in a minority in some settings (ageism, racism, sexism). Advocates for the rights of disabled individuals have used the term "handicapism" to describe a similar prejudice and discrimination directed at disabled members of our society. The greater the disability, the greater the evinced prejudice. A disability (not able) does not translate the same as a handicap (hindrance, not at an advantage). The words should not be used interchangeably. A person who is not able to do something (walk, see, hear) has a disability but does not have to be handicapped. Society imposes handicaps (hindrances) by preventing the person with the disability from functioning in an alternative way. Thus, if a person who cannot walk can instead locomote in a wheelchair, he or she is not handicapped. However, if a building has no ramps, and is inaccessible to a wheelchair user, then society has imposed a handicap by preventing access to that particular property of the environment. There are millions of ways in which properties of our environment, and characteristics of our behavior, prevent persons with disabilities from functioning up to their potentialities. Therefore, society is "handicappist" and practices handicapism.

Public schools have resisted the regular education initiative (REI) that calls for general education classes rather than special education classes to be primarily responsible for the education of students with disabilities. The inclusive school movement, which supports the REI, would have special education teachers become consultants, resource specialists, collaborative teachers, or itinerant teachers rather than full-time special education teachers. While arguments for and against the REI have not been resolved, most educators agree that an appropriate education for each child with a disability may require a continuum of services. Some children, especially those with multiple disabilities, may require an environment more restrictive than a general education classroom in which to have the types of assistance they need to function up to their potentialities. Teacher education typically does not offer comprehensive preparation for working with children with MD who require extensive special educational services. In addition, children with MD often require related services (for example, chemotherapy, physical therapy, psychotherapy, transportation) to enable them to learn in a classroom environment.

Many children and youth with MD suffer from a lack of understanding, a lack of empathy, and handicapist attitudes that are directed at them. They present very special problems that few teachers are equipped to solve. Often the message they hear is, "Just go away." The challenge of writing an appropriate individualized education plan (IEP) is enormous. Updating the IEP each year and preparing an individualized transition plan (ITP), which will allow the child with MD to function as independently as possible after age 21, is mandated by law. These children will not go away. They must be served. Excuses such as no time, no money, and no personnel to provide appropriate services are unacceptable.

The first article in this unit suggests team teaching as one way to provide inclusionary opportunities for learners with MD. Melissa Jones and Laura Carlier acknowledge the difficulties of including students with MD, who have numerous areas of special need, in their regular classrooms. They present their own cognizance of and experience with this dilemma in an interesting way. They chose cooperative learning techniques as they carefully planned and initiated their program. Their successful experiment contains many insights for prospective teachers of students with MD.

The second article of this unit on multiple disabilities reports on the unexpected benefits of high school peer tutoring. The authors describe a peer tutoring program which has achieved phenomenal success in Danville, Kentucky, since its initiation in 1983. They describe how to set up a program and how to evaluate its usefulness, citing research documenting its effectiveness as a learning and a social tool. Students with multiple disabilities are not the only recipients of benefits from peer tutoring. The students, parents, teachers, and the community all have positive outcomes from high school peer tutoring programs.

The unit's final article discusses the uses of new technology to make appropriate, individualized services to students with disabilities more feasible in general education classes. Computers can be adapted to make many areas of instruction more applicable to their specific needs. The author, A. Edward Blackhurst, reviews the dramatic evolution of technology in education and presents information on the technology of teaching, as well as medical, instructional, and assistive technology.

Multiple Disabilities

Creating Inclusionary Opportunities for Learners with Multiple Disabilities:

A

Team-Teaching

Approach

Melissa M. Jones • Laura Little Carlier

Students with multiple disabilities often have severe learning delays combined with other difficulties. These students may have orthopedic or health impairments, visual impairments, or hearing or speech disabilities. They may use unconventional behavior to communicate a basic need or desire, or they may have any combination of disabilities. Because these students present numerous areas of need, many general educators express concerns about including learners with multiple disabilities in their classrooms. These concerns are realistic—the inordinate amount of time these learners take away from their peers without disabilities and the traditionally required high learner/teacher ratios (Schaffner & Buswell, 1991). Providing a least restrictive environment for students with multiple disabilities has often been problematic.

To alleviate some of these concerns and to increase and improve inclusionary practices for learners with multiple disabilities in our school, we devised a plan to use team-teaching and cooperative learning activities in a combined classroom. (One author is a special education teacher and the other is a general education teacher.) Our purpose was to teach learners with multiple disabilities alongside students without disabilities in a general classroom setting. In this article, we describe how we planned and initiated a successful inclusionary program.

The concept of using cooperative learning techniques with general education learners and learners with multiple disabilities was chosen because of the wide range of benefits to all learners, whether identified as having a disability or not. As described by Cohen (1986) and Putnam (1993), benefits include increased skills in conceptual learning, planning, individual accountability, creative problem solving, self-esteem, oral language proficiency, and socialization. In addition, cooperative learning as a teaching tool assists in stressing traditional areas of curriculum content. These outcomes are also often common goals shared by parents and special education teachers for learners with multiple disabilities. By using cooperative learning, teachers are able to identify individual learner needs and ability levels to establish teacher expectations for each learner.

■ Planning for Inclusion

In the beginning of the fall semester, we worked together to plan and facilitate an inclusionary cooperative learning program involving team teaching. Because we instituted this program in a previously established classroom in a public school setting, it required no additional funding.

Planning began informally as we brainstormed ideas for lessons, scheduling, physical arrangement of the classroom, and teaching techniques. Planning became more formalized as we began to determine which of the learner goals and objectives on current individualized education programs (IEPs) and from the graded course of study would be best met in our program. As a result of this planning, we selected communication and behavior goals from the various IEPs and language arts objectives from the sixth grade course of study.

Learner Description

We planned activities for students with ranges in ability, from learners with multiple disabilities (IQ in low 50s) to sixth graders without disabilities (with a mean school ability index = 94). The school ability index, based on the Otis-Lennon School Ability Test, is used in this school district to predict a learner's achievement ability in school instead of a standard IQ score. A 94 on this scale roughly translates to a low-average ability level. The students with multiple disabilities are exempt from taking this standardized test from which the ability index is derived. The ages of all the learners range from 10 to 13 years.

Scheduling

The program was originally scheduled for a minimum of 1 hour per week. With increased success, we revised the schedule mid-year to 1 hour per day, four to five times per week. Often the learners become so involved in the group projects that they requested additional time to continue working on them. Emphasis

quickly moved from the counting of minutes spent in the general education classroom to the amount of quality instruction in a particular subject area.

Program Goals

We identified two basic program goals before we designed our inclusionary program:

1. To increase the amount of time learners with multiple disabilities spend in the general classroom.

2. To improve the quality of functional instruction given to learners with multiple disabilities while in the general classroom.

Learner Goals

Before implementing our proposed lessons, we identified learner goals and objectives by reviewing current IEPs and the Sixth Grade Competency-Based Graded Course of Study for Language Arts developed by the County Office of Education. The primary focus of the program for the learner with multiple disabilities is the improvement of language development and social development. For the learner without disabilities, the focus is on improving language arts skills. We use language experiences during groupwork to implement specific learner goals and objectives (see box).

Although the general education learners are expected to accomplish the goals and objectives written in the graded course of study, each special education learner has an IEP. Therefore, goals and objectives may vary according to each learner's individual needs.

■ Inclusionary Activities

The activities designed for this inclusionary program center around language arts. Initially, the class is trained in basic groupwork concepts, such as the delineation and responsibility of specific roles within the groups.

Forming Groups

At the beginning of each activity, which might take 4–5 days to complete, learners are individually assigned the role of leader, recorder, presenter, facilitator, timekeeper, or participant. The *leader* is expected to keep the group members on task and to be sure the assignment gets completed. The *recorder* has the job of writing down everyone's ideas and providing a visual representation of the group's progress. The *presenter* has the responsibility of sharing the group's final product with the rest of the class. The *participants* are those group members without a specific role and have the job to create new ideas and to help the group problem solve. The *facilitator*, for the purpose of this program, has the responsibility of making sure that the ideas of the learners with multiple disabilities are heard and used. The *timekeeper* keeps group members aware of how much time is available for the task.

In our classroom, the students are divided into six groups of five to six learners per group. Using strategies for composing groups from Cohen (1986), we chose to group heterogeneously by gender and by ability level. To start, we place one strong resource person in each group. A resource person is not necessarily someone who is successful according to academic criteria, but rather someone who may be successful in other areas. These areas may include being creative, articulate, a flexible thinker, or maybe even someone who has personal experience with the task or some feature of the task (Cohen). We then assign a special education learner to the group. We place other students in the various groups, depending on the students' social and problem-solving skills and needs.

Designing Lesson Plans

Each activity is designed with the sixth grade course of study in mind, concentrating on the story development and writing aspects of the course of study. We feel it is important not to water down the sixth grade curriculum in any way, but rather to present the material in such a way so that

---

Learner Goals and Objectives for Groupwork

1. The learner will learn appropriate communication skills for daily living. For example, the learner will:

   a. demonstrate verbal expression by independently using language to predict, describe, and/or give cause and effect.

   b. interact conventionally with others by interacting with one to one, peers, and/or in small groups.

   c. develop comprehension skills by following directions that apply to group activities.

2. The learner will demonstrate conventionally social behavior in the school and work environment. For example, the learner will develop interpersonal skills necessary to relationships and successful employment by maintaining conventional social distance, making only necessary body movements (if appropriate), respecting the rights and property of others, joining in group activities, initiating conversations, communicating clearly, and/or cooperating with peers and teachers.

3. The learner will participate in small-group discussions.

4. The learner will give an oral presentation.

5. The learner will speak to entertain. For example, the learner will retell a story and/or dramatize.

6. The learner will demonstrate attention to delivery. For example, the learner will use conventional eye contact; vary volume, rate, and pitch; and/or maintain an appropriate demeanor.

7. The learner will recognize characterization.

8. The learner will identify setting, mood, and plot.

9. The learner will write imaginatively. For example, the learner will write in the form of a narrative, description, and/or a short story.

all the learners participate more actively during their learning experiences. Teacher expectations of learners vary per learner and even vary per activity depending on the amount of experience each person has had with the material presented. We devise lesson plans with these various expectations in mind. The tasks assigned to the groups vary from writing a sequel for a published story or book, to creating a story from a magazine picture, creating a play, or practicing storytelling skills.

An example of such an activity is writing a sequel to a trade book such as *Jumanji*, by Chris Van Allsburg. After listening to one of the teachers read the book, students conduct a classwide brainstorming session to generate a variety of possibilities of successive events that could be used to create a sequel to the story. The learners then begin the small-group work, continuing the brainstorming process to discuss additional ideas for events that will be included in their sequel.

Once consensus within the individual groups has been reached as to which events to include, the actual writing of the sequel begins. Various groups may add illustrations. Some groups may choose to create a book, some may have a series of posters or smaller drawings, or some may develop a more elaborate method of publishing this work. The groups then orally share their sequels with the entire class.

Evaluating Groupwork

The teachers meet at least once a week to review the success of the previous activities, note problem areas, share in problem solving, and devise the activities for the succeeding lessons. To document changes in learner behavior during the inclusionary groupwork, we designed checklists for each of the students with multiple disabilities. These checklists (see Figure 1 for an example) list individual IEP objectives used to document such changes. These checklists also demonstrate the various expectations teachers can have for each learner with multiple disabilities, aside from the expectations dictated by the graded course of study.

The teachers and speech therapist share the responsibility of observing and documenting language use and behavioral changes noted during the group processes, as stated in the learner objectives.

The general education learners are taught to monitor and evaluate their own progress in terms of the entire group process. Group members use an evaluation form to help them evaluate their work after they have completed the assignment. (See box for self-evaluation goals for the group process.)

In addition to self-evaluations by each group, we ask the class members to make positive remarks about each presentation.

Figure 1. Sample Checklist

This checklist can be used for documenting changes in behavior of students with multiple disabilities during groupwork.

Learner's Name: _____

Date:

Use of meaningful word combinations up to four

Answering yes/no questions

Use of scripts to communicate wants/needs

Initiate/return a greeting

Answer "what" questions

Answer "where" questions

Follow one–step verbal directions

Initiate a conversation

The general education teacher writes down all comments and compiles them for the group. She then includes these comments in a narrative evaluation, which is used in conjunction with the group's self-evaluation to derive a grade. The recorded grade is an average of the two grades given, one from the teacher and one from the group.

After each activity, we evaluate the group processes as a whole. Sometimes we need to design an activity that might help to remediate any problem areas groups may have encountered during a particular activity. (See flowchart in Figure 2.)

For example, to help learners develop the skill of coming to consensus, we use an activity called "Shipwreck" (Cohen, 1986). This is a one-day activity in which the students are presented with a paragraph describing a hypothetical shipwreck. Within their groups, the learners must prioritize a list of items they will take with them to a nearby deserted island to assist them in their survival. Group members must also be prepared to state reasons for the choices they make as a group.

We have noted that each time an activity such as "Shipwreck" is done, the sophistication of the learner's knowledge about group processes increases, including that of some of the learners with multiple disabilities.

■ Outcomes and Conclusions

We originally thought that the learners with multiple disabilities would most likely keep the role of participant throughout the course of the school year. We noted, however, that the sixth graders without disabili-

ties were not satisfied with such unequal distribution of duties. The special education learners are now serving as presenters and timekeepers as well. In fact, we no longer have to assign roles to students because the learners share responsibilities, alternating roles to create an interdependence among group members.

We have found that team teaching of special educators with general educators, using cooperative learning techniques, helps to eliminate some of the common concerns teachers may have for placing special education learners in the general classroom. These techniques have resolved the issues of time being taken away from other learners and learner/teacher ratios that might be too high. Normally, the general education teacher involved in this program has 25 learners in the classroom. The special education teacher brings to the classroom 6–7 additional learners, as well as a teaching assistant, and thus actually lowers the learner/teacher ratio to 10:1. In addition, as we move from group to group, facilitating the group process and offering individual assistance as needed, we believe that quality time with all learners is enhanced instead of forfeited. This form of interdependency among teachers proves to be effective for including learners with multiple disabilities in the general education classroom, as well as being an effective cooperative model for learners to follow.

Through this experience, the special education teacher has the opportunity to see and better understand grade-level expectations for socialization and language development. This increased knowledge assists the special education teacher in determining goals and objectives relevant to each learner's environment when writing IEPs for the following school year.

Individual learner gains were noted during the first year of this program's implementation. Students from the special education class showed progress by increasing the number of interactions they initiated or responded to, and by exhibiting increased confidence. Initially, the learners with multiple disabilities had an overall baseline average of initiating 0–2 interactions with peers during a 30-minute period and responding to peer questions an average of one out of five times during the same 30-minute period. After 5 months of participating in this program, the overall learner-initiated interactions with peers increased to 2–8 interactions during a 30-minute period. Responses to peers also increased to an average of three out of five responses. Learners with multiple disabilities who exhibited behavioral concerns showed a marked decrease in the number of less-conventional types of behavior, such as aggression and noncompliance, occurring during the groupwork process. One learner actually decreased her usual verbal outbursts to extinction during the groupwork activities and demonstrated a 25% increase in her attention to task.

We also observed gains in the sixth graders without disabilities as their confidence and ability levels improved. We attributed these gains not only to the groupwork activities, but also to the new relationships formed between these learners and the learners with multiple disabilities. We noted that the social attitudes of the sixth graders also changed over the course of the first year of this program. In the beginning, these children wanted to "help" the learners with disabilities; but during the year, they began to demonstrate an attitude of equality among learners, sharing the knowledge and resources that all learners possess. The children without disabilities now speak more often of likenesses between themselves and the children with disabilities, rather than looking for and responding to differences.

The successes we have realized for the learners in their classroom have not come without difficulty and some frustration. Communication between learners remains the biggest challenge to meaningful interactions. The teachers have had to problem solve ways to include the ideas of learners with autism who have poor expressive and receptive language skills, to intervene and redirect aggression used to communicate needs, and to encourage participation from learners who either verbally or nonverbally refuse to participate as a means of controlling their environment. By using a collaborative method of problem solving, these teachers feel they have been better able to find solutions to these difficulties than if they had been trying to problem solve alone.

■ Future Implications

As this program demonstrates, the thrust for including learners with disabilities in the general education classroom should not stop with learners who exhibit only mild disabilities. Learners with multiple disabilities can also benefit from programs that increase the amount of quality interactions they have with their peers without disabilities. Although current schoolwide involvement in this inclusionary program is still limited, additional possibilities for expansion to other classrooms and settings exist.

For expansion to be possible, it is essential that general and special educators work together to discover methods that can be used to teach all learners side by side in a productive setting. By doing so, not only will the learners with disabilities benefit by becoming active participants in the class activities, but so may other learners benefit who are deemed at risk for school success. Cooperative groupwork and team-teaching are efficient ways in which the individual needs of all learners can be met without sacrificing quality instruction.

Beyond the scope of the classroom, there exist sociocultural implications of inclusion. In our society, people often view learners with disabilities as needing help, always receiving and rarely giving. Through the use of cooperative learning and inclusion, the contrary can be realized as each member of the group contributes to the function and uniqueness of that group. With an increase in inclusionary practices, perhaps the next generation will learn to value all people as participating members in society instead of as separate groups of givers and receivers. To promote such social changes, future endeavors to create programs that destratify and desegregate current homogeneous classrooms should be encouraged.

■ References

Cohen, E. (1986). *Designing groupwork.* New York: Teachers College Press.

Putnam, J., (1993). *Cooperative learning and strategies for inclusion: Celebrating diversity in the classroom.* Baltimore, MD: Paul H. Brookes.

Schaffner, B., & Buswell, B. (1991). *Opening doors: Strategies for including all students in regular education.* Colorado Springs, CO: Peak Parent Center, Inc.

■

Melissa M. Jones (*CEC Chapter #11*) *was a Special Education Teacher for learners with multiple disabilities, Clermont Northeastern Intermediate School, and now supervises programs for learners with severe behavior handicaps, Clermont County Office of Education, Cincinnati, Ohio.* Laura Little Carlier, *General Education Teacher, Clermont, Northeastern Intermediate School, Batavia, Ohio. The work the authors began, including learners with disabilities in general education, continues with the help of a team of exceptional general and special educators.*

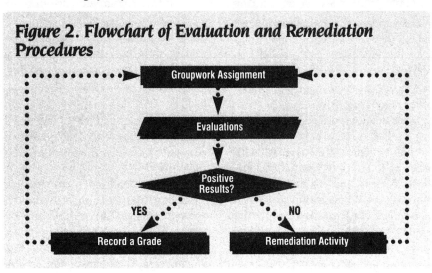

Figure 2. Flowchart of Evaluation and Remediation Procedures

The Unexpected Benefits of High School Peer Tutoring

Amy Wildman Longwill
Harold L. Kleinert

Flexible scheduling, course credits, and alternative assessments are some characteristics of an innovative peer tutoring program in Danville, Kentucky. And students with disabilities, who receive the tutoring, are not the only beneficiaries.

This article describes how high school peer tutoring programs can enhance educational outcomes, including increased academic performance, for students both with and without moderate and severe disabilities. Moreover, we describe how peer tutoring programs can play an important role for all participants as high schools increasingly undergo fundamental educational restructuring. Finally, we note how peer tutoring programs can promote greater levels of general education class participation and community inclusion for students with significant disabilities.

Fundamental Changes in High School Programs

Over the past decade, significant changes in best practices have occurred at the high school level in both general and special education services for students with moderate and severe disabilities. In general education, restructuring has resulted in the following strategies:

Interdisciplinary projects
Block scheduling
Alternate portfolios
Reciprocal teaching and learning
Course credit for peer tutoring
Student-produced adaptations
Cooperative learning
Natural supports
Community links
Developing career interests
Genuine friendships

- *Block scheduling,* for example, students attending four classes per semester, with each class lasting 90 minutes instead of 60, to allow for greater in-depth exploration of specific topics.
- *Increased interdisciplinary learning opportunities,* for example, an ecology assignment in which students are required to integrate writing, mathematics, and biology skills into a single, applied project on recycling and its impact on pollution in their own community.
- *Performance-based assessment,* in which students are evaluated more by the solutions they develop to address actual problems rather than the knowledge they can feed back on more tra-

ditional pen-and-pencil tests (Brandt, 1992; Falvey, Gage, & Eshilian, 1995).

Best practices for high-school age students with moderate and severe disabilities have likewise undergone a significant shift during this time. Following a renewed focus on essential life outcomes (Hardman, McDonnell, & Welch, 1997) teachers have placed greater emphasis on the development of social interaction skills, genuine friendships, and support networks for students with significant disabilities at the high school level, and the importance of learning *along with* (and not always *from*) their peers without disabilities (Coots, Bishop, Grenot-Scheyer, & Falvey, 1995; Giangreco, Cloninger, & Iverson, 1993). Moreover, reflected in the newly enacted 1997 Amendments to the Individuals with Disabilities Education Act (IDEA) is the requirement that the learning results of students with significant disabilities be included in general state and district student assessment measures—that these students' educational outcomes are a part of school accountability, too.

These fundamental changes in school practice at the national level have had their counterpart in Kentucky. As a result of the Kentucky

From *Teaching Exceptional Children,* March/April 1998, pp. 60-65. © 1998 by The Council for Exceptional Children. Reprinted by permission.

*H*igh school peer tutoring programs can enhance educational outcomes, including increased academic performance, for students both with and without moderate and severe disabilities.

Education Reform Act of 1990 (KERA), educators have established a set of 57 learner outcomes, or academic expectations. These outcomes are meant for *all* students, including students with moderate and severe disabilities. Thus *all* students, including those with severe disabilities, take part in the state's performance-based assessment and accountability system (Steffy, 1993; Ysseldyke, Thurlow, & Shriner, 1992). While students with and without *mild* disabilities are collecting their best work for their required math and writing accountability portfolios, students with *moderate and severe* cognitive disabilities are participating in the state's assessment system through the Alternate Portfolio (Kleinert, Kearns, & Kennedy, 1997).

Finally, these national and state reforms have had a significant impact at the local level. For example, Danville, Kentucky, High School (DHS) incorporated block scheduling for all students at the start of the 1995–96 school year. To emphasize a more interdisciplinary curricular approach, the principal implemented a school-wide policy that students must complete one entry for their required writing portfolio from *every* class, including electives. At the same time, students with moderate and severe disabilities had begun developing their own Alternate Portfolios, as an integral part of the school's score in Kentucky's mandatory assessment and accountability system.

All these changes—for students with moderate and severe disabilities and for general education students—have prompted educators in Kentucky to take a new look at high school peer tutoring. Specifically, we needed to ask how peer tutoring can focus on these essential outcomes for all students, with activities designed so that students are learning with and from each other.

Peer Tutoring in Danville

Peer tutoring is not a new program at Danville High. In fact, peer tutoring, as a formal credit elective, originated in Kentucky at DHS in 1983. As was typical in many such programs, peer tutoring at DHS was initially set up to provide social interactions between students with and without disabilities. Students without disabilities enrolled in peer tutoring to receive academic course credit. The course required students to complete a series of self-study modules in such areas as beliefs and attitudes, legal rights of people with disabilities, educational programming needs, and family issues; take multiple choice type tests on their readings; and do class projects (Guiltinan & Kleinert, 1987; Kleinert et al., 1991). Students also received grades for their daily work and their interactions with the students with moderate and severe disabilities for whom they acted as tutors. The instructors hoped that, from these more formally structured interactions, friendships would develop (and, sometimes, real friendships did occur).

With the emergence of both general and special education reforms, however, it was time to make changes in peer tutoring, as well. What has evolved at DHS is a series of activities and assignments that allow peer tutors to learn about issues of concern to people with disabilities, to learn with students with disabilities as they work on projects together, and to develop deeper insights into

What the Research Says About Peer Tutoring

Extensive research on peer tutoring can be viewed in three categories:

- Peer tutoring is a well-recognized strategy for increasing instructional effectiveness in programs for students with moderate and severe cognitive disabilities and enhancing interactions with peers without disabilities (Haring, 1991; Haring, Breen, Pitts-Conway, Lee, & Gaylord-Ross, 1987; Helmstetter, Peck, & Giangreco, 1994; Salisbury, Gallucci, Palombaro, & Peck, 1995; Sprague & McDonnell, 1984; Thousand & Villa, 1990).
- Peer tutoring offers many benefits to students both with and without disabilities, as well as to their parents and teachers (see Figure 1), as noted extensively throughout the literature.
- Much of the research has focused on social and educational outcomes for the *tutee* (Helmstetter, Peck, & Giangreco, 1994; Kishi & Meyer, 1994).

the nature of human relationships and social policy (e.g., inclusion, full community participation). These activities have allowed peer tutors to develop an awareness of significant life issues and to develop their own opinions and beliefs about these issues. (See box "Setting Up a Peer Tutoring Program.")

Some of the peer tutor topics for both reading and writing assignments have included the desirability, benefits, and potential drawbacks of including students with severe disabilities in general education classes at the high school level; opportunities for peer tutors to develop their *own* strategies for adapting and modifying general education class activities to meet the needs of a student with a moderate or severe disability; the meaning and importance

Figure 1

Benefits of Peer Tutoring

For Students with Moderate and Severe Disabilities:
- Opportunities for sustained, positive interactions and friendships (Haring, 1991; Stainback, Stainback, & Wilkinson, 1992)
- Increased opportunities to practice needed skills (Sprague & McDonnell, 1984)
- Age-appropriate role models (Kleinert, Guiltinan, & Farmer, 1991)
- Development of prosocial behaviors and communication skills (Staub & Hunt, 1993)
- Promotion of equity among students and the discovery of hidden strengths of students with significant disabilities (Salisbury, Gallucci, Palombaro, & Peck, 1995)

For Peers Without Disabilities:
- Increased acceptance of individual differences (Helmstetter, Peck, & Giangreco, 1994)
- A deeper sense of social justice and advocacy for others (Falvey, Gage, & Eshilian, 1995)
- Increased self-esteem and knowledge of self (Peck, Donaldson, & Pezzoli, 1990; Helmstetter et al., 1994)
- Better understanding of how to communicate with and provide assistance to people with moderate and severe disabilities (Clayton, 1993; Staub & Hunt, 1993)

For Special Education Teachers:
- Increased instructional time for students in school and community settings (Sprague & McDonnell, 1984)
- More age-appropriate expectations for their students (Kleinert et al., 1991)
- Opportunities to become more personally and professionally integrated into the school's general education programs (Clayton, 1993)

For Parents of Students with Moderate and Severe Disabilities:
- Increased skill gains for their son or daughter
- Enhanced opportunities for the development of friendships for their son or daughter (Kleinert et al., 1991)

For Parents of General Education Students:
- An interest in pursuing a career in the helping professions on the part of their son or daughter
- Increased enthusiasm for school on the part of their son or daughter (Kleinert et al., 1991)

of friendships in all of our lives; and the pros (or cons) of the Americans with Disabilities Act as an instrument of social justice and basic human rights. The new peer tutoring assignments relate closely to the academic expectations that have been identified for all Kentucky students (Steffy, 1993). For example, here are two of these outcomes:

- Students recognize issues of justice, equality, responsibility, choice, and freedom, and apply these democratic principles to real-life situations.
- Students use critical thinking skills in a variety of situations that will be encountered in life.

Each activity requires peer tutors to develop a written product, usually from a reading assignment and always from a writing prompt. Students are required to relate the topics to their own experiences and to their activities in peer tutoring; they are graded on both the quality and

logic of their ideas, as well as the clarity of their writing.

Indeed, one of the most valuable aspects of peer tutoring in Kentucky today is that peer tutors are often providing assistance to students with moderate and severe disabilities in the development of Alternate Portfolio entries, while the students without disabilities are simultaneously able to complete requirements for their *own* portfolios. Peer tutoring has thus evolved more into a context of learning *together*, helping one another and supporting each other's efforts. Such a context provides a more fertile ground for the development of genuine friendships, and lessens the potentially negative impact of peer tutors seeing themselves as extensions of the teacher, as opposed to participating as true learning partners of students with significant disabilities (Kleinert, 1996).

For example, all students at DHS are required to take a Writing Workshop Class as a part of developing their school accountability portfolios. Together, peer tutors and students with significant disabilities work on their "Letters to the Reviewer" (a state requirement for both general writing portfolios and Alternate Portfolios). They also work together to compile their own Table of Contents, design their own Cover Page, and assemble their portfolio entries. For a student with a significant disability whose primary mode of communication is a picture communication system, a peer may help that student to develop a written description of what the student has communicated through pictures.

For many of the same reasons, peer tutoring also provides an excellent framework for increasing the meaningful participation of students with moderate and severe disabilities in general education classes. If a peer tutor is enrolled in the same class as a student with a disability, that peer tutor can be an excellent source of natural support for the student with a disability. Indeed, one of the required peer tutor assignments (identifying potential adaptations in general education class activities)

Setting Up a Peer Tutoring Program

1. Create with your school administration and other interested faculty a framework for a high school peer tutoring course. Develop a course syllabus, including course overview, learning objectives, and required activities and assignments, and decide who may enroll in the class (at DHS enrollment is usually limited to 11th and 12th graders).
2. Include the new course in your high school's description of course offerings. Make sure that eligible students, faculty, and guidance counselors are all aware of the new elective.
3. Ensure that students can enroll in the peer tutoring course through the same process that they register for their other courses. (Some teachers have also found it helpful to personally interview prospective peer tutors.)
4. Do not accept more peer tutors than you can actively engage in learning activities with students with disabilities, and limit the number of peers who may sign up for the course during each scheduled period of the day.
5. On the first day of class, give peer tutors the essential information they need about the course (e.g., grading, assignments, behavioral expectations). Stress the importance of learning together and that students are expected to support each other.
6. Schedule writing assignments (based on required readings and school and community learning experiences) approximately every 2 weeks. Initial assignments are due weekly; toward the end of the course, more in-depth projects are due at approximately 3-week intervals.
7. Make writing assignments reflective and insist on the student's best work. You may want to coordinate the development and grading of these assignments with members of your school's English faculty.
8. Ensure that students with significant disabilities and peer tutors are given a range of opportunities throughout the course to engage in cooperative learning activities in both school and community settings, as well as the opportunities to develop friendships.
9. For students who have completed the peer tutoring course but who wish to continue their learning, consider offering a more advanced course on an independent study basis (this should be developed as an individualized learning contract between the student, teacher, and school principal).
10. Frequently evaluate the impact of your peer tutoring program; seek the input of students (with and without disabilities), parents, and other teachers, as well as your own observations and data on student learning.

provides a wealth of ideas for both special and general education teachers. In the context of that assignment, students read an article about curricular modifications to enhance general education class participation for students with significant disabilities (see Tashie et al., 1993). Students must then develop ways, through the use of a general education class activity analysis (Roger, Gorevin, Fellows, & Kelly, 1992), to adapt one of their *own* classes for an individual student with a significant disability. Peers have developed a number of practical and innovative strategies for adapting course content and instruction across a variety of classes (e.g., English,

art, history, and music). Here are some of their ideas:

- In art class, instead of having Richard, who has severe disabilities, draw a picture, he could paste pictures from magazines.
- When completing research papers, Tony could work with picture symbols on a topic or theme of his choice. He could use the pictures, arranged or copied from his communication system, for a research report.
- When a large reading assignment is required, peers could write summaries of each reading for Karla. This would help the student who was developing the summary learn the material and

help Karla understand the basic themes or ideas.

- In typing class, when there are longer assignments, Tom could type his personal identification information or what he did in the community that day.
- As a part of the yearbook class, Lauren could classify photographs into activity categories such as school classes, clubs, and sports.
- In biology, for an oral research presentation to the class, Derrick could develop a collage of local fruits and vegetables, and the best places to purchase the seeds for those plants.

Besides providing an essential link to academic classes, peer tutors can also provide a natural link to the community for students with significant disabilities. Many peer tutors work in the community on a part-time basis and introduce students with disabilities to their co-workers in their own jobs. Peers also may provide support to students with disabilities in their respective job searches. For example, one of the requirements of the peer tutoring class is that both peer tutors and students with disabilities develop their own job resumes; of course, they work on this together.

Yet it is important to remember that this community-linking goes both ways. Because students with significant disabilities usually participate in community-based instruction (CBI) extensively at the secondary level, many of them are already familiar with their community. For example, when a new discount store opened in Danville, students with moderate and severe disabilities often chose that new store as a site to work on their purchasing skills. Two of the peer tutors, assigned to provide assistance with shopping and budgeting skills, commented what a help the students (with disabilities) were to them in learning their way around the new store.

Peer tutors love to go on community-based instruction themselves,

Reflections of a Peer Tutor

This is my second semester as a peer tutor. That in itself says a lot about my feelings toward the class. You don't see me signing up for plant physiology for a second semester! I have learned more about my true identity and aspirations in this class than I ever dreamed to. The values and experiences that I have gained will be important to me for years to come. It is easy to express my growth as a person through writing about peer tutoring. Several pieces that I have written will be included in my senior writing portfolio.

The particular prompt I am writing from instructs me to write an introduction to peer tutoring for future peer tutors. It will include advice, suggestions, and examples of what it takes to be a successful peer tutor.

Day one. I know what you are thinking, unless you have had a personal encounter with students with disabilities prior to now, you feel the same way that everyone else does. You are somewhat nervous, intrigued, and even frightened. Don't be—sit back, take a deep breath, and get over it!

It will take time and patience to become a good peer tutor. It will not happen overnight. The students will not magically adjust to you, or fall in love with you, neither you with them, but it won't take long....

I can honestly say that I know I have gained just as much from being a peer tutor as the students have from me. I have grown immensely as a peer tutor, and filled an empty place in my heart....

Soon I will be moving on to college, and few classes have prepared me for the next phase of my life like peer tutoring. I have learned about happiness, diversity, patience, strength, determination, and above all, life in its true essence.

Katie Corcoran
Danville High School

and the longer class periods facilitated by block scheduling has increased opportunities for their participation. In addition to providing carefully planned assistance on targeted CBI skills to students with moderate and severe disabilities, peer tutors continue to gain skills in budgeting, nutrition, banking, and overall shopping. Peers continue to comment about how much they learn when they go on CBI with students with disabilities.

Evidence of Learning Together

As noted previously, students with moderate and severe disabilities in Kentucky must complete Alternate Portfolios as the students in the general assessment system simultaneously complete writing and math portfolios. For students in the Alter-nate Portfolio assessment, the special education teacher must enable these students to show evidence of extensive interactions with peers and reliance on natural supports, as well as clear documentation of students' performance of learned skills across a wide range of school and community settings. This evidence is presented through a series of portfolio entries (see Kleinert et al., 1997).

Peer tutors are valued resources in documenting each of these Alternate Portfolio assessment requirements. Peer tutors frequently develop friendships with students with disabilities that go well beyond the classroom. Peers collaborate with students with disabilities within and outside of the school, in such activities as going to youth group, out for pizza on Saturday night, or to the movies; researching topics at the school and public libraries; and going Christmas shop-ping together. Peers collaborate on community instruction while shopping, banking, eating at a fast food restaurant, and participating in community recreation and leisure activities. Each of these instances can provide an appropriate context for showcasing both learned skills and valued social relations at an exemplary performance level for students in Kentucky's alternate assessment system (Kleinert et al., 1997). This documentation can take the form of written or photographic entries (e.g., a portfolio entry centered on community recreation/ leisure activities in which the student engages), course projects developed together, or examples of instructional programming and student self-evaluation data across school and community settings. Finally, peer tutors may assist students with moderate and severe disabilities in completing their entries and assembling the entries into a finished portfolio.

As peer tutors provide this support, they also are developing their own portfolio entries. Essays on the meaning and purpose of friendship, the essential need for all students to be an integral part of their community, or what they have learned from their peer tutoring experience have provided the context for outstanding writing entries. Students have even used their peer tutoring assignments as a part of their college admission application, as evidence of their best writing.

Encouraging Self-Evaluation

As a culminating activity for their peer tutoring experience, tutors are required to complete a self-evaluation matrix during the latter part of the semester. For this assignment, each peer determines five characteristics they believe essential for a peer tutor. They then must describe that characteristic, as it would be shown at four different performance levels (novice, apprentice, proficient, and distinguished—the four levels that are used to score students' work in Kentucky's overall assessment and accountability system). Finally, using their own rubric, peers must evaluate their performance. They must also complete a written explanation for their score. Here are some of their final comments on the course and on their own performance:

- This class will have more meaning than *any* other classes on your schedule.... Expect the class to be one you will remember for a lifetime."
- "You are there for support, not to do students' work, a job they are supposed to be doing.... You will have learned that students with disabilities are capable of doing anything you are."

Peer tutoring continues to evolve at DHS in a way that reflects rapidly changing educational practices and paradigms for students both with and without moderate and severe disabilities. The teachers have experienced a renewed excitement and challenge related to peer tutoring, as they attempt to integrate the learning experiences of their students into a curriculum reflecting high expectations for all.

References

Brandt, R. (1992). On performance assessment: A conversation with Grant Wiggins. *Educational Leadership, 49*(8), 35–37.

Clayton, J. (1993). *Peer power manual for middle school students.* Lexington: Kentucky Statewide Systems Change Project, Human Development Institute, University of Kentucky.

Coots, J., Bishop, K., Grenot-Scheyer, M., & Falvey, M. (1995). Practices in general education: Past and present. In Falvey, M. (Ed.). *Inclusive and heterogeneous schooling: Assessment, curriculum, and instruction* (p. 18). Baltimore: Paul Brookes.

Falvey, M., Gage, S., & Eshilian, L. (1995). Secondary curriculum and instruction. In Falvey, M. (Ed.), *Inclusive and heterogeneous schooling: Assessment, curriculum, and instruction* (p. 355). Baltimore: Paul Brookes.

Giangreco, M., Cloninger, C., & Iverson, V. (1993). *Choosing options and accommodations for children.* Baltimore: Paul Brookes.

Guiltinan, S., & Kleinert, H. (1987). *High school peer tutoring manual.* Frankfort: Division of Exceptional Children Services, Kentucky Department of Education.

Hardman, M., McDonnell, J., & Welch, M. (1997). Perspectives on the future of IDEA. *Journal of the Association for Persons with Severe Handicaps, 22,* 61–76.

Haring, T. (1991). Social relationships. In Meyer, L., Peck, C., & Brown, L. (Eds.), *Critical issues in the lives of people with severe disabilities* (p. 204). Baltimore: Paul Brookes.

Haring, T., Breen, C., Pitts-Conway, V., Lee, M., & Gaylord-Ross, R. (1987). Adolescent peer tutoring and special friend experiences. *Journal of the Association for Persons with Severe Handicaps, 12,* 280–286.

Helmstetter, E., Peck, C., & Giangreco, M. (1994). Outcomes of interactions with peers with moderate or severe disabilities: A statewide survey of high school students. *Journal of the Association for Persons with Severe Handicaps, 19,* 263–276.

Kishi, G., & Meyer, L. (1994). What children report and remember: A six-year follow-up of the effects of social contact between peers with and without severe disabilities. *Journal of the Association for Persons with Severe Handicaps, 19,* 277–289.

Kleinert, H. (1996). *Kentucky classrooms—Everyone's welcome: A practical guide to learning and living together.* Lexington: Human Development Institute, University of Kentucky.

Kleinert, H., Guiltinan, S., & Farmer, J. (1991). *High school peer tutoring manual—revised edition.* Frankfort: Division of Exceptional Children Services, Kentucky Department of Education.

Kleinert, H., Kearns, J., & Kennedy, S. (1997). Accountability for *all* students: Kentucky's Alternate Portfolio assessment for students with moderate and severe cognitive disabilities. *Journal of the Association for Persons with Severe Handicaps, 22,* 88–101.

Peck, C., Donaldson, J., & Pezzoli, M. (1990). Some benefits nonhandicapped adolescents perceive for themselves from their social relationships with peers who have severe handicaps. *Journal of the Association for Persons with Severe Handicaps, 15,* 241–249.

Roger, B., Gorevin, R., Fellows, M., & Kelly, D. (1992). *Schools are for all kids: School site implementation level II training.* San Francisco: California Research Institute, San Francisco State University. (ERIC Document Reproduction Service No. ED 365 052)

Salisbury, C., Gallucci, C., Palombaro, M., & Peck, C. (1995). Strategies that promote social relations among elementary students with and without severe disabilities in inclusive schools. *Exceptional Children, 62,* 125–137.

Sprague, J., & McDonnell, J. (1984). *Effective use of secondary age peer tutors: A resource manual for high school teachers.* Eugene: Center on Human Development, University of Oregon.

Stainback, W., Stainback, S., & Wilkinson, A. (1992). Encouraging peer supports and friendships. *TEACHING Exceptional Children, 24*(2), 6–11.

Staub, D., & Hunt, P. (1993). The effects of social interaction training on high school peer tutors of schoolmates with severe disabilities. *Exceptional Children, 60,* 41–57.

Steffy, B. (1993). Top-down—bottom-up: Systemic change in Kentucky. *Educational Leadership, 51*(1), 42–44.

Tashie, C., Shapiro-Barnard, S., Schuh, M., Jorgensen, C., Dillon, A., Dixon, B., & Nisbet, J. (1993). *From special to regular, from ordinary to extraordinary.* Concord: Institute on Disability/University Affiliated Program, University of New Hampshire. (ERIC Document Reproduction Service No. ED 387 963).

Thousand, J. & Villa, R. (1990). Sharing expertise and responsibilities through teaching teams. In Stainback, W., & Stainback, S. (Eds), *Support networks for inclusive schooling: Interdependent, integrated education.* (p. 162). Baltimore: Paul Brookes.

Ysseldyke, J., Thurlow, M., & Shriner, J. (1992). Outcomes are for special educators too. *TEACHING Exceptional Children, 25*(1), 36–50.

Books Now

To order books marked by an asterisk (*), please call 24 hrs/365 days: 1-800-BOOKS-NOW (266-5766) or (702) 258-3338 and ask for ext. 1212; or visit them on the Web at http://www.BooksNow. com/TeachingExceptional.htm. Use VISA, M/C, or AMEX or send check or money order + $4.95 S&H ($2.50 each add'l item) to: Books Now, 660 W. Charleston Blvd., Las Vegas, NV 89102.

Amy Wildman Longwill, *Teacher, Danville High School, Kentucky.* **Harold L. Kleinert,** *Training Director, Human Development Institute, University of Kentucky, Lexington.*

Address correspondence to Harold L. Kleinert, Human Development Institute, University of Kentucky, 126 Mineral Industries Bldg, Lexington, KY 40506-0051 (e-mail: haroldk@ ihdi.uky.edu).

Authors' Note: As of this writing, Kentucky is the only state in which all students, including students with moderate and severe cognitive disabilities, are fully represented in school and district accountability indexes (Kleinert et al., 1997). Yet the 1997 Amendments to the Individuals with Disabilities Education Act (IDEA) require that all states develop alternate assessments for those students who cannot participate in general state and district educational assessments, and that these alternate assessments be in place no later than July 1, 2000.

Preparation of this article was supported, in part, by the U.S. Department of Education Office of Special Education and Rehabilitation Services (Grant No. H086J20007). However, the opinions expressed do not necessarily reflect the position or policy of the U.S. Department of Education, and no official endorsement should be inferred.

PERSPECTIVES ON
TECHNOLOGY
in Special Education

During the past 25 years, we have seen a dramatic evolution of technology in education: microcomputer technology, research on instructional procedures, and many new assistive devices and equipment.

A. Edward Blackhurst

My special education career began in 1960 as a teacher of adolescents with mild mental retardation in a self-contained classroom in an inner-city school. My students were between the ages of 12 and 14, and their academic achievement levels were between Grades 1 and 4. The school district supplied me with a basal reading series, and I was instructed to teach the students how to read. (This was before individualized education programs, or IEPS, were required by federal law.) Although my students needed to develop basic reading skills, these teenagers did not respond well to the "baby stuff" in the texts. I became frustrated by the lack of age-appropriate instructional materials that could be used to teach basic skills.

While casting about for resources to support my teaching, I attended a demonstration of a device called a *tachistoscope*. This was an overhead projector equipped with a camera shutter that could control the speed at which visual images, such as words and phrases, could be projected (as quickly as $1/100$ of a second). It struck me that the use of such a device might be useful in capturing and holding the attention of my students when I was teaching them how to read basic sight vocabulary words.

I arranged to to borrow a tachistoscope and designed a research study to determine whether it was useful as a supplement to reading instruction. The results of that study indicated that the tachistoscopic training was effective (Blackhurst,

1967). My interest in technology applications for students enrolled in special education programs was born.

That interest was nurtured while attending graduate school, where I had the opportunity to work with an early pioneer in programmed instruction, Robert Glaser, who coined the term "student-subject matter interface." He was interested in enhancing learning by conceptualizing devices that would make it easier for students to interact with subject matter. I became intrigued with this concept and began to speculate about potential interface devices that might be developed to address the unique needs of students with disabilities (Blackhurst, 1965).

Since those early experiences, much of my professional career has been devoted to exploring the potential that technology has for teaching students with disabilities and for preparing special education professionals to work in a variety of different roles. This article represents perspectives I have developed over the years as a participant-observer in the evolution of technology applications in special education—ways to view technology, the role technology plays in the field of special education, and some of the forces that have affected the development of technology applications. (For historical and descriptive information, see Alliance for Technology Access, 1996; Baumgart, Johnson, & Helmstetter, 1990; Behrmann, 1984; Beukelman & Mirenda, 1992; Blackhurst & Hofmeister, 1980; Church & Glennen, 1992; Cook & Hussey, 1995; Flippo, Inge, & Barcus, 1995; Galvan & Scherer, 1996; Lewis, 1993; Lindsey, 1997; Male, 1994; Margalit, 1990; Silverman, 1995; Taber, 1983).

Perspectives on the Technology Continuum

To many people, the term *technology* conjures up visions of computers and other high-tech devices, both expensive and complicated. Often, such perspectives focus solely on hardware and equipment and overlook the procedures that teachers use in the classroom.

We need to view technology as a tool that can be used to solve problems in the education of their students. I like to think of solutions as a continuum—ranging from "high-tech" to "no-tech":

High-tech solutions involve the use of sophisticated devices, such as computers and interactive multimedia systems.
Medium-tech solutions use less complicated electronic or mechanical devices, such as videocassette players and wheelchairs.
Low-tech solutions are less sophisticated aids, such as adapted spoon handles, Velcro fasteners, or raised desks that can accommodate a wheelchair.
No-tech solutions require no devices or equipment. These might involve the use of systematic teaching procedures or the services of related services personnel such as physical or occupational therapists.

In making decisions about the type of technology tools or supports a particular student might require, a good approach is to start with no-tech or low-tech solutions and then work up the continuum as needed. Too often, when people make technology decisions in IEP meetings, they tend to *start* at high-tech solutions. For example, if a student has difficulty writing legibly, IEP planners may recommend providing the student with a laptop computer to take from class to class (cost: $1,500–3,000). In reality, an electronic keyboard with memory that can be downloaded into a desktop computer later in the day may be more appropriate (cost: about $300). Although the student in this example may eventually need a laptop computer, the electronic keyboard may be a better place to start.

Perspectives on Types of Technology

In 1926, Pressey developed the first "teaching machine." Was this the first example of educational technology? Not necessarily—as the congressional Commission on Instructional Technology (1970) concluded: In addition to devices and equipment, instructional technology also involves a systematic way of designing and delivering instruction.

During the past 25 years, we have seen a dramatic evolution of technology in education: microcomputer technology, research on instructional procedures, and many new assistive devices and equipment. In addition to technology productivity tools such as word processors, researchers and educators today recognize four types of technology: the technology of teaching, medical technology, instructional technology, and assistive technology (Blackhurst & Cross, 1993):

The technology of teaching includes systematically designed procedures and strategies that are applied in precise ways. They typically include well-defined objectives; precise instructional procedures based on the tasks students are required to learn; small, sequenced units of instruction; a high degree of teacher activity; high levels of student involvement; liberal use of reinforcement; and careful monitoring of student performance. These technologies include direct instruction, applied behavior analysis, competency-based instruction, learning strategies, and response prompting (see, e.g., Alberto & Troutman, 1995; Carnine, Silbert, & Kameenui, 1990; Wolery, Ault, & Doyle, 1992).

Medical technology continues to amaze us, with almost miraculous surgical procedures and new devices that keep people alive. For example, new technologies provide respirator assistance (oxygen supplementation, mechanical ventilation, positive airway pressure devices) and surveillance of vital signs (cardiorespiratory monitors, pulse oximeters) (Batshaw & Perret, 1992).

Instructional technology includes various types of hardware and software, combined with innovative teaching methods, to accommodate learners' needs in the classroom. Such technology may include videotapes, computer-assisted instruction, or complex hypermedia programs in which computers are used to control the display of audio and visual images stored on videodisc (Blackhurst & Morse, 1996). The use of telecommunication systems, particularly the Internet (Williams, 1995) and its World Wide Web (Williams, 1996), has great promise for use in classrooms and for distance education.

Assistive technology includes various services and devices designed to help people with disabilities function within the environment. Examples include communication aids, alternative computer keyboards, adaptive switches, and services such as those that might be provided by speech/language pathologists. To locate such services, educators can use computer databases such as HyperABLEDATA (Trace Center, 1996) and the Adaptive Device Locator System (Academic Software, 1996).

Creative and knowledgeable educators—or teams of educators and other professionals—often use these technologies in combination. For example, students who are unable to use their hands to operate a computer keyboard may use a voice-operated computer (assistive technology) that provides instruction from a software program that was designed to deliver spelling instruction (instructional technology) using a constant time delay response prompt fading instructional procedure (technology of teaching).

A Functional Perspective About Technology

Unfortunately, many decisions about applications of technology in special education are "device driven." As new devices appear on the market, it is not uncommon to find consumers, parents, vendors, and professionals advocate strongly for their acquisition and use with different students—often with less than satisfactory results. Instead of getting caught up in the allure of new products with intriguing features, a better perspective is to focus on problems that children have in functioning within the environment. For example, a preschooler with cerebral palsy may lack the fine muscle control that will permit her to fasten buttons so that she can get dressed independently. A boy with a visual impairment may be unable to use printed material that is being used for instruction in an English class. Another student, due to unknown cause, may be unable to solve math problems. Similarly, a child who has been in an automobile accident may have had a severe head injury that has impaired her ability to speak clearly.

In all of these cases, environmental demands have been placed on the children to perform some function that they will find difficult to execute because of a set of unique circumstances or restriction in functional capability caused by the lack of personal resources. For example, the above children lack the physical or mental capability to button, read, calculate, or speak.

Many variables, which interact in very complex ways, are involved in making decisions about the provision of special education and related services and the selection and use of technology. Figure 1 illustrates those variables and their interrelationships.

When making planning decisions, there is the need to know things such as the nature of the demands that are being placed on the child from the environment and how those demands create the requirements to perform different human functions, such as learning, walking, talking, seeing, and hearing. It is important to know how such requirements are—or are not—being met by the child and how factors such as the child's perceptions and the availability of personal resources such as intelligence, sight, hearing, and mobility can affect the responses the child can make. In addition, it is important to understand how availability of external supports, such as special education, different types of therapy, and technology can impact on the child's ability to produce functional responses to the environmental demands.

Although each exceptional child will be unique, the common challenge is to identify and apply the best possible array of special education and related services that will provide support, adjustment, or compensation for the child's functional needs or deficits. A variety of responses may be appropriate. For example, Velcro fasteners may be used to replace buttons on garments for the child having difficulty with buttoning. Braille or audio materials may be provided for the child who cannot read conventional print. The student who has difficulty calculating may require specialized, intense direct math instruction, while a computerized device that produces speech may enable the child who cannot talk to communicate. Monitoring and evaluation provide feedback about the personal changes that have occurred in order to determine whether additional modifications may be required.

The model in Figure 1 places technology in its proper perspective: as an external support. Functions that can be aided by technology include existence, communication, body support and positioning, travel and mobility, environmental adaptation, education and learning, rehabilitation, and sports, leisure, and recreation. Additional information about this functional approach and how it relates to special education and technology applications can be found elsewhere (Blackhurst & Cross, 1993; Blackhurst & Lahm, 1997).

Perspectives on Federal Initiatives

Over the years, the federal government has stimulated technology applications in special education. Federal laws and regulations have included technology mandates and funding to support a variety of technology research and development, training, and service activities.

Legislated support for technology can be traced back to Public Law 45-186 in 1879, which awarded $10,000 to the American Printing House for the Blind to produce Braille materials. Although many other laws were established to support services to people with disabilities, four acts—and their amendments—have had the greatest impact for technology applications.

The Individuals with Disabilities Education Act (IDEA, P.L. 94-142 and its amendments) guarantees the right of all children with disabilities to a free and appropriate education in the least restrictive environment. As part of the IEP planning process,

Figure 1 Model for Planning Special Education and Technology Services

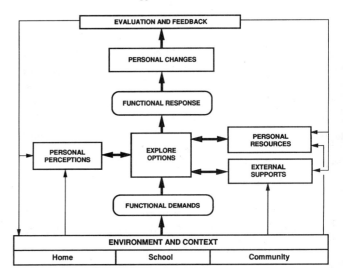

parents, teachers, and administrators are required to consider technologies that may help a child meet the IEP objectives.

P.L. 99-506 amended the Rehabilitation Act of 1973 by adding Section 508. This amendment ensures access to computers and other electronic office equipment in places of federal employment. The guidelines ensure that users with disabilities can access and use the same databases and applications programs as do other users. Users with disabilities also will be able to manipulate data and related information sources to attain the same results as other users and will have the necessary adaptations needed to communicate with others on their system.

P.L. 101-336, the Americans with Disabilities Act, broadened the definition of those who are considered to have disabilities. It also broadened the types of agencies and employers covered by Section 508 requirements and mandates additional protections, such as accessible public transportation systems, communication systems, and access to public buildings.

> **The technology of teaching includes systematically designed procedures and strategies that are applied in precise ways.**

P.L. 100-407, the Technology-Related Assistance for Individuals with Disabilities Act, was signed into law in 1988. Under the auspices of that Act, a number of states are developing systems for providing a variety of technology assistance to children and adults with disabilities and their parents and guardians. The purpose of P.L. 100-407 is to provide financial assistance to the states to enable them to conduct needs assessments, identify technology resources, provide assistive technology services, and conduct public awareness programs, among others. It also provided a definition of assistive technology devices and services that was added to IDEA in one of its amendments.

In addition to these legislative actions, other federal assistance includes the funds that various government agencies have provided to support technology-related projects. The agency that has been the most active is the Division of Innovation and Development of the Office of Special Education Programs (OSEP) in the U.S. Department of Education. [See Kallas (1996) for a listing of projects that were being supported in 1996.]

U.S. schools and districts need knowledgeable staff to implement technology applications in special education. The Division of Personnel Preparation in OSEP has supported many projects to fund technology-training programs for teachers, administrators, leadership personnel, and parents.

Many of the technology advances that have occurred would not have been possible without federal support. Legislators and professionals in the executive branch of the federal government should be commended for their past support of technology initiatives and should be strongly encouraged to continue their efforts. The results of past federal initiatives have paid rich dividends to people with disabilities.

Perspectives on CEC's Role in Technology

In commemoration of CEC's 75th anniversary, we need to recognize some of the contributions that the Council has made to the growth and development of technology applications in special education. The Council's membership—along with federal funding—has supported many activities.

CEC has operated the Educational Resources Information Center (ERIC) Clearinghouse on Disabilities and Gifted Education since 1966. This Clearinghouse is responsible for reviewing and abstracting much of the world's literature on special education and related topics. In addition to contributing data for ERIC's publications and electronic database, CEC's Clearinghouse maintains its own electronic database and publishes *Exceptional Child Education Resources (ECER),* which abstracts all literature reviewed by that project. ERIC's online and CD-ROM resources contain only a sampling of ECER resources; complete listings from ECER's databases are available on CD-ROM in many libraries (Barbara Sorensen, CEC-ERIC Clearinghouse, personal communication; SilverPlatter Information, 1996). The CEC ERIC Clearinghouse also publishes mini-bibliographies in various topical areas, including technology (e.g., ERIC Mini-Bib, 1996).

From the mid-1960s through the late 1970s, the Coordinating Office for the national Instructional Materials Center Network for Handicapped Children and Youth (IMC Network) was housed at CEC. (For more information, see the September 1968 issue of *Exceptional Children.*)

This journal, *TEACHING Exceptional Children (TEC),* is a direct outgrowth of work done with the IMC Network. A committee was formed to find ways to provide practical information about teaching exceptional children. The committee developed a publication prospectus (Blackhurst, 1968), and *TEC* was born. The first issue (see above) appeared in the fall of 1968. A primary goal of *TEACHING Exceptional Children* is to help translate theory and research into effective practice (Blackhurst, 1968).

CEC was an early leader in exploring satellite technology for distance education. In 1978, broadcasts from the First World Congress on Special Education in Stirling, Scotland, were transmitted to sites in the United States, thus enabling those who were unable to travel abroad to benefit from that international conference.

The Technology and Media (TAM) Division became affiliated with CEC in 1984 and received its charter as an official division in 1989. TAM's annual conferences, special initiatives, and *Journal of Special Education Technology* are invaluable resources to both its members and professionals from related fields. TAM also monitors and responds to pending federal legislation and regulations related to technology through its political action network.

CEC has operated federally funded technology projects, such as the Special Education Technology Center (1987–1991) and Project Retool (1983–1992). Hundreds of people have attended research symposia and training programs and received resource documents from these projects.

CEC is a leader in publications on educational technology—journal articles, books, monographs, and special reports. The first book on applications of microcomputers in special education was published by CEC (Taber, 1983).

From Then to Now

When I began writing about the implications of technology for special education more than 30 years ago, it was fun speculating about what the future might hold. Although some of the devices I speculated about eventually were developed in one form or another, I missed the mark badly on others because I

> Instead of getting caught up in the allure of new products with intriguing features, a better perspective is to focus on problems children have in functioning within the environment.

did not anticipate the development of personal computers and the many marvelous applications that were developed as extensions to them.

In projecting technology developments as we move to the 21st century, we can say few things with certainty. On the high-tech side, microprocessors will continue to get smaller and faster; and telecommunication systems will be developed with greater capacity and speed. Costs of computers and related equipment will decline. Software developers will develop smarter software, and computer memory and file storage requirements will increase. Interconnectivity among classrooms and schools will improve—and people will develop products that we cannot even conceptualize today.

On the no-tech side, people will become more knowledgeable about the various technologies and their application. Educators and other team members will pay more attention to the implications of technology when planning IEPs for individual students. Technology specialists and support systems will become more available in schools; more technology in-service training programs will be provided for special education teachers and related personnel; and colleges and universities will add instruction about technology for people who are preparing for special education positions and those who are involved in providing related services.

Ingenious computer scientists, creative engineers, clever software programmers, and talented tinkerers have produced—and will continue to produce—an amazing array of low-tech to high-tech devices that can help people who have severe medical problems to stay alive and function in our society, enable people who have difficulty speaking to communicate, assist people who cannot hear to use the telephone system, assist people who have limited muscle control to operate machinery and appliances, aid people who cannot walk move from place to place, help people who cannot see listen to machines that can read for them, and provide children who have difficulty learning with effective instruction. Many applications that once seemed futuristic are already available: expert systems (Aldinger, Warger, & Eavy, 1995), virtual reality (Inman, 1996a, 1996b), robotics (Cook & Hussey, 1995), voice recognition systems (Cavalier & Ferretti, 1996), and telecommunication systems (Slaton & Lacefield, 1991) to name a few.

Many of the current technology applications in special education reflect the "state of the art." A major challenge facing us for the future is to move those applications to the point where they reflect a "state of the science." We must continue to conduct research and study the application of technology devices and services in objective ways so that we can make informed decisions about their use.

References

Academic Software, Inc. (1996). Adaptive device locator system [Computer program]. Lexington, KY: Author.

Alberto, P. A., & Troutman, A. C. (1995). *Applied behavior analysis for teachers* (4th ed.). Columbus, OH: Merrill.

Aldinger, L. E., Warger, C. L., & Eavy, P. W. (1995). Expert systems software in special education. *TEACHING Exceptional Children, 27*(2), 58–62.

Alliance for Technology Access. (1996). *Computer resources for people with disabilities: A guide to exploring today's assistive technology* (2nd ed.). Alameda, CA: Hunter House.

Batshaw, M. L., & Perret, Y. M. (1992). *Children with disabilities: A medical primer.* Baltimore: Paul H. Brookes.

Baumgart, D., Johnson, J., & Helmstetter, E. (1990). *Augmentative and alternative communication systems for persons with moderate and severe disabilities.* Baltimore: Paul H. Brookes.

Behrmann, M. (1984). *Handbook of microcomputers in special education.* San Diego, CA: College-Hill Press.

Blackhurst, A. E. (1965). Technology in special education: Some implications. *Exceptional Children, 31*, 449–456.

Blackhurst, A. E. (1967). Tachistoscopic training as a supplement to reading instruction for educable mentally retarded children. *Education and Training of the Mentally Retarded, 2*, 121–125.

Blackhurst, A. E. (1968). Dissemination: TEACHING Exceptional Children. *Exceptional Children, 35*, 315–317.

Blackhurst, A. E., & Cross, D. P. (1993). Technology in special education. In A. E. Blackhurst & W. H. Berdine (Eds.), *An introduction to special education* (3rd ed., pp. 77–103). New York: HarperCollins.

Blackhurst, A. E., & Hofmeister, A. M. (1980). Technology in special education. In L. Mann & D. Sabatino (Eds.). *Fourth review of special education* (pp. 199–228). New York: Grune and Stratton.

Blackhurst, A. E., & Lahm, E. A. (1997). Foundations of technology and exceptionality. In J. E. Lindsey (Ed.), *Technology for exceptional individuals* (3rd ed.). Austin, TX: PRO-ED.

Blackhurst, A. E., & Morse, T. E. (1996). Using anchored instruction to teach about assistive technology. *Focus on Autism and Other Developmental Disabilities, 11*, 131–141.

Carnine, D. W., Silbert, J., & Kameenui, E. J. (1990). *Direct instruction reading* (2nd ed.). Columbus, OH: Merrill.

Cavalier, A. R., & Ferretti, R. P. (1996). Talking instead of typing: Alternate access to computers via speech recognition technology. *Focus on Autism and Other Developmental Disabilities, 11*, 79–85.

Church, G., & Glennen, S. (1992). *The handbook of assistive technology.* San Diego, CA: Singular Publishing Group.

Commission on Instructional Technology. (1970). *To improve learning: A report to the President and the Congress of the United States.* Washington, DC: U.S. Government Printing Office.

Cook, A. M., & Hussey, S. M. (1995). *Assistive technologies: Principles and practice.* St. Louis, MO: Mosby.

ERIC Mini-Bib. (1996). *Readings on the use of technology for individuals with disabilities.* Reston, VA: ERIC Clearinghouse on Disabilities and Gifted Education, Council for Exceptional Children.

Flippo, K. F., Inge, K. J., & Barcus, J. M. (Eds.). (1995). *Assistive technology: A resource for school, work, and community.* Baltimore: Paul H. Brookes.

Galvan, J. C., & Scherer, M. J. (1996). *Evaluating, selecting, and using appropriate assistive technology.* Gaithersburg, MD: Aspen.

Inman, D. (1996a). A virtual reality training program for motorized wheelchair operation. In A. Kallas (Ed.), *Innovation and development in special education: Directory of current projects.* Reston, VA: ERIC Clearinghouse on Disabilities and Gifted Education, Council for Exceptional Children. (ERIC Document Reproduction Service No. ED 392 224)

Inman, D. (1996b). Science education for secondary students with severe orthopedic impairments using virtual reality. In A. Kallas (Ed.), *Innovation and development in special education: Directory of current projects.* Reston, VA: ERIC Clearinghouse on Disabilities and Gifted Education, Council for Exceptional Children. (ERIC Document Reproduction Service No. ED 392 224)

Kallas, A. (Ed.). (1996). *Innovation and development in special education: Directory of current projects.* Reston, VA: ERIC Clearinghouse on Disabilities and Gifted Education, Council for Exceptional Children. (ERIC Document Reproduction Service No. ED 392 224)

Lewis, R. B. (1993). *Special education technology.* Pacific Grove, CA: Brooke Cole Publishers.

Lindsey, J. E. (Ed.). (1997). *Technology for exceptional individuals* (3rd ed.). Austin, TX: PRO-ED.

Male, M. (1994). *Technology for inclusion: Meeting the special needs of all students* (2nd ed.). Needham Heights, MA: Allyn & Bacon.

Margalit, M. (1990). *Effective technology integration for disabled children: The family perspective.* New York: Springer-Verlag.

Silverman, F. H. (1995). *Communication for the speechless* (3rd ed.). Needham Heights, MA: Allyn & Bacon.

SilverPlatter Information. (1996). *Exceptional child education resources* [CD-ROM]: Norwood, MA: Author.

Slaton, D. B., & Lacefield, W. E. (1991). Use of an interactive telecommunications network to deliver inservice education. *Journal of Special Education Technology, 11,* 64–74.

Taber, F. M. (1983). *Microcomputers in special education: Selection and decision making process.* Reston, VA: Council for Exceptional Children. (ERIC Document Reproduction Service No. ED 228 793)

Trace Center. (1996). *HyperABLEDATA* [CO-NET CD-ROM program]. Madison: University of Wisconsin, Author.

Williams, B. (1995). *The Internet for teachers.* Foster City, CA: IDG Books Worldwide.

Williams, B. (1996). *The World Wide Web for Teachers.* Foster City, CA: IDG Books Worldwide.

Wolery, M., Ault, M. J., & Doyle, P. M. (1992). *Teaching students with moderate and severe disabilities: Use of response prompting procedures.* White Plains, NY: Longman.

A. Edward Blackhurst *(CEC Chapter #180), Professor, Department of Special Education and Rehabilitation Counseling, University of Kentucky, Lexington. Blackhurst chaired the committee that conceptualized* TEACHING Exceptional Children *and served as the Chairperson of its first Editorial Advisory Board.*

Address correspondence to the author at the University of Kentucky, Department of Special Education and Rehabilitation Counseling, 229 Taylor Education Building, Lexington, KY 40506-0001 (e-mail: blakhrst@pop.uky.edu).

Preparation of this article was supported by Grant H180U50025, Examination of the Effectiveness of a Functional Approach to the Delivery of Assistive Technology Services in Schools, from the Division of Innovation and Development, Office of Special Education Programs, U.S. Department of Education. The perspectives presented herein do not necessarily reflect the official position of the U.S. Department of Education.

Unit 9

Key Points to Consider

❖ Can children with severe motor disabilities benefit from the same activities as their nondisabled peers in the classroom? How can this be accomplished?

❖ How can school-home partnerships assist children with disabilities?

❖ Why do browsers make it more difficult for people with orthopedic impairments to access the Web? How can Web sites be made more accessible?

 **Links** | **www.dushkin.com/online/**

These sites are annotated on pages 4 and 5.

The word "handicapped" used to be applied indiscriminately to all persons who needed assistive devices (e.g., braces, canes, wheelchairs) to walk after about the age of two. Old dictionaries defined "handicapped" as inferior and in need of an artificial advantage. People were described as handicapped if they were encumbered by physical limitations. Today, describing a person as "handicapped" is derogatory. People who need medical assistance or assistive devices are not inferior. They are equal to other persons but have somewhat different functional abilities. The correct way to describe such a person is to say he or she has a disability. The preferred order is person first, disability second; e.g., Tom with quadriplegia, Harry with diabetes. It is also polite to describe all of the things the person can do with the stress on abilities, not disability. Handicap is synonymous with hindrance. If a property of the environment prevents a person with an orthopedic or health impairment from functioning to the best of his or her abilities, then the environment has imposed a handicap.

Children and youth with orthopedic and health impairments can be divided into classifications of mild, moderate, and profound. Within most impairments, the same diagnosis may not produce the same degree of disability. For example, children with cerebral palsy may be mildly, moderately, or profoundly impaired. Orthopedic impairments are usually defined as those that hinder physical mobility and/or the ability to use one or more parts of the skeletomuscular system of the body. Health impairments are usually defined as those that affect stamina and predominantly one or more systems of the body: cardiovascular, respiratory, gastrointestinal, endocrine, lymphatic, urinary, reproductive, sensory, or nervous systems. Orthopedic and health impairments are not always mutually exclusive. Many times a child with an orthopedic impairment also has a concurrent or contributing health impairment, and vice versa. In addition, children with orthopedic and health impairments may also have concurrent problems (the addition of one or more other disorders such as learning disability, mental retardation, behavioral disorder, speech and language impairments, or sensory disorders).

Some children with orthopedic and health impairments have only transitory impairments; some have permanent but nonworsening impairments; and some have progressive impairments that make their education more complicated as the years pass and may even result in death before the end of the developmental/educational period.

Each of the dimensions defined in the preceding paragraphs makes educational planning for children with orthopedic and health impairments very individualistic. The Individuals with Disabilities Education Act (IDEA) and its amendments mandate a free and appropriate public school education in the least restrictive environment for all children with orthopedic and health impairments from the age of diagnosis until age 21, if needed. This may require only minimal special education, as in the cases of children with mild impairment, with only one problem, or with a transitory disability. On the other end of the spectrum, children with profound or progressively worsening disabilities may need maximal special education services over a very long period of time. Between these two poles lie the majority of children with orthopedic and health impairments. They have widely differing needs (qualitatively and quantitatively), depending on the nature of their impairments.

Orthopedic problems may have a neurological etiology (injury or dysfunction of the brain or spinal cord) or a skeletomuscular etiology (injury or dysfunction of an area of the muscles or skeletal bones). Regardless of etiology, the child with an orthopedic impairment usually has a problem with mobility. A child with a mild impairment may be able to walk alone. A child with a moderate impairment may need crutches or other aids in order to walk. A child with a more profound orthopedic disability will probably be in a wheelchair.

Children with health impairments usually have to take medicine or follow a medical regimen in order to have the energy or salubrity required to attend school. The degree of impairment (mild, moderate, profound) is usually based on limitations to activity (none, some, many), duration of problem (temporary, chronic, progressive), and extent of other problems (none, some, many).

When orthopedic or health impairments are diagnosed in infancy or early childhood, an interdisciplinary team usually helps plan an individualized family service plan (IFSP) that includes working with parents, medical and/or surgical personnel, and preschool special education providers. When the orthopedic or health impairment is diagnosed in the school years, the schoolteachers collaborate with outside agencies, but more of the individualized educational programming (IEP) is in their hands. Children who have orthopedic and/or health impairments need psychological as well as academic support. Teachers need to help them in their peer interactions and encourage their friendships. Teachers should also work closely with parents and significant others in the lives of children to ensure a smooth transition toward a lifestyle that fosters independence and self-reliance.

The first unit article presents information about inclusive educational programming for children with orthopedic and health impairments. Kristyn Sheldon is concerned with how to adapt the classroom so that it is more user-friendly to children with limited motor abilities.

The next article suggests helpful ways to design the most appropriate IEP for each child with an orthopedic or health impairment. Linda Davern advises talking to parents frequently.

The last selection in this unit considers the benefits of computer technology in breaking down some of the barriers faced by students with physical disabilities. The author points out that educators may need to help students with disabilities use computers. "All Web designs should be accessible to all people," according to Stacy Peters-Walters.

Orthopedic and Health Impairments

Early Childhood Special Education

"Can I Play Too?" Adapting Common Classroom Activities for Young Children with Limited Motor Abilities

Kristyn Sheldon[1,2]

This paper offers suggestions on adapting common classroom activities found in early childhood classrooms to increase participation of young children with limited motor abilities. It stresses the importance of de-emphasizing differences among children and highlighting that all children, even those with severe disabilities, can benefit from the same activities.

KEY WORDS: adapting activities; inclusion; limited motor abilities.

INTRODUCTION

Amber, eager to attend her first day of school in her new classroom, enters the room ready to play. The art easel looks like a good place to start, but she discovers she cannot reach the paint. Amber tries the dramatic play area next, but her wheelchair will not fit in the space and she accidently bumps toys and shelves everywhere. She would like to play with puzzles, but is unable to manipulate the small pieces. Amber attempts to play at the sensory table, but it is too high and her wheelchair gets in the way. Circle time is no better. There is nowhere for her to sit and she is unable to participate in the group activities.

Many children with special needs are enrolled in early childhood programs. Such enrollment is a wonderful learning opportunity for all, but it involves more than placing children together in the

same program (Odom & McEvoy, 1990). Many early childhood educators are open to the inclusion of preschoolers with mild to moderate disabilities, but may be hesitant to include children with severe disabilities because they believe extensive modifications will be needed (Demchak & Drinkwater, 1992). Teachers are constantly challenged with arranging the environment to allow young children with physical impairments to participate and engage in the environment. These special challenges include increasing the amount and quality of participation for young children with limited motor abilities (Bigge, 1991).

Although there are an increasing number of children with motor difficulties integrated into early childhood classrooms, many early childhood teachers have limited experience and training in working with these children. Existing day care services and preschool

settings provide natural and rich environments for early education experiences with only minor modifications or adaptations needed in daily activities to accommodate children with limited motor ability (Klein & Sheehan, 1987). This article provides suggestions on adapting common classroom activities found in early childhood classrooms to increase participation of young children with limited motor abilities.

DEFINITION OF LIMITED MOTOR ABILITY

The term, limited motor ability, is used in this article to define any movement difficulty that negatively affects a child's participation in an activity (Bigge, 1991). For example, Randy, age 4, has cerebral palsy that affects his equilibrium and ability to control his

From *Early Childhood Education Journal,* Winter 1996, pp. 115–120. © 1996 by Human Sciences Press, Inc. Reprinted by Permission.

movement. Jamar, age 5, has cerebral palsy which has limited his ability to walk, run, or even sit up by himself. Kelly, a 3-year-old girl, has spina bifida and no sensation below her waist. She wears braces on her legs, uses a walker for mobility, and depends on her upper body for engaging in most activities. Sara uses a wheelchair, has only minimal use of her left arm, and needs support to sit upright in her chair. What is important to remember about children with special needs such as Randy, Jamar, and Kelly is not their physical limitations but their abilities.

Neisworth and Madle (1975) stressed the importance of de-emphasizing differences and highlighting that all children, even those with severe disabilities, can benefit from the same activities. Developmentally Appropriate Practice guidelines currently followed in early childhood classrooms are also appropriate for children with disabilities (Bredekamp, 1987). The guidelines for developmentally appropriate practice (Bredekamp, 1987) and the curriculum and assessment guidelines with NAEYC and NAECS/SDE (1991) clearly recognize the importance of individual differences and the need to adapt the curriculum to those differences (Wolery, Strain, & Baily, 1992). The guidelines are the context in which appropriate early education of children with special needs should occur; however, a program based on the guidelines alone is not likely to be sufficient for many children with special needs. Programs that use the guidelines may be good places for children with special needs to receive early education, but those programs must be adjusted to be maximally beneficial to those children (Wolery et al. 1992). Adaptations are usually needed so children with special needs, especially children with limited motor abilities, can participate.

It is not always necessary for children to participate in an activity to the same degree as children without disabilities for the activity to be enjoyed. Partial participation is a valid goal as long as meaningful participation is encouraged. The principle of partial participation states that, regardless of severity of disability, individuals can be taught to participate in [a] variety of activities to some degree, or activities can be adapted to allow participation (Baumgart, Brown, Pumpian, Nisbet, Ford, Sweet, Messina, & Schroeder,

1982). Activities and materials should be adapted or modified, and/or personal assistance strategies used. Have a child with a disability and a peer without a disability play together to allow the child with a disability to participate in the activity to the maximum extent appropriate.

SPECIAL ADAPTATIONS

In planning activities for children with limited motor ability, start with typical activities planned for all children. When special adaptations are needed, they should be designed to include other children whenever possible (Chandler, 1994). Special activities such as speech or physical therapy, if needed, should be provided in addition to, not instead of, typical program activities. In successfully integrated preschools, teachers strive to use the least intrusive, natural prompts, and contingencies needed to help children participate actively and meaningfully in the routines of the preschool (Drinkwater & Demchak, 1995). Encourage and assist the child to participate as fully as possible in activities such as circle time, art, books, sensory play, fine motor activities, dramatic play, snack, and gross motor activities. Some suggestions are provided below.

Circle Time

Circle time is a popular activity in early childhood classrooms, but certain environmental adaptations may be needed during circle to ensure that everyone can participate. Some problems children with limited motor abilities experience at circle time are difficulties in finding a place to sit, a difference in eye level from other children, and the possibility of being unable to communicate with the other children or the teacher. During circle time, children often sit on the floor or on carpet squares. This can become a problem for children in a wheelchair or children unable to sit independently on the floor. They may not be able to physically fit in the circle area or the children with limited motor abilities may not be comfortable. Remember children in a wheelchair will be at a different eye level than the rest of the group. It is important to recognize this when presenting circle time activities or

reading books. Children with limited motor abilities often have communication difficulties, so adaptations must be used to ensure all children are able to communicate with the teacher and their peers.

Suggestions for Circle Time

- To facilitate the integration of children in wheelchairs have the children and teacher sit in chairs at circle time. This will allow all children's eye level to [be] more similar and make children in wheelchair[s] "less different."
- Include modalities of communication other than verbal language. For example, a song board can be incorporated for all of the children to select what songs they want to sing. The board can have pictures of the songs the children sing during circle and both children with limited motor abilities and typical peers can use this board to choose a song.
- Use songs that can involve the children interacting with one another. For example, "If you're happy and you know it, hug a friend, give them five."
- Use books which talk about and include children with disabilities.
- Seat children with disabilities next to their peers to provide natural opportunities for interaction (Hanline, 1985).

Art

Children with physical disabilities have difficulties coloring and painting for many reasons. Some children with limited motor ability have problems because they cannot grasp and hold the tools or they are unable to maintain their arms and hands in the necessary angle or position to draw, color, or paint (Bigge, 1991). Others cannot reach the materials or enter the art area. A common problem for children who are nonambulatory is their inability to reach the standard art easel typically used in classrooms.

Suggestions for Art

- Provide a variety of areas and surfaces for children to paint. For example, place the paper on the floor or more easily accessible surfaces such as a window, wall, refrigerator, etc.

- Cut off the legs of an art easel so children can crawl to or kneel at the easel.
- Use adaptations such as velcro or yarn to fasten a paint brush to the child's hand or wrist.
- Encourage children to paint using their fingers, feet, and other body parts.
- Use edible paint for those who engage in hand mouthing. For example, paint with jello and water, marshmallow whip or pudding. Food coloring can be added with many edible painting mediums.
- Assign a buddy to be paired with a child with disabilities to encourage meaningful participation (Drinkwater & Demchak, 1995).
- Use age appropriate clothing for activities. For example, use a paint shirt as a cover-up and not a bib (Drinkwater & Demchak, 1995).

Specific Art Activity Suggestions

- *Funnel painting.* Place a large funnel made of paper over a table and allow the children to push the funnel back and forth, dripping paint out of the funnel onto a large piece of paper.
- *Record player art.* Place a piece of paper on a record player and have the children hold a crayon, pencil, or paint brush on the paper as the record player turns.
- *Swing art.* This activity allows a child with limited motor ability to color or paint a large piece of paper. The child is placed in a seater swing and a crayon or paint brush is attached to the swing. As the child is slowly pushed back and forth a drawing is created.
- *Contact paper collages.* This activity is appropriate for children with limited motor movement because they do not have to manipulate any tools, they simply drop or place items onto the sticky surface of the contact paper. A piece of contact paper is taped on a flat surface and the child is given different materials to drop onto the sticky side of the contact paper. Contact paper collages can be made with a variety of different materials such as, feathers, torn colored paper, uncooked macaroni or beans, cotton balls, etc.
- *Glue activities.* Glue activities can be challenging for children with limited hand movement and control. In order

to increase the participation of children in these activities, have the children brush the glue onto the paper or materials instead of using squeeze bottles. The glue can be provided in foil pie dishes or bowls.

Sensory Play

The use of sensory play (water, sand, cornmeal, shaving cream, cotton, etc.) is a wonderful activity for young children with limited motor abilities. Many times children are unable to reach the sensory table where the items are commonly placed or are hesitant to explore a sensory activity because of the textures involved. When adaptations for this activity are implemented, children with limited motor abilities can actively participate and engage in sensory play.

Suggestions for Sensory Play

- Arrange some of the sensory items in a messy tray on the floor or use a sensory table that is wheelchair accessible.
- Place sensory items in a zip lock bag and tape it to the table or tray on the children's wheelchairs for exploration.
- Place sensory items directly on the children's tray.
- Encourage children to touch the sensory items with their feet or rub it on their arms or legs.
- Use large mirrors to increase engagement in the activity. For example, place a mirror on the table, spray shaving cream on the mirror, and allow children to explore with their fingers or toys (small cars, paint brushes, etc.).
- Encourage the children to explore the object with a variety of senses.

Specific Sensory Activity Suggestions

- *Tactile stimulation.* Provide sponges, honey, peanut butter, marshmallow fluff, mashed bananas, cotton candy, snow, whipped gelatin, etc. for children to experience various textures.
- *Visual stimulation.* Blow bubbles, play with bubble wands, or use automatic blowers for children who may have difficulty in blowing. Paint on black paper with fluorescent paint and use lights to show off the child's art.

- *Auditory stimulation.* Play music with regular classroom activity or help children make shakers with uncooked beans and macaroni.
- *Aromatic stimulation.* Let the class feel and smell cut fruit, flowers, and spices. For example, oranges, lemons, fresh flowers, herbs, spices in jars, etc.

Books

Children with limited motor abilities often have difficulty engaging in book time or playing in the book area. The books may be too difficult to manipulate, out of their reach, or not stimulating enough. Some books have very thin pages which are difficult for young children with limited motor abilities to manipulate. High and unstable book shelves are often found in an early childhood classroom. This arrangement makes it difficult for children to have access to books and the area.

Suggestions for Book Area

- Arrange shelves at different levels so the materials are accessible to everyone.
- Provide headphones and tapes so children can listen to the stories.
- Add a bookstand to hold the book for children unable to hold the book.
- Incorporate textured books (homemade or commercial) to book selection.
- Encourage the use of musical books that include individual sounds, songs, and voices.
- Provide books in several areas of the classroom, especially if the book area is in a loft.

Fine Motor

Fine motor activities are often difficult for young children with limited motor movement because many of the fine motor activities involve the manipulation of small pieces and materials. Puzzles are usually a fun activity for young children, but sometimes the pieces are too small or there are too many. Also, if the activity is done on a table top, items may slip around on the table causing difficulties for children with limited motor abilities to complete the task.

Suggestions for Fine Motor Area

- Select puzzles that have large knobs on the tops of the pieces and only three to four pieces per puzzle.
- Provide puzzles with auditory stimulation. For example, puzzles that play music when children place the puzzle piece in the correct place or take it out.
- Select musical shape sorters with auditory stimulation. For example, a song plays when the child places the correct shape into the holder.
- Try to keep the fine motor items large enough for the children to manipulate. The size can be changed as the children progress with the activity. For example, large chalk, crayons, pencils, and pegs can be used.
- Use Velcro to prevent materials from sliding around on the table or their tray. Velcro can be placed under the toy or puzzle.

Dramatic Play

Some problems young children with limited motor abilities may experience in the dramatic play area of a preschool classroom are difficulties in participating in the social games, the area may not be wheelchair accessible, and the toys may be too difficult to manipulate. Social interactions typically occur during dramatic play. However, children with limited motor abilities often also have language and communication delays which make social interactions more difficult. Also, the dramatic play area often contains many pieces of furniture which limits space and accessibility for children with limited motor abilities. If a child needs additional or different type of space modifications, they should be made only if necessary. This is so attention is not called to the child's disability and opportunities for children to move around in and accommodate to physical barriers in the natural environment are not lost (McCormick & Feeney, 1985).

Suggestions for Dramatic Play Area

- Make this section of the room accessible to children with limited motor abilities.
- Incorporate items such as hats, dishes, and utensils that are large and easy to manipulate.

- Label shelves with pictures as well as words so children do not have to be able to read to participate in clean up.
- Encourage peers to include and play with the children with limited motor ability. For example, plan integration experiences and activities for the children (Chandler, 1994).
- Allow children to use adaptive equipment on the dolls and their peers in the dramatic play area. For example, the children can explore and play with wheelchairs, walkers, and braces. Monitor this activity so equipment is not damaged (Chandler, 1994). Children can gain a sense of what equipment feels like and will likely be less fearful or anxious about the apparatus and the child who uses it.
- Create opportunities for children with motor impairments to interact with their normally developing peers. For example, provide materials and toys that promote play, engagement, and learning (Sainato & Carta, 1992).
- Structure the social dimensions of the environment to include peer and adult models.
- Facilitate proximity to responsive and imitative adults (Odom, McConnell, & McEvoy, 1992b).

Snack

Some problems children with limited motor abilities encounter during snack are cups that easily tip, bowls that slide on the table, difficulty finding a seat, communicating their needs and overall inclusion in the activity. Regular cups and bowls can cause frequent spills. Also, children with limited motor ability are sometimes unable to communicate their wants and needs.

Suggestions for Snack

- Encourage peers to help the children with limited motor ability. For example, peers can help the child communicate or eat.
- Use bowls with suctions to avoid table sliding and sipper cups to avoid spills.
- Design a job board to include jobs for all children. For example, include children with limited motor ability by allowing them to pass out the cups, napkins, or bowls at snack.

- Include all of the children at the table during snack, even if not all the children are eating.

Gym and Playground

Playground and gym time can be very difficult for children with physical impairments. Most children are running, jumping, and climbing during this time. Children with limited motor abilities may become frustrated at not being able to perform these skills. Young children with limited motor abilities may not be able to sit safely in a swing, have access to the sand box, or engage in social games.

Suggestions for Gym and Playground

- Provide scooter boards for the children to sit on. The children can either push themselves around or be pulled by a peer.
- Include a pool of balls for the children to sit in and explore.
- Encourage wagon, blanket, and sheet pulls. The child with limited motor ability can be in the wagon, blanket or sheet while the peer pulls them around.
- Provide adaptive tricycles (adaptive pedals or hand cycles) and/or roller skates.
- Make sand tables and swings accessible for everyone.

Computers and Technology

Computers and related technology can help provide the means to adapt classroom areas and activities in order to provide for children's diverse needs. Technology can provide young children with and without disabilities the opportunity for maximum participation in the social and educational environment of the early childhood setting. Young children with limited motor abilities who have difficulty communicating, playing, and/or interacting with their environment can benefit from technology in a number of ways (Brett, 1995).

Suggestions for Computer Use

- Use battery-operated toys, switches, and computer games to provide children with and without disabilities to play together.

- Use alternative keyboards or switches with speech output for children who are nonverbal to participate in language development activities.
- Provide children with exploratory and open-ended computer programs to provide children the opportunity to play together.
- Include modifications of the standard keyboard, alternative keyboards, touch-sensitive screens, hand-held devices, switches, and voice input (Brett, 1995).

Modifications for the Standard Keyboard

- Place stickers on keys for a particular program to help children locate them more easily.
- Set a template or overlay over a keyboard so that only certain keys show.
- Place a keyguard over a standard keyboard to allow only one key to be hit at a time (Brett, 1995).

Alternative Keyboards

- Muppet Learning Keys feature large keys in alphabetical order with pictures that designate functions.
- The PowerPad is a large touch-sensitive board which can be divided into squares of various sizes. Each square can be easily programmed to generate voice and visual output.
- Condensed keyboards or minikeyboards are small enough so children with a limited range of motion can reach the keys.
- Unicorn Keyboard is a touch-sensitive membrane keyboard which has 128 squares that can be programmed to operate in several different ways, including imitation of the standard keyboard.
- A touch-sensitive screen such as Touch Window is an input device which allows children to point to their selections on the screen.
- Hand-held devices, such as the mouse and the joystick, are input devices which require less fine motor skill than a keyboard.

- Switches are on-off devices that are activated by contact or by detection of motion, sound, or light.
- Voice input allows an individual to speak commands into the computer and have the computer carry out these commands (Brett, 1995).

CONCLUSION

Teachers in typical early childhood settings need to provide an effective learning environment for children who exhibit a wide range of abilities within the context of the naturally occurring activities. Adaptations to activities can enhance opportunities for interactions and increase the quality of participation among children with limited motor ability. As part of a developmentally appropriate program, these adaptations can be integrated into the curriculum to make the preschool environment stimulating and interesting for all children.

ACKNOWLEDGMENTS

Support for this research was provided by a Leadership Training Grant (H029D10054) from the Office of Special Education and Rehabilitation Services, U.S. Department of Education.

REFERENCES

Baumgart, D., Brown, L., Pumpian, I., Nisbet, J., Ford, A., Sweet, M., Messina, R., & Schroeder, J. (1982). Principle of partial participation and individualized adaptations in educational programs for severely handicapped students. *Journal of the Association for the Severely Handicapped, 7*(2), 17–27.

Bigge, J. L. (1991). *Teaching individuals with physical and multiple disabilities* (3rd Ed.). New York: Macmillian Publishing Company.

Bredekamp, S. (Ed). (1987). *Developmentally appropriate practice in early childhood programs serving children from birth through age 8.* Washington, D.C.: National Association for the Education of Young Children.

Brett, A. (1995). Technology in inclusive early childhood settings. *Day Care and Early Education, 10,* 8–11.

Chandler, P. A. (1994). *A place for me.* Washington, D.C.: National Association for the Education of Young Children.

Demchak, M., & Drinkwater, S. (1992). Preschoolers with severe disabilities: The case against segregation. *Topics in Early Childhood Special Education, 11*(4), 70–83.

Drinkwater, S., & Demchak, M. (1995). The preschool checklist integration of children with disabilities. *Teaching Exceptional Children, 28*(1), 4–8.

Diamond, K., Hestenes, L., & O'Conner, C. (1994). Integrating young children with disabilities in preschool: Problems and promises. *Young Children, 49*(2), 68–75.

Hanline, M. F. (1985). Integrating disabled children. *Young Children, 40*(2), 45–48.

Janney, R. E., Snell, M. E., Beers, M. K., & Raynes, M. (1995). Integrating students with moderate and severe disabilities into general education classes. *Exceptional Children, 61*(5), 425–439.

Klein, N., & Scheehan, R. (1987). Staff development. A key issue in meeting the needs of young handicapped children in day care settings. *Topics in Early Childhood Special Education, 7*(1), 13–27.

McCormick, L., & Feeney, S. (1995). Modifying and expanding activities for children with disabilities. *Young Children, 50*(4), 10–17.

Newsworth, J. T., & Madle, R. A. (1975). Normalized day care: A philosophy and approach to integrating exceptional and normal children. *Child Care Quarterly, 4,* 163–171.

Odom, S. L., & McEvoy, M. A. (1990). Mainstreaming at the preschool level: Potential barriers and tasks for the field. *Topics in Early Childhood Special Education, 10*(2), 48–61.

Odom, S. L., McConnell, S. R., & McEvoy, M. A. (1992). *Social competence of young children with disabilities: Issues and strategies for intervention.* Baltimore, MD: Paul H. Brooks.

Sainato, D. M., & Carta, J. J. (1992). Classroom influences on the development of social competence in young children with disabilities. In S. L. Odom, S. R. McConnell, & M. A. McEvoy, (Eds.) Social competence of young children with disabilities: Issues and strategies for intervention (pp. 93–109). Baltimore: Paul H. Brooks.

Snell, M. E. (1993). *Instruction of students with severe disabilities* (4th ed.). New York: Merrill/Macmillan.

Wolery, M., Holcombe, A., Venn, M., Brookfield, J., Huffman, K., Schroeder, C., Martin, C., & Flemming, L. (1993). Mainstreaming in early childhood programs: Current status and relevant issues. *Young Children, 49*(1), 78–94.

Wolery, M., & Wilbers, J. S. (1994). *Including children with special needs in early childhood programs.* Washington, D.C.: National Association for the Education of Young Children.

Wolery, M., Strain, P., & Baily, D. (1992). *Reaching potentials: Appropriate curriculum and assessment for young children.* Washington, D.C.: National Association for the Education of Young Children.

Listening to Parents of Children with Disabilities

Linda Davern

Linda Davern is an Assistant Professor, Education Department, The Sage Colleges, Troy, NY 12180.

Interviews with parents of mainstreamed children shed light on building effective school-home partnerships.

A growing number of children with disabilities are becoming members of general education classes. As someone involved in teacher preparation, I am particularly interested in what teaching teams can do to build productive alliances, or strengthen existing relationships, with the parents or caregivers of these children.

To explore this issue, I conducted a series of in-depth interviews with 15 families (21 parents) whose children were fully included in general education programs—mostly at the elementary level. Many of these children needed a great deal of support and modification to participate successfully in general classes. Overall, these parents were extremely pleased with the impact that inclusion had on their children. They also offered suggestions for improving the quality of home-school relationships.[1] The following recommendations to teaching teams come from an analysis of these parents' perspectives.

■ *Convey a clear, consistent message regarding the value of the child.* How school personnel talk about children in both formal and informal interactions early in the school year has a significant impact on the development of relationships with their families. Several parents in this study valued the ability of teachers to see different aspects of a child's personality aside from academic achievement. As Gail put it,

> For teachers to say to me, "I really like your kid," or "You know, he really has a great sense of humor"... lets me know that they really care about him as a person.

These parents also commended personnel who focused on the individual child's progress, rather than using other children as a reference for comparison. As Anna said:

> So our child's not going to be the top of her class in gym. We understand that. Just take her for who she is. Find space for her.

Members of the teaching team need to convey clear, consistent messages that they are happy to have this child in the classroom and that they hold high expectations for the child's achievement.

■ *Put yourself in the shoes of the parent.* The parents I interviewed valued the efforts of school personnel to try to understand what it is like to have a child with a disability—for example, to have to negotiate both the general and special education bureaucracies in order to gain access to classes, accommodations, and support services. Several of these parents felt that some staff did not understand their anger and frustration with educational systems. While one mother felt more strongly than others I spoke with, she expressed the sense of detachment experienced by families of children in special education:

> Parents hate special ed.... Parents hate it because the kids hate it.... They hate the isolation of it.

Parents often felt they were viewed as impatient. They wanted staff to better understand their frustration with the slow pace of school improvement efforts related to inclusive practices. School staff who attempt to understand the parent's frame of reference are less likely to assume the judgmental attitudes that can be damaging to the home-school relationship.

■ *Expand your awareness of cultural diversity.* Building an awareness of cultural diversity will strengthen school personnel's ability to teach as well as connect successfully with families. Marguerite believed that "a lot of teachers have never had . . . training in multiculturalism or diversity." Through effective staff development, schools can help personnel examine "the cultural base of their own belief system" in relation to children and families (Harry 1992, p. 23), and how these beliefs affect relationships.

Harry and colleagues emphasize that cultures are greatly influenced by generational status, gender, social class, education, occupational group, and other variables (1995, p. 106). Such an approach to professional development will help personnel be aware of the cultural lenses through which they make judgments about children and families.

■ *See individuals, challenge stereotypes.* A few parents felt that some teachers made assumptions about them and their parenting skills simply because their child had a disability. Doria saw some of these attitudes arising from a lack of understanding of some types of disabilities such as emotional disturbance. Marguerite felt that school personnel frequently "lumped parents together"—working from inaccurate assumptions about single parents and parents who were not of European heritage. School personnel need opportunities to explore the impulse to stereotype, and encouragement and support to challenge this tendency in themselves as well as their colleagues.

■ *Persevere in building partnerships.* While federal law requires school teams to invite parents into the planning process for their children with disabilities, the collaborative outcome envisioned by the legislation does not always materialize. Several parents thought that schools gave up too soon—that personnel were quick to dismiss parents who didn't attend meetings, and were cynical about the possibilities for change. Parents felt that building partnerships took commitment and vision over the *long* term. As one father stated, "The first year you make a decision to team with parents, maybe you're not going

> ## Schools will not become proficient in building alliances with these families until general class membership, with adequate supports, is the norm for children with disabilities.

to get all the parents . . . but give it a little time, nurture it along."

Parents suggested looking at how schools share information with parents, using more flexibility in setting up meeting times with them, and assisting parents in connecting with other parents who might share child care responsibilities to free one another to attend planning meetings.

■ *Demonstrate an authentic interest in the parent's goals for the child.* A first step in establishing dialogue is to connect with parents as individuals. Participants in the study commended some staff as very skilled in diminishing the psychological distance between parents and professionals. These teachers were able to create an atmosphere where parents did not feel that they had to "watch their p's and q's," as one parent put it. Staff did this through their choice of language, as well as their interaction styles. Their interest in parents' ideas felt authentic.

Parents also mentioned interactions that they viewed as evidence of an "expert syndrome." In these cases, parents felt that the attitude coming from staff was, "You couldn't possibly know what you're talking about." One parent described a critical distinction between those personnel who talk with parents as opposed to those who talk at them. Teachers can maintain their expertise as educators while fully acknowledging the information and insights held by parents. The interplay of these complementary roles can greatly enrich the outcome for students.

■ *Talk with parents about how they want to share information.* Successful collaboration requires effective ongoing communication between

home and school. Some participants thought that having one school person as the primary contact would be helpful. Several parents in this study did not want their primary contact to be a special educator, for fear that this would lessen the feelings of ownership on the part of the general educator for the child's progress. Yet consistent communication with a person who really knew the child and his or her unique learning characteristics was important.

Teachers need to ask parents which school representative they would like to communicate with, how frequently, and through which means (for example, combinations of meetings, phone calls, and written communication). Moreover, parents' preferences for involvement may change over time given a variety of factors such as the child's age and the family's circumstances.

Several families found home visits by school staff very helpful. Parents felt that opportunities to visit with children in their homes might give staff insight into children's capabilities that had not been demonstrated at school.

■ *Use everyday language.* Parents often felt excluded from the planning process when professionals used unfamiliar educational terms when discussing test results, staffing patterns, and ways of organizing and identifying services. One parent referred to this practice as "blowing all that smoke." As another put it:

> What does it mean "30 minutes three times a week," "one plus one," "parallel curriculum"? . . . When you do that stuff you just close out the parent. As soon as

you use language that's exclusive of parents, they're gone.

It is an unfortunate irony that in order to graduate from many teacher preparation programs, preservice teachers must master a professional lexicon that ultimately creates significant barriers to being effective in their professions.

■ *Create effective forums for planning and problem solving.* Yearly review meetings, mandated by law, are held for each child with an Individualized Education Plan (IEP). During these meetings, school personnel and parents (and students at the secondary level) review assessments, make placement decisions, determine children's services, and identify individual goals. The parents I interviewed described these formal meetings as some of the most difficult interactions they experienced during the year. They used such phrases as "very intimidating" to describe them, adding that they felt at times like token participants in discussions about their children.

In contrast to these formal yearly reviews, at least six of the children involved in this study were the focus of regularly scheduled team meetings, composed of teachers, parents, related service providers, and occasionally teaching assistants. Although evaluations of these meetings varied greatly, parents indicated that, compared to the formal meetings, they felt more comfortable discussing their children in an atmosphere that recognized achievements, friendships, interesting stories, and humorous anecdotes. As one mother put it,

> **Successful collaboration requires effective ongoing communication between home and school.**

When we go to team meetings, a lot of times it *is* a celebration. That's how it feels. By George, we're doing something *right* here— it's working!

The literature offers direction for districts interested in developing their expertise in the arena of team planning for individual children (Giangreco 1996, Giangreco et al. 1993, Thousand and Villa 1992).

■ *Build long-term schoolwide plans that offer full membership to all children.* Several of the parents I interviewed had advocated extensively for a general class placement for their child. Schools will not become proficient in building alliances with these families until general class membership, with adequate supports, is the norm for children with disabilities. These findings reinforce calls from parents and others in the educational community for districts to develop long-term schoolwide plans to offer full membership to all students, not just set up programs for children in response to the requests of individual parents (Gartner and Lipsky 1987, Stainback and Stainback 1990). Teachers can actively support such restructuring (with appropriate safeguards to ensure adequate resources). Such efforts will result in inclusive settings becoming available to those children whose parents are not in a position to pursue such extensive advocacy actions.

[1]Parents' names are pseudonyms.

References

Gartner, A., and D. Lipsky. (1987). "Beyond Special Education: Toward a Quality System for all Students." *Harvard Educational Review* 57, 4: 367–395.

Giangreco, M. F. (1996). *Vermont Interdependent Services Team Approach: A Guide to Coordinating Educational Support Services.* Baltimore: Paul H. Brookes.

Giangreco, M. F., C. J. Cloninger, and V. S. Iverson. (1993). *Choosing Options and Accommodations for Children (COACH).* Baltimore: Paul H. Brookes.

Harry, B. (1992). *Cultural Diversity, Families, and the Special Education System.* New York: Teachers College Press.

Harry, B., M. Grenot-Scheyer, M. Smith-Lewis, H. Park, F. Xin, and I. Schwartz. (1995). "Developing Culturally Inclusive Services for Individuals with Severe Disabilities." *The Journal of The Association for Persons with Severe Handicaps* 20, 2: 99–109.

Stainback, S., and W. Stainback. (1990). "Inclusive Schooling." In *Support Networks for Inclusive Schooling,* edited by W. Stainback, and S. Stainback. Baltimore: Paul H. Brookes.

Thousand, J. S., and R. Villa. (1992). "Collaborative Teams: A Powerful Tool in School Restructuring." In *Restructuring for Caring and Effective Schools,* edited by R. A. Villa, J. S. Thousand, W. Stainback, and S. Stainback. Baltimore: Paul H. Brookes.

Accessible Web Site Design

Stacy Peters-Walters

The World Wide Web (WWW) is a wonderful tool for classroom use. Students can explore many virtual libraries and museums and conduct research. The WWW has the ability to bring information to everyone who has access to a computer. The Web and other telecommunications applications like e-mail can help students with disabilities in many ways. When a Web site is designed correctly, there is very little discrepancy between users with disabilities and those people temporarily without disabilities. Computers and the WWW can be a great equalizer in the classroom and in the world. Figure 1 provides information about users with disabilities who have used telecommunications applications to overcome barriers (U.S. Department of Commerce, 1994).

The Importance of Web Site Design

Many people with disabilities have difficulties accessing information over the Internet because of poor Web site designs. Many of the site designs actually create barriers for information access (Paciello, 1996). Students with visual and cognitive disabilities have the greatest barriers to overcome to gain access to information (Paciello). There is very little that users can do to change site design to accommodate their own needs. Site designers must accommodate the user. Educators who wish to create Web sites that are accessible need to follow a few simple site design rules so that all students can access information.

Figure 1

Technology Can Break Down Barriers

Reduced Barriers to Full Participation in Society

I am a C7 quadriplegic who has completed a course in desktop publishing. I have been disabled for 2 years and am very eager to get back into the work force. I have learned I'm still employable regardless of my disability. I recently learned about telecommunications and the different networks for communicating. With electronic mail, I communicate with various people from all around the world. My life has really opened up with my career change and the electronic information systems.

Reduced Barriers to Business and Employment

I am a C5 quadriplegic living in the Silicon Valley and a current intern with the Networking and Communication Department. I have been disabled for 10 years from a motor vehicle accident in 1983. I use computer telecommunications daily in numerous functions. Telecommunications has opened up a new world, allowing me to communicate via e-mail with colleges, government agencies, and organizations. The future success of telecommunications is phenomenal, especially for the disabled community. It not only allows a person unable to go out into the community to access endless amounts of information, but also permits persons with disabilities, such as myself, to eventually return to the work force (via telecommuting) and become productive citizens again.

Reduced Communication Barriers

I am 17 years old. I am an oral, profoundly hearing impaired student who is fully mainstreamed in the 12th grade. I did not really have access to e-mail until early October, when a friend of mine proposed we e-mail each other. . . . E-mail turned out to be easier than I thought, and it has been wonderful because it has enabled me to communicate with my friends from around the Atlantic Seaboard region.

The "electronic super highway" is a boon for deaf/hearing impaired people because it enables them to communicate via the written word, which is a very effective alternate means of obtaining vital information in a relatively short period of time. It is my hope that the White House will make access to the information highway universal.

Reduced Barriers to the "Basics" in an Information Society

Rodney, a senior, has no use of his arms or legs and uses a mouth wand to operate a computer. He began using a computer at age 6, and learned to read and write in this manner.

When asked a question, Rodney balances his wand on a box strategically placed near his terminal. "A computer," he says, "is sort of like running water. You don't know what you'd do without it."

From *Teaching Exceptional Children*, May/June 1998, pp. 42-47. © 1998 by The Council for Exceptional Children. Reprinted by permission.

Table 1

HTML Coding

HTML is the programming language used to create WWW pages. HTML can be hand coded by using a word processor or created by an HTML generator. All suggestions in this article can be hand coded. Some of the suggestions can be created using an HTML generator, depending on the generator's complexity and quality.

Below are a few hand coded tags for programming in HTML. All HTML tags are placed within brackets when hand coding. Tags without the "/" are placed at the end of the text or image that is to be formatted. When hand coding, all tags are formatted using capital letters.

Tag	Placement	Function
<HTML></HTML>	These are placed at the beginning and ending of a document.	These tags tell the browser that it will be reading an HTML document.
<HEAD></HEAD>	These are placed inside the HTML tags. They surround the TITLE tags.	These tags tell the browser that this is prologue information.
<TITLE></TITLE>	These are placed before and after the text of the title.	These tags tell the browser that the text they surround is part of the title bar and not the actual page.
<BODY></BODY>	These are placed before and after the entire body text.	These tags tell the browser that everything within these tags is body text.
<P></P>	These tags surround each paragraph.	These tags tell the browser to format the text like a paragraph.
<A HREF = "url name"></A>	These tags surround text that is to be linked to the URL named in the quotation marks.	These tags tell the browser that the text enclosed by tags is a link to the URL specified within the quotes.
<H1></H1> to <H6></H6>	These tags surround the text that the user wants to be displayed as headers.	These tags (H1, H2, H3, H4, H5, H6) tell the browser that the text they surround is a header. The text displays the text in a larger size and as bold. H1 specifies the largest while H6 specifies the smallest.
<IMG SRC = "image.gif">	These tags are placed anywhere the user wants to place an image.	These tags tell the browser to read and display the images specified within the quotes.

Web Barriers to Overcome

- Some barriers that people with *visual disabilities* face is not being able to access information because of its graphical format.
- People with *auditory problems* cannot access the information in sound files.
- People with *attention deficit disorder* can become easily distracted from the information by the use of continual animations.
- Users with *cognitive disabilities* may become lost due to poor navigation controls.
- People with *physical disabilities* face the barrier of not being able to run the browser that would give them access to the information.

browser that would give them access to the information.

Visual Disabilities

People with visual disabilities have difficulties accessing information published on the WWW because the Web is a highly visual medium. Web pages are designed to be visually stimulating which can make them difficult to read. Many people with visual disabilities access information from the WWW by using screen readers or refreshable Braille displays. These machines can only access and read text. When the machine arrives at a graphic, the machine either ignores the graphic or informs the user that it is reading a graphic and has no description to read. This cuts down on

- Educators can run "Bobby" (http://www.cast.org/bobby) to find out whether their site designs are accessible. "Bobby" is a Web site validator (Center for Applied Special Technology, 1997).
- Users who wish to validate their Web site with accessibility requirements type the specific URL they want validated into the form provided.
- "Bobby" goes to that URL and validates whether it meets the accessibility requirements. Images of a blue hat with the "handicapped" sign on them appear next to areas that are not accessible.
- "Bobby" also provides written reports as to what is wrong and how to fix the problem.
- "Bobby" also contains an advanced validator that validates the code for specific browser types.

If a site meets with "Bobby" specifications, the site designers are invited to use the "Bobby Approved" logo on the site (Center for Applied Special Technology, 1997).

Second, educators can help students indirectly by educating site designers about information-access barriers on the WWW and how to overcome those barriers. A barrier that people with visual disabilities face is not being able to access the information because of its graphical format. People with auditory problems cannot access the information in sound files. People with attention-deficit disorder can become easily distracted from the information by the use of continual animations. Users with cognitive disabilities may become lost due to poor navigation controls. People with physical disabilities face the barrier of not being able to run the

Many people with disabilities have difficulties accessing information over the Internet because of poor Web site designs.

the usability of the WWW because graphics are used to convey much information.

Graphics. Web site designers can alleviate the problem of interpreting graphics for people with visual disabilities by using the IMG ALT tag when creating WWW pages (see Table

Table 2

Sample Table

Student	Sue	Joe	Matt
Math Grade	A	B	C
Science Grade	C	B	A

Web Tutorials

There are many products on the market to help people build Web pages. When deciding what to purchase, educators must look at how much time and money they would like to invest in Web page development.

For those educators serious about Web page development and willing to learn how to hand code, Laura Lemay has published several informative tutorials on the different aspects of Web page design. Lemay speaks in layman's terms so that the user is not fumbling through computer jargon. Each book contains lessons for the user to try and examples for the user to view. Lemay's book Learn HTML in 14 Days covers the wide range of HTML programming that most beginners are willing to use.

While learning to hand code is beneficial for any HTML programmer, learning to hand code can be time-consuming. For those educators who do not have the time to learn hand coding, there are HTML generators. There are several types of HTML generators, most of which can be found in any software store. These programs range in price from thirty dollars to several hundred dollars. For the most part, the more a person pays for these programs, the more features the programs have.

HTML generators usually come with some type of documentation to explain how they work. There are also multitudes of books about each generator. Many of these books follow a lesson format like Lemay's books.

1 for an illustration of this tag). This tag allows the designer to embed a text description of the image into the image source code so that a screen reader will be able to describe the picture. Example code for the IMG ALT tag is <IMG SRC = "cat.gif" ALT = ["A big black cat is perched on the windowsill looking outside at the trees blowing in the wind. It is a sunny day outside."] > The IMG SRC = "cat.gif" is telling the browser that it will be viewing the picture cat.gif. The ALT tag tells the browser that if a user is browsing the Web in text mode or through a screen reader, instead of viewing the graphic, the text should read: "Graphic: A big black cat is perched on the windowsill looking outside at the trees blowing in the wind. It is a sunny day outside."

Graphic Links. Graphics that link one page to another page can be troublesome for people with visual disabilities. Because the screen reader cannot orally "read" the graphical link, people with visual disabilities do not have a description of the link that they will be visiting. The user will have to click the link and scan the page to decide whether the information on the page is what the user was looking for. This can amount to wasted time for the user when he or she is trying to access information. To help users with visual disabilities, all graphical links should have an alternate text link beside or beneath the graphical link.

Text links should be short yet descriptive. An example of a short descriptive link is "WWW and Visual Disabilities." Text links should not be placed in horizontal lines like Home Education Sites Student Work. While the screen reader can read the links, it can make comprehension difficult. The screen reader will not pause between the links, but read the links like a sentence (Paciello, 1996). It is difficult for the person listening to decide whether the link is the home page, which contains the educational sites and student work, or three separate links.

Video Files. More and more WWW pages are embedding video files that

Other Devices to Enable People with Disabilities to Access Computers

- **Dragon Dictate**
- **Dragon Naturally Speaking**
- **Microsoft "Access Pack"**
- **Word Prediction Software**
- **Mouth stick**
- **Switches (hand, head, mouth)**
- **Eyegaze**
- **Screen readers**
- **Refreshable Braille Screens**
- **Stickybear ABC and Talking Stickybear**
- **Muppet Learning Keys**
- **IntelliKeys**
- **Touch Windows**

users can access. While a user with visual disabilities can hear the audio in the movie, the user will not be able to view the video. Because much of the information in video files is accessible only by viewing the video, without ad-

Use "Bobby" (http://www.cast.org/bobby) to find out whether your Web site designs are accessible.

aptations the user will be unable to use much of the informational content of the video. WWW designers can add a text file that gives the full transcription of the audio and a description of all visual elements in the video. Site designers can create a text file and then provide a link to it beside the link to the video.

Imagemaps. Another problem for screen readers and other adaptive devices is reading imagemaps. An imagemap is a large picture that has hot spots, or links, embedded into the image. When a user runs a cursor over the imagemap, there are certain areas, the hot spots or links, where the cursor turns into a hand and can access another page of the site. Because screen readers and other adaptive devices cannot access pictures, the person with a visual disability will not be able to access the links. The user will not be able to follow the informational links if he or she cannot access the links within imagemaps. If WWW designers want to use imagemaps for their visual appeal, designers need to make text links that correspond with the links in the imagemap and place those links beneath the imagemap.

Tables. Tables are another difficulty for screen readers and other adaptive devices to interpret. A screen reader will not read the information in each separate cell as one entity. The screen reader will read across the table from left to right. For example, a simple table like Table 2 will be difficult for the screen reader to interpret. Rather than reading that Sue received an A in math and a C in science, the user will read: "Student Sue Joe Matt Math Grade A B C Science Grade C B A." If possible, tables should be avoided. A designer who wants to use a table should also provide an alternate, text-only page that provides the same information but not in a table format. Some designers prefer to build their entire sites using tables. Users should be notified of the table format and a text-based site needs to be provided.

Sites that are meant to be wonders of design should have an alternate site built specifically for accessibility.

Table 3

Keyboard Commands for Tool Bar Functions in the Microsoft Internet Explorer

Function	Keyboard Commands	Description
Access Menu Bar	F10	Open and view menus
Reload Page	F5	Reload current page
View Previous URLs	F4	View list of URLs previously visited
Help	F1	Access help menu
Stop	Esc	Stop page download
Open New Window	Ctrl + N	Open new window
Open URL	Ctrl + O	Type URL to visit
Print	Ctrl + P	Print current page
Save	Ctrl + S	Save current page
Find	Ctrl + F	Find keyword on current page
Go Back	Alt + Left Arrow	Move back a page
Go Forward	Alt + Right Arrow	Move forward a page
Next Anchor (Link)	Tab	Move to next anchor (link) and stop at end of document
Previous Anchor (Link)	Shift + Tab	Move to previous anchor and stop at beginning of document
Scroll Line Up	Up arrow key	Change view of document by one line up
Scroll Line Down	Down arrow key	Change view of document by one line down
Scroll Page Up	PageUp key	Change view of document by one height up
Scroll Page Down	PageDown key	Change view of document by one height down
Top of Page	Home key	Change view to beginning of document
Bottom of Page	End key	Change view to end of document

Forms. Screen readers also have difficulty reading online forms. Online forms allow the user to enter information online in a guest book, request information through a form, use search engines, and register for shareware computer application. Forms should be available as a text file to download to the user's hard drive and then to be mailed either through e-mail or postal mail. All forms should list the e-mail address that the form is being sent to. Users who cannot download forms will then be able to write directly to the address.

Colors and Backgrounds. Color and background patterns are another difficulty for people with visual disabilities. Pages with too many color combinations can be difficult to read for anyone, especially people with low vision and other visual disabilities. To decide whether the color combinations are difficult to read, designers need to view their pages in 256 shades of gray. Designers can adjust their monitors in the Control Panel to read only 256 shades of gray. While viewing the pages in gray, designers need to ask themselves whether they can read and distinguish the differences between colors on the basis of only lightness and darkness. Designers should also ask a person who has not helped to design the site to read the information on the site and to distinguish between the different shades of gray.

Another problem is the use of the color combinations of blue/yellow and red/green for text and backgrounds. People who are colorblind cannot see what is on these pages. Designers must never use these color combinations, unless they are providing an alternate site. The link to this alternate site should never be in blue, yellow, red, or green.

Background patterns can also create difficulty for people with low vision or other visual disabilities. A background that has many images on it or a pronounced texture is too decorative for the text to show well. Long pages of unbroken text are also a disadvantage for people with visual disabilities.

Unbroken Text. Long pages of unbroken text are difficult to skim for content for anybody, but especially for people with visual disabilities because it takes longer to read a passage. Long pages of text can be broken up by the use of headers (tags H1 to H6), which will help with the skimming process (see Table 1 for examples of tags used in HTML coding).

Frames. A major problem for people with visual disabilities is the use of frames. Although frames that are well designed can be visually stimulating, frames make an already small computer screen smaller. Also, frames act

Table 4

Keyboard Commands for Tool Bar Functions in the Netscape Navigator

Function	Keyboard Commands	Description
Access Menu Bar	F10	Open and view menus
Reload Page	Ctrl + R	Reload current page
View Previous URLs	F4	View list of URLs previously visited
Help	F1	Access help menu
Stop	Esc	Stop page download
Open New Window	Ctrl + N	Open new window
Open URL	Ctrl + O	Type URL to visit
Print	Ctrl + P	Print current page
Save	Ctrl + S	Save current page
Find	Ctrl + F	Find keyword on current page
Increase Font	Ctrl +]	Increase font size
Decrease Font	Ctrl + [	Decrease font size
Page Source	Ctrl + U	View page source code
Page Info	Ctrl + I	View information about page
Next Anchor (Link)	Tab	Move to next anchor (link) and stop at end of document
Previous Anchor (Link)	Shift + Tab	Move to previous anchor and stop at beginning of document
Scroll Line Up	Up arrow key	Change view of document by one line up
Scroll Line Down	Down arrow key	Change view of document by one line down
Scroll Page Up	PageUp key	Change view of document by one height up
Scroll Page Down	PageDown key	Change view of document by one height down
Top of Page	Home key	Change view to beginning of document
Bottom of Page	End key	Change view of end of document

like tables for a screen reader, which causes confusion. Designers should avoid the use of frames. If frames must be used, designers need to provide an alternate site without frames.

Auditory Disabilities

Currently, people with auditory disabilities have few problems accessing information on the WWW. This is because Web design is primarily visual. More and more, however, Web designers are incorporating audio and video files into their pages. These formats pose problems for people with auditory disabilities.

Audio and video files should have full-text transcriptions of the audio. If possible, movies should be created that have a person signing the audio. The video of the person signing can either be added to the video file by using video editing software or as a separate file from the original video file. This will help the user—more than just reading the transcription—because the user can watch the movie and the signing at the same. Designers can also add closed captioning to the video.

Cognitive Disabilities

Navigating the WWW is currently very difficult; it is not an intuitive process. Not only are browsers difficult to use, but most Web page navigation is poorly designed. Site designers can make navigating a WWW page or site more intuitive by creating small menus at the top of the page for users to follow. Graphical "You Are Here" site maps can also be created using a graphics/drawing package and placed in each page.

Students who have difficulty reading will not receive much benefit from the WWW since the majority of the information is in a text format. Although it is extra work for Web designers, creating an audio file of the information on the page will alleviate the problem of long reading time or a lack of comprehension due to poor reading skills. The audio file can be designed as a downloadable option so that users who like to read text will not have to listen to the audio. Designers can add audio files by using sound recording and editing software and a computer microphone to create the files and then use an HTML generator to link the files into the site.

Long Web pages filled with unbroken text are difficult for users with cognitive disabilities to skim for information. Long pages of text can be broken up by the use of Headers (tags H1 to H6) and by graphics. Headers allow users to skim for the important parts of the document so that they will not have to read the entire document. Graphics break up the monotony of the pages and add another dimension to the user's understanding of the text.

Attention Deficit Disorder

The WWW has the ability to focus the attention of people with attention deficit disorder (ADD) by using graphics to lead the user through the information. But some Web designers create difficulties for people with ADD.

Multiple or long pages of unbroken text cannot keep people focused on the task of reading. Web designers can alleviate this problem by using descriptive headers (tags H1 to H6) to differentiate between important pieces in the document. Descriptive graphics can also be used to break up the monotony of long pages of text.

Many WWW pages are designed so that it is difficult to remain focused on an informational piece of text or graphic due to blinking text, scrolling marquees, or continual animation. This is a simple problem for Web designers to control. The designer can either not use the continual movements or can design an alternate page that does not contain the continual movements. Designers who wish to use continual movements for focusing the user's attention on one section can program the continual animations to stop after a few seconds. This will focus the user's attention to what the designer wants the user to view first, but will not become a distraction.

Physical Disabilities

Browsers make it difficult for people with limited mobility to access Web pages. Most browsers are designed for mainly mouse input. For people with limited mobility, mouses are difficult to use because they require fine motor skills of the fingers, hand, and arm.

For ease of navigation, many browsers are incorporating keyboard commands that function like mouse commands. Tables 3 and 4 list some of the keyboard commands for navigating the WWW with the Microsoft Internet Explorer and the Netscape Navigator.

Design and Accessibility

Because the WWW is a visual place where design is highly respected, many designers may want to focus more on design rather than accessibility. Sites that are meant to be wonders of design should have an alternate site built specifically for accessibility. These sites should allow users to access the alternate site or alternate pages on the first page of the site and then on every page throughout the site. For example, Page 1 of a site would contain a link to Page 1 of the alternate site. Page 2 of the graphical site would contain links to Pages 1 and 2 of the alternate site. Page 3 of the graphical site would contain links to Pages 2 and 3 of the alternate site, and so on. This enables users to move through sites at their ease, rather than at the designer's ease.

To many WWW designers, it may seem easier to create alternate text-only pages for users with disabilities. Though many users with disabilities (and users with slow modem connections) may use only the alternate pages, it is best to provide both alternate pages and the accessibility tips listed here. In this way, there will not be two standards and levels of quality for WWW design. All Web designs should be accessible to all people.

References

Center for Applied Special Technology. (1997, December 6). *Bobby* [Web site]. URL = http://www.cast.org/bobby/

Lemay, L. (1996). *Teach Yourself Web Publishing with HTML 3.2 in 14 Days* (Professional Reference Edition). [Web site]. URL = http://www.mcp.com/sansnet/

Paciello, Mike (1996; 1997, August 20). *Making the Web accessible for the blind and visually impaired* [Web site]. URL = http://www.yuri.org/webable/mp-blnax.html

Paciello, Mike (1996; 1997, August 20). *People with disabilities can't access the Web* [Web site]. URL = http://www.yuri.org/webable/mp-pwdca.html

Trace Research and Design Center. (1997, December 6). *Trace research and design* [Web site]. URL = http://www.trace.wisc.edu/

U.S. Department of Commerce, Technology Administration, National Institute of Standards and Technology. (1994; 1997, August 18). *People with disabilities and NII: Breaking down barriers, building choice* [Web site]. URL = http://www.itpolicy.gsa.gov/coca/SB_paper.htm

Stacy Peters-Walters, *Instructional Assistant, Governor's Technology for Teaching and Learning Academy, College of Education, Dakota State University, Madison, South Dakota.*

Address correspondence to the author at RR3, Box 28, Madison, SD 57042 (e-mail: peterss@triton.dsu.edu).

Unit Selections

Key Points to Consider

❖ How can preschool teachers encourage special gifts and talents?

❖ What ideas do gifted students have about their own education?

❖ How can regular education teachers provide full-time special educational programming for gifted students in their classrooms on a part-time budget?

 **Links** | **www.dushkin.com/online/**

These sites are annotated on pages 4 and 5.

Children with special gifts and talents do not qualify for special educational services under the Individuals with Disabilities Act (IDEA). The U.S. Omnibus Education Bill of 1987 provided modest support for gifted and talented identification and education. It required, however, that each state foot the bill for the development of special programs for children with special gifts and talents. Some states have implemented special education for the superabled. Most states have not.

Since many textbooks on exceptional children include children with special gifts and talents, and since these children are exceptional, they will be included in this volume. Instructors who deal only with the categories of disabilities covered by IDEA may simply omit coverage of this unit.

Are children with super-ability really at a disadvantage in our society? Do their powerful abilities and potentialities in some area (or areas) leave them bored in a regular classroom? Are they disabled by their potencies? Many professional educators, researchers, and experts in the area of creative genius argue that children with special gifts and talents are excluded from the mainstream. Their exceptionalities do, in fact, deprive them of some of the opportunities with which less exceptional children are routinely provided. Giftedness can be viewed as both a blessing and a curse. Problems of jealousy, resentment, misunderstanding, embarrassment, indignation, exasperation, and even fear are often engendered in the people who live with, work with, or get close to a child with exceptional knowledge or accomplishments.

Children and youth with special gifts and talents often test the patience of parents, teachers, peers, and even of special tutors or mentors, who are asked to help them in their areas of exceptionality. Gifted students tend to ask a lot of questions and pursue answers with still more questions. They can be incredibly persistent about gathering information about topics that interest them. They may, however, show no interest at all in learning about topics that do not. They may be very competitive in areas where they are especially skilled, competing even with teachers and other adults. They may seem arrogant about their skills, when, in their minds, they are only being honest.

Many children and youth with special gifts and talents have extraordinary sensitivity to how other people are reacting to them. As they are promoted through elementary school into middle school and high school, many such children learn to hide their accomplishments for the secondary gain of being more socially acceptable or more popular. Because they have been underchallenged and/or discouraged from achieving at their highest potentialities, many gifted high school students are underachievers. They have poor study habits as a result of not needing to study in elementary school. They are unmotivated, intensely bored, and discouraged by the educational programs available to them.

Researchers who have studied creative genius and exceptional giftedness found that most accomplished high achievers share one similarity in childhood. Their parents recognized their special abilities early and found tutors who would help them develop their skills. This is true not only of mathematicians and scientists but also of world class sports players, musicians, artists, performers, writers, and other producers of note.

Educational programs that refuse to find tutors or mentors, or to encourage original work, or to provide special education in the skill areas of gifted students are selling short the future society's potential producers.

The earlier children with special talents are recognized the better. The sooner they are provided with enriched education the more valuable their future contributions will become. Children from all ethnic backgrounds and socioeconomic levels, and of both sexes, can have exceptional talents. One cannot predict from parents' productivity whether or not their child will have an area of special giftedness. Researchers who have reported that parents of gifted persons recognize talent early, have not, concurrently, reported that the parents had any special talents of their own.

The assessment of children with special gifts and talents, especially in the early childhood years, is fraught with difficulties. Should parents nominate their own children when they see extraordinary skills developing? How objective can parents be about their child's ability as it compares to the abilities of other same-aged children? Should measures of achievement be used (e.g., recitals, performances, art, reading levels, writings)? Do all parents want their children to have special gifts or talents? The evidence suggests that, to the contrary, many parents are embarrassed by their child's extraordinary aptitudes. They would rather have their child be more like his or her peers.

The first article in this unit emphasizes the importance of enriching the education of children with special gifts and talents as soon as they are identified. The author, Suzanne Foster, provides preschool teachers with many practical activities that can enrich the education of gifted and talented children and help them to develop their potentials before they begin regular education. She also gives hints on assessment, and she stresses the need for all children to learn through the medium of play.

Lugene Polzella, in the second article, asks "What ideas do gifted students have about their own education?" The answers given by these students may come as a surprise. Most of the students surveyed wanted more work and more challenges. They like evening and weekend adventures in learning. They like pursuing their individual interests with adult mentors. They want flexible, hands-on work experiences with other people of similar intellect. And they want access to libraries, laboratories, and equipment that will enhance their learning experiences.

The last selection included in this unit answers the query, "How can a school provide full-time services on a part-time budget to students with special gifts?" Susan Winebrenner and Barbara Devlin answer several other questions about providing special services to students who are already far ahead of their peers. In addition, this article explains the cluster group model of education and gives explicit directions for becoming a cluster group teacher.

MEETING THE NEEDS OF GIFTED AND TALENTED PRESCHOOLERS

Suzanne M. Foster

Suzanne M. Foster is a Doctoral Fellow in the Department of Elementary Education, Ball State University, Muncie, Indiana. She assists in the supervision of undergraduates who teach reading to local elementary school students.

Gifted preschool children are rarely served by special preschools for the gifted. There is a shortage of these kinds of programs in the United States. In 1982 there were only 18 such programs identified (Karnes & Johnson, 1991). If they are in preschool programs, gifted children may or may not be receiving enrichment. The current emphasis on inclusion makes it doubtful that preschool programs for the gifted will be publicly funded in the near future. Preschool teachers need to take responsibility for meeting the needs of this group, as well as the needs of other special needs children in their classroom. How can teachers help these children develop their potential? What kinds of things can be done in the regular preschool classroom?

Gifted preschoolers enjoy many of the same activities that non-gifted children enjoy but to a greater degree and in more depth and detail (Wolfe, 1989). If the preschool class is studying a unit on the human body, the teacher could go into more detail for the gifted children. This can be done through a learning center with models of the heart, brain and lungs. Many of the gifted and non-gifted children would love to see and touch the models. The gifted children would be able to understand the concepts in greater depth as their curiosity and thinking were stimulated. While these models would interest many of the children, they would also meet the needs of the gifted children.

Information Lovers

Many gifted preschoolers love to learn information. They are like sponges in their ability to absorb concepts and new ideas. Samantha, for example, loved dogs and focused for weeks on learning all about the different breeds. She loved to go to the grocery store and read the dog food labels and collect pictures of dogs. The teacher can provide enrichment by focusing on the special interests of children like Samantha and integrating these interests into the curriculum.

Through books, field trips, the arts and resource people, a teacher can expand gifted children's knowledge and introduce them to new ways of thinking about a subject they are interested in.

For example, gifted children who are interested in bees can be enriched by a unit on bees. The book corner could have books of various levels of difficulty on bees and related insects. The teacher could discuss wasps and help the children see the similarities and differences between bees and wasps. The teacher could stretch the children's knowledge through discussions, asking both higher and lower level questions. Materials such as empty wasp nests and honeycombs could be displayed on the science table. A beekeeper could be invited to the school to relate his/her experiences with the children. The gifted children would be fascinated by all the details as the other children benefited as well.

Many gifted preschoolers are very verbal; they easily absorb new vocabulary and are often interested in learning to read. Many show a fascination with books and some gifted children teach themselves to read before they enter kindergarten. Activities that intro-

From *Children Today,* Vol. 22, No. 3, 1993, pp. 28–30. Reprinted by permission of *Children Today,* a publication of the Administration for Children and Families, U.S. Department of Health and Human Services.

duce advanced vocabulary would be an excellent source of enrichment for gifted preschoolers. A unit on the oceans could be expanded for the gifted children by showing all the children a video of coral reefs. The gifted children would enjoy learning the names of the animals that live in the reefs—names like banner fish, anemones and clown fish. The teacher could print word cards with the names of the animals that live in the reef so the gifted children could use them to make sentences and stories.

The Need For Play

Play is one of the best ways for children to learn. According to Johnson, Christie and Yawkey (1987) children need at least a 30- to 50-minute block of uninterrupted time during their free play period to enact an episode in dramatic or consecutive play. It takes time for them to organize themselves and their materials and work out their ideas. Gifted preschoolers especially need these longer time blocks because they often are able to create extensive sociodramatic play episodes and build complicated block structures. They may get so involved in their play that they are reluctant to stop and move on to something else. They need to play with their intellectual peers to experience the joys of playing with someone who can understand them and help create these dramatic play episodes.

For example, five-year-old Jane often played at home with Megan, a non-gifted friend. Megan was not as advanced in her dramatic play as Jane was and would play the same role again and again with little imagination or variation. Jane would try to involve Megan in more complicated roles but would give up and go off to read a book by herself when Jane didn't respond. When Jane played with Beth, her gifted peer, the dramatic play would last for hours, with both children playing joyfully. Dramatic play can be especially enriching for gifted preschoolers who have the

imaginations and concepts to carry out elaborate play episodes.

Thematic Units

Thematic units in science and social studies are an excellent way to meet gifted children's intellectual needs. The units, along with appropriate field trips, can provide much of the enrichment a gifted preschooler needs. The block and dramatic play areas, art, music and literacy centers can all be coordinated around the theme. Some possible themes are:

- Pioneers
- The Ocean
- Dinosaurs
- Space
- Animals and Habitats.

Depending on the children's interest levels, the thematic unit can be as much as a month long. The unit should allow for more detail for the gifted preschoolers. For example, if the class is studying space exploration, props such as pieces of dryer hose for breathing equipment, space helmets, walkie talkies, a refrigerator box for a space ship and food in plastic bags could be put in the dramatic play center. The gifted children in the center will probably be organizing the play and helping the others create more complicated story lines. If the children are absorbed in their dramatic play, extending the play time will benefit all the children while meeting the needs of the gifted children.

Reading the children such books as *The Magic School Bus Lost in the Solar System,* and then inviting all of them to dictate individual stories using this theme to make their own books is a way to extend this theme. Later, the teacher could read to the gifted children more of the details in this book, which has two levels. This activity suits the needs of the gifted child, who may dictate more elaborate stories and spend more time illustrating them.

A field trip to a planetarium would fascinate most children while it enriches the gifted preschoolers, who would love learning the names of the stars and constellations. A visit from an aerospace engineer or an astronomer who could share how their occupations related to space would be another way to provide enrichment.

Activities For Gifted Preschoolers

There are many other activities teachers or parents can do with gifted preschoolers. Examples of these are:

- reading higher level books to the children. Gifted 4-year-olds might enjoy listening to such books as *The Trumpet of the Swan* by E. B. White. They often enjoy paging through books about science and nature. The book corner should have books reflecting different interests and reading levels.
- teaching the children to use computers. Some programs such as *Dinosaurs and Facemaker* are enjoyed by gifted young children (Alvino, 1988).
- introducing them to music appreciation by letting them listen to Vivaldi, Bach and Raffi.
- introducing them to art appreciation by teaching them about great artists and different art styles, taking them to the art gallery, and reading them picture books with high quality illustrations such as *Animalia* by Graeme Base.
- providing a variety of manipulative materials—such as parquetry blocks, peg boards and Jumbo Cuisenaire Rods—to encourage math development (Alvino, 1989).
- teaching critical thinking skills and problem solving by introducing them to simple logic puzzles and mazes.
- providing art activities rather than crafts. A craft activity can intimidate gifted children, who are perfectionists and become frustrated when their project doesn't look like the model.

Ideas From Parents

Parents of gifted preschoolers are an ideal source of ideas. Here is a list of activities collected from parents of gifted preschoolers:

- Teach them to play card games of all kinds, e.g. War, Slap Jack, checkers, *Monopoly, Chutes and Ladders* and chess. They learn to read words and numbers, count and reason from these activities.
- Immerse them in literature by having books in every room to encourage their desire to learn to read.
- Leave writing and drawing materials out at all times for them to use, and have a special drawer of "junk" materials that can be used to create projects.
- Let them be chemists: Give them your old spices, vinegar and baking soda and let them see what happens.
- Make a list with them of all the materials they would need if they were buying a pet; figure the costs with them and take them comparison shopping.
- Give them coupons and let them choose items they would like to buy.
- Let them plan a party of their choice, designing the invitations, making the guest list and arranging for the activities and refreshments. Then hold the party.

Conclusions

Gifted preschoolers provide a special challenge to teachers and parents alike. Child care specialists, childhood development workers and educators need to remember that although gifted preschoolers may think like 8-year-olds, they are still preschoolers. The key to enriching gifted preschoolers lies in knowing their interests and offering activities and materials to expand these interests. Gifted preschool children can test the patience of both parents and teachers. Interesting and challenging activities at home and in preschool will help channel their energy and intellectual curiosity in positive ways. It is the job of parents and teachers to see to it that these children receive appropriate educational experiences so that boredom and underachievement don't occur (Koopmans-Dayton and Feldhusen, 1987).

References

Alvino, J. (1989). *Parents' Guide to Raising a Gifted Toddler.* Boston: Little, Brown and Company.

Base, G. (1986). *Animalia.* New York: Harry N. Abrams, Inc.

Cole, J. (1991). *The Magic School Bus Lost in the Solar System.* New York: Scholastic.

Karnes, M.B. and Johnson, L.J. (1991). The Preschool/Primary Gifted Child. *Journal for the Education of the Gifted,* 14(3), 267–283.

Koopmans-Dayton, J.D. and Feldhusen, J.F. (1987). A Resource Guide for Parents of Gifted Preschoolers. *Gifted Child Today,* 10(6), 2–7.

White, E.B. (1970). *The Trumpet of the Swan.* New York: Harper & Row.

Wolfe, J. (1989). The Gifted Preschooler: Developmentally Different but Still 3 or 4 Years Old. *Young Children,* 44(3), 41–48.

Gifted Students Suggest Reforms for Education

Listening to gifted students' ideas

by Lugene Polzella

At this time of concern for basic skills, educational standards, achievement testing, and curriculum guides, there is little interest in the educational needs of brighter students. Budget cuts have made programs for the gifted in public schools practically obsolete. Still, these able students remain in the classroom, sitting in the background, bored with the slow pace, questioning their own special needs as learners, and often feeling isolated and alone. Schools today are seriously limited in their ability to meet the needs of these able children. Some teachers, on the other hand, are particularly sensitive to the unique aspects of gifted children and plan an open-ended curriculum. Often parents need to become directly involved in order to encourage experiences that match the interests and learning styles of their gifted children.

Summer programs for gifted students often provide the necessary components for them to advance in their learning and to feel good about themselves (Feldhusen & Clinkenbeard, 1982; VanTassel-Baska, Landau, & Olszewski, 1984). However, it is unfair that these students have to spend 10 months out of the year suffering in low level, single-faceted courses (Kunkel, Chapa, Patterson, & Walling, 1992) to have their educational needs met for only a few weeks in the summer (Lenz & Burruss, 1994). American public school education is free for

From *Gifted Child Today*, July/August 1997, pp. 30-35. © 1997 by The Gifted Child Today. Reprinted by permission.

everybody and should more accurately meet the needs of a diverse population of learners (Nielsen, 1993). Parents of brighter students should not have to pay extra for their children to get a quality education. Their regular schools must provide the intellectual stimulation they need during the traditional school year. We as educators have just as much responsibility to brighter students as to all other levels of students. When asked, the students themselves offer a wide range of suggestions for ways of enhancing their own educational experiences. It is time we start listening to the gifted students themselves and put energy toward ensuring their successes, both academic and social/emotional, in their regular schools.

Fifty returning students in grades 4–11 at the 1995 Bryn Mawr College session of the Summer Institute for the Gifted completed a survey containing three open-ended questions: Why did you return to the Summer Institute? What is your favorite area of interest—both academic and cultural? Which aspects of the program would you like to have as part of your regular school year experience?

Informal interviews were also conducted to obtain more qualitative information. Student responses that related to school improvements and reform were given emphasis, rather than the quantity of similar responses.

When asked their primary reason for returning, the most popular response was to further their education. Many students mentioned that their attendance in this program would help them "get ahead" in life. The second most popular response was that the program was fun. They most enjoyed the mixture of academic and recreational aspects. The third most popular response was that they were able to make new friends, and most notably, from among their intellectual peers. Lastly, students mentioned that this program were something productive to do in the summer. By far the most popular reasons for attending this program were academic; however, friendships, exciting dorm experiences, and the chance to be more

independent were also important to this group of students.

When students were asked to indicate their favorite areas of interest, the most popular responses indicated enjoyment of the following classes: drama and theater, swimming and water games, SAT preparation, mock trials and the justice system, tennis, and several of the science classes. It seemed that the popularity of some classes and experiences related somewhat to their novelty. Many students do not attend schools with the type of facilities a college campus can afford. Tennis courts and an Olympic-size pool, a full-sized computer lab with a wide range of available software, and a full-size auditorium with a large stage, are luxuries for upper elementary, middle, and high school students. Many students mentioned they enjoyed their computer classes and use of the computer lab during free time. Clearly they enjoyed taking full advantage of the available facilities. The SAT prep courses were important to the students because of the test's mandatory requirement for college entry. Most interesting was the enthusiasm for science classes, which were challenging and offered students a hands-on approach. As one student wrote: "I like my science classes a lot because there is a lot of hands-on lab education." This is an area in particular need of improvement in the regular schools, and was clearly appreciated by these students.

When asked "Which aspects of the program they would like to have as part of their regular school year experience?" the most popular response indicated the students' enjoyment of the evening special programs and the weekend trips. Special programs of this summer program ranged from a '50s singing group, to a man pretending to be Mozart, a woman playing Harriet Tubman, a masked man who explained and cleverly modeled the uses for masks, a theater sports group, a talent show, a brain bowl, and two dances, each with themes. The weekend "get away days" ranged from the

Hershey amusement park, a Renaissance Faire, river rafting on the Delaware River, a historical tour of Philadelphia, exploring museums, and several different trip choices in Washington, DC, including the Smithsonian Institute, Air and Space museum, a tour of the White House, and the Lincoln Memorial. Each of these trips offered countless opportunities for extending the imagination, knowledge, and understanding of bright young people.

The second most important aspect these students would like to see incorporated into their regular school experience was more challenging coursework in their classes. Some specifically mentioned the opportunity to take college level courses early if ready. These students were hungry for a challenge, which in turn challenged their teachers to offer more rigorous, complex, meaningful, applications to their curricula.

The third aspect mentioned by several students was more free time, and most specifically, more time between classes. One student wrote: "I liked that we had 15 minutes between our classes to relax or look over things before class." Several others mentioned that they enjoyed the "greater freedom around campus." Students often have trouble making transitions from one subject to another because regular school time is tightly structured. Their comments clearly mirrored this idea. Students need time to unwind from one course, and appreciate the chance to prepare mentally for the next.

Several other interesting responses that have a direct influence on our desire to improve regular school experiences are worth noting. Students particularly loved the chance to choose their own courses and felt they deserved that freedom during the school year. They also appreciated the support they felt from other students within the classroom environment, the excitement and love for learning generated by dedicated, young teachers, the small, low-stress classes, and finally, the emphasis on hands-on learning.

Often as administrators, parents, and teachers, we feel we know what is best for students. Unfortunately, in the public schools of today, the reality of overcrowded classes, budget cuts in staffing, programming and supplies, and frequent resulting teacher burn-out makes serving the needs of exceptionally bright children a difficult challenge. Often, we fail to ask the students about their needs. If we take the time to really listen, their requests and needs are obtainable. Clearly, the gifted students of this study have much to teach us about how we can better serve them during the regular school year. Here are some suggestions based on their ideas:

1. **Curriculum-related field trips.** On-site visits to local community areas of particular interest and intrigue spark the imaginations and create innovative ideas in our brightest students. Trips to museums, experiences in nature, and historical tours are an essential part of an enriched curriculum. Students need the exposure to the real world, and want the chance to interact with people in the field of study they are pursuing. Many such trips are inexpensive, and often only require coordination and parent volunteers.

2. **Serving individual student interests.** Sometimes the needs of a particular individual require a careful listening ear and strong advocates willing to extend themselves in providing specific growth experiences. Using community resources to help make those experiences happen is an effective way of serving our brightest. For example, taking an aeronautics enthusiast to a local airport and linking him or her with a pilot willing to explain the intricacies of flying and offering him or her a flying lesson, may make all the difference to an eager learner. Fostering the enthusiasm of excited students and matching their interests to experiences, will bring learning to life for our most able students.

3. **Use of college campus facilities.** Local college campuses often provide equipment and facilities that better suit the needs and abilities of young people with advanced talents or aspirations. Weekend programs offered to the community could include these students. Arrangements for special students to attend seminars, work with trainers and coaches, and obtain acting parts in local productions are possibilities. Pairing a college student with an advanced gifted student with similar interests would afford the gifted student a learning partner and advocate. Those who are ready should attend college classes and be allowed to obtain college credit for their efforts.

4. **Flexible school policies and teacher planning.** Several other requests revolve around school policy and administrative decision-making. Students need greater freedom in their course selections and require more time between classes. A small class size initially seems unobtainable, but with effective coordination of other staff members, school volunteers, and administrators, small groups could be possible, at least for part of the class time experience. For example, if the librarian, the computer teacher, and the principal each work with a group of students from the same class, the homeroom teacher would then have a quarter of the students at a time. Such an arrangement could supplement and enrich the learning experience for the students by involving other subject area teachers. Smaller groups increase student-to-teacher and student-to-student interactions and allow more time for student response. Student-to-student interactions also increase in smaller classes. These are ways to make that "comfortable feel of small class size" happen.

Several students were impressed with the expertise of their teachers and their integrated, open-ended teaching styles. Many developed lasting friendships with their summer program teachers as a result of their willingness to involve their students directly and to listen carefully to their ideas. Teacher training in the areas of the educational needs of gifted students and curriculum integration methods are necessary for gifted students to feel comfortable with the teachers in their regular classes. Teacher sensitivity to the unique qualities and needs of gifted individuals helps create an atmosphere in which bright children feel more comfortable getting involved.

5. **Hands-on science and technology.** Emphasis on hands-on learning is of key importance in

teaching today. Students need to experience the world in both concrete and abstract ways and must have enthusiastic, capable teachers to facilitate their learning. Particularly in the sciences, students need a strong background in technology, computers, and the sciences to experience first-hand the questions or problems they wonder about. Teachers must be knowledgeable and supportive, guiding students toward inherent challenges. A flexible curriculum with direct student contribution allows for individual differences. Gifted students have an opportunity to express themselves creatively when they have a chance to play around with ideas. The result is a crucial unspoken message to the brighter students that their ideas and input are vital to the success of the curriculum.

6. **Opportunities for gifted students to spend time working together.** One of the most important aspects of the summer experience for these students was the chance to work on meaningful areas of pursuit with their intellectual peers. Often as classroom teachers we distribute the brightest students across several groups in order to have a wide range of abilities within each group. This heterogeneous grouping is often detrimental for the brighter students who often end up tutoring the slower students in the group to the group's level, or doing more than their fair share of the work. When brighter children in a class work together in one group, they have a chance to enrich their experiences and incorporate a more abstract, complex view of the curriculum presented. By sharing their work with others, gifted students are able to show the entire class a more advanced way of learning.

In middle school and high school, certain times of the year (often for a week at a time) are designated for presenting concepts and ideas from an interdisciplinary perspective. A topic or theme for the unit is chosen which incorporates several disciplines. An example might be: "Man's Influence On His Environment In Turn Causes His Change." Teachers from various classes meet to generate ideas for projects and explore new methods for creating meaning for the students. Individual disciplines are taught from this perspective as students are invited to suggest ways to explore the theme. A variety of forms of expression of their ideas are encouraged. This open-ended approach to exploring ideas helps gifted students present their ideas in a less rigid educational forum.

The Governor's Scholars Program (GSP) in Kentucky presents a superb example of this interdisciplinary style of teaching. Eleventh graders are given the opportunity to participate in "an intensive living-learning experience." During this five-week summer program, students explore a variety of disciplines, and apply their learning to the real world. Work and play become one. Students attend non-traditional classes held in unique settings at different times of the day. For example, "Some teachers remove the furniture from the rooms; some conduct class peripatetically, teaching while walking through a town at dawn; some meet their students in the dining commons or dormitory lounges" (Riegelman, Wolf, & Press, 1991, p. 7). Students elect to "major" in one of 12 disciplines, but also take courses that seem antithetical. If they choose a major in the humanities, they must also take some science and math classes. Courses are taught from an interdisciplinary perspective. Emphasis is on hands-on learning in the real world. Some examples include: "A history class studies the Civil War by becoming Civil War soldiers at a nearby battlefield—eating beans and hardtack, drilling in 100 degree heat, wearing authentic wool uniforms, and sleeping in pup tents between patrols. A biology class studies the environment by analyzing water samples from a polluted stream and researching waste treatment alternatives, later forming an active organization to lobby for environmental change. A philosophy class, after discussing the ethical implications of current medical decisions, decides to spend time in a crippled children's hospital" (Riegelman et al., pp. 7–8). This type of enriched, involving, relevant educational experience will guide our brightest students toward becoming concerned, informed experts in their chosen fields.

Students spend the majority of their educational life in their regular hometown school. In most cases, this is public school with limited funding and resources. Often teacher attention revolves around the needs of the average and special education students with frequent neglect of the brighter students. It is imperative that we as teachers and administrators take the time to include enriching, challenging, dignifying experiences for our gifted students. These experiences often are easily obtained. By listening to the suggestions of students attending a summer camp experience especially tailored to the needs of the gifted, we can create strategies designed to help make the dreams of all gifted students a reality.

References

Feldhusen, J. F., & Clinkenbeard, P. R. (1982). Summer programs for the gifted: Purdue's residential programs for high achievers. *Journal for the Education of the Gifted, 5*(3), 178–184.

Kunkel, M. A., Chapa, B., Patterson, G., & Walling, D. D. (1992). Experience of giftedness. "Eight great gripes" Six years later. *Roeper Review, 15*(1), 10–14.

Lenz, K., & Burruss, J. D. (1994). Meeting affective needs through summer academic experiences. *Roeper Review, 17*(1), 51.

Nielsen, B. (1993). An attempt to make a difference: Overlooked disadvantaged gifted Appalachian children. *Roeper Review, 16*(1), 62–64.

Reigelman, M., Wolf, K., & Press, L. (1991). Creating an effective learning environment. *Gifted Child Today, 14*(3), 6–11.

VanTassel-Baska, J., Landau, M., & Olszewski, P. (1984). The benefits of summer programming for gifted students. *Journal for the Education of the Gifted, 8*(10), 73–82.

From the ERIC clearinghouse

CLUSTER GROUPING OF GIFTED STUDENTS:

HOW TO PROVIDE FULL-TIME SERVICES ON A PART-TIME BUDGET

Susan Winebrenner and Barbara Devlin

ERIC Digest #E538 • EC304950 • ED397618

What does it mean to place gifted students in cluster groups?

A group of five to eight identified gifted students, usually those in the top 5% of ability in the grade level population, are clustered in the classroom of one teacher who has training in how to teach exceptionally capable students. The other students in that class are of mixed ability. If there are more than eight to ten gifted students, two or more clusters should be formed.

Isn't cluster grouping the same as tracking?

No. In a tracking system, all students are grouped by ability for much of the school day, and students tend to remain in the same track throughout their school experience. Gifted students benefit from learning together and need to be placed with similar students in their areas of strength (Hoover, Sayler, & Feldhusen, 1993; Kulik & Kulik, 1990; Rogers, 1993). Cluster grouping of gifted students allows them to learn together, while avoiding permanent grouping arrange-ments for students of other ability levels.

Why should gifted students be placed in a cluster group instead of being assigned evenly to all classes?

When teachers try to meet the diverse learning needs of all students, it becomes extremely difficult to provide adequately for everyone. Often, the highest ability students are expected to "make it on their own." When a teacher has several gifted students, taking the time to make appropriate provisions for them seems more realistic. Furthermore, gifted students can better understand and accept their learning differences if there are others just like them in the class. Finally, scheduling out-of-class activities is easier when the resource teacher has only one cluster teacher's schedule to work with.

What are the learning needs of gifted students?

Since these students have previously mastered many of the concepts they are expected to "learn" in a given class, a huge part of their school time may be wasted. They need exactly what all other students need: consistent opportunity to learn new material and to develop the behaviors that allow them to cope with the challenge and struggle of new learning. It is very difficult for such students to have those needs met in heterogeneous classes.

Isn't gifted education elitist?

Gifted students need consistent opportunities to learn at their challenge level—just as all students do. It is inequitable to prevent gifted students from being challenged by trying to apply one level of difficulty for all students in mixed-ability classes. When teachers can provide opportunities for all students, including those who are gifted, to be challenged by rigorous curriculum, there is nothing elitist about the situation.

Don't we need gifted students in all classes so they can help others learn through cooperative learning, peer tutoring, and other collaborative models?

When gifted students are placed in mixed-ability groups for cooperative learning, they frequently become tutors. Other students in these groups may rely on the gifted to do most of the work and may actually learn less

From the ERIC Clearinghouse is a regular feature sponsored by the ERIC Clearinghouse on Disabilities and Gifted Education. Its purpose is to inform readers about the many resources available through ERIC. The column is prepared with funding from the U.S. Department of Education, Office of Educational Research and Improvement, and the Office of Special Education Programs, Contract No. RR93002005. The opinions expressed in this column do not necessarily reflect the position or policies of OERI, OSEP, or the Department of Education.

than when the gifted students are not in their groups. When gifted students work in their own cooperative learning groups from time to time on appropriately challenging tasks, they are more likely to develop positive attitudes about cooperative learning. At the same time, other students learn to become more active learners because they are not able to rely so heavily on the gifted students. When the learning task focuses on content some students already know, those students should be learning how to cooperate in their own groups on extension tasks that are difficult enough to require cooperation. When the cooperative task is open-ended and requires critical or divergent thinking, it is acceptable to include the gifted students in heterogeneous cooperative learning groups.

If gifted students are not placed in some classes, won't those classes lack positive role models for academic and social leadership?

Research on role modeling (Schunk, 1987) indicates that to be effective, role models cannot be drastically discrepant in ability from those who would be motivated by them. Teachers overwhelmingly report that new leadership "rises to the top" in the non-cluster classes. There are many students, other than identified gifted students, who welcome opportunities to become the new leaders in groups that no longer include the top 5% of a grade level group. This issue becomes a problem only when more than 5 to 10% of students are clustered. As classes are formed, be sure the classes without clusters of gifted students include several highly capable students.

How does the cluster grouping concept fit in with the inclusion models that integrate students with exceptional educational needs into general education classes?

The Inclusion model, in which students with exceptional learning needs are integrated into general education classrooms, is compatible with the concept of cluster grouping of gifted students, since both groups have exceptional educational needs. The practice of cluster grouping allows educators to come much closer to providing better educational services for groups of students with similar exceptional learning needs. In non-cluster classrooms, teachers report they are able to pay more attention to the special learning needs of those for whom learning may be more difficult. Some schools choose to avoid placing students with significant learning difficulties in the same class that has the cluster group of gifted students. A particular class may have a cluster of gifted students and a cluster of special education students as long as more than one adult is sharing the teaching responsibilities.

Won't the presence of the clustered gifted students inhibit the performance of the other students in that class, having a negative effect on their achievement?

When the cluster group is kept to a manageable size, many cluster teachers report that there is general improvement in achievement for the entire class. This suggests the exciting possibility that when teachers learn how to provide what gifted students need, they also learn to offer modified versions of the same opportunities to the entire class, thus raising the level of learning for all students, including those who are gifted. The positive effects of the cluster grouping practice may be shared with all students over several years by rotating the cluster teacher assignment among teachers who have had gifted education training and by rotating the other students so all students eventually have a chance to be in the same class with a cluster group.

How should students be identified for the cluster group?

If there will be one cluster, its highly capable students should be those who have demonstrated that they will need a curriculum that exceeds grade level parameters. Traditional measures such as standardized tests may also be used, but not as the sole criterion. If there will be more than one cluster, those highly capable in specific subjects might be grouped together in separate clusters. Profoundly gifted students should always be grouped together, since there will rarely be more than two such students in any grade level. Identification should be conducted each spring with the help of someone with training in gifted education.

What specific skills are needed by cluster teachers?

Since gifted students are as far removed from the "norm" as are students with significant learning difficulties, it is necessary for teachers to have special training in how to teach children of exceptionally high ability. Cluster teachers should know how to

- recognize and nurture behaviors usually demonstrated by gifted students.
- create conditions in which all students will be stretched to learn.
- allow students to demonstrate and get credit for previous mastery of concepts.
- provide opportunities for faster pacing of new material.
- incorporate students' passionate interests into their independent studies.
- facilitate sophisticated research investigations.
- provide flexible grouping opportunities for the entire class.

Should the cluster grouping model replace out-of-class enrichment programs for gifted students?

No. Cluster grouping provides an effective complement to any gifted education program. Gifted students need time to be together when they can just "be themselves." The resource teacher might also provide assistance to all classroom teachers in their attempts to differentiate the curriculum for students who need it. As a matter of fact, this resource person is being called a "Schoolwide Enrichment Specialist" in many schools instead of a "Gifted Program Coordinator" in recognition of the fact that so many students can benefit from "enriching" learning opportunities.

Is clustering feasible only in elementary schools?

No. Cluster grouping may be used at all grade levels and in all subject areas. Gifted students may be clustered in one section of any heterogeneous class, especially when there are not enough students to form an advanced section for a particular subject. Cluster grouping is also a welcome option in rural settings, or wherever small numbers of gifted students make appropriate accommodations difficult. Keep in mind, however, if your school has enough gifted students for separate sections in which curriculum is accelerated, such sections should be maintained. Many middle schools have quietly returned to the practice of offering such sections. Placement in cluster groups is gained by demonstrating that one needs a differentiated curriculum—not by proving one is "gifted."

How are records kept of the progress made by students in cluster groups?

Differentiated Educational Plans (DEP) should be maintained for gifted students and filed with their other ongoing records. In some schools, teachers develop a DEP for the cluster group, rather than for individual students. These plans briefly describe the modifications that are planned for the group and should be shared with parents regularly.

What are the advantages of cluster grouping?

Gifted students feel more comfortable when there are other students just like them in the class. They are more likely to choose more challenging tasks when other students will also be eligible. Teachers no longer have to deal with the strain of trying to meet the needs of just one precocious student in a class. The school is able to provide a full-time, cost-effective program for gifted students, since their learning needs are being met every day.

What are the disadvantages of cluster grouping?

There may be pressure from parents to have their children placed in a cluster classroom, even if they are not in the actual cluster group. Gifted students may move into the district during the school year and not be able to be placed in the cluster classroom. These situations may be handled by

- providing training for all staff in compacting and differentiation so parents can expect those opportunities in all classes.
- requiring parents to provide written documentation of their child's need for curriculum differentiation instead of requesting the placement by phone.
- rotating the cluster teacher assignment every 2 years among teachers who have had appropriate training so parents understand that many teachers are capable of teaching gifted students.
- rotating other students into cluster classrooms over several years.

Another disadvantage might arise if the cluster teachers are not expected to consistently compact and differentiate the curriculum. Their supervisor must expect them to maintain the integrity of the program, and must provide the needed support by facilitating regular meetings of cluster teachers, and by providing time for the enrichment specialist to assist the cluster teachers.

Conclusion

There is an alarming trend in many places to eliminate gifted education programs in the mistaken belief that all students are best served in heterogeneous learning environments. Educators have been bombarded with research that makes it appear that there is no benefit to ability grouping for any students. The work of Allan (1991); Feldhusen (1989); Fiedler, Lange, & Winebrenner (1993); Kulik and Kulik (1990); Rogers (1993) and others clearly documents the benefits

of keeping gifted students together in their areas of greatest strength for at least part of the school day. It appears that average and below average students have much to gain from heterogeneous grouping, but we must not sacrifice gifted students' needs in our attempts to find the best grouping practices for all students.

If we do not allow cluster groups to be formed, gifted students may find their achievement and learning motivation waning in a relatively short period of time. Parents of gifted students may choose to enroll their children in alternative programs, such as home schooling or charter schools. The practice of cluster grouping represents a mindful way to make sure gifted students continue to receive a quality education at the same time as schools work to improve learning opportunities for all students.

References

Allan, S. (1991). Ability grouping research reviews: What do they say about grouping and the gifted? *Educational Leadership, 48*(6), 60–65.

Feldhusen, J. (1989). Synthesis of research on gifted youth. *Educational Leadership, 46*(6), 6–11.

Fiedler, E., Lange, R., & Winebrenner, S. (1993). In search of reality: Unraveling the myths about tracking, ability grouping, and the gifted. *Roeper Review,16*(1), 4–7.

Hoover, S., Sayler, M., & Feldhusen, J. (1993). Cluster grouping of gifted students at the elementary level. *Roeper Review, 16*(1), 13–15.

Kulik, J. A., & Kulik, C-L. C. (1990). Ability grouping and gifted students. In N. Colangelo & G. David (Eds.), *Handbook of gifted education* (pp. 178–196). Boston: Allyn and Bacon.

Rogers, K. (1993). Grouping the gifted and talented. *Roeper Review, 16*(1), 8–12.

Schunk, D. H. (1987). Peer models and children's behavioral change. *Review of Educational Research, 57*, 149–174.

Susan Winebrenner, is the author of *Teaching Gifted Kids in the Regular Classroom.* She is a full-time consultant in staff development (1–888–327–3477) and author of several books and articles.

Barbara Devlin, is Superintendent of Schools in Richfield, Minnesota.

ERIC Digests are short reports that provide a basic overview, with references, on topics of interest to the broad educational community. They are in the public domain and may be freely reproduced and disseminated. ERIC EC Digests may be obtained for $1 each from the ERIC Clearinghouse on Disabilities and Gifted Education (800–328–0272), and they are available free of charge on the Internet at the following URL: http://ericae.net/

Unit Selections

Key Points to Consider

❖ What services are needed to make transition from primary to middle school work?

❖ What do we know about the transition successes and failures of students who received special education just before the onset of ITPs (1987–1990)? What can we learn from this data?

❖ Why should students with disabilities have transition services that focus on self-development and citizenship as well as on employment?

 **Links** www.dushkin.com/online/

These sites are annotated on pages 4 and 5.

The 1990 amendment to the Individuals with Disabilities Education Act (IDEA) extended special educational services to students from the completion of their public school education through age 21. This extension of services is to prepare students with disabilities to make a successful transition from the dependent status of student to a more independent status as community member and participant in the world of work.

The implementation of this amendment, Public Law 101-476, is still in its infancy. Many teachers, special educators, vocational counselors, and employment mentors (job coaches) are not sure how much vocational preparation should be given in the public schools, or when. Should children with disabilities start planning for their futures in elementary school, in middle school, in high school, throughout their education, or just before they finish school? Should there be a trade-off between academic education and vocational education for these students? Should each student's vocational preparation be individualized according to his or her needs and abilities, with no general rules about the wheres and whens of transitional services?

These and other questions about implementation of transitional services for children with exceptionalities abound. The U.S. government defined transitional services as outcome-oriented, coordinated activities designed to move students with disabilities from school to post-school activities such as college, vocational training, integrated employment, supported employment, adult education, adult services, independent living, and community participation. Choices are not either/or, but rather multiple: to help students with disabilities move from school to successful adulthoods. While some students may only be able to achieve partial independence and supported employment, others may achieve professional degrees and complete self-sufficiency.

Public Law 101-476, the transition amendment, stipulates that every student have an individualized transition plan (ITP) added to his or her individualized education plan (IEP) by age 16. This mandate defines the upper limit for beginning transition planning, but not the lower boundary. Transition planning may begin in elementary school.

The transition from student to employee in the work world usually receives a great deal of attention. The transitions from child living at home to adult living away from parents, and from noncommunity participant to full participant in community activities, should also be supported in an ITP.

The transition to the world of work may take the form of supported employment (mobile work crew, clustered or enclave placement, on-site training and supervision by a job coach, group providing a specific service product) or of sheltered employment (in a workshop). Many students with disabilities can make a transition from school to competitive employment. If they will eventually work side by side with nondisabled coworkers, they may need transitional services such as assertiveness training, negotiating skills, and personal empowerment counseling.

The transition to independent living requires careful planning, with goals and objectives as detailed as those for the transition to employment. Independent living may range from complete autonomy in a home or apartment, to partial autonomy with a spouse or roommate, to residence with a live-in aide or a part-time aide, to residence in a group home. Just a few years ago, adults with disabilities were expected to live in institutions or with parents, siblings, or extended family members. This is no longer considered appropriate. Each individual with a disability should be encouraged to be as autonomous as possible in adulthood. Self-sufficiency is enhanced by providing education in life skills such as meal preparation and cleanup, home deliveries (for example, mail) and delivery pickups (for example, trash), using money and paying bills, making household repairs, and following home safety precautions.

The transition from noncommunity participant to fully participating member of society requires ITP modifications quite different from IEP academic goals. Students with exceptional conditions may need more than the usual amount of assistance in learning to drive a car or to use public transportation. They need to know how to read maps and schedules. They need to be able to assert their right to vote in secret (for instance, ballot in Braille or computerized for their software), and to marry, divorce, reproduce, sue, defend themselves, or even run for public office. They should know social conventions (greetings, conversation skills, manners), grooming fashions, and clothing styles. They deserve to have the same access to health settings, religious locales, social activities, and information services (telephone, television, computer networks) as do persons without disabilities. While much has been done since the passage of PL 101-476, much is still left to be done to ensure a better life for adults with disabilities.

The first essay included in this unit on transition offers insights into the collaborative efforts required of administrators, staff, regular and special education teachers, and the student body, when a child with special needs transfers into a middle school. It reports the findings of a 2-year research project on transition. It identifies key issues that must be faced, addresses school policies and practices that can enhance or detract from a smooth transition, and discusses the dangers of resegregation of children with special needs.

The second article in this unit, by Mary Wagner and Jose Blackorby, addresses the current status of transition. It reports the results of a U.S. longitudinal study of how special education students have been faring in the transition from school to work. Success correlates are given as well as the factors that are more strongly related to poor outcomes.

Three interrelated goals for transition planning—self-development, citizenship, and employment—are the focus of the last article in this unit. Michael Hartoonian and Richard Van Scotter argue that students should be educated with an eye toward "learning a living," not just earning a living.

Transition

Making Comprehensive Inclusion of Special Needs Students Work in a Middle School

Paul D. Deering

More and more middle level schools are taking on the challenge of an inclusion approach to educating their special needs students (Bergen, 1993; Rothenberg, 1995). Inclusion, also known as mainstreaming, places students who have special educational needs in regular classrooms with peers who have no such identified needs. This is in contrast to the traditional self-contained approach in which special needs students are grouped together in separate rooms with special education teachers for all or most of the school day. The shift to an inclusion approach presents middle level schools with complex challenges as they attempt to shift the locations and methods for meeting all their students' needs. This article offers insights from a two-year study that may help schools to identify key issues, policies, and practices in serving the needs and bringing forth the talents of all of their on-site educational constituents—special needs and mainstream students, special education and mainstream teachers, administrators, and staff.

The widespread shift to inclusion was prompted by Public Law 94-142, the Education of the Handicapped Act of 1975, and its more recent updates (P.L. 99-457 of 1986; P.L. 101-476 of 1992). Based on the premise that mandating separate educational contexts for special needs students is inherently unequal, these laws require that special needs students be educated "in the least restrictive environment possible," in other words, in regular educational contexts with non-special needs students (Kellough & Kellough, 1996). Special educational needs defined by these acts may include any combination and degree of the following: autism, hearing impairment, mental impairment, orthopedic impairment, health impairment, emotional disturbance, learning disability, speech impairment, and visual impairment. Other special educational needs identified and served by many schools include giftedness and limited English proficiency. Inclusion of a particular child can range from partial, encompassing some fraction of the school day, to full—the entire school day. This is generally determined jointly by special education and mainstream teachers, counselors, and the child's parents (Kellough & Kellough, 1996).

Inclusion is especially important to middle schools as it is in concert with their fundamental embracing of diversity (e.g., National Middle School Association, 1995; Stevenson, 1997). The kinds and degree of physical, emotional, and academic diversity among students in the various special education categories are often not that different from what is found in the mainstream young adolescent population, so it makes sense for all-inclusive educational contexts to be the norm. Furthermore, all young adolescents need to broaden social horizons as part of their development of identity and social skills. Inclusion can support this development by providing students opportunities to interact with others different from themselves and to see others who are just as "different" as they are.

While middle school educators may wish to move from a self-contained special education approach to an inclusion model, it is no simple task. The shift to inclusion profoundly affects both teachers and students, not only in classrooms, but throughout the school environment. All of a sudden, persons who are not used to interacting with one another find themselves face-to-face on a regular basis.

Paul D. Deering teaches at the University of Hawaii at Manoa.

Mainstream teachers and special program teachers who have never worked with each other, much less each other's students, are often called upon to collaborate closely. Similarly, special needs and mainstream students who have minimal contact with one another find themselves in the same classrooms and social settings (Bradley & Fisher, 1995). Thus, inclusion of special needs students implies more than a policy decision, it entails a profound shift in the ways people view themselves, their actions and their peers in and around school. By examining one school's efforts with this process, we can learn about some of its challenges and promise.

A Study of Inclusion

I spent two years studying school culture at "Banner Middle School" (a pseudonym, by agreement with the participants). One of the focuses of my study was Banner's approach to inclusion of its special needs students who were from the following categories: developmentally disabled (DD); emotionally-behaviorally disabled (EBD); English as a second language (ESL); gifted and talented (GT); learning disabled (LD); multiple handicapped (MH); and severe learning handicapped (SLH). Banner is located in a large Western metropolitan area in the United States. Its 750 students were approximately equally distributed between Caucasians and Latinos, almost all of whom were from lower-middle class and low-income families.

I used ethnographic methods in this study, including participant and non-participant observation, formal and informal interviews, surveying the physical environment, and collecting artifacts (Bogdan & Biklen, 1992; Erickson, 1996). I observed more than 300 class sessions and school-related events in classrooms, the cafeteria, the school grounds, and the neighborhood. In my data analysis, I searched for patterns and recurring themes, then built tentative assertions to explain them. I focused on the interplay between policies and practices, and between local contexts, such as classrooms, and broader ones, such as the school grounds. As I developed tentative assertions I would return to the field to confirm, disconfirm, or alter them, often checking them directly with participants (Goetz & LeCompte, 1984).

The issues discussed in this article deal primarily with social relations in the classrooms and school relative to the inclusion process.

Although academic learning is not the primary focus, it is explored in terms of students' access to learning opportunities, since access is strongly affected by the social structures constructed in classrooms and throughout schools (Heath, 1983; McDermott, 1977). For example, it is widely accepted that teacher-directed recitation where students compete to get called on, places students with limited English proficiency and other special needs at a disadvantage; they simply cannot respond quickly enough to compete with their mainstream peers (Kellough & Kellough, 1996; Mehan, 1979). By contrast, cooperative or collaborative learning approaches are widely recommended for heterogeneous learning contexts as they offer students more equal access to discussions (Johnson & Johnson, 1987; Slavin, 1983).

Insights into Comprehensive Inclusion

Comprehensive inclusion denotes that all students—special needs and mainstream—are consistently provided with positive opportunities for social and academic development. This means that all students have equal access to successfully participating in meaningful social and academic interactions with a variety of peers. Comprehensive inclusion necessitates two conditions—coordination and scaffolding. Each is explained with examples below. Briefly, coordination exists when policies and practices within and between the levels of the classroom and the school are in concert with each other, and not at odds—that is, they consistently support inclusion. Scaffolding entails providing "just enough" assistance for a learner to succeed at a task (Vygotsky, 1978). In the context of inclusion, scaffolding is evidenced in classroom and institutional policies that help students successfully bridge the gulf between special needs and mainstream to establish positive social and academic relations.

Comprehensive inclusion is a multi-level process requiring coordination of institutional policies and classroom practices to address students' social and academic interactions.

Actions of school participants must be in concert at the school and classroom levels in order for there to be comprehensive inclusion of special needs students. Coordination of policies and practices across these levels is necessary to ensure that students are able and encouraged to interact with each other in ways that include all. By contrast, lack of co-ordination can undermine the best intentions of both educators and students. The examples provided illustrate the need for a comprehensive approach to inclusion.

School Level

An inclusion policy is a good start, but only a start.

An institutional policy of inclusion is a good first step at fully including special needs students in the academic and social life of a school. It provides the opportunity for inter-group contact to take place and for positive relations to develop between special program and mainstream students.

Banner's *School Vision* called for inclusion of its special needs students, and all spent at least a substantial portion of their school day in heterogeneous classrooms. The more profoundly handicapped students, those in the

The shift to inclusion profoundly affects both teachers and students, not only in classrooms, but throughout the school environment.

DD, MH, and SLH programs, were in mainstream classes for about one-third of their day while the GT students were mainstreamed for all but a two-hour, weekly pull-out program. All the compensatory (non-GT) special needs students met in resource rooms with specially certified teachers for one or more class periods per day, and were usually accompanied by support staff when in mainstream classes.

The potential of intergroup contact to spontaneously spark new friendships was illustrated at Banner by Freddie and Joe, two boys with cerebral palsy. Freddie walked with a pronounced limp and drooled, and Joe was confined to a support wheelchair. They could easily have been objects of ridicule among their status-conscious peers, but instead, both boys were incredibly popular. Wherever they went, boys and girls called out greetings, waved, and came over to talk with them. Neither boy was ever harassed or teased by anyone—and how many young adolescents can say *that*?

The inclusion policy clearly benefited Freddie, Joe, and their able-bodied peers, judging from all of their smiles and laughter. However, it appeared that these boys enjoyed special status because of the severity of their disabilities. Their less dramatically disabled peers did not enjoy the same kind of celebrity status and, in fact, were often excluded from classroom and social groups. Thus, an inclusion policy can start the process of broadening students' social relations, but is insufficient by itself to promote comprehensive inclusion. At least some special education students' needs will not be addressed by merely placing them out in the mainstream; they and their mainstream peers require scaffolding in order to succeed together socially.

Mainstream and special program students need scaffolding in order to develop positive social and academic relationships with each other.

Middle level students have difficulty transcending the boundaries of their group identities, whether defined by gender, special program, ethnicity, or other factors. (Eder & Parker, 1987; VanHoose & Strahan, 1988). This social difficulty is especially profound for the "more different" special needs students, such as those in DD, ESL, MH, and SLH programs. As noted, these students are not as different or "special" as Freddie and Joe, yet they are not as "normal" as those in GT or LD programs so they have a harder time blending in with their mainstream peers.

As an example of this phenomenon, Banner's DD, MH, and SLH students ate lunch at a table by themselves in the cafeteria, assisted by their adult aides. Meanwhile, the ESL students sat in an isolated group at another table. Only rarely did anyone from either group interact with the hundreds of other non-special program students surrounding them. This was especially ironic for the ESL students since so many of their peers were bilingual. For lack of social scaffolding, each group of special program students remained an island in a sea of mainstream peers.

One way in which Banner was beginning to scaffold student interactions across the special program-mainstream gulf was through peer tutoring. In this program, mainstream student volunteers helped special needs students with their school work, both in the special education resource rooms and in mainstream classrooms. The program became so much a part of the school life during the course of the study that it was almost a rarity to enter a classroom and not see it occurring. The social benefits of peer tutoring were evident in the non-classroom settings such as the cafeteria and school dances. It became increasingly common to see tutors and tutees laughing and talking together in these settings, thanks to the scaffolding that their working relationship had provided.

Peer tutoring can thus provide an accessible, meaningful structure to scaffold the development of both academic *and* social relationships among participants. At the same time, peer tutors provide modeling for their other mainstream peers that interaction with special program students can be non-threatening and even rewarding. The comments of Nina, a seventh grade peer tutor underscore the importance of this modeling, "When I'm around the mentally retarded kids or the slow learners I feel good, 'cause I like to help them. Sometimes mean kids make fun of them."

Other schools with which I have worked have scaffolded lunch room social relations with exploratory activities such as homeroom-based intramurals and participatory careers presentations. Others have "buddy programs" where an established student helps a newcomer or special needs student to get acquainted with the school and peers. Regardless of how it is done, some form of social scaffolding can help students to overcome their shyness and cliqueishness to form relationships across the special education barrier.

Classroom Practice

Teachers must examine their practices in light of the bigger picture of comprehensive inclusion.

Comprehensive inclusion requires that teachers take a broad, school-wide view of their roles. They must consider more than the academic and in-class impact of their practices. They must examine the effects of students' social relations. In addition, they must consider the degree to which their practices support comprehensive inclusion rather than undermining it, as illustrated in the following examples.

Heterogeneous group learning can support inclusion.

Numerous studies have confirmed the effectiveness of cooperative and collaborative group learning approaches for promoting

positive intergroup relations among students and stimulating impressive academic gains (see reviews by Johnson, Johnson, Maruyama, 1983; Slavin, 1983, 1990). However, group learning is no panacea for comprehensive inclusion, nor for any other educational aims. *How* it is done is just as important as if.

PHOTO BY DOUG MARTIN

Working in heterogeneous groups can provide an excellent opportunity for building meaningful relationships between special program and mainstream students, as well as for academic learning. This was apparent in many Banner classrooms. Those in which students built positive relationships via group work and other activities were characterized by a spirit of warmth and collaboration. In these contexts, there was a high degree of positive interaction between the special program and mainstream students in their peer work groups. Ideas and materials flowed so freely that it was often difficult to tell who was in which program. Discussion, laughter, and excitement permeated these classrooms, and students often left them talking enthusiastically with group mates from across the special education divide. A nerdy boy in the LD program who had lots of problems with persecution by peers described his work group mates as, "Nice, they're polite. They don't bully people around. They know stuff and tell you how to do it."

Teachers in the classrooms have confirmed where group work "clicked" did not simply focus on "warm fuzzies." They were also quite demanding regarding behavior and effort. They clearly communicated high academic expectations, both verbally and in writing. In addition, they quickly intervened in a firm but low-key manner when student behavior got out of line. In other words, they were nice *and* tough. Students appreciated having high behavioral expectations as expressed by Bobby, a seventh grader in the LD/EBD program:

> I like working in groups, but sometimes they play around and I want to get done. Sometimes I play around too, but I'm trying to pass! I like it with Mr. Moc. People work because he's got a loud voice.

Interestingly, these teachers also made sparing use of formal cooperative learning structures, only occasionally drawing upon the approaches of Kagan (1989) and the Johnsons (1987). Usually the teachers just instructed students to "work together," sometimes with some modeling or discussion of appropriate ways to interact. Perhaps most importantly, the learning tasks were active, varied, and challenging so that collaboration was useful and even *necessary*. Composing and illustrating myths, researching and building Native American villages, and finding examples and making collages of advertising propaganda drew rigorously upon multiple intelligences (Gardner & Hatch, 1989) so that all students' weaknesses and strengths were exposed. Thus, the special program students often provided the artwork or the breakthrough idea that eluded their mainstream peers. Several students described quite sophisticated and egalitarian outlooks on the processes of working in heterogeneous groups:

> You can ask your group if you don't understand. If you get stuck on a question they'll tell you more about the question and you figure it out from their information . . . not just give you the answer. (Steven, 7th grader, LD program)

> They can give to you and you give to them . . . maybe I don't know about mountains so I ask someone who knows about them. They could explain about them, and I could tell them about Mexico. It helps when you explain stuff 'cause you learn how to get along with others. (Mike, 7th grader, GT program)

The teachers in these classrooms provided several crucial forms of scaffolding for the building of positive social and academic relations between and among their special needs and mainstream students. In addition to the opportunity for face-to-face contact in heterogeneous groups, they provided scaffolding for meaningful interactions in the form of clear,

high, social, and academic expectations, and interesting, multi-dimensional tasks that motivated and required the participation of all members.

Competition undermines inclusion—"I don't mind the special ed kids except when we're in a competition" (seventh grade boy).

Numerous studies have criticized overt classroom competition for sorting students into winners and losers (Goldman & McDermott, 1987; Johnson & Johnson, 1987; Kohn, 1986; Sapon-Shevin, 1994). Those on the social and academic margins, such as special education and minority students, are especially susceptible to being made consistent losers in competitive school environments. The findings of this study add still more evidence to the case against overt classroom competition. The only class at Banner in which mainstream students staunchly resisted working in groups with special program peers was one in which the teacher used a team competition approach to cooperative learning. Based on Slavin's (1990) methods, the approach required students to calculate group members' grade averages to determine improvement points. The points were to be tallied for team competitions for pizza parties. A couple problems emerged with this cooperative learning approach. For one, the accounting procedures were so complex that few students ever figured how to calculate improvement points properly. Thus, they never saw how low-achieving teammates could contribute improvement points as readily as high-achievers. As a result, mainstream and GT students resisted working in groups with other special program students. The competition heightened this resistance, as Nick, a GT student, explained:

> It's fun when you're in a group when people are willing to work and know how. When I'm in a group where people don't know how or don't care and we're in a competition, it gets frustrating. Usually we know, so we'll get in a group with real intelligent kids.

Students like Nick frequently dealt with these concerns by taking over group materials while special program students looked on passively or engaged in disruption.

It may be that clarification of the accounting procedures would have gotten this cooperative learning program operating more smoothly. This might then have helped the mainstream students to view their special program peers more positively. Nevertheless, the team-versus-team competition added an extra level of tension that short-circuited students' ability to focus on anything but the contest and the pizza. Thus, it seems reasonable to conclude from this and the many prior studies that explicit classroom competition should be viewed very skeptically in an inclusion environment.

Be wary of resegregation

There are myriad ways in which inclusion can be undermined. While a school-level inclusion policy can place special needs students into the mainstream they can all too readily be resegregated within teams and classrooms. Ironically, the rationales for such practices can make perfectly good sense on some levels while appearing ill-advised on others. Coordination of philosophy, policies, and practices within and across contexts can help to avoid resegregation.

Banner educators wrestled with resegregation of special program students in several ways. For example, the seventh grade was divided into two teams, one of which had all of the DD, EBD, GT, LD, and SLH students and the other all of the ESL students. This decision had the unfortunate effect of concentrating Latino students in the latter team, creating what one teacher called, a "brown track/white track" effect. In addition, this division made the former team into this "special ed" team in the eyes and words of students. The rationale for this arrangement was that it would cut down on the running around demanded of the special program teachers, thus allowing them to focus more of their energy on their students. Unfortunately, this worthwhile goal came with the cost of making both the minority and special education students more concentrated and identifiable. The school addressed this problem the following year, opting to maximize inclusion with a more random distribution of students even though this was not as convenient for the teachers.

The seventh grade "special ed" team grappled with other resegregation issues as well. The teachers placed all of the GT, LD, and EBD students into a single class for all of the core subjects reasoning that this would make it easier to challenge the GT students and would minimize the running around by the LD/EBD resource teacher. In math class, the teachers went one step further by placing the GT students on one side of the room and the other special

program students on the other. Not surprisingly, this heightened teachers' and students' awareness of special program identities. One boy in the LD program illustrated this by referring to the "smart half of the room and the not-so-smart half." They found it too hard to plan and teach with the schizophrenic class distribution and also found that the EBD students were reinforcing each others' undesired behavior. After one grading period the team dispersed all of the special needs students across their four classes. The teachers subsequently found it easier to maintain appropriate behavior with the EBD students and

Comprehensive inclusion means that all students have equal access to successfully participating in meaningful social and academic interactions with a variety of peers.

found no big drawback to the resource teacher's covering more ground with the dispersed placement approach.

Resegregation of special needs students can also occur during group work. For example, when Banner students chose their own groups, they invariably chose others from the same special program and gender, although they showed no ethnic preferences. In addition, some teachers assigned special program students to work together in their own groups. For example, one kept the ESL students in a separate group with their translator during both direct instruction and group work. This may have been useful during direct instruction for translation, but it was unnecessary during group work with so many bilingual students present. This in-class segregation cost the ESL students several important social and academic opportunities: (a) interactive, discourse-based learning of mathematics (Webb, 1989); (b) active use of English in a meaningful context (McGroarty, 1989); and (c) building of intergroup friendships (Johnson & Johnson, 1987).

I should clarify that I am not advancing an argument that cooperative groups should always be heterogeneous. Work by Webb (1982, 1989) and Palincsar and Brown (1984) strongly suggests that homogeneous groups can sometimes be highly beneficial for student learning. Nonetheless, it is abundantly clear from this and much prior work that student work groups should not *always* be homogeneous, as this eliminates the face-to-face interaction necessary for the development of intergroup friendships (Johnson & Johnson, 1987). Still more, consistent homogeneous grouping reinforces the social and academic divisions among students rather than bridging them.

It is apparent that resegregation of special needs students can occur inadvertently as a by-product of well-intentioned decisions. This illustrates the complexity of balancing inclusion goals with other important priorities, and by extension, the need for coordination of inclusion practices and policies at all levels of the school. The concentration of certain special needs students in one or the other of the seventh grade teams conflicted with the school's broader goal of fully including special needs students in the social and academic life of the school. So too did the in-class grouping of LD and EBD students and of ESL students. Prior research (Johnson, Johnson, Maruyama, 1983; Slavin, 1983, 1990) suggests that these students' isolation in the cafeteria and other school contexts could have been reduced if they had had more regular classroom opportunities to interact with non-special program peers. A coordinated, whole-school approach to inclusion, a comprehensive approach, could help ensure such opportunities at all levels of the school.

Inclusion benefits everyone.

One of the clearest conclusions to be drawn from this study is that the "special" students are not the only beneficiaries of an inclusion program. *All* students and educators can benefit from the broader, richer social interactions that inclusion can provide. Again, this is especially important for young adolescents as it addresses their developmental need to socialize with a wide variety of others (National Middle School Association, 1995; Stevenson, 1997). Banner Middle School was a far richer community for having the various special needs students, first of all, in the building and, secondly, out among their peers. Having seen the school's promising, trial-and-error struggles with inclusion, it is hard to imagine going back to "quarantining" the special needs students in self-contained classrooms.

The benefits to mainstream students from interacting with peers such as Freddie, Joe, and others in the special programs can

scarcely be overestimated. Instead of reacting with fear or rejection toward disabled peers, they were learning to reach out to them. Mike, the GT student quoted earlier, had his eyes opened by working in heterogeneous groups to the potential for *all* other students to contribute unique and important ideas. No "curriculum" can promote such learning the way experience can.

Peer-tutoring similarly benefits all participants, not just the targeted special needs students. Tutors develop broader social relations just as their tutees do. They also gain a well-founded sense of accomplishment as well as compassion. Nikki, a seventh grader described her experiences with peer tutoring as follows: "Things come easier for me, and having a sister, I can understand how it is. So I like to help kids. I don't really get anything out of it except when a kid does better. That feels good." The gains in self-esteem can be especially dramatic for peer tutors who are themselves in special programs. Banner teachers found students in the EBD program to be exceptionally patient and compassionate tutors for their peers in the DD and SLH programs. This gave the EBD students a much-needed opportunity to be needed and appreciated by someone. Their special program teacher noted that this boost in self-esteem carried over outside the tutoring sessions in much calmer demeanor for her student tutors.

Inclusion belongs to everyone.

Students need help in bridging the long-standing social gulf that has separated "special program" and "mainstream," regardless of which side they are on. They need educators to provide scaffolding that will help them to interact in meaningful ways with peers from across programs. By bridging the social gap, students and educators will be taking a giant step toward closing the academic gap between "special" and "mainstream" education. When all students have equal access to the social and academic benefits of widespread interaction in school, all will be better served.

Such a goal, comprehensive inclusion, requires that all of a middle school's participants take ownership of the process at both classroom and institutional levels. Simply "doing one's job" in the classroom and ignoring the institutional level of policy and scheduling is not enough. Leaving students' social relations in non-classroom contexts to take care of themselves is not enough. In order for comprehensive inclusion to occur, classroom practices and institutional policies must be coordinated to consistently work for inclusion, rather than against it.

Comprehensive inclusion requires that middle level educators use "bifocal lenses" to see both the immediate and broader implications of their practices. Only then, will classroom and institutional practices be coordinated to consistently scaffold the academic and social functioning of special needs and mainstream students. Only then will all of us—students and educators, special program and mainstream—reap the full benefits of inclusion.

References

Bergen, D. (1993). Teaching strategies: Facilitating friendship development in inclusion classrooms. *Childhood Education, 69*, 234–36.

Bogdan, R. C., & Biklen, S. K. (1992). *Qualitative research for education.* Boston: Allyn & Bacon.

Bradley, D. F., & Fisher, J. F. (1995). The inclusion process: Role changes at the middle level. *Middle School Journal, 26*(3), 13–19.

Eder, D., & Parker, S. (1987). The cultural production and reproduction of gender: The effect of extracurricular activities on peer-group culture. *Sociology of Education, 60*, 200–213.

Erickson, F. (1986). Qualitative methods in research on teaching. In M. Wittrock (Ed.), *Handbook of research on teaching* (3rd ed.) (pp. 119–161). New York: Macmillan.

Gardner, H., & Hatch, T. (1989). Multiple intelligences go to school: Educational implications of the theory of multiple intelligences. *Educational Researcher, 18*(8), 410.

Goetz, J. P., & LeCompte, M. L. (1984). *Ethnography and qualitative design in educational research.* Orlando, FL: Academic Press.

Goldman, S. V., & McDermott, R. (1987). The culture of competition in American schools. In G. D. Spindler (Ed.), *Education and cultural process: Anthropological approaches* (2nd ed.) (pp. 282–300). Prospect Hts., IL: Waveland Press.

Heath, S. B. (1983). *Ways with words: Language, life, and work in communities and classrooms.* Cambridge: Cambridge University Press.

Johnson, D. W., & Johnson, R. T. (1987). *Learning together and alone: Cooperative, competitive and individualistic learning* (2nd ed.). Englewood Cliffs, NJ: Prentice Hall.

Johnson, D. W., Johnson, R. T., & Maruyama, G. (1983). Interdependence and interpersonal attraction among heterogeneous and homogeneous individuals: A theoretical formulation and a meta-analysis of the research. *Review of Educational Research, 53*, 5–54.

Kagan, S. (1989). *Cooperative learning: Resources for teachers.* San Juan Capistrano, CA; Resources for Teachers.

Kellough, R. D., & Kellough, N. G. (1996). *Middle school teaching: A guide to methods and resources.* Englewood Cliffs, NJ: Prentice-Hall.

Kohn, A. (1986). *No contest: The case against competition.* Boston: Houghton Mifflin.

McDermott, R. P. (1977). Social relations as contexts for learning in school. *Harvard Educational Review, 47*, 198–213.

Mehan, H. (1979). *Learning lessons: Social organization in the classroom.* Cambridge, MA: Harvard University Press.

McGroarty, M. (1989). The benefits of cooperative learning arrangements in second language instruction. *National Association of Bilingual Education Journal, 13*, 127–143.

National Middle School Association. (1995). *This we believe: Developmentally responsive middle level schools.* Columbus, OH: Author.

Palincsar, A. S., & Brown, A. L. (1984). Reciprocal teaching of comprehension-fostering and comprehension-monitoring activities. *Cognition and Instruction, 1*, 117–175.

Rothenberg, D. (1995). Inclusion in the middle school: An update. *Middle School Journal, 27*(1), 56–58.

Sapon-Shevin, M. (1994). Cooperative learning and middle schools: What would it take to really do it right? *Theory into Practice, 33*(3), 183–190.

Slavin, R. E. (1983). *Cooperative learning.* New York: Longman.

Slavin, R. E. (1990). *Cooperative learning: Theory, research, and practice.* Boston: Allyn & Bacon.

Stevenson, C. (1997). *Teaching ten to fourteen year olds* (2nd ed.). New York: Longman.

Van Hoose, J., & Strahan, D. (1988). *Young adolescent development and school practices: Promoting harmony.* Columbus, OH: National Middle School Association.

Vygotsky, L. S. (1978). *Mind in society development of higher psychological processes.* M. Cole, V. John-Steiner, S. Scribner, & E. Souberman (Eds). Cambridge, MA: Harvard University Press.

Webb, N. M. (1982). Group composition, group interaction, and achievement in cooperative small groups. *Journal of Educational Psychology, 74*, 475–484.

Webb, N. M. (1989). Peer interaction and learning in small groups. *International Journal of Educational Research, 13*, 21–40.

The author wishes to thank the students, educators, and families of Banner Middle School and the Industry community for welcoming him among them. Thanks also to Margaret A. Eisenhart, Michael S. Meloth, Evelyn Jacob and the C.U. College of Education Anthropology Group for helping develop this research.

Transition from High School to Work or College: How Special Education Students Fare

Mary M. Wagner
Jose Blackorby

Mary M. Wagner, Ph.D., is program manager of education and human services research at SRI International, Menlo Park, CA.

Jose Blackorby, Ph.D., is a research social scientist at SRI International Menlo Park, CA.

Abstract

Results are reported from the National Longitudinal Transition Study of Special Education Students. Dropout rates were high: 30% of students with disabilities dropped out of high school, and another 8% dropped out before entering high school. The average dropout with disabilities was 18 years old at the time of leaving but had earned less than half the credits needed to graduate.

Employment successes were strongly related to taking a concentration (four courses) in vocational education. Youths with learning disabilities or speech impairments were most likely to approach the rate of employment found in the general population. Postsecondary education was low: 37% of high school graduates with disabilities had attended a postsecondary school, compared with 78% of high school graduates generally. Students with hearing or visual impairments were most likely to attend college.

Students with disabilities were significantly more likely to be poor than were youths in the general population, and poverty tended to exacerbate the impact of having a disability. Impoverished students with disabilities were less likely than wealthier students with disabilities to be enrolled in those postsecondary education and training programs that could enable them to break out of poverty. When employed, the poorer students with disabilities earned significantly less per year than did those from wealthier families.

Placement in regular education (rather than special education) was associated both with better and worse postschool outcomes. Students with sensory or motor disabilities appeared to benefit from regular education placement. However, for many students, more time in regular education was associated with a higher likelihood of course failure, which was a strong predictor of dropping out of school.

Reprinted with permission from *The Future of Children,* Spring 1996, pp. 103–120. © 1996 by the Center for the Future of Children of the David and Lucile Packard Foundation. *The Future of Children* journals and executive summaries are available free of charge by faxing mailing information to: Circulation Department (650) 948-6498.

In 1983, the first generation of children to go entirely through elementary school under the provisions of the Education for All Handicapped Children Act (Public Law 94-142) was approaching secondary school. The secondary school students with disabilities who had preceded them had left school, and disquieting reports were surfacing in some states and communities regarding how they were faring as workers, postsecondary students, and citizens.[1-3] Graduation and employment rates were low, and so were wages. Most students were not furthering their educations after high school. Social adjustment often was difficult.

How widespread were these problems? Were students with particular characteristics more prone to have difficulty making the transition from school to adult life? What could schools or service agencies do to support students in making that transition more effectively?

The absence of answers of these kinds of questions prompted the U.S. Congress to direct the Department of Education to commission a study of "a sample of handicapped students, encompassing the full range of handicapping conditions, examining their educational progress while in special education and their occupational, educational, and independent living status after graduating from secondary school or otherwise leaving special "education" (Public Law 98-199, section 618). In 1985, SRI International, under contract to the Office of Special Education Programs, began to develop the design, sample, and instruments for the National Longitudinal Transition Study of Special Education Students (NLTS). In 1987, under a separate contract, SRI initiated the NLTS, the largest single investment in research ever made in the special education field.

Since 1987, the NLTS has helped define much of what is known about the experiences of young people with disabilities nationally while they were in secondary school and in the early years afterward. The results of this study provided solid measures of the frequency of critical school experiences[4] and accurate indicators of student performance.[5] From the NLTS, researchers also learned the extent to which youths followed various life paths after high school, moving into postsecondary education, employment, residential arrangements of various kinds, and marriage and parenthood.[6]

The NLTS includes a nationally representative sample of more than 8,000 youths with disabilities,[7-10] drawn from the rosters of special education students in more than 300 school districts nationwide. All sample members were special education students between the ages of 15 and 21 in the 1985–86 school year. Data were collected about them in 1987 and again in 1990. School records of sample members, telephone interviews with their parents and with the students themselves when possible, and surveys of the principals and teachers who served them all have contributed to a rich database about young people with disabilities in secondary school and early adulthood.

In describing their experiences, the NLTS reports percentages of youths with a particular status (for example, the percentage employed). Percentages reported in the NLTS and in this article have been weighted to represent youths nationally; they are not percentages of the sample, but estimates for the population of youths with disabilities as a whole and for students in each of the 11 federal special education disability categories in use in 1985. The distribution of disability categories within the full population of youths with disabilities nationally is depicted in Figure 1. Note that youths with learning, cognitive, and emotional disabilities predominate; physical and sensory disabilities are low-incidence conditions. Thus, for example, values for youths with learning disabilities are weighted more heavily than those for youths with visual impairments when discussing youths with disabilities as a group because of the significantly greater number of those with learning disabilities in the population.

Given this large and representative sample and its broad scope and multiple sources of data, the NLTS is a firm basis for understanding how youths with disabilities fared in their early postschool years in furthering their educations or finding work. Specifically, the following questions are considered here:

■ What were the goals of young people with disabilities for their early postschool years?

■ What did special education students bring with them to their adult roles by way of education and training?

■ To what extent did youths with disabilities participate in postsecondary education and in the workforce in their early years after secondary school?

■ What factors contributed to more positive adult outcomes for youths with disabilities?

Postschool Goals of Young People with Disabilities

In interpreting the outcomes of young people with disabilities in their early postschool years, it is important to have an understanding of what

Figure 1

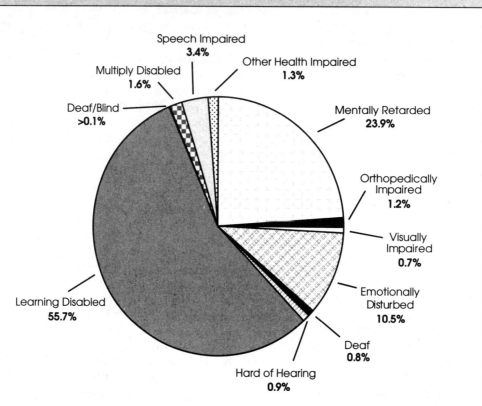

Primary Disability Category of Secondary Special Education Students Reported by the NLTS

Speech Impaired
3.4%

Other Health Impaired
1.3%

Multiply Disabled
1.6%

Deaf/Blind
>0.1%

Mentally Retarded
23.9%

Orthopedically Impaired
1.2%

Visually Impaired
0.7%

Emotionally Disturbed
10.5%

Learning Disabled
55.7%

Deaf
0.8%

Hard of Hearing
0.9%

The distribution of secondary-school-age students with disabilities by primary disability category that is shown in this figure differs somewhat from the distribution for elementary-school-age students. Among elementary students with disabilities, those with speech impairments are a much larger proportion of students than among secondary school students. This results from the fact that many articulation disorders (for example, lisps and stutters) are ameliorated or outgrown by the time students reach secondary school, the tendency for schools to determine that remaining articulation disorders no longer require special education, or the tendency to conclude that speech/language processing disorders are actually learning disabilities and to reassign students to that category. Also apparent is an increase in the category of serious emotional disturbance among older students, the disability that is more likely than any other to surface in adolescence.

Source: Wagner, M., D'Amico, R., Marder, C., et al. *What happens next? Trends in postschool outcomes of youth with disabilities. The second comprehensive report from the National Longitudinal Transition Study of Special Education Students.* Menlo Park, CA: SRI International, 1992.

they hoped to achieve. What goals did students have for after high school?[11] Examining their intended postschool paths provides an appropriate yardstick against which to assess the outcomes they achieved.

The majority of high school students with disabilities intended to enter the workforce upon leaving school.[12] In many ways, high school was a difficult academic environment for students with disabilities,[5] and the world of work may have offered them a wider variety of activities at which

they could succeed. Among 12th-graders with disabilities, more than half (56%) had a goal of finding competitive employment after leaving high school, 10% had a goal of obtaining supported employment,[13] and 2% sought sheltered work.[13] Even among those who did not intend to go to work immediately, training for work held dominance over academic pursuits. More than one-fourth of 12th-graders with disabilities (28%) had a goal of postsecondary vocational training, compared with 23% having college attendance as their postsecondary goal. Only among youths with speech or sensory impairments did one-third or more students have college attendance as their postschool goal. Given the prevalence of employment-oriented goals, one would expect to see students with disabilities pursuing vocational programs with greater emphasis than college-preparatory academic programs, an expectation born out in the course-taking experiences of many high school students with disabilities.

Secondary School Education and Training

Young people with disabilities who graduated from high school on average earned 22 high school credits, as did high school graduates with no identified disabilities.[14] Twelve of the credits earned by graduates with disabilities were in academic subjects,[15] somewhat fewer than the fifteen credits earned by students in the general population.[14] Reflecting their emphasis on vocational goals, the average secondary school student with disabilities earned five credits in vocational education, one more than typical high school students. One credit was earned in a life skills course, and the remaining four credits were earned in other subjects, such as physical education or the arts. With the exception of high school graduates with mental retardation or multiple disabilities, this pattern of credits earned did not vary significantly for students with different kinds of disabilities, largely due to the standardization imposed on high school course taking by state and school district graduation requirements.

Although virtually all high school students with disabilities spent the majority of their class time taking academic courses, few of them took courses that were indicative of college-preparatory programs.[16] For example, graduates with disabilities averaged 2.5 credits in mathematics, only marginally less than the 2.9 credits earned by typical high school students.[14] Yet, throughout four grades of high school, only 12% of students with disabilities had taken any advanced mathematics (which includes algebra, geometry, trigonometry, or calculus), courses often required for college entrance. Similarly, only 18% of students with disabilities had taken a foreign language at any time in high school. Further, only 7 of the 12 academic credits earned by graduates with disabilities as a group were in regular education academic courses. Special education courses may have conferred different kinds or levels of preparation for postsecondary education and other adult roles than courses taken in regular education.

Yet, these aspects of academic course taking varied widely for students with different kinds of disabilities. For example, among students with visual impairments, 51% took advanced mathematics at some time in high school, and 62% took a foreign language, reflecting the fact that postsecondary education was a more common intention among these students than among students with disabilities as a whole. Further, 13 of the 15 academic credits earned by students with visual impairments were in regular education classes, suggesting that more of their high school course work was comparable to that of typical students than was true for students with disabilities as a whole.

In addition to academic courses, virtually all students with disabilities (99%) who stayed in high school for four grade levels took some kind of vocational education during that time.[17] However, many fewer (34%) took a "concentration" of vocational education—that is, four or more semester courses in the same skill area (for example, auto repair or computer programming). Most students (62%) took one or more survey courses—that is, beginning courses in a content area, with little or no follow-up in the same area to more fully develop the skills needed for employment in that field.

Vocational concentration was most common for students with learning disabilities (40%) and speech impairments (30%). It was least common for those with multiple (16%) or visual impairments (19%). However, these groups had different explanations for having relatively few vocational concentrators. As noted previously, students with visual impairments were the most likely to be taking college preparatory classes; vocational courses may have been inconsistent with their college ambitions, and there may have been little room in their schedules to include them. In contrast, students with multiple disabilities were among the most severely impaired and may not have had the functional abilities to pursue advanced skill training in many vocational areas.

Vocational concentration also was significantly more common among male students than among females (40% versus 23%; $p < 0.001$) and among white students than among African-American students (38% versus 16%; $p < 0.001$). The extent to which these differences reflect differences in the preferences and goals of students and/or differences in the resources or programs available to them is unclear. Trade and industry was the most popular skill area among male vocational concentrators, 81% of whom concentrated in that skill area, whereas 62% of female students with disabilities who had a concentration in vocational education did so in office occupations. Virtually

At the time they entered high school, more than three-fourths of students with disabilities were at least a year older than their age peers.

all students (92%) who concentrated in vocational education took those courses as regular education classes. More than one-third of students with disabilities (38%) combined their vocational instruction with a work-study program; however, the majority of that work experience was school based, rather than community based.

Dropping Out of High School

The discussion thus far has considered the secondary school training of students with disabilities who had stayed in high school through four grade levels. They exited high school with a diploma, 22 credits, and a mixed bag of academic and vocational experiences. However, these students were fewer than 60% of those with disabilities who started high school: 30% of exiters from secondary school with disabilities dropped out of high school; another 8% dropped out before ever reaching high school.[18] Among those who started high school but did not finish, the average age was 18 at the time of school leaving. Thus, dropouts with disabilities stayed in school as long as most of their peers who graduated, but at the time they left, they had earned only an average of 10 credits, fewer than half of the credits they needed to graduate.

Course failure and dropping out were most common for students with serious emotional disturbances.

This poor record of credits earned resulted from repeated course failure on the part of many students with disabilities. At the time they entered high school, more than three-fourths of students with disabilities were at least a year older than their age peers, indicating that they may have been retained at grade level at some earlier point in their school careers. During four grade levels of high school, 64% failed at least one course.

Course failure was found in the NLTS analyses to be among the strongest predictors that students would eventually drop out of school.[5] Course failure and dropping out were most common for students with serious emotional disturbances, among whom more than three-fourths failed a course in high school and almost half dropped out. In contrast, among deaf students, 44% failed one or more courses, and 11% dropped out.

Postschool Outcomes

Here the extent to which students with disabilities achieved their employment and postsecondary education goals is considered. Outcomes for a cohort of young people with disabilities when the group had been out of high school from three to five years are examined. Where comparable data are available, the outcomes of this cohort are compared with those of youth without identified disabilities who had been out of school a similar length of time.[19]

Postsecondary Education

Most American high school seniors expect to attend at least some college, and almost half of the youths in the general population expect to complete at least a bachelor's degree.[20] The pervasiveness of the expectation of postsecondary education reflects the reality of the increasing technical complexity of our economy. School may be even more important for people with disabilities than for others. In the employment arena, educational credentials attest to skills, knowledge, and a work ethic that can help direct an employer's focus toward a person's abilities rather than disabilities.

Federal activities reflect a recognition of the important role of postsecondary education in helping persons with disabilities achieve adult independence and economic productivity. For example, the HEATH (Higher Education for Adult Training for People with Handicaps) Resource Center, a federally funded center of information about education for individuals with disabilities, publishes a resource directory and operates the National Clearinghouse on Postsecondary Education for Handicapped Individuals. Federal legislation such as the Americans with Disabilities Act (Public Law 101-336), also supports the transition of youths with disabilities from secondary to postsecondary education.

Despite such legislation and information services, by definition, youths in special education have disabilities that make aspects of the educational process more difficult for them than for

Figure 2

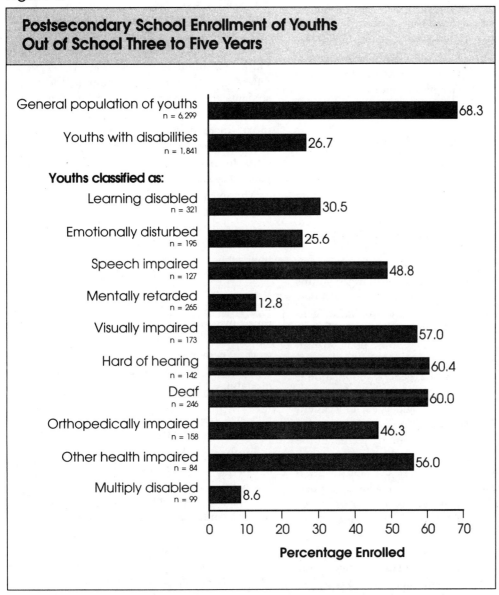

Postsecondary School Enrollment of Youths Out of School Three to Five Years

General population of youths — n = 6,299 — 68.3
Youths with disabilities — n = 1,841 — 26.7

Youths classified as:

Learning disabled — n = 321 — 30.5
Emotionally disturbed — n = 195 — 25.6
Speech impaired — n = 127 — 48.8
Mentally retarded — n = 265 — 12.8
Visually impaired — n = 173 — 57.0
Hard of hearing — n = 142 — 60.4
Deaf — n = 246 — 60.0
Orthopedically impaired — n = 158 — 46.3
Other health impaired — n = 84 — 56.0
Multiply disabled — n = 99 — 8.6

Percentage Enrolled (0, 10, 20, 30, 40, 50, 60, 70)

Source: Wagner, M., D'Amico, R., Marder, C., et al. *What happens next? Trends in postschool outcomes of youth with disabilities. The second comprehensive report from the National Longitudinal Transition Study of Special Education Students.* Menlo Park, CA: SRI International, 1992.

other youths. Thus, it is not surprising that the educational attainment of youths with disabilities is considerably lower than that of youths in general.[21] Only 27% of youths with disabilities had been enrolled in postsecondary school at any time when they had been out of high school three to five years (see Figure 2). This enrollment percentage compares with an attendance rate of 68% for youths in the general population out of high school the same length of time.

Several factors may contribute to this sizable disparity between youths with disabilities and youths in the general population. One factor clearly is the nature of the disability the youths had. The majority of youths with disabilities had learning disabilities, mental retardation, or emotional disturbances (see Figure 1). Young people in these categories had among the lowest rates of postsecondary school attendance of any youths with disabilities. In contrast, young people with visual or hearing disabilities, for example, attended postsecondary schools at close to the same rate as youths in general.

Confounding this apparent relationship between disability and school attendance, however, is the fact that youths with learning disabilities, mental retardation, or emotional disturbances also had among the highest dropout rates of any youths with disabilities. Perhaps it was the absence of a high school diploma that created a barrier to further postsecondary education. However, the post-secondary enrollment rates of high school graduates with disabilities argues against this explanation. Even among graduates, only 37% of those with disabilities had enrolled in postsecondary schools, compared with 78% of high school graduates in the general population who had been out of school for the same length of time.

Only youths with learning or speech impairments began to approach the employment rates of youths as a whole.

One further potential contributing factor to lower rates of postsecondary education for youths with disabilities involves the demographic differences between these youths and youths in general. Secondary school students with disabilities were significantly more likely to be poor, African American, and from single-parent households than were youths in the general population.[22] These factors may have created social or economic barriers to postsecondary school attendance, which were more pronounced among youths with disabilities than among youths in the general population. However, when analyses were performed by the NLTS to adjust statistically a national sample of youths in the general population to match the gender, ethnic, and socioeconomic distribution of youths with disabilities, virtually none of the difference in postsecondary enrollment disappeared. The adjusted sample of youths in the general population, which was equally African American, poor, and from single-parent households, still had enrolled in postsecondary schools at a rate more than twice as high as youths with disabilities (62% versus 27% when youths had been out of school three to five years; p < 0.001).

When youths with disabilities did go on to postsecondary schools, it rarely was to four-year colleges. Only 4% of youths with disabilities had ever attended a four-year college at the time they had been out of high school three to five years. Two-year college attendance was more common (only 12% of youth had ever attended), but postsecondary vocational training was the most common form of postsecondary education (16%). Thus, the employment-related goals of high school seniors with disabilities continued to be reflected in their educational choices several years after leaving high school.

Employment

American society has expressed increasing concern about the quality of its high school graduates and their ability to help the country be competitive in a global economy. The 1994 School-to-Work Transition Act (Public Law 103–239) is a reflection of the country's commitment to support students in acquiring high-end vocational skills and in transitioning to the kinds of jobs needed in an increasingly information-based economy. Provisions in that legislation explicitly require states to include students with disabilities in the plans they develop for school-to-work programs.

This inclusion of students with disabilities in employment-related transition programs reflects an understanding of the difficult time many of them have finding a place in the workforce after high school.[23] When youths with disabilities had been out of high school between three and five years, 57% were working competitively (see Figure 3), and the majority (43%) were doing so full time. Just over one-third of youths were not working (36%); many (17%) were not looking for work. These rates of participation in the work place lagged behind those of their peers without disabilities. More than two-thirds of youths (69%) in the general population were employed when they had been out of secondary school three to five years (p < 0.001).

Further, employment successes were not experienced by all youth with disabilities. As shown in Figure 3, only youths with learning or speech impairments began to approach the employment rates of youths as a whole. These were the categories of youths most likely to have taken a concentration of vocational education in high school. Successes also were most apparent for those who had graduated from high school. Almost two-thirds of graduates (65%) were employed competitively three to five years after high school compared with only 47% of dropouts. Three to five years after high school, employment also was significantly more common for young men with disabilities than for young women (64% versus 40%; p < 0.001) and for white youths than for African-American or Hispanic youths (61% versus 47% and 50%, respectively; p < 0.05).

Labor force participation did not necessarily translate into financial independence for youths with disabilities. The median hourly wage for working youths with disabilities was $5.72 three to five years after high school (1990), and only 40% of working youths with disabilities were earning more than $6.00 per hour. Wage levels were similar for most categories of youths except those with mental retardation or orthopedic im-

Figure 3

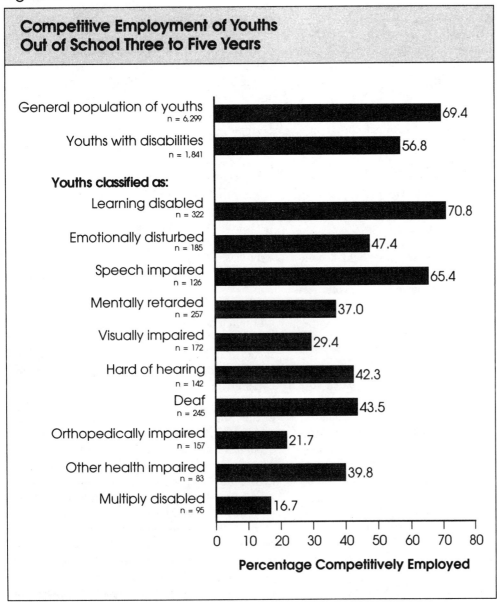

Competitive Employment of Youths Out of School Three to Five Years

General population of youths — n = 6,299 — 69.4
Youths with disabilities — n = 1,841 — 56.8

Youths classified as:

Learning disabled — n = 322 — 70.8
Emotionally disturbed — n = 185 — 47.4
Speech impaired — n = 126 — 65.4
Mentally retarded — n = 257 — 37.0
Visually impaired — n = 172 — 29.4
Hard of hearing — n = 142 — 42.3
Deaf — n = 245 — 43.5
Orthopedically impaired — n = 157 — 21.7
Other health impaired — n = 83 — 39.8
Multiply disabled — n = 95 — 16.7

Percentage axis: 0 10 20 30 40 50 60 70 80

Percentage Competitively Employed

Source: Wagner, M., D'Amico, R., Marder, C., et al. *What happens next? Trends in postschool outcomes of youth with disabilities. The second comprehensive report from the National Longitudinal Transition Study of Special Education Students.* Menlo Park, CA: SRI International, 1992.

pairments, among whom only 13% and 14%, respectively, were earning more than $6.00 per hour when they had been out of school three to five years. Almost twice as many young men as women with disabilities were earning more than $6.00 per hour (44% versus 23%; $p < 0.05$), and more than three times as many white working youths as African-American youths were earning that much (46% versus 14%; $p < 0.001$). Although graduates were significantly more likely than dropouts to have found jobs, they were not significantly more likely to be earning more than $6.00 per hour (42% versus 38%).

What Hurts? What Helps?

The previous sections have described the postsecondary education and employment outcomes of young people with disabilities. But describing outcomes is only the first step to understanding how public policy, educational programs, and related services can be used more effectively to help young people improve those outcomes. To go further, it is necessary to know what experiences in school helped students achieve their goals after leaving school. And it is necessary to know whether some school programs or experiences benefitted particular kinds of students most. In addressing these questions, the following aspects of postschool outcomes are examined:

■ Postsecondary education participation

1. Enrollment in an academic program—whether at any time since the youth left high school he or she had been enrolled in a four-year college or in a two-year college program, which the parent or youth described as primarily academic.

2. Enrollment in a vocational program—whether at any time since the youth left high school he or she had been enrolled in a postsecondary vocational school (public or private) or in a two-year college program, which the parent or youth described as primarily vocational.

■ Employment

1. Whether the youth currently held a competitive job outside the home for which he or she was paid (sheltered, supported, and volunteer work were not included as competitive paid employment).

2. An estimate of the annual total compensation youths received for their work.[24]

These postschool outcomes were related to a variety of aspects of the school programs and experiences of youths while they were in secondary school, as identified through multivariate statistical analyses, described below. The sample of youths (about 1,200) included in these analyses had been out of high school up to three years.

NLTS findings confirm that students from low-income households experienced poorer postschool outcomes than students with disabilities from higher-income households.

Many aspects of the secondary school experiences of young people with disabilities are closely related to the nature and severity of their disability. For example, placement in regular education classrooms is more common for less severely impaired youths than for those with multiple disabilities. Other characteristics of youths also are interrelated, such as the close connection between a student coming from a poor family and attending a school with a large proportion of students from low-income households. These interrelationships make it difficult to disentangle the inde-

pendent relationships of school factors from postschool outcomes. Multivariate statistical techniques often are employed for just this purpose—to identify the relationship between a particular independent variable (for example, attending a special school) and an outcome, holding constant the variety of other factors included in the analysis. The results of multivariate analyses are reported here as the difference in the estimated probability of a particular outcome (for example, being competitively employed) between youth with a particular characteristic (for example, those who took vocational education) and those who did not have that characteristic, with the values of all other variables in the analysis held at their means. Thus, the analysis in essence creates "statistical twins," allowing researchers to understand how outcomes would differ for youths who were "average" on all other factors in the analysis but differed on the school factor under consideration.

The remainder of this article reports findings on the relationship of school factors to postschool outcomes, independent of differences between them, in disability category, self-care skills, functional mental skills, gender, ethnic background, coming from a single- or two-parent household, whether the youth was a parent, and the length of time the young person had been out of secondary school.[25] Results are reported for youths with disabilities as a whole and for youths in four disability clusters, to identify whether particular high school experiences were more effective in supporting the transition of students with particular kinds of disabilities. Because considering each of the 11 disability categories separately would severely fragment the sample for these analyses, youths have been combined into broader groupings. The "mild" disability cluster incudes youths with learning, speech, and emotional disabilities and mild mental retardation. Youths with visual or hearing impairments comprise the "sensory" disability cluster, whereas the "physical" disability cluster includes youths with orthopedic or other health impairments. Deaf/blind youths and those with moderate or severe mental retardation or multiple disabilities are included in the "severe" disability cluster.

The Effects of Poverty

Considered here are the relationships to postschool outcomes of two aspects of poverty: attending a high-poverty school and individual household income.

Attending schools with relatively larger proportions of low-income students made no signifi-

Table 1

	All Youths with Disabilities	Type of Disability[b]			
Estimated Difference in Postschool Outcomes Associated with Household Income[a]					
		Mild	**Sensory**	**Physical**	**Severe**
Comparing youths from households with incomes of less than $12,000 with those from households with incomes of $38,000 to $50,000, the estimated difference in					
The percentage enrolled in post-secondary academic programs	-9.3[c]	-7.4[d]	-13.1[e]	-11.6	-5.0
The percentage enrolled in post-secondary vocational programs	-5.3	-3.4	-5.0	-1.5	-2.0
The percentage competitively employed	-2.9	-0.2	-3.3	-13.4	-13.1
The total dollar compensation earned from employment	-$760[d]	-$1,144[d]	-$379	-$1,103	-$1,548[e]

[a] Income is the annual household income for 1986.

[b] The "mild" disability cluster includes youths with learning, speech, and emotional disabilities and mild mental retardation. Youths with visual or hearing impairments comprise the "sensory" disability cluster, whereas the "physical" disability cluster includes youths with orthopedic or other health impairments. Deaf/blind youths and those with moderate or severe mental retardation or multiple disabilities are included in the "severe" disability cluster.

[c] $p < 0.001$

[d] $p < 0.05$

[e] $p < 0.01$

Note: Negative numbers on the chart indicate that students from low-income households were less likely to be enrolled or employed than were their wealthier peers.

Source: Wagner, M., Blackorby, J., Cameto, R., and Newman, L. *What makes a difference? Influences on postschool outcomes of youth with disabilities. The third comprehensive report from the National Longitudinal Transition Study of Special Education Students.* Menlo Park, CA: SRI International, 1993.

cant additional difference in postschool outcomes for students at those schools, independent of the poverty levels and other characteristics of the individual students themselves. However, household income is strongly associated with how youths from those households fare in their early postschool years.

NLTS findings confirm that students from low-income households experienced poorer postschool outcomes than students with disabilities from higher-income households, as shown in Table 1. Youths with disabilities from low-income households were significantly less likely to attend postsecondary education programs, particularly academic programs, independent of other factors, confirming a relationship also apparent for youths in the general population.[26] These relationships are consistent in direction across all disability groups and statistically significant for youths with mild or sensory impairments. Thus, students from low-income households were less likely than their wealthier peers to have access to the advanced education and training that could enable them to break out of the poverty of their childhood.

Controlling for other factors, economically disadvantaged youths were not significantly less

Michael Rosenfeld/Tony Stone Images

ther education after high school and because enrollment in such courses was indicative of a relatively high level of cognitive functioning on the part of the students enrolled in them. The relationship between academic, high school course taking and postsecondary school enrollment was strongest for youths with mild and physical disabilities; those taking advanced, high school academic classes were 27 and 26 percentage points ($p < 0.001$ and 0.05) more likely to enroll in postsecondary academic programs, respectively, than those with similar disabilities who did not take advanced academic courses in high school. A weaker relationship is noted for youths with sensory impairments (a 19-percentage-point difference, $p < 0.001$), and the relationship for youths with severe disabilities was not statistically significant (9 percentage points).

Consistent with the contribution of advanced course work to later enrollment in academic programs, youths who had college preparatory programs in high school were somewhat less likely than others to enroll in postsecondary vocational programs (9 percentage points), and significantly so for youths with physical disabilities (19 percentage points, $p < 0.05$). The level of academic preparation in high school was unrelated to either of the employment measures. Perhaps in their early postschool years, students with disabilities were not getting the kinds of jobs for which advanced course work was necessary or beneficial. Alternatively, youths who had taken advanced high school courses might still have been in college and, therefore, not yet experiencing employment effects of their earlier course taking.

Vocational Course Taking

The intention of vocational education is to benefit youths both in finding postschool employment and in the wages they earn. Table 2 shows that there were strong positive contributions of both survey and concentrated vocational training to the probability of competitive employment (20- and 19-percentage-point-high probabilities for vocational students). Although both concentrating on vocational courses and taking unrelated survey courses contributed to higher employment rates in this analysis, additional NLTS analyses suggest that employment gains grew over time for youths taking a concentration of courses, whereas the employment rate was fairly stable over time for those taking unrelated survey courses, suggesting greater long-term benefits of concentrated vocational training.[23]

Further, taking a concentration of vocational classes was related to larger incomes; concentra-

likely than others to be employed, but poorer youths earned less per year than did those from wealthier families, suggesting that they may have worked in lower-quality jobs than youths with disabilities from higher-income households. Compensation gaps were largest for youths with both mild and severe impairments. These findings regarding the pervasive negative effects of family poverty are particularly disturbing in light of the growing number of children, with and without disabilities, who are growing up poor.

Enrollment in Academic Programs

Participation by students with disabilities in higher-level academic classes in high school (that is, advanced mathematics or a foreign language) related positively to enrollment in postsecondary academic programs. Among students with disabilities overall, those who took such classes in secondary school were 22 percentage points more likely to have enrolled in postsecondary academic programs than peers who did not take advanced academic courses, independent of other factors. It is likely that this relationship occurred both because those courses often were required for fur-

tors were estimated to earn $1,851 more than other students. Again, wage gaps increased over time in favor of those taking a concentration of vocational education.[23] These postschool benefits of concentrated vocational education are an encore to the positive outcomes associated with such training while students were still in secondary school.[5]

The largest benefits for both kinds of vocational course taking accrued to youths with mild disabilities, as expected, among whom vocational students had a probability of competitive employment almost 40 percentage points greater than that of students without vocational experiences in secondary school, independent of other differences between them. Further, for those youths, a concentration in vocational education was especially lucrative; concentrators were estimated to earn $6,247 more annually than nonvocational or prevocational students. Youths who took survey vocational courses also earned more—nearly $4,000 per year—than peers who took none. No statistically significant benefits of vocational training were identified for youths with severe disabilities or for youths with sensory disabilities.

Vocational education experiences were unrelated to postsecondary vocational education for all groups (not included in the table) and to postsecondary academic enrollment for youths as a whole. However, some differences in the relationship to academic education were observed for youths with different types of disability. For example, for youths with physical disabilities, taking either a concentration of vocational courses or participating in a work experience program was related to a significantly lower likelihood of pursuing postsecondary academic training, presumably because of greater emphasis on employment.

Contrary to expectations, Table 2 shows that, when other variables were included in the analyses, work experience did not make a significant added contribution to any outcomes for youths with disabilities as a group. It is likely that the skills and foci of work experience programs and vocational education in general were similar and that the two factors became confounded when youths with disabilities were considered overall. However, work experience was positively and significantly associated with employment for youths with physical impairments and, to a lesser extent, those with mild disabilities.

Placement in Special or Regular Education Classes

The NLTS examined the relationships to postschool outcomes of two aspects of high school placement: whether youths attended special schools that served only students with disabilities and the percentage of class time students spent in regular education classes.

Overall, 8% of secondary school students with disabilities attended special schools, ranging from only a few percent of students with learning disabilities to about two-thirds of those who were deaf. The educational experiences of students in special schools clearly differed markedly from those of their peers in regular schools.[27] However, these differences did not manifest themselves in differences in postschool outcomes. The NLTS has found little relationship between postschool outcomes and attending special schools. Even for youths in the sensory disability categories who were most likely to do so, attending special school seems to have conferred no particular advantage.

No benefits of regular education placements occurred for youths whose disabilities involved explicit learning problems or cognitive deficits.

However, controlling for other differences between youths, more time spent in general education classrooms was positively related to employment (see Table 3). For example, youths who spent all of their school day during secondary school in regular education settings were 11 percentage points more likely than their peers, who spent half of their time there, to be competitively employed and were estimated to have higher earnings ($2,095). However, these employment advantages accrued only to youths with sensory or physical disabilities, not to the largest group of youths, those with mild impairments, or to severely impaired youths. This difference in impacts supports the notion that regular education benefits youths cognitively equipped to absorb regular high school course work as it is presented in regular education classes. No benefits of regular education placements occurred for youths whose disabilities involved explicit learning problems or cognitive deficits.

Time spent in regular education also was associated with a greater likelihood of post-secondary vocational enrollment for youths with mild disabilities (10 percentage points).

Table 2

Estimated Difference in Postschool Outcomes Associated with High School Vocational Education and Work Experience Programs				
	All Youths with Disabilities	Type of Disability[a]		
		Mild	Sensory	Physical[b]
Comparing youths who completed vocational education **survey courses** in high school with nonvocational or prevocational[c] students, the estimated difference in				
The percentage enrolled in post-secondary academic programs	10.3	3.6	2.3	—
The percentage competitively employed	19.8[d]	35.6[e]	16.6	—
The total dollar compensation earned from unemployment	$1,097	$3,993[d]	$1,021	—
Comparing youths who **concentrated in vocational education**[f] in high school with nonvocational or prevocational[c] students, the estimated difference in				
The percentage enrolled in post-secondary academic programs	2.0	-5.7	-2.6	-28.6[d]
The percentage competitively employed	19.0[d]	39.9[g]	15.3	-5.3
The total dollar compensation earned from unemployment	$1,851	$6,247[g]	$1,071	$2,009[d]
Comparing youths who had taken a high school **work experience program** with those who had not, the estimated difference in				
The percentage enrolled in post-secondary academic programs	-9.3[d]	-7.3	1.0	30.9[d]
The percentage competitively employed	-2.0	10.4	-11.3	32.6[d]
The total dollar compensation earned from unemployment	$542	$1,379	-$697	$4,196[g]

[a] There were no consistent or significant relationships between vocational education experiences and postschool outcomes for youths with severe disabilities; they are included in "all youths," but relationships are not reported for them separately.

[b] The distribution of the vocational education variables for the physical disability cluster did not allow the inclusion of both variables. Thus, for this cluster, models included only concentration in vocational education.

[c] Prevocational courses covered a significantly different curriculum from standard vocational education courses and so were considered separately.

[d] $p < 0.05$

[e] $p < 0.01$

[f] A concentration is at least four semesters of vocational education in the same content area (for example, trade and industry, office occupations).

[g] $p < 0.001$

Source: Wagner, M., Blackorby, J., Cameto, R., and Newman, L. *What makes a difference? Influences on postschool outcomes of youth with disabilities. The third comprehensive report from the National Longitudinal Transition Study of Special Education Students.* Menlo Park, CA: SRI International, 1993.

Table 3

Estimated Difference in Postschool Outcomes Associated with the Amount of Time Spent in Regular Education Classes				
	All Youths with Disabilities	**Type of Disability**[a]		
		Mild[a]	**Sensory**	**Physical**
Comparing youths who spent all of their class time in regular education classes with those who spent half of their time there, the estimated difference in				
The percentage enrolled in postsecondary academic programs	3.2	10.4[b]	-4.0	15.0
The percentage competitively employed	11.2[b]	1.9	15.0[c]	43.2[b]
The total dollar compensation earned from unemployment	$2,095[d]	$683	$1,550[b]	$1,664[c]

[a] There were no consistent or significant relationships between regular education placement and postschool outcomes for youths with severe disabilities; they are included in "all youths," but relationships are not reported for them separately.

[b] $p < 0.01$

[c] $p < 0.05$

[d] $p < 0.001$

Source: Wagner, M., Blackorby, J., Cameto, R., and Newman, L. *What makes a difference? Influences on postschool outcomes of youth with disabilities. The third comprehensive report from the National Longitudinal Transition Study of Special Education Students.* Menlo Park, CA: SRI International, 1993.

Two caveats must be offered in interpreting these findings. First, one should not interpret these relationships as implying that regular education necessarily caused improvements in outcomes. Rather, it is possible that disabled youths who spent all of their time in regular education were more competent in ways not measured by the NLTS and that these differences contributed to their positive outcomes.

Second, these analyses reflect in large measure the experiences of youths who had succeeded sufficiently in regular education classrooms to graduate from high school. But many students did not do well enough in regular education classes to graduate. Findings from other NLTS research showed that spending more time in regular education was associated with a higher likelihood of course failure, which in turn contributed greatly to a higher likelihood of students' dropping out of school.[5] Those who did not succeed in regular education settings and dropped out experienced negative postschool outcomes, as described below. Thus, regular education appears to confer advantages on those who suc-

ceed in it and graduate, but the negative effects of dropping out dominate the experiences of those who do not succeed in regular education settings.

Successful Completion of Secondary School

Dropouts with disabilities had consistently poorer postschool outcomes than did their peers who persisted in school, independent of other differences between them. Dropouts were less likely to enroll in postsecondary vocational programs (a 14-percentage-point difference compared with nondropouts) and academic programs (a 12-percentage-point difference), particularly among youths with mild disabilities, those most likely to have dropped out (a 14-percentage-point difference). A pattern of negative, though weak, relationships was found between dropping out of secondary school and employment outcomes for youths with disabilities as a group when other factors in the analyses were controlled. These findings underscore for students with dis-

Regular education academic courses are difficult for many students with disabilities, and when they fail there, students are more likely to drop out of school.

abilities the importance of successfully completing secondary school as a platform for success in adulthood.

Summary

These analyses from the NLTS document the early postschool outcomes that were achieved by young people with disabilities who had gone through secondary school in the mid to late 1980s. The secondary school programs they experienced influenced, sometimes considerably, some of their later outcomes. What schools do can make a difference in what students later achieve.

Yet a variety of school reform policies may be inconsistent with findings regarding what helps students with disabilities achieve more positive postschool outcomes. For example, raising academic course requirements for graduation might encourage students to take more advanced academic courses, and data show benefits are associated with this kind of course taking for some students in terms of supporting their enrollment in postsecondary education programs. However, policies that foster academic course taking may leave little room in students' schedules for the vocational courses that are more attuned to the employment goals of a majority of students with disabilities. Vocational courses were strongly related to lower probabilities that students would drop out of school and, independent of school completion, also were strongly related to positive employment outcomes. Can course-taking policies be developed that permit flexibility in course choices rather than forcing students with disabilities to trade off the potential benefits of academic versus vocational courses?

Further, any courses, whether academic or vocational, only benefit those who can succeed in them. A consistent message of NLTS findings is that regular education academic courses are difficult for many students with disabilities, and when they fail there, students are more likely to drop out of school.[5] Findings presented here confirm the negative postschool path taken by many students with disabilities who dropped out of school. Perhaps the greatest positive contribution schools can make to the postschool success of students with disabilities is to contribute to the in-school success of those students, regardless of the placement of their courses. As the inclusion movement gains momentum, great care must be paid to issues of quality and support. Placement in regular education offers little postschool benefit to students who cannot succeed in these courses.

Finally, NLTS analyses of contributions to outcomes for students with different kinds of disabilities confirm that there is no "magic bullet" that offers benefits to all students. Vocational education appears to have benefitted students with mild disabilities but not those with sensory impairments. Academic course taking benefitted those with sensory impairments but not those with severe disabilities. Regular education placement appears to have advantages in some outcome areas for students with physical disabilities but to be less helpful to those with either mild or severe disabilities. In shaping policy and programs for students with disabilities, a range of options, tailored to the individual needs of students, continues to be the most effective approach to meeting the wide range of needs, preferences, and abilities of students who participate in special education. No principle that is held to be appropriate for all students, with or without disabilities, is likely to succeed in helping all students meet their needs. A diversity of students requires a diversity of program choices if students are to benefit from their educations and make a successful transition to adulthood.

1. Mithaug, D.E., and Horiuchi, C.N. *Colorado statewide follow-up survey of special education students.* Denver: Colorado Department of Education, 1983.
2. Hasazi, S.B., Gordon, L.R., and Roe, C.A. Factors associated with the employment status of handicapped youth exiting high school from 1979–1983. *Exceptional Children* (1985) 51: 455–69.
3. Edgar, E., Levine, P., and Maddox, M. *Washington state follow-up data of former secondary special education students.* Seattle: University of Washington, 1985.
4. Wagner, M., ed. *The secondary school programs of students with disabilities. A report from the National Longitudinal Transition Study of Special Education Students.* Menlo Park, CA: SRI International, 1993.
5. Wagner, M., Blackorby, J., and Hebbeler, K. *Beyond the report card: The multiple dimensions of secondary school performance of students with disabilities. A report from the National Longitudinal Transition Study of Special Education Students.* Menlo Park, CA: SRI International, 1993.
6. Wagner, M., D'Amico, R., Marder, C., et al. *What happens next? Trends in postschool outcomes of youth with disabilities. The second comprehensive report from the National Longitudinal Transition Study of Special Education Students.* Menlo Park, CA: SRI International, 1992.

7. Javitz, H., and Wagner, M. *The National Longitudinal Transition Study of Special Education Students: Report on sample design and limitations, wave 1 (1987)*. Menlo Park, CA: SRI International, 1990.

8. Javitz, H., and Wagner, M. *The National Longitudinal Transition Study of Special Education Students: Sample characteristics and procedures, wave 2 (1990)*. Menlo Park, CA: SRI International, 1993.

9. Wagner, M., Newman, L., and Shaver, D. *The National Longitudinal Transition Study of Special Education Students: Report on procedures for the first wave of data collection (1987)*. Menlo Park, CA: SRI International, 1989.

10. Marder, C., Habina, K., and Prince, N. *The National Longitudinal Transition Study of Special Education Students: Report on procedures for the second wave of data collection (1990)*. Menlo Park, CA: SRI International, 1992.

11. Postschool goals were reported in written questionnaires completed by teachers of 12th-grade students with disabilities who were familiar with the students' school programs and transition plans.

12. Cameto, R. Support services provided by secondary schools. In *The secondary school programs of students with disabilities. A report from the National Longitudinal Transition Study of Special Education Students*. M. Wagner, ed. Menlo Park, CA: SRI International, 1993.

13. Supported employment often involves working in competitive jobs but with the wages earned being subsidized by public funds to provide an incentive to employers to hire persons with disabilities. Those in supported employment also may receive support services such as job training or supervision or advocacy from an employment "coach" or counselor. Sheltered employment is work in settings in which most or all other workers have disabilities; wages are generally below those earned in competitive jobs.

14. Hayward, B.J., and Thorne, J. *The educational programs of high school special education students*. Research Triangle Park, NC: Research Triangle Institute, 1990.

15. Hebbeler, K. Overview of the high school experiences of students with disabilities. In *The secondary school programs of students with disabilities. A report from the National Longitudinal Transition Study of Special Education Students*. M. Wagner, ed. Menlo Park, CA: SRI International, 1993.

16. Newman, L. Academic course-taking. In *The secondary school programs for students with disabilities. A report from the National Longitudinal Transition Study of Special Education Students*. M. Wagner, ed. Menlo Park, CA: SRI International, 1993.

17. Blackorby, J., Participation in vocational education by students with disabilities. In *The secondary school programs of students with disabilities. A report from the National Longitudinal Transition Study of Special Education Students*. M. Wagner, ed. Menlo Park, CA: SRI International, 1993.

18. Unlike students in the general population, who either graduate or drop out, students with disabilities have those two school-leaving options, as well as being able to "age out," that is, stay in high school until the maximum age allowed (usually 21 years) without earning the credits to graduate.

19. Wagner, M., D'Amico, R., Marder, C., et al. *What happens next? Trends in postschool outcomes of youth with disabilities. The second comprehensive report from the National Longitudinal Transition Study of Special Education Students*. Menlo Park, CA: SRI International, 1992.

20. Gardner, J. A. *Transition from high school to postsecondary education: Analytical studies*. Washington, DC: Center for Education Statistics, 1987.

21. Marder, C. Education after secondary school. In *What happens next? Trends in postschool outcomes of youth with disabilities. The second comprehensive report from the National Longitudinal Transition Study of Special Education Students*. M. Wagner, R. D'Amico, C. Marder, et al. Menlo Park, CA: SRI International, 1992.

22. Marder, C., and Cox, R. More than a label: Characteristics of youth with disabilities. In *Youth with disabilities: How are they doing? The first comprehensive report from the National Longitudinal Transition Study of Special Education Students*. M. Wagner, L. Newman, R. D'Amico, et al. Menlo Park, CA: SRI International. 1991.

23. D'Amico, R. The working world awaits: Employment experiences during and shortly after secondary school. In *Youth with disabilities: How are they doing? The first comprehensive report from the National Longitudinal Transition Study of Special Education Students*. M. Wagner, L. Newman, R. D'Amico, et al. Menlo Park, CA: SRI International. 1991.

24. In calculating an estimate of total compensation, unemployed youths were considered to receive no compensation. Estimates for paid workers involved multiplying the reported hours typically worked per week by the reported hourly wage; a typical work year was assumed to involve 49 work weeks for those who did not receive paid sick leave or vacation. For workers who received paid sick leave and vacation, the work year, for purposes of calculating total compensation, was assumed to include 52 paid weeks. Medical insurance received as an employment benefit was valued at 6.1% of wages, as commonly calculated by the U.S. Bureau of the Census. *Statistical abstract of the United States*. 110th ed. Washington, DC: U.S. Department of Commerce, Bureau of the Census, 1990.

25. Wagner, M., Blackorby, J., Cameto, R., and Newman, L. *What makes a difference? Influences on postschool outcomes of youth with disabilities. The third comprehensive report from the National Longitudinal Transition Study of Special Education Students*. Menlo Park, CA: SRI International. 1993.

26. Stage, F.K., and Hossler, D. Differences in family influences on college attendance plans for male and female ninth graders. *Research in Higher Education* (1989) 30: 301–14.

27. Wagner, M. Secondary school programs. In *Youth with disabilities: How are they doing? The first comprehensive report from the National Longitudinal Transition Study of Special Education Students*. M. Wagner, L. Newman, R. D'Amico, et al., eds. Menlo Park, CA: SRI International, 1991.

School-to-Work

A Model for Learning a Living

BY MICHAEL HARTOONIAN AND RICHARD VAN SCOTTER

Individuals embark on the path toward learning (a living) by embracing active scholarship, citizenship, and artisanship—all three together. We cannot distinguish where one characteristic ends and another begins, Messrs. Hartoonian and Van Scotter maintain.

I know of no safe depository of the ultimate powers of the society but with the people themselves; and if we think them not enlightened enough to exercise their control with a wholesome discretion, the remedy is not to take power from the people, but to inform their discretion through instruction.
—*Thomas Jefferson*[1]

THE FUNDAMENTAL purpose of education in any society is to maintain the cultural heritage and to improve both society and the individual. Thus the nature of schooling and the form it takes are defined within the context of a particular society. In the United States education serves to promote the interrelated goals of self-development, citizenship, and employment.

The Role of Education In a Democratic Republic

Our democratic republic is built on the idea of "enlightened citizens." Such individuals are aware of their cultural heritage and possess a working knowl-

MICHAEL HARTOONIAN is a professor of education and liberal studies in the Graduate School, Hamline University, St. Paul, Minn. RICHARD VAN SCOTTER is vice president of education policy, marketing, and evaluation with Junior Achievement, Colorado Springs, Colo.

edge of the economic, political, and social conditions that make up our human ecosystem. For example, they understand the concepts of the basic rule of law, legal limits to freedom, and majority rule with minority rights. They also realize that, in addition to being a legal document, the U.S. Constitution serves as a symbol of the story of America that provides its citizens with meaning and a moral light. They themselves display, and expect in others, such characteristics as fairness, cooperation, integrity, responsibility, and the performance of high-quality work.

Without a conscious effort by society to teach and learn these cultural and civic virtues, a democratic capitalistic republic will not long endure. Thus this nation's first priority and public policy goal must be to ensure our republic's survival as a free nation by developing in the minds and hearts of its students the qualities of good scholars, citizens, and workers.

Education's Response To Global Markets

The dynamics of economic cycles affect virtually every aspect of society, and education is no exception. Similarly, the U.S. domestic economy is embedded within the tides and currents of the global economic ocean. In fact, to speak of a domestic economy today is outmoded. Economic activity is essentially global; we all inhabit one economic world. As a result, education must address both broader and higher standards.

As global markets ebb and flow, business and government leaders have applied pressure to American schools to help maintain and expand the international economic competitiveness of the U.S. This relationship between markets and education is a theme that dates back more than 100 years, to the time when the United States became a minor and then a major player in the global economic network. In the closing decades of the 19th century, authorities criticized schools as the United States continued to lose market share to the Germans in the machine tool industry. Then, in the 1930s, educators were told that, if schools had better educated students for employment, we might have avoided the Great Depression. Needless to say, reasonable and discerning observers understood that government policy and corporate practices had much more to do with these economic conditions than did school curriculum.

With the end of World War II and the beginning of the Cold War, critics led by Vice Admiral Hyman Rickover demanded that schools help keep the U.S. militarily ahead of the Soviet Union. Rickover argued that "education is even more important than atomic power in the Navy."[2] Rickover blamed professional educators for creating an anti-intellectual atmosphere in schools and claimed that schools were the weakest link in America's overall defense strategy. When the Soviets put Sputnik I into space in 1957, a shocked nation, influenced largely by business and government officials, demanded that schools develop stronger science and mathematics programs. In the late 1950s and early 1960s educators embarked on, and the public endorsed, major curriculum reform efforts, believing that the nation's schools were using outdated learning materials. And in the wake of the economic recession of the late 1950s, assessment of schooling was linked to the performance of the economy.

In the early 1970s another recession, fueled by the oil embargo of 1973, ushered in a call for "back to basics." Again, this simplistic reaction to a complex economic issue failed to address the essential philosophical principles that underlie our democratic capitalist system and failed to acknowledge the merits of citizenship, scholarship, and artisanship.

A decade later, coinciding with another recession and stiff competition in global markets, particularly from the Japanese, the National Commission on Excellence in Education issued *A Nation at Risk,* a report that brutally detailed the poor quality of American schools.[3] The influence of business leaders and their education agendas since then testifies to the continued strength of the belief in the link between schools and the economy. Yet the purposes of education in America have always been much broader than preparing efficient workers and serving the goal of economic competitiveness—as important as these objectives are. In fact, we can't nurture a high-quality work force in the absence of informed, responsible, and ethical citizens.

Our nation benefits immensely from the legacy of Thomas Jefferson and from that of Adam Smith, who gave us the simple yet profound precept that free markets cannot function unless they are grounded in ethics.[4] And most of the reports on school reform in recent years, including *A Nation at Risk,* acknowledge the broader purposes of schooling. As the members of the National Commission on Excellence in Education wrote, "Our concern . . . goes well beyond matters such as industry and commerce. It also includes the intellectual, moral, and spiritual strengths of our people which knit together the very fabric of our society."[5] However, this type of message receives little attention from the media. As a result, the public—including many educators—is reluctant to build school programs around the intellectual, moral, and spiritual strengths of our traditions, opting instead for the quick fix of skills training.

School-to-Work Issues

As an organization, agency, or school system explores the challenge of developing a new secondary program grounded in school-to-work opportunities, it will need to address underlying cultural issues. In addition, any sound school-to-work model must create smooth pathways from learning in schools to learning in the workplace.

But any school-to-work effort, despite good intentions and hard work, will be disappointing if participants take what communications and media expert Neil Postman calls "a rearview mirror" approach to reform. Fundamental change in schools, classrooms, and students won't occur if we drive into the 21st century looking into the rearview mirror—attempting to do what apparently worked a decade or even a generation ago.

First, we need to recognize that the school can be a place both where students learn and where they carry on productive work. In turn, the workplace ought not to be just a business where people develop products, provide services, and collect a paycheck, but one in which they continuously learn, grow, and create. Such environments would be fertile ground for genuine school-based learning and work-based learning, two educational components that are called for in the School-to-Work Opportunities Act of 1994.

This is the message that management reformers such as Peter Senge and the late W. Edwards Deming (father of Total Quality Management) have persuasively put forward in recent years. To use Senge's language, the healthy, productive business or school is a "learning organization." Likewise, Theodore Sizer, founder of the Coalition of Essential Schools, proposes an engaging, productive learning environment that features students as workers and teachers as coaches.

Second, we must be aware that preparing young people for the workplace is like "shooting at a moving target." By this we mean that concentrating just on job skills and career opportunities will leave us off the mark 20, 10, or even five years from now. Willard Daggett, director of the International Center for Leadership in Education, points out, "As the waves of technological change break faster and faster, the technologies we teach today may be outdated by the time students graduate. Furthermore, using technology to do a better job of teaching the old curriculum misses the point of first addressing whether that curriculum is still appropriate."[6]

Next, our culture emphasizes what we possess and what we do. It falls short in building character, in helping people to understand who they are. Good school-based learning and good work-based learning both can help us to develop this third dimension, thereby fostering the growth of psychologically healthy workers and people, enriching the learning place, and enhancing our lives.

John Gardner explained, "A society that scorns excellence in plumbing because it is a humble activity and tolerates mediocrity in philosophy because it is an exalted activity will have both bad plumbing and [bad] philosophy. Neither its pipes nor [its] theories will hold water."

Finally, it is dangerous and disingenuous for schools to promise high-paying jobs to young people. We corrupt students when we use extrinsic motivation. Furthermore, neither the U.S. nor any industrialized nation can promise high-paying, high-skilled jobs to all its able workers. It should surprise no one that an increasingly service-oriented U.S. economy requires people with a range of job skills and includes a significant proportion of humble, low-paying jobs.

As researchers at the Sandia National Laboratories found, U.S. schools are supplying future workers whose levels of schooling are strikingly consistent with the requirements of employers. "The education system," they report, "turns out in today's youth roughly 26% as college graduates, an additional 60% with 12 to 15 years of schooling, and the final 14% with less than a high school diploma."[7] The researchers add that these percentages correlate with the findings in both the Hudson Institute's report on near-term work-force requirements, *Workforce 2000,* and the report by the Commission on the Skills of the American Workforce, *America's Choice: High Skills or Low Wages!*

The culture we inhabit plays a powerful role in fostering an egocentric, narcissistic, materialistic, and individualistic vision rather than a common one. And schools collaborate in this spurious mission when they stress such things as normative grading, standardized tests, college tracks, and an assortment of honors. But without a common vision, we are not likely to have a healthy community. The purpose of schooling is not to help people to be *better off,* but to be *better*—better scholars, citizens, and workers.

A New School-to-Work Model

People in the work force and those preparing to enter the work force will require three distinct but interrelated attributes or qualities: scholarship, citizenship, and artisanship. This triad serves as a model to prepare a productive and enlightened work force and could guide the development of school-to-work programs.

Scholarship. This characteristic involves learning by doing and the ability to apply knowledge. Proponents of school-to-work plans, particularly those in industry, stress that students need to be prepared with essential academic, problem-solving, and interpersonal skills for the "Age of Electronic Communications." (Curiously, some policy makers refer to the high-tech era of instant communications as the "Information Age." This is misleading. The Information Age began when the printing press was invented in the 15th century.)

As an example of the kinds of skills being sought by industry, the BellSouth Corporation's definition of core academic skills includes the ability to

- understand and interpret written information;
- locate data to answer questions;
- apply mathematical methods to multistep problems;
- listen to, interpret, and respond to verbal messages; and
- organize ideas and speak in a concise, accurate manner.[8]

No doubt, the most fundamental core academic skill is the ability to communicate thoughts, information, and opinions in writing, using clear, concise style and sound grammar. The late Ernest Boyer expressed this idea nicely when he said, "Clear writing leads to clear thinking; clear thinking is the basis for clear writing. Perhaps more than any other form of communication, writing holds us responsible for our words and makes us more thoughtful human beings."[9]

In turn, problem-solving skills include the ability to

- organize and plan multiple tasks;
- generate new ideas, display imagination, and apply ideas to new situations;
- make decisions that account for obstacles and choose among best alternatives; and
- analyze problems and devise plans of action.[10]

In effect, this means that students should be able to think, write, and communicate with the clarity, conciseness, variety, complexity, and richness that are appropriate for high-quality work. Likewise, students should develop habits of mind that include curiosity, speculation, thoughtfulness, and imagination. Unfortunately, as Sizer notes, most students, including many so-called high achievers, fall short. "Many are lively, well-intentioned, and adept at cranking out acceptable test scores," he explains, "but

they are without habits of serious thought, respectful skepticism, and curiosity about much of what lies beyond their immediate lives."[11]

In the ideal environment, learning becomes a shared responsibility between teacher and student. Rather than serve as providers of information, teachers stimulate and coach students, ultimately holding them responsible for their own learning. Likewise, teaching becomes a sophisticated form of learning. In the process, young people acquire skills and attitudes—including a love of learning—that will sustain lifelong learning. We are not likely to inculcate such attitudes unless students are involved in projects, simulations, role playing, demonstrations, internships, and other hands-on activities.

Citizenship. What employers desire—and our economy needs—are people who bring to the workplace a strong work ethic, characterized by dependability and perseverance. We also call for civilized and virtuous behavior. In fact, the literature from employers on school-to-work preparation increasingly stresses the importance of personal characteristics in the workplace. Behaviors that employers expect of their employees including being at work each day, on time; accepting responsibility for one's own actions and decisions; demonstrating understanding, friendliness, adaptability, and concern for others; working with minimal supervision; displaying integrity and honesty; and showing a willingness to take risks and to learn new things.[12]

In a recent survey of human resource executives in the Minneapolis-St. Paul area, conducted by Northwestern Mutual Life Insurance Company, respondents cited shortcomings in personal characteristics as the greatest deficiency that recent high school graduates bring to the workplace. New workers, they said, tend to be undependable; they lack commitment, a strong work ethic, experience in the business world, and a good attitude. In addition, cooperative behavior and teamwork are becoming increasingly important in the workplace. Business knows that students need more than knowledge and skills to contribute substantially in the workplace. They must also exhibit civility.

Alongside the intellectual skills espoused by business, most employers believe that interpersonal skills are essential for workers. Again, if the BellSouth Corporation represents the sentiments of other employers, they would have schools prepare young people to understand the needs of others (customers), to participate cooperatively as team members, to perform at high levels, to

negotiate agreements and mediate differences, and to work with others from diverse cultural backgrounds.[13] Needless to say, these specifications from employers reinforce the efforts many schools are making to implement such strategies as cooperative learning; the use of projects, demonstrations, and simulations; and authentic assessments.

The Sandia researchers corroborated these views in their study of skill requirements for the work force. They found from investigations by the Commission on the Skills of the American Workforce that only 5% of employers feel that education and skill requirements are increasing significantly. Likewise, only 15% of the employers surveyed said that they had difficulty finding skilled workers, and such shortages generally occur in chronically underpaid occupations. Finally, when businesses complain about workers' "skills," they are generally referring to lack of a work ethic and poor social skills.[14]

Ours is a political economy in which civic virtues, economic behavior, and government policy are intertwined. A recent National Youth Survey conducted by the Gallup Organization for Junior Achievement revealed that young people have little confidence in most U.S. institutions. While secondary school students indicated modest confidence in religious institutions and public schools, they appeared soundly disenchanted with big business, the media, and the federal government.[15] No doubt, their views reflect those of the general public. As Robert Bellah and his associates explain, "Individualistic Americans fear that institutions impinge on their freedom. . . . Yet, if this is our only conception of institutions, we have a very impoverished idea of our common life."[16]

Artisanship. Producing high-quality goods and services requires that everyone take immense pride in being a craftsperson or artisan, regardless of one's trade or profession. Artisanship, both in school and on the job, taps a person's gifts and talents, reveals what one is very good at, commands deep involvement in and respect for work, and gives one's work meaning. With opportunities to do high-quality work, learning and working become inseparable.

Craftsmanship was the basis of the tech schools that every major U.S. city established in the early 1990s. The emphasis these schools placed on "learning by doing" paralleled the practices of such educational organizations as Junior Achievement, which initiated its Company Program in 1919. Through study and work, students in these schools and programs practiced a craft and learned much about themselves.

Within the past two decades Junior Achievement has been at the vanguard of developing K–12 school programs that involve students in hands-on learning.

When Vince Lombardi, the legendary football coach, was asked what distinguished his Green Bay Packers from other teams, he replied, "Love." His players, he elaborated, had a deep love for one another and for their craft. As Coach Lombardi explained, the Packers never lost a game, they just ran out of time on a few occasions, and they always performed to the best of their ability.

Not surprisingly, young people today do not appear to be learning that the route to fulfillment and happiness is paved with moderation and meaningful work. Instead, distracted by the abundance pervasively displayed in society, they place importance on acquiring material goods and prestige. The Junior Achievement-Gallup youth survey revealed that most young people expect to have a professional or managerial career; fewer than 10% say that their chosen vocation will be in the services or skilled crafts. Virtually all those surveyed (99%) expect to be "as well off" as or "better off" than their parents. The other 1% "don't know." Likewise, young people view higher education as the key to professional and financial rewards—82% plan to enter a college or university. Only small numbers of those surveyed desire to enter work training (4%), seek a job immediately (6%), or enter the armed forces (4%). In reality, closer to 50% of U.S. high school graduates will attend college, with approximately one-half of those students eventually receiving a bachelor's degree.[17]

From another perspective, this optimism and naiveté suggest that young people are crying out to be prepared for what many of them view as a mysterious world of work. Increasingly over the past generation, this work has taken place in large private and governmental organizations operating within the steel-and-glass towers of the urban skylines.

As school programs and curricula incorporate characteristics of this scholarship/citizenship/artisanship triad, we have the opportunity to demystify the modern corporate environment. In turn, the school would come to look and feel much like a creative, productive, humming, and learning workplace. Likewise, a healthy workplace can look much like a school—a good school. In short, this is a schoolplace-to-workplace model in which students develop not only worthy habits of mind and of hand but also habits of the heart.

Implications for School-to-Work Programs

The pedagogical ideas underlying the "School-to-Work: Learning a Living" model and embodied in the scholarship/citizenship/artisanship triad can lead to a variety of program components suitable for the sciences, technology, English and communication, the humanities, and other curricula. Here are six components or units that might be integrated into a high school program designed to help students understand the political/economic system of the U.S. and the world of business:

- studying the history of the political and economic thought of democratic capitalism,
- exploring democratic and ethical behavior in business by interviewing corporate CEOs,
- evaluating personal characteristics and career opportunities,
- looking at economic trends and policy making,
- examining philosophical issues related to politics and the economy, and
- acquiring firsthand knowledge of businesses through internships and mentorships.

History of political and economic thought. One unit of study in a high school program would survey ideas from political economists and intellectual statespeople who helped shape our democratic capitalist system. The roots of democratic capitalism might be traced to ancient Greece and the works of Plato and Aristotle. From there the story could move to the Middle Ages—specifically, to the 12th and 13th centuries—to tell the role that Christianity played in political and economic thought, largely through the intellectual work of St. Thomas Aquinas.

The historical trail of our democratic capitalist heritage would highlight the contributions of such "worldly philosophers" as Thomas Jefferson and Adam Smith, while illustrating the enlightened views of Robert Owen and John Stuart Mill regarding a moral economy and workplace. It could also contrast the practices of the democratic capitalist James J. Hill with those of the mercantilist Jay Gould. This path could extend to contemporary thinkers, including Milton Friedman and John Kenneth Galbraith. This historical unit would be designed to reveal fundamental principles that have come to define the U.S. economy today. In addition it would provide a valuable background to the issues that the students will consider in the program's philosophical unit.

Democratic and ethical behavior. High school students being prepared for the working world would conduct interviews with current and retired CEOs of major corporations. These business leaders would be selected because of their trailblazing efforts to promote economic democracy in their firms or to set standards of ethical behavior, or both. Among the questions that might be explored during these interviews would be the following:

- Does ethical behavior enhance or erode profits, and why?
- In what ways can modern companies give workers a stronger voice in management practices and workplace policies?
- Does a firm need a mission statement that addresses democratic and ethical responsibility?
- How can employees and employers continue to learn on the job?
- In what ways does this personal growth help the company, if it does?
- What is the proper relationship between a firm and the community?

Personal characteristics and career opportunities. Students would take part in a variety of classroom activities designed to help them understand their personal learning styles, gifts, talents, and vocational strengths. Some activities would be conducted individually, but many would involve working together and sharing insights with classmates. The aim of these experiences would be to help students find their authentic selves and discover what intrinsically motivates them to display vigor in work and play. In addition, this component would help students understand the cultural forces that encourage them to be consumption-oriented, outer-directed, and distracted from engaging in that which is good for self and society.

Social and economic trend data. In this component, students would work with economic, social, and demographic data that reveal national and global trends. These analyses could help students perceive the nature of the emerging local, regional, national, and global society they are inheriting. Likewise, the data would help them have as clear a view as possible into the living, learning, and working places that lie ahead in the coming century. Students would learn how these data can be used to make personal decisions and public policy. In the process, they would examine such questions as, How should U.S. population trends be used to devise policies on immigration, economic development, workplace diversity, government spending, and taxation? And what relationship exists between national and international trends and personal decisions about careers, location of work, and living?

Philosophical issues. Informed and responsible citizens must be capable of addressing fundamental questions if we are to maintain a healthy democratic capitalist system. The following questions are examples of topics that could be discussed.

- What is the proper relationship between one's private (economic) life and one's public (civic) life?
- What is the relationship between socioeconomic status and forms of government?
- What is the relationship between the health of institutions and the well-being of citizens?
- What is the importance of embracing inclusiveness and abandoning separateness in our organizations, communities, and nation?
- What degree of responsibility does the individual have for the community, and what degree of responsibility does the community have for the individual?

Business internships and mentorships. The indifference many young people today display toward business, politics, and various economic values that older generations tend to cherish probably stems from both bewilderment and a moral inner voice. Young people seem to have acquired a conscientiousness, compassion, creativity, and idealism—fostered by a musical and visual subculture—that their elders don't appreciate. In turn, the world of large organizations and institutions that adults understand and in which they feel comfortable appears abstract to young people.

Providing internships and matching students with mentors can intimately engage young people in the modern workplace and help clarify this mysterious world for them. In addition, being deeply involved in the workplace helps young people identify their genuine vocational talents and desires and prepares them for productive and rewarding careers.

In his extensive research into human learning, Harvard psychologist Howard Gardner has demonstrated how ill-suited traditional school materials and practices are to our natural ways of learning. By the time children enter school at age 5, Gardner maintains, they have developed theories that help them make sense of their social and physical worlds. However, "these understandings are often immature, misleading, or fundamentally misconceived." The learning that takes place in schools, including colleges, does little to divest students of the misconceptions they possess about science, of their mechanical approach to mathematics, of the problems they have with economics, and of the stereotypes and simplifications they carry about history, literature, and the arts. Until we become "disciplinary experts" (or skilled persons), a stage of knowing that for many applies only to their vocation and is reached well after their school years, we do not have an accurate understanding of the world.[18]

In contrast to the accepted approach to education, Gardner submits that the best path to genuine understanding for young children is through children's museums. For older children, it is through apprenticeships. We would add that the various curriculum applications described here—including internships, mentorships, and apprenticeships—can lead to deeper and more meaningful understanding of the disciplines.

Finally, Mortimer Adler reminds us that "all genuine learning is active, not passive. It involves the use of the mind, not just memory. It is the process of discovery, in which the student is the main agent, not the teacher."[19] Adler took care to clarify what is meant by active learning, while reminding us of a lesson that John Dewey had imparted. In so doing, he also described how learners acquire expertise, craftsmanship, and artisanship.

> What John Dewey had in mind was not exclusively physical doing or even social doing—engagement in practical projects of one kind or another. The most important kind of doing, as far as learning is concerned, is intellectual or mental doing. In other words, one can learn to read or write well only by reading and writing. . . . To learn how to do any of these things well, one must not only engage in doing them, but one must be guided in doing them by someone more expert in doing them than oneself.[20]

Likewise, individuals embark on the path toward learning (a living) by embracing active scholarship, citizenship, and artisanship—all three together. We cannot distinguish where one characteristic ends and another begins. Dewey might well agree that this approach would be the best preparation for living and, because of it, the best preparation for the world of employment.

1. Thomas Jefferson, "Letters to William Charles Jarvis," in Paul L. Ford, ed., *The Writings of Thomas Jefferson* (New York: Putnam's, 1892–99), vol. 10, p. 161.
2. Edward R. Murrow, Foreword to Hyman G. Rickover, *Education and Freedom* (New York: Dutton, 1959), pp. 5–7.
3. National Commission on Excellence in Education, *A Nation at Risk: The Imperative for Educational Reform* (Washington, D.C.: U.S. Department of Education, 1983).
4. Adam Smith, *Theory of Moral Sentiments* (1759; reprint, New York: A. M. Kelley, 1966).
5. National Commission on Excellence in Education, p. 7.
6. Willard R. Daggett, "Everything New Looks Old Again," *Vocational Education Journal,* September 1994, p. 26.
7. C. C. Carson, R. M. Huelskamp, and T. D. Woodall, "Perspectives on Education in America: An Annotated Briefing," *Journal of Educational Research,* May/June 1993, pp. 293–94.
8. *Hook-up: Job Skills for the Information Age* (a booklet produced by BellSouth in cooperation with the U.S. Department of Education, Southern Regional Education Board, and Georgia Department of Education), p. 3. Copies of *Hook-up* can be obtained free of charge by phoning 800/631–1586.
9. Ernest L. Boyer, *High School: A Report on Secondary Education in America* (New York: Harper & Row, 1983), p. 57.
10. *Hook-up*, p. 3.
11. Theodore R. Sizer, *Horace's School: Redesigning the American High School* (Boston: Houghton Mifflin, 1992), p. 1.
12. *Hook-up*, p. 12.
13. Ibid., p. 3.
14. Carson, Huelskamp, and Woodall, p. 294.
15. Richard Van Scotter, "What Young People Think About School and Society," *Educational Leadership,* November 1994, pp. 72–73.
16. Robert N. Bellah et al., *The Good Society* (New York: Alfred A. Knopf, 1991), p. 10.
17. Van Scotter, p. 75.
18. Howard Gardner, *The Unschooled Mind: How Children Think and How Schools Should Teach* (New York: Basic Books, 1991), pp. 6–11.
19. Mortimer Adler, *The Paideia Proposal: An Educational Manifesto* (New York: Macmillan, 1982), p. 50.
20. Ibid., p. 52.

AE Article Review Form

We encourage you to photocopy and use this page as a tool to assess how the articles in **Annual Editions** expand on the information in your textbook. By reflecting on the articles you will gain enhanced text information. You can also access this useful form on a product's book support Web site at **http://www.dushkin.com/online/.**

NAME: _____   DATE: _____

TITLE AND NUMBER OF ARTICLE: _____

BRIEFLY STATE THE MAIN IDEA OF THIS ARTICLE: _____

LIST THREE IMPORTANT FACTS THAT THE AUTHOR USES TO SUPPORT THE MAIN IDEA:

WHAT INFORMATION OR IDEAS DISCUSSED IN THIS ARTICLE ARE ALSO DISCUSSED IN YOUR TEXTBOOK OR OTHER READINGS THAT YOU HAVE DONE? LIST THE TEXTBOOK CHAPTERS AND PAGE NUMBERS:

LIST ANY EXAMPLES OF BIAS OR FAULTY REASONING THAT YOU FOUND IN THE ARTICLE:

LIST ANY NEW TERMS/CONCEPTS THAT WERE DISCUSSED IN THE ARTICLE, AND WRITE A SHORT DEFINITION:

ANNUAL EDITIONS revisions depend on two major opinion sources: one is our Advisory Board, listed in the front of this volume, which works with us in scanning the thousands of articles published in the public press each year; the other is you—the person actually using the book. Please help us and the users of the next edition by completing the prepaid article rating form on this page and returning it to us. Thank you for your help!

ANNUAL EDITIONS: Educating Exceptional Children 99/00

ARTICLE RATING FORM

Here is an opportunity for you to have direct input into the next revision of this volume. We would like you to rate each of the 35 articles listed below, using the following scale:

1. Excellent: should definitely be retained
2. Above average: should probably be retained
3. Below average: should probably be deleted
4. Poor: should definitely be deleted

Your ratings will play a vital part in the next revision. So please mail this prepaid form to us just as soon as you complete it. Thanks for your help!

RATING

ARTICLE

1. Inclusion of Children with Disabilities: Seeking the Appropriate Balance
2. What Are Special Education Teachers Made Of?
3. What Do I Do Now? A Teacher's Guide to Including Students with Disabilities
4. Four Inclusion Models That Work
5. From Philosophy to Practice in Inclusive Early Childhood Programs
6. Together Is Better: Specific Tips on How to Include Children with Various Types of Disabilities
7. "Buddy Skills" for Preschoolers
8. Dyads and Data in Peer Coaching
9. Learning Disabilities
10. Pyramid Power for Collaborative Planning
11. Mega-Analysis of Meta-Analyses: What Works in Special Education and Related Services
12. Distinguishing Language Differences from Language Disorders in Linguistically and Culturally Diverse Students
13. Language Interaction Techniques for Stimulating the Development of At-Risk Children in Infant and Preschool Day Care
14. The 1992 AAMR Definition and Preschool Children: Response from the Committee on Terminology and Classification
15. Collaborative Planning for Inclusion of a Student with Developmental Disabilities
16. Facilitating the Socialization of Children with Autism
17. Getting the Student with Head Injuries Back in School: Strategies for the Classroom
18. Group Development for Students with Emotional/Behavioral Disorders

RATING

ARTICLE

19. How to Prevent Aggressive Behavior
20. How to Defuse Defiance, Threats, Challenges, Confrontations . . .
21. Preschool Orientation and Mobility: A Review of the Literature
22. A Child with Severe Hearing Loss Joins Our Learning Community
23. Multimedia Stories for Deaf Children
24. Creating Inclusionary Opportunities for Learners with Multiple Disabilities: A Team-Teaching Approach
25. The Unexpected Benefits of High School Peer Tutoring
26. Perspectives on Technology in Special Education
27. "Can I Play Too?" Adapting Common Classroom Activities for Young Children with Limited Motor Abilities
28. Listening to Parents of Children with Disabilities
29. Accessible Web Site Design
30. Meeting the Needs of Gifted and Talented Preschoolers
31. Gifted Students Suggest Reforms for Education: Listening to Gifted Students' Ideas
32. Cluster Grouping of Gifted Students: How to Provide Full-Time Services on a Part-Time Budget
33. Making Comprehensive Inclusion of Special Needs Students Work in a Middle School
34. Transition from High School to Work or College: How Special Education Students Fare
35. School-to-Work: A Model for Learning a Living

(Continued on next page)

We Want Your Advice

BUSINESS REPLY MAIL
FIRST-CLASS MAIL PERMIT NO. 84 GUILFORD CT

POSTAGE WILL BE PAID BY ADDRESSEE

**Dushkin/McGraw-Hill
Sluice Dock
Guilford, CT 06437-9989**

ABOUT YOU

Name _____ Date _____

Are you a teacher? ☐ A student? ☐
Your school's name _____

Department _____

Address _____ City _____ State ____ Zip ____

School telephone # _____

YOUR COMMENTS ARE IMPORTANT TO US !

Please fill in the following information:
For which course did you use this book?
_____

Did you use a text with this *ANNUAL EDITION*? ☐ yes ☐ no
What was the title of the text?
_____

What are your general reactions to the *Annual Editions* concept?
_____

Have you read any particular articles recently that you think should be included in the next edition?
_____

Are there any articles you feel should be replaced in the next edition? Why?
_____

Are there any World Wide Web sites you feel should be included in the next edition? Please annotate.
_____

May we contact you for editorial input? ☐ yes ☐ no
May we quote your comments? ☐ yes ☐ no